Handbook of Professional and Ethical Practice for Psychologists, Counsellors and Psychotherapists

D0169100

Closer regulation of psychological counselling means that an awareness of the professional, legal and ethical considerations is vital.

The Handbook of Professional and Ethical Practice brings together leading therapists and psychologists who have a wealth of knowledge and experience of their subjects. Each chapter places particular emphasis on the current codes of practice and ethical principles underpinning safe ethical practice and the implications for practitioners. Comprehensive coverage of the legal, clinical and ethical considerations involved in research and training is provided and the reflective questions at the end of every chapter serve to prompt further discussion of the issues. The following subjects are covered:

- Professional Practice and Ethical Considerations
- Legal Considerations and Responsibilities
- Clinical Considerations and Responsibilities
- Working with Diversity – Professional Practice and Ethical Considerations
- Research, Supervision and Training

This innovative handbook provides a supportive guide to the major professional, legal and ethical issues encountered by trainees on counselling, clinical psychology and psychotherapy courses, as well as providing an invaluable resource for more experienced therapists and other members of the helping professions.

Rachel Tribe is a Senior Lecturer, Chartered Psychologist and Course Director in the School of Psychology at the University of East London.

Jean Morrissey is a Registered Counsellor (BACP) and a lecturer at the School of Nursing & Midwifery Studies, Trinity College Dublin.

Contributors: Nicola Barden, Nicola Barry, Jane Boden, Tim Bond, Robert Bor, Michael Carroll, Adrian Coyle, Malcolm Cross, Emmy van Deurzen, Gráinne Ní Dhomhnaill, Amanda Evans, Peter Forster, Tim Gallagher, Irvine S. Gersch, Andrew Grimmer, Rebecca Haworth, Peter Jenkins, Martin Milton, Lyndsey Moon, Shirley Morrissey, John Newland, Eleanor O'Leary, Camilla Olsen, Nimisha Patel, David Purves, Digby Tantam, Allan Winthrop, Joanne Wood.

Handbook of Professional and Ethical Practice for Psychologists, Counsellors and Psychotherapists

Edited by Rachel Tribe and Jean Morrissey

Brunner-Routledge
Taylor & Francis Group

HOVE AND NEW YORK

First edition published 2005 by Brunner-Routledge
27 Church Road, Hove, East Sussex, BN3 2FA

Simultaneously published in the USA and Canada
by Brunner-Routledge
270 Madison Avenue, New York, NY 10016

Brunner-Routledge is an imprint of the Taylor & Francis Group

© 2005 Rachel Tribe & Jean Morrissey

Typeset in Times by RefineCatch Limited, Bungay, Suffolk
Printed and bound in Great Britain by TJ International Ltd,
Padstow, Cornwall

Paperback cover design by Lisa Dynan

British Library Cataloguing in Publication Data
A catalogue record for this book is available from the British Library

Library of Congress Cataloging-in-Publication Data
Handbook of professional and ethical practice for psychologists,
   counsellors, and psychotherapists / edited by Rachel Tribe and
   Jean Morrissey.
     p. cm.
   Includes bibliographical references and index.
   ISBN 1–58391–968–6 (hbk.)—ISBN 1–58391–969–4 (pbk.)
   1. Psychologists – Professional ethics.   2. Counsellors –
Professional ethics.   3. Psychotherapists – Professional ethics.
I. Tribe, Rachel.   II. Morrissey, Jean.   III. Title.
   BF76.4.H365   2004
   174'.915 – dc22   2004007118

ISBN 1–58391–968–6 (hbk)
ISBN 1–58391–969–4 (pbk)

Rachel Tribe would like to dedicate this book to the memory of Richard Brian Kenyon. To quote his son Kieron, 'He did so much for so many and never wanted reward or recognition.' He was a very special person and we miss him very much.

Jean Morrissey would like to dedicate this book to Mary and Patrick Morrissey and Colin Brett: thank you all for everything.

Contents

List of tables and figures

Tables

Figures

Contributors

Editors

Rachel Tribe is a Chartered Counselling and Organisational Psychologist, currently employed as Course Director on the Counselling Psychology course at the University of East London. She has published widely and regularly contributes to national and international conferences. She has worked in the UK and a number of other countries.

Jean Morrissey is a Registered Counsellor (BACP) and a lecturer at the School of Nursing & Midwifery Studies, Trinity College Dublin (formally an associate professor at the Chinese University of Hong Kong). She originally trained and worked as a general and psychiatric nurse before becoming a counsellor and supervisor. She has worked as a counsellor and supervisor in voluntary, educational and hospital settings in the UK, Ireland and Hong Kong. She has published on issues relating to training supervision.

Authors

Nicola Barden is currently Head of Counselling at the University of Portsmouth. A registrant of both UKCP and BACP, she is Deputy Chair of BACP and chairs its Professional Standards Committee. She was Editor of the *CPJ* from 2000 to 2002. Previous publications include 'The responsibilities of the supervisor in BACP's codes of ethics and practice' in Wheeler and King, *The Responsibility of the Supervisor* (Sage 2000), and *Rethinking Gender and Therapy* (Open University Press 2001), co-edited with Susannah Izzard.

Nicola Barry MA is a Registered Psychologist and College Lecturer in the Department of Applied Psychology, University College Cork. She is the Assistant Course Director of the Higher Diploma in Guidance and Counselling and co-author of articles in the area of Gestalt reminiscence therapy.

Jane Boden is an Accredited Counsellor with the BACP working within both public and private sectors. She is also the principal infertility counsellor for the Hull IVF Unit and Accredited Cruse Bereavement Counsellor and Supervisor. Jane lectures at the University of Hull, where she gained her MSc in Counselling, and is currently reading for a PhD.

Tim Bond is a Fellow of BACP and a Reader in Counselling and Professional Ethics at the Graduate School of Education, University of Bristol. He was chair of BACP 1994–96. He has numerous publications but his two most significant recent ones are *Standards and Ethics for Counselling in Action* (second edition) (Sage 2000) and *The Ethical Framework for Good Practice in Counselling and Psychotherapy* (BACP 2002). He is a leading writer in the area of practice and ethical issues in therapy.

Robert Bor is a Consultant Clinical Psychologist at the Royal Free Hospital, London, where he works in the Infection and Immunity Directorate. He is a Chartered Clinical, Counselling and Health Psychologist as well as a UKCP Registered Family Therapist. He is also Emeritus Professor of Psychology at London Metropolitan University and a Visiting Professor at City University, London. He has many years of experience of working with individuals, couples and families affected by acute and chronic illness. He has published numerous books and academic papers on this and related topics.

Michael Carroll is a Fellow of the BACP, a Chartered Counselling Psychologist and a BACP Senior Registered Practitioner. He works as a counsellor, supervisor, trainer and consultant to organisations in both public and private sectors, specialising in the area of employee well-being. He is Visiting Industrial Professor in the Graduate School of Education, University of Bristol, and the winner of the 2001 BPS Award for Distinguished Contributions to Professional Psychology. He has published widely particularly in the areas of clinical supervision and counselling in organisations His most recent book is *Integrative Approaches to Supervision* (edited with Margaret Tholstrup; Jessica Kingsley, 2001).

Adrian Coyle is Senior Lecturer and Research Tutor for the Practitioner Doctorate in Psychotherapeutic and Counselling Psychology in the Department of Psychology, University of Surrey. His research interests include lesbian and gay psychology, identity, spirituality/religion, bereavement and qualitative research approaches. To date, he has (co-)written 35 journal articles and 16 book chapters and co-edited *Lesbian and Gay Psychology: New Perspectives* (BPS Blackwell, 2002).

Malcolm Cross is Director of Counselling Psychology Programmes, City University, London. He is also a UKCP Registered Psychotherapist and Chartered Counselling Psychologist. An active practitioner and researcher with numerous academic articles, book chapters and books to his name. His most recent book is *Reporting in Counselling and Psychotherapy: A trainee's Guide to Preparing Case Studies and Reports*, prepared in collaboration with Papadopoulos and Bor.

Emmy van Deurzen directs the New School of Psychotherapy and Counselling in London, where she is a Professor in Psychotherapy with Schiller International University. She is also Co-Director, of the Centre for the Study of Conflict and Reconciliation at the University of Sheffield. She has written extensively on the application of philosophical ideas to psychotherapy and runs a private practice. She founded the Society for Existential Analysis and created numerous courses in psychotherapy for academic institutions. She is a fellow of the BACP and BPS and has also been external relations officer to the European Association for Psychotherapy.

Gráinne Ní Dhomhnaill is employed as a Lecturer in Psychology in the Education Department, University College Dublin. Her work involves training educational psychologists as well as the initial and continuing professional development of teachers. She has served as President of the Psychological Society of Ireland, and is a former Course Director of the professional training programme for educational psychologists. Gráinne has presented papers at international conferences, and retains an international perspective on the development of educational psychology.

Amanda Evans initially trained as a humanistic counsellor and later as a Counselling Psychologist and has worked as a counsellor in secondary healthcare for 16 years. She specialised in working with people affected by HIV infection including patients, partners, families and children from widely diverse backgrounds and at all stages of HIV infection from initial diagnosis to death. She is involved in co-coordinating the training and supervision of counselling staff in a busy HIV testing clinic and the training of counsellors specialising in this field.

Peter Forster is employed in Tower Hamlets, East London, on the community team for learning disabilities. He is a Chartered Counselling Psychologist and has extensive experience of working in a number of clinical settings, which include mental health, primary care, and learning disabilities.

Tim Gallagher is a Chartered Counselling Psychologist with experience of working in independent therapy practice, NHS adult mental health, clinical health and primary care in various locations. He also worked as a manager in the NHS and voluntary sector and has published in the areas of stress and coping strategies.

Irvine S. Gersch has worked as a schoolteacher, university lecturer, and principal educational psychologist. He is Course Director of the MSc professional course of training for educational psychologists. He has published widely in the fields of SEN, school systems, behaviour management, listening to children, conciliation, and training, educational leadership and management. He is a member of the Government advisory group on the future training of educational psychology and a Fellow of the BPS. In 2002 he was awarded the distinguished award by the BPS for professional practice in psychology, in recognition of his pioneering work.

Andrew Grimmer is an accredited BACP Counsellor and a full member of the New Zealand Association of Counsellors. He works as a counsellor in a tertiary education counselling service and in private practice. He has a particular interest in mandatory personal therapy and has carried out research on the subject with counselling psychologists. He currently lives in Auckland, New Zealand.

Rebecca Haworth, Chartered Clinical Psychologist, has experience of working in a private consultancy – specialising in child and adult mental Health, including an expert witness service. She has also worked in a range of NHS settings for over 10 years, and has particular interest working with adults, families and children in primary care settings. She has undertaken a range of additional training in brief solution-focused therapy with individuals and families, psychoanalytic psychotherapy and group work. She has published several journal papers.

Peter Jenkins is a Lecturer in Counselling at the University of Manchester and a member of the Professional Conduct Committee of the British Association for Counselling and Psychotherapy. He is the author of *Counselling, Psychotherapy and the Law* (Sage 1997), co-author with Debbie Daniels of *Therapy with Children* (Sage 2000), and editor of *Legal Issues in Counselling and Psychotherapy* (Sage 2002).

Martin Milton UKCP Reg is Course Director (Practice) of the University of Surrey Practitioner Doctorate in Psychotherapeutic and Counselling Psychology. He is also Consultant Counselling Psychologist and Registered Psychotherapist with North East London Mental Health Trust. His research and specialist interests include lesbian and gay affirmative psychology and psychotherapy, HIV-related psychotherapy and existential psychotherapy. He has previously served on the committee of the BPS Lesbian and Gay Psychology section and was one of the co-editors of its Newsletter. He is currently one of the Division of Counselling Psychology's representatives to the Admissions Committee of the BPS and consulting editor to *Counselling Psychology Review*.

Lyndsey Moon is a Chartered Counselling Psychologist and Fellow of the University of Newcastle. She is External Examiner for the University of

Teesside and a former lecturer in counselling psychology. She has worked for the NHS in the field of substance misuse and addictions and for a lesbian, gay and bisexual alcohol counselling project in Soho, London.

Shirley Morrissey is a Clinical and Health Psychologist in private practice in Australia. She was previously course director for an MSc programme in counselling psychology in the UK. She is a member of the APS, BPS, BABCP and AACBT. She has won several awards during her career in Australia, including a grant for research into ethical dilemmas with an honours student. She conducts workshops in CBT, supervision, and ethical practice, has presented numerous conference papers, and is well published.

John Newlands is a Chartered Clinical Psychologist. He has worked for over 10 years in the multicultural London Borough of Islington. He has a strong interest in promoting inclusive thinking and practice for black and minority ethnic people with learning disabilities. Within the Division of Clinical Psychology, he held the post of elected Chair of the 'Race' & Culture Special Interest group from 1994 to 1998. His published work focuses on understanding ethnic identity. He is a visiting lecturer to several clinical psychology training courses.

Eleanor O'Leary is Director and Principal Investigator of the Cork Older Adult Intervention Project at University College Cork. She has written and researched extensively on the subject of older adults. Her work has been translated into Greek, Italian, Chinese and Uzbek. Her book, *Counselling Older Adults*, is one of two key international books in the area.

Camilla Olsen is a Chartered Counselling Psychologist. She is currently employed in a Community Mental Health Team and is involved as a therapist with a psychosis relapse prevention study carried out by Professor Garety and Professor Kuipers at the Institute of Psychiatry at Maudsley Hospital. She is a Visiting Lecturer at City University, teaching students on a certificate course in counselling psychology and at Surrey University teaching students on PsychD in Psychotherapeutic and Counselling Psychology.

Nimisha Patel is a Senior Lecturer in Clinical Psychology at the University of East London, a Consultant Clinical Psychologist, and Head of Clinical Psychology at the Medical Foundation caring for victims of torture. She also worked for many years in the NHS as a practitioner/clinician and researcher and in developing clinical practice and services for a multi-ethnic population. She has published widely on issues of working with difference and discrimination in psychological health services.

David Purves is a Principal Lecturer in Counselling Psychology at London Metropolitan University. He gained his doctorate from Oxford University in 1994. Since that time he has become both a Chartered Counselling Psychologist and Psychotherapist. Dr Purves has a long-held interest in ethics and teaches a popular course on this topic. He also has both research and practice interests in the field of posttraumatic stress disorder and maintains an NHS practice in this field. He has published and spoken both nationally and internationally on this subject.

Digby Tantam is Clinical Professor of Psychotherapy at the University of Sheffield. He is a practising psychotherapist, psychiatrist and psychologist. He is Co-Director of the Centre for the Study of Conflict and Reconciliation at the University of Sheffield, and a partner in Dilemma Consultancy in Human Relations. He served as Registrar of the European Association of Psychotherapy (1999–2001) and Chair of the UKCP (1995–98). He has published extensively; his most recent book is *Psychotherapy and Counselling in Practice. A narrative approach* (Cambridge University Press 2002).

Allan Winthrop is Director of Counselling Psychology programmes at Teesside University. He is a Consultant Chartered Counselling Psychologist. He previously worked in the NHS and is now a partner in a private psychology practice. He has a postgraduate diploma in law and holds the Common Professional Exam (CPE) in law. He is a full member of the Society of Expert Witnesses and is recognised as a psychology provider by various health insurance schemes.

Joanne Wood is an Associate Lecturer at City University, London, and practises as a Psychologist in a child and adolescent mental health service. She has extensive experience working in primary and secondary adult mental health settings and also within specialist addiction agencies. Prior to training as a counselling psychologist, Joanne worked as a professional human resources specialist for a number of blue chip companies in the city of London. Her current research interests are related to the training and development of counsellors and therapists and the application of theory to practice.

Acknowledgements

We have received help, support and encouragement from many people in writing this book, particularly Irene So, Dorcas Shuen and Robert Sherman. We would like to thank all the contributors who have given so generously their time and effort to writing their chapters. We are indebted to Andrew Kilburn who kindly agreed to act as a reader for this book and made valuable and insightful comments on the text. Our gratitude also goes to Ken Fisher for his artistic skills and humour.

As editors, we particularly value the support and encouragement we gave to each other throughout this project, which at times presented some unexpected challenges. We acknowledge and value the knowledge and experience we have gained from all the clients, supervisees and trainees we have worked with in the UK and abroad.

Finally, we want to thank email, which enabled us to communicate across continents and time zones with such great speed and success; without it this book may not have been completed.

Part I

Professional practice and ethical considerations

Chapter 1

Introduction

Rachel Tribe and Jean Morrissey

There is no doubt that professional and ethical practice is a potent and dynamic area. Changes in research and practice, legislation, and professional and ethical guidelines may all mean incremental and paradigm shifts. In addition, changing professional codes of practice, culture, and personal belief systems, as well as the demands of clinical governance, lifelong learning and the likelihood of statutory registration, will also impact upon professional and ethical practice. Accordingly, we believe that the challenges in this area of practice are among the things that make it an interesting and vibrant one. The juxtaposition of the personal and professional is central to professional and ethical practice and is written about in this book by a number of authors. Our aim in producing this book was to make it as comprehensive as possible; inevitably constraints of space (and therefore price) meant that we had to omit areas we might ideally have liked to include. Therefore, we decided to include the areas which, we believe, are of most importance both to trainee therapists, psychologists, and counsellors, and to experienced practitioners. An issue within this area which we believe is vital but did not warrant an entire chapter in this book is the necessity of practitioners taking responsibility for their own continuing professional development (CPD). While different professional bodies have slightly different views and conditions about this, the recognition of continuing professional development for all therapists is becoming mainstream and is in our view an essential requirement of professionalism.

Throughout this book particular emphasis is placed in each chapter on the current codes of practice and ethical principles underpinning safe ethical practice and the implications for practitioners. Therefore each author was asked to focus on the particular professional and ethical issues in his or her area of expertise and on the challenges they present in clinical practice. The importance of considering diversity is also paramount and this theme runs throughout the book. Different audiences may be guided by different ethical codes, cultures of practice and training, among which there are many similarities and some differences. Notwithstanding this, the importance of ethical awareness and practice for all therapists or practitioners working in therapeutic environments share a common underlay. Given the boundaries of this book, it was not feasible to cover all eventualities related to professional and ethical practice or the contexts in which they occur. Instead, this book aims to foster the professional judgement of the reader, which is required to manage the often complex and challenging ethical issues unique to each situation. The latter is illustrated throughout the various clinical case examples in the respective chapters.

The book is divided into five parts. Each chapter is written by someone who is an experienced practitioner or specialist in the area of practice that they have written about. The authors represent different constituencies, including BACP, BPS, and UKCP, as well as a range of theoretical orientations. Part I entitled 'Professional practice and ethical considerations', describes the development and monitoring of professional ethics in contemporary Britain and the USA as well as in various European countries and what we might learn from them. The following chapter addresses issues concerning the concept of professional contracts with and within organisations and how they can be negotiated to create healthier relationships and more positive working environments. The final chapter in this section discusses the 'person' in ethical decision making and the varying degrees of discomfort that can arise between ethical principles and personal values as well as its impact on the therapeutic work. The first two chapters in Part II, 'Legal considerations and responsibilities', provide a comprehensive overview of the professional responsibilities as they relate to the legal context of therapy. The following chapters focus on specific professional and legal considerations and responsibilities of record keeping, writing a report for use in court reports and appearing as an expert witness. Part III, 'Clinical considerations and responsibilities', covers specific areas and the accompanying professional and ethical challenges that apply to the practice of therapy, including managing referrals and complaints, fitness to practise, suicide risk and working in a multidisciplinary team in a healthcare setting. The penultimate part, 'Working with difference – professional practice and ethical considerations', focuses on issues of working with diversity, including age, sexual orientation, disability and race, and the importance of such issues in the consulting room. The final part, 'Research, supervision and training', highlights the importance of research and the challenges of undertaking research in clinical practice. Current debates surrounding evidence-based practice are also discussed. This is followed by an examination of personal therapy, the teaching of ethics and professional practice and clinical supervision as key components in the process of becoming a psychologist, counsellor or psychotherapist. The final chapter presents trainees' perspectives of professional and ethical issues based on their experiences in clinical practice.

Finally, as editors we hope the reflective questions at the end of each chapter will act as a springboard for ongoing discussion, reflection and learning concerning the many complex and challenging professional and ethical issues each therapist is confronted with in an ever-changing therapeutic environment.

Chapter 2

Developing and monitoring professional ethics and good practice guidelines

Tim Bond

Why do we have codes of ethics? What purpose do they serve? How can we distinguish better approaches to developing ethics and good practice guidelines from poorer ones? These are the questions I want to address in this chapter. They are ones that have preoccupied me over the last few years as I worked on rewriting the ethical framework for the second largest professional body for the talking therapies worldwide, the British Association for Counselling and Psychotherapy (BACP). However, these questions are equally applicable to other major professional bodies in the talking or psychological therapies in Britain such as the British Psychological Society (BPS) or the United Kingdom Council for Psychotherapy (UKCP). Indeed there is no reason why these questions should be confined to these therapeutic professional bodies. The challenge of being ethical is shared by many different professions. They are generic questions that open the possibility of learning from one another in very different professional roles and contexts.

I propose to approach this chapter in this spirit and to draw on examples from medicine and accountancy to inform possible ways of discriminating between better and worse approaches to professional ethics. However, before doing so, I want to set out some of the assumptions that inform this chapter. Firstly, I do *not* want to imply a direct correspondence between statements of ethics published by professional bodies and the quality of ethical practice delivered by practitioners, as its practitioners may not necessarily implement what the professional body espouses. The publication of ethical statements is only the most visible element of creating an infrastructure to support ethical practice. Secondly, there is a complex dynamic at work between practitioners and their professional body that can be more or less supportive of the development of ethical practice. The published codes and guidelines provide only a very partial glimpse of what this dynamic might be. This is one of the issues that need to be borne in mind in developing and monitoring the ethical well-being of any profession. The examples I have selected illustrate the challenge of creating a positive dynamic between practitioner and professional body that enhances and supports ethical practice.

CHANGING THE LOCUS OF RESPONSIBILITY IN PROFESSIONAL ETHICS

Until the events I am about to recount took place, the ethics for medical practitioners depended very much on a personal sense of honour and the character of the person concerned. Two factors encouraged this focus on the individual. The word 'profession' has Latin roots meaning 'declared publicly', originally in the form of an oath sworn to establish one's occupation to a tax collector. The Hippocratic Oath is the most famous of these and has for long periods of European history been the defining ethical hallmark of members of the medical profession, which commits medical practitioners to special obligations to their patients (Jonsen 1999). As oaths are sworn in the first person they foster a view of ethics as a personal responsibility. This focus on the individual was further reinforced by the medieval European cultural heritage with its stress on honour, reinforced by ideas of chivalry and the importance of character. In the eighteenth century, any hint of a slur on a professional's character was to question his/her ethical integrity and once a slur gained credence it was considered to be irreparable. As a consequence, practitioners fought ferociously to protect 'their good name and reputation' by litigation, 'pamphlet wars', and sometimes duelling to the death.

This is the background to a festering dispute between surgeons that was fuelled by the production of hostile and provocative pamphlets (Leake 1975). This disagreement concerned how best to care for people during an epidemic of typhus (typhoid). Two senior surgeons took it as an affront to their honour when a hospital board decided to appoint additional medics to assist with overstretched services. They resigned their posts in the midst of an epidemic in 1792 with the consequence that the Manchester Infirmary was closed to all admissions. The trustees of the hospital were deeply concerned that desperate patients were turned away at a time when they most needed healthcare. They sought the help of a well-respected physician and President of the Manchester Philosophical Society. Thomas Percival (1740–1804) was already renowned in Manchester for humanitarian campaigns on behalf of public health, including improved sanitation and water supply, and his opposition to slavery. They invited him to lead a committee to find ways of preventing a recurrence of the problem of a hospital closing its doors in the height of an epidemic. It took Percival three years to produce the prototype of all codes of medical ethics. He was the first person to use the terms 'medical ethics' and 'professional ethics' and more significantly his writings marked a major change in the way that professional ethics are conceptualised and implemented. He relocated the ethical locus of responsibility from the individual to the profession as a whole. In the case of medicine, he envisaged a collective professional responsibility for the care of the sick as a greater ethical priority than any individual practitioner's honour.

The voice of the documents written by Percival was very different from anything that preceded them. They were written in the second and third person rather than the first, which was characteristic of oaths. Professional obligations were set out as numbered duties, some of which were quite detailed. The first version was written as a pamphlet in 1794 and circulated privately before the publication of an expanded version in 1803. The expanded version was to have considerable impact on both sides of the Atlantic. In re-edited versions, it was adopted initially by local medical associations and eventually embryonic national medical associations, first by the newly formed American Medical Association in 1847, and then the British Medical Association in 1856, followed by the General Medical Council in 1858. Although codes of medical ethics have been extensively revised many times since Percival's day, they have retained the same voice and character as the original version. There is an unmistakable shift from ethics residing in an individual's sense of honour to a collective commitment to care for the sick. This shift has been deployed to serve many purposes. These include creating a collective moral authority for the professional to exert against employers in order to protect their ethical 'space' to practise and to influence the circumstances of their work. For example, Percival's codes created a duty to challenge parsimonious trustees who overcrowded patients on wards or required the use of inferior drugs to save money (Percival 1803/1975: 74). The assertion of a professional collective ethic also provided the means to develop a shared baseline for ethical standards and practice and thus a potentially clearer demarcation between acceptable practice and professional malpractice or misconduct.

PROFESSIONAL ETHICS: RULES OR PRINCIPLES?

The circumstances that inspired Percival to construct professional ethics on a collective professional sense of duty favour rule-making. Something that is so manifestly unethical and reprehensible as excluding sick people from hospital in a time of emergency surely requires an authoritative countermanding remedy. Excessive reliance on an individualised honour code was replaced by duties that quickly became rules in an emerging system of professional self-regulation as the collective ethic is reinforced by the creation of unified national professional bodies. However, there are dangers in rules becoming too dominant as a method of constructing ethics. Recent events in the United States demonstrate that the type of discourse in which professional ethics are constructed is not merely of academic interest but can have considerable and far-reaching impact on many people's lives.

The financial collapse of Enron in the United States in 2001 is a tragedy on an enormous scale. Harvey Pitt, the Chairman of the US Securities and Exchange Commission (SEC) commented that 'the large number of people callously injured is shocking' (Pitt 2002: 1). However, it has taken on significance beyond being one of the largest financial collapses to date. The cause of the collapse has shaken the trust of the financial markets in company accounts worldwide and is a contributing factor to the current depressed and volatile state of many national economies. In particular, the way Enron constructed its accounts had the effect of understating and concealing its indebtedness and liabilities, as well as exaggerating its profitability on a massive scale. The systems for achieving this were constructed by company lawyers and accountants and were approved by auditors who are responsible for inspecting and verifying the company accounts, so that lenders, investors and other interested parties can be reasonably confident of financial status of that company. Nonetheless it is quite possible that the professionals concerned are not guilty of legal wrongdoing or acting in breach of their professional ethics. In media interviews shortly after the collapse, the Chief Executive of British Petroleum compared the way accountants approached their ethics in the USA and Britain. He suggested that one of the causes of the collapse was the way professional ethics in the USA tend to be constructed as rules. In other words, what is not explicitly forbidden is permitted. One of the consequences of constructing professional ethics as rules is that the locus of ethical responsibility is devolved to the body that constructs the ethics and regulates the profession. The professional is merely required to comply with precise rules and indeed may gain merit and income by exploiting any gaps in the rules. In contrast, he suggested the British approach to accountancy ethics gave greater significance to principles, in part due to the profession's critical reflections on earlier scandals associated with Robert Maxwell and his exploitation of pension funds in his company finances. If the auditor's role is guided by the principles that they approve accounts as being both accurate and honest, this establishes a moral context against which any rules ought to be interpreted or even overturned.

TALKING THERAPIES: RULES OR PRINCIPLES?

These excursions into the history of medical ethics and a current crisis in financial ethics may seem rather remote from the world of psychological and talking therapies. However, there are parallels. Any comparison between the published ethics in the United States and Britain reveals that there are differences in the way professional bodies construct their ethics. Both the American Counseling Association (ACA 2002) and the American Psychological Association (APA 2002) tend to produce much longer and more behaviourally prescriptive codes that are worded in such a way as to demand compliance over the issues specifically considered within them. They are more *rule-driven*. (For a comparison between the way BACP and ACA approach privacy and confidentiality see Table 2.1.)

Table 2.1 Comparison between ACA and BACP ethical guidance on confidentiality

BACP (2001) Guidance on Good Practice in Counselling and Psychotherapy	*ACA (2002) Code of Ethics*
Keeping Trust 16. Respecting client confidentiality is a fundamental requirement for keeping trust. The professional management of confidentiality concerns the protection of personally identifiable and sensitive information from unauthorised disclosure. Disclosure may be authorised by client consent or the law. Any disclosures should be undertaken in ways that best protect the client's trust. Practitioners should be willing to be accountable to their clients and to their profession for their management of confidentiality in general and particularly for any disclosures made without their client's consent.	**Section B Confidentiality** **B.1. Right to Privacy** a. Respect for Privacy. Counselors respect their clients' right to privacy and avoid illegal and unwarranted disclosures of confidential information. (See A.3.a. and B.6.a.) b. Client Waiver. The right to privacy may be waived by the client or his or her legally recognized representative. c. Exceptions. The general requirement that counselors keep information confidential does not apply when disclosure is required to prevent clear and imminent danger to the client or others or when legal requirements demand that confidential information be revealed. Counselors consult with other professionals when in doubt as to the validity of an exception. d. Contagious, Fatal Diseases. A counselor who receives information confirming that a client has a disease commonly known to be both communicable and fatal is justified in disclosing information to an identifiable third party, who by his or her relationship with the client is at a high risk of contracting the disease. Prior to making a disclosure the counselor should ascertain that the client has not already informed the third party about his or her disease and that the client is not intending to inform the third party in the immediate future. (See B.1.c and B.1.f.) e. Court-Ordered Disclosure. When court ordered to release confidential information without a client's permission, counselors request to the court that the disclosure not be required due to potential harm to the client or counseling relationship. (See B.1.c.) f. Minimal Disclosure. When circumstances require the disclosure of confidential information, only essential information is revealed. To the extent possible, clients are informed before confidential information is disclosed.

continued...

BACP (2001) Guidance on Good Practice in Counselling and Psychotherapy	ACA (2002) Code of Ethics
	g. Explanation of Limitations. When counselling is initiated and throughout the counseling process as necessary, counselors inform clients of the limitations of confidentiality and identify foreseeable situations in which confidentiality must be breached. (See G.2.a.) h. Subordinates. Counselors make every effort to ensure that privacy and confidentiality of clients are maintained by subordinates including employees, supervisees, clerical assistants, and volunteers. (See B.1.a.) i. Treatment Teams. If client treatment will involve a continued review by a treatment team, the client will be informed of the team's existence and composition . . .

When I have discussed the preference for behaviourally prescription with American colleagues they attribute this, at least in part, to the litigious nature of their culture. The categorical voice of rules appears to offer greater protection and reassurance to the professional members of these organisations who are concerned to avoid being caught up in unforeseeable litigation. To date each new edition of the ACA and APA codes has become longer and more detailed. Comparable documents in Britain tend to be written at a greater level of generality and are behaviourally less prescriptive. There are rules in the sense of professionally enforceable injunctions that clearly expect compliance, for example prohibition on sex with clients (BACP 2002: 7; BPS 2000: 5; UKCP 1998: 1) and a requirement to receive supervision (BACP 2002: 7; BPS 2001: 2.1.1–9) but such categorical imperatives are exceptional. More typically, ethics produced by any of the major professional bodies in the talking therapies in Britain are written at the level of, and in the style of, principles. Principles tend to be less behaviourally prescriptive than rules by leaving some scope for the practitioner to interpret them according to the context in which they are working. Principles are a way of expressing a general ethical commitment to a value in ways that are action-orientated.

The type of ethical discourse that is adopted collectively by a profession is a significant contributor to the way in which ethical practice is strengthened or weakened. Rules position the person who is subject to them in subservient compliance to an external authority. The only issue to be addressed is whether something is forbidden or mandatory. There may be scope for the exercise of professional judgement by creative interpretation of what is stated or using the spaces left between different rules. However, the predominant position of someone subject to rules is compliance, even if this means overriding their own sense of what is right or wrong.

There is no direct encouragement to foster a personal and professional sense of ethical responsibility beyond skilled and informed obedience. It is arguable that there is a strong connection between how Percival sought to resolve a major ethical challenge in his time with the recent financial collapse of Enron. This is not the first time that the limitations of rules and compliance have been exposed. One of the defences offered by people standing trial in Nuremberg for their role in the Holocaust during the Third Reich of Germany was that they were merely obeying orders. This defence provides a clear illustration of how externalising ethical responsibility onto a superior authority can extinguish any sense of personal ethical responsibility. When professions are under the pressure of media scrutiny following the exposure of major misconduct or malpractice, it is tempting to resort to rules in order to provide an authoritative position that seems to countermand any recurrence of the unacceptable behaviour.

Enron and Nuremberg provide salutary reminders that rules may only give the appearance of resolving the cause of concern and may in the longer term weaken the ethical health of the profession. At the very least, rules ought only to be used sparingly to address major areas of concern such as the vulnerability of clients to exploitation in the talking therapies. Some other form of ethical discourse is required if the profession seeks to foster ethical awareness and practice by its members.

FOSTERING ETHICAL MINDFULNESS

The circumstances in which most practitioners of talking therapies work demand a strong sense of personal and professional ethical responsibility. Most work is undertaken in private and seldom observed directly by anyone outside the practitioner–client relationship. The client is vulnerable psychologically and relatively powerless as the person seeking help in comparison to the person offering help. The interactive nature of the work between client and practitioner makes it a less predictable process than some physical or technical interventions. Each therapeutic relationship is to a greater or lesser extent unique. The good practitioner of talking therapy is capable of making sound therapeutic and ethical judgements that are appropriate to a particular client in a specific moment of his/her work together. The role of the professional body in these circumstances is to:

- set a baseline for acceptable practice, especially where issues of public safety are involved, and
- promote ethical practice within the profession.

The first of these is challenging and typically requires a means of setting the baseline and procedures for determining whether the baseline has been breached by means of a complaints or disciplinary adjudication. From experience, I consider that the second challenge is just as demanding and potentially of greater significance to clients, as most work by reasonably conscientious practitioners will be in varying degrees above the baseline of acceptable practice. Most practitioners in the talking therapies set out quite highly motivated by a desire to be of beneficial service to clients. However, the challenge for professional bodies is how to build on this. Good intentions are not enough, they need to be developed by an ability to recognise ethical issues and to be able to apply ethical insight in practice. The phrase that best captures this is 'fostering ethical mindfulness' (Bond 2000: 242). It directs both the practitioners' and the professional body's attention to the interplay between external loci of ethical control and the intrinsic ethics that are incorporated within the work with clients that rely heavily on the practitioner's own internal locus of ethical control. Anyone who is involved with professional complaints and disciplinary procedures would be struck by how often the blurring of boundaries in relationships has contributed to those cases where the client has suffered harm. This might lead to a very jaundiced view of dual relationships and a suspicion that the holding of more than one type of relationship with a client is invariably harmful.

The combination of a sexual and therapeutic relationship is stereotypical of the potential for emotional confusion, power imbalance and the therapist's self-gratification at the expense of the client. This has led most professional bodies to use their collective extrinsic authority to prohibit sexual relationships between therapist and client. This raises the question of how far should other types of dual relationships be prohibited? Other combinations have been problematic in specific instances. Examples include simultaneously combining social acquaintance and therapist, therapeutic psychologist and assessor of psychological harm following an accident for an insurance claim, psychiatric nurse and psychotherapist, clinical trainer and supervisor, or welfare advisor and counsellor. Would it be appropriate to prohibit all these combinations because in one or more instances they have contributed to the harming of some clients? I consider that this would be an over-reaction. These are all instances where the ethical awareness and professional competence of the practitioner is critical to the outcome for the client. It is the intrinsic ethical mindfulness of the practitioner that makes the decisive difference. A practitioner working in an urban area with many alternative sources of services available may be better placed to avoid potentially problematic dual relationships, but they still need to be assessed in terms of their potential for benefit or harm. For example some particularly vulnerable or stigmatised clients may only begin to consider seeking talking therapy when they meet a practitioner who has shared their problematic experience and has gained respect for having overcome or resolved some of the difficulties and challenges of that condition. I have witnessed practitioners working very effectively with clients who share life experiences around particular mental and physical illnesses, addictions or social marginalisation. The sharing of a problematic life experience can break down the client's sense of isolation and being the only one who is failing to cope. Meeting a therapist who is more resolved around the issue can instil hope that improvement is possible. Used wisely and competently these can be powerful therapeutic forces for good but they are only possible because of the combination of acquaintanceship and the therapeutic relationship.

Other types of dual relationships may not only require attentiveness to how the relationship is managed within the therapeutic alliance but also in the contact outside that relationship. For example, a practitioner in a rural community may not be able to avoid contact with a client in the village shop or when collecting children from the local school. Here the ethical context of the range of relationships is more analogous to doctors or clergymen who live in the community in which they work. The way in which they live their lives and manage the boundaries between different aspects of their lives can assist or undermine their effectiveness in their professional role.

Dual relationships represent a considerable challenge to professional bodies and their members. Extrinsic authority alone cannot adequately regulate them. The professional body can prohibit the blatantly exploitative relationships. But so much depends on the individual judgement and competence of the practitioner concerned that the task of the professional body in most cases is to support and develop the ethical mindfulness of its members on such a variably challenging issue. The same sort of challenge for professional bodies arises in triangular relationships between client, practitioner and agency where these occur. Extrinsic authority alone cannot resolve all the potential challenges of multiple accountability. The intrinsic ethical mindfulness of the practitioner and agency staff is essential to securing best practice.

QUALITY CRITERIA IN PROFESSIONAL ETHICAL GUIDANCE

The interplay between extrinsic and intrinsic ethics requires a greater degree of sophistication than simply transferring individual ethical responsibility to a collective professional ethic. Excessive reliance on either mere compliance to rules or highly individualised ethics would undermine the potential positive dynamic between extrinsic and intrinsic ethics by privileging one over the other. The dual aims of ensuring public safety and fostering ethical mindfulness direct attention beyond merely writing codes to developing additional strategies for promoting ethical awareness in the profession. These might well include incorporating ethics in initial training and continuing professional development, researching ethical issues, alerting the profession to new issues as they emerge in practice, and promoting dialogue about ethics in seminars, conferences and journals. Nonetheless the codification of ethics can provide a valuable focus for all these activities even if it cannot be the whole solution. This raises the third question with which I opened this chapter. How can we distinguish better approaches to developing ethics and good practice guidelines from poorer ones? In other words, what are the quality criteria for statements about the moral and ethical purpose of a profession?

1   It provides an adequate basis for protecting the public from harm caused by professional malpractice and misconduct. The sense of moral purpose identifies and challenges what is manifestly unconscionable behaviour.
2   The locus of ethical authority endorsed by the statement of professional ethic mediates between the collective sense of moral purpose held by the profession and the capacity of individual practitioners to be ethically responsible. (The Manchester Infirmary scandal cautions against excessive reliance on the latter and the collapse of Enron on the former.)
3   The ethical statement acts as the basis for fostering ethical mindfulness across all the circumstances in which the services are delivered. It is a tough standard to meet but a core ethical statement ought to validate all well-founded ethical practice within its scope. This criterion seems more achievable when phrased negatively. The ethical statement ought to avoid invalidating any ethically justifiable variations in practice.
4   The espoused ethics of the profession ought to contain regulatory, educational and inspirational elements in order to address the range of legitimate expectations of professional ethics. An excessive concern with regulation will merely establish the boundary between adequate and inadequate practice without advancing the practice of probably the majority of most professionals who actively strive to be ethical and wish to be ethically informed. Promoting and enhancing good practice requires actively addressing this positive ethical commitment.
5   A core ethical statement for a profession ought to be capable of acting as a platform on which other activities to promote the ethical mindfulness of practitioners can be based.

Anyone who has been involved in the writing of ethical codes and guidelines will know how hard it is to produce a document that informs and influences practice. These quality criteria ought not only to be of use to prospective authors but also to practitioners seeking to evaluate the guidance available to them. They have emerged from the history of ethical endeavour and are offered as indications of best practice in the current context.

REFLECTIVE QUESTIONS

1   What are the sources of your own sense of ethical commitment?
2   How does your professional body's published ethical guidance influence your practice as a talking therapist?
3   To what extent do external sources (to determine what is ethically appropriate) relate to your personal sense of what is ethically right or wrong in your practice as a talking therapist?
4   Review your professional body's guidance on professional ethics for your practice. How far does it meet the quality criteria for ethical guidance suggested in this chapter?

REFERENCES

ACA (2002) *Code of Ethics and Standards of Practice*. Alexandria, VA: American Counselling Association.
   http://www.counseling.org/resources/ethics.htm#eh
APA (2002) *Ethical Principles of Psychologists and Code of Conduct*. Washington, DC: American Psychological Association.
BACP (2002) *Ethical Framework for Good Practice in Counselling and Psychotherapy*. Rugby, UK: British Association for Counselling and Psychotherapy.
   http://www.bacp.co.uk/members_visitors/members_visitors.htm
Bond, T. (2000) *Standards and Ethics for Counselling in Action*. London: Sage.
BPS (2000) *Code of Conduct, Ethical Principles and Guidelines*. Leicester: British Psychological Society.
   http://www.bps.org.uk/documents/Code.pdf
BPS (2001) *Professional Practice Guidelines*. Leicester: Division of Counselling Psychology, British Psychological Society.
   http://www.bps.org.uk/documents/couns_guidelines.pdf
Jonsen, A. R. (1999) *A Short History of Medical Ehics*. New York: Oxford University Press.
Leake, C. D. (ed.) (1975) *Percival's Medical Ethics*. New York: Robert E. Krieger.
Percival, T. (1803/1975) Medical ethics or, a code of institutes and precepts adapted to the professional conduct of physicians and surgeons, in C. D. Leake (ed.) *Percival's Medical Ethics*. New York: Robert E. Krieger, pp. 61–205.
Pitt, H. (2002) Remarks on Enron at the Winter Bench and Bar Conference of the Federal Bar Council, Puerto Rico, February 19, 2002.
   http://www.polinitics2.com/page819275.htm
UKCP (1998) *Ethical Requirements for Member Organisations*. London: United Kingdom Council for Psychotherapy.

Chapter 3

European guidelines to professional and ethical issues

Digby Tantam and Emmy van Deurzen

Counselling and psychotherapy are types of trade in which the principal activity is talking, with the aim of creating a professional relationship and to use it to relieve distress or to enable personal development. Anyone may call themselves a counsellor or psychotherapist in any European country, except for the Netherlands and Finland where the title of psychotherapist is restricted. More countries restrict the title of psychologist. Psychologists have a common background training, but undertake many different kinds of work. Psychotherapists and counsellors, by contrast, are so named because they carry out a particular kind of work, and not because of having had a particular kind of training. Psychotherapy or counselling may therefore be undertaken by psychologists, medical practitioners, priests, teachers, and others.

Psychologists in Europe are represented by the European Association of Professional Psychology Associations (EFPA), psychotherapists by the European Association for Psychotherapy (EAP), and counsellors by the European Association for Counselling (EAC). All of these organizations have a federal structure, like the European Union, since an increasing number of countries also have national bodies for the regulation of these professions. In the UK, these are the British Psychological Society, the United Kingdom Council for Psychotherapy, the British Association for Counselling and Psychotherapy and the BCP specifically for psychoanalytic psychotherapists.

There is an increasing trend in Europe towards unification. This has had its effect in the fields of psychology, psychotherapy and counselling, with national organizations increasingly being influenced by European standards. In this chapter we shall be considering these European frameworks as they apply to training, ethical, and practice standards. This chapter will provide information on practice in other European countries, and some pointers on how the situation might evolve in the future.

BACKGROUND

In a survey of European psychotherapy training and practice (the SEPT study), we found the provision, type, and funding of psychotherapy varied enormously between different European countries (Tantam *et al.* 2001). This heterogeneity in psychotherapy provision reflects a considerable economic, social and health heterogeneity (Council of Europe 2003b). Health statistics show a similar pattern, with fourfold variation in infant mortality (Council of Europe 2003b; World Bank Group 2003) between different European countries.

Forty-four European states have ratified the European Convention for the Protection of Human Rights and Fundamental Freedoms and 43 have signed the Social Charter, although only 32 of these have ratified it (Council of Europe 2003a). These two documents impose a right of European citizens to certain basics of health and social care provision, although there is no correlative duty of governments to make these provisions. Neither the Convention nor the Social Charter mention psychotherapy, or indeed any specific treatment method. However, rights to some treatments and treatment conditions have been established in the European Court of Human Rights that interprets and applies the Convention and the Charter in the case of those countries that ratify it, and for those sections that the particular country has ratified.

The subject of psychotherapy has not so far been considered by the court, although we have argued (Tantam & van Deurzen 1999) that there is a case for interpreting the 'right to social and medical assistance' (Article 7 of the social charter) to include a right to psychotherapy since the article specifies that states undertake 'to provide that everyone may receive . . . such advice and personal help as may be required to prevent, to remove, or to alleviate personal or family want'. The SEPT study mentioned above involved a questionnaire survey of qualified psychotherapists in 6 European countries and interviews with key informants in 34. Information on the modalities or approaches to psychotherapy being practised in each country was obtained from 31 countries (Zerbetto & Tantam 2002). There were many approaches that were practised in only one country. For example, in the UK the key informants quoted a figure of 143 different approaches, but only 23 of these were practised in other countries. The most widely practised approach, with practitioners in 28 of the 31 European countries was 'psychodynamic', and the second most common was 'systemic' or family therapy (see Table 3.1).

REGULATION BY THE EUROPEAN UNION (THE EU)

The EU, a union of 25 autonomous European states, allows free mobility within its borders for citizens of EC member states. Free mobility for professionals required a procedure for recognizing qualifications. Initially this

Table 3.1 Range of modalities being practised in European countries

Modality	Percentage of countries in which practised (N = 31)
Psychodynamic	90.6%
Systemic family	84.4%
Gestalt	81.3%
Behavioural and cognitive	78.1%
Freudian psychoanalysis	46.9%
Transactional analysis	43.8%
Client-centred	37.5%
Psychodrama	31.3%
Group analysis	28.1%
Hypnotherapy	28.1%
Existential and logotherapy	25.0%
Integrative	25.0%
Adlerian psychoanalysis	21.9%
Jungian analytical psychology	15.6%
Body therapy and bioenergetics	15.6%
Art therapies	15.6%
Psychosynthesis	12.5%
Lacanian psychoanalysis	9.4%
Autogenic therapy	9.4%
Constructivist	9.4%
Sophia analysis	6.3%
Catathymic imaginary	6.3%
Cognitive analytic	6.3%
Psycho-organic analysis	6.3%

was done by a vertical strategy of defining sectors, such as medicine, and developing specific sectoral directives (Schneider 2000). Criteria for training in psychotherapy were included in the medical directives, but only as they applied to medical practitioners. The specific sectoral directives specified training requirements, but were found to be extremely time-consuming to apply in practice. They were therefore superseded by general directives that established a system for recognizing qualifications, but placed the onus for setting the standards for the qualification on the individual member state, rather than the EU. General directives therefore provide a framework, or common platform, for the recognition of qualifications, but do not make the EU the body that accredits training: the EU on 'designated authorities' confers this power. The first general directive (89/48/EEC) applies to qualifications or diplomas conferred after completion of at least three years of tertiary education. More recently, there has been a second general directive (92.51.EEC) for qualifications and diplomas conferred after less then three years tertiary education. The European Association for Counselling has developed its own qualification the European Certificate for Counsellor Accreditation.

There are only two designated authorities in the UK relevant to the area being considered by this chapter: the BPS, which is the designated authority for psychology, and the Association of Child Psychotherapists which is the designated authority for child psychotherapy. A designated authority must accept the qualification or diploma awarded by another designated authority but may add requirements that reflect professional practice in the country to which the professional is moving. So, if a psychologist is qualified in another European country but wishes to practise in the UK they must submit details of their training and experience to the BPS who can:

1   accept the application and accord the professional the right to practise and use the title 'psychologist',
2   require the professional to produce evidence of further professional experience,
3   require the professional to take an aptitude test or undergo a period of supervised practice (maximum three years),
4   reject the application.

PSYCHOTHERAPY, THERAPEUTIC COUNSELLING, AND COUNSELLING: THE SAME OR DIFFERENT?

UKCP and BACP both participated in the Lead Body on Advice, Guidance, Counselling, and Psychotherapy, one of many Lead Bodies created at the initiative of the UK Government to develop qualifications that would be based on demonstrated competencies ('outputs') rather than on training received ('inputs'). The theoretical advantage of such qualifications were that training could be carried out on the job, that competencies that had been acquired through work would be recognized, and that a qualification would provide a guarantee of practical skill as well as academic achievement. Establishing competencies meant mapping the core skills of a counsellor and a psychotherapist. The mapping process proved time-consuming and difficult, but it did establish that there were no differences in the specific skills that counsellors and psychotherapists used, but there were differences in generic skills like creativity and research. These generic skills were particularly relevant to level 5, the highest level of the NVQ, corresponding to the competencies that may be expected after three years of higher education. All psychotherapists and therapeutic counsellors can be expected to have the equivalent of a level 5 qualification, but not all counsellors can. Possibly in recognition of these findings, the British Association of Counselling added 'and Psychotherapy' to its title.

Counselling has not developed as a separate profession in Europe and the EAC only has membership from nine European countries. Several members of the EAC are also members of the EAP, reflecting the overlapping aims and goals of the two organizations. The person-centred approach often thought of as the paradigmatic counselling approach in the UK, is represented in Europe in the Network of Person-Centred and Experiential Psychotherapy and Counselling. We shall in this chapter refer to 'counselling and psychotherapy' as a single activity, and this reflects our own description of our own teaching and practice. For example, when we founded a new training institute we called it the New School of Psychotherapy and Counselling.

THE RELATIONSHIP BETWEEN 'PSYCHOLOGY' AND 'COUNSELLING AND PSYCHOTHERAPY'

Many psychologists practise psychotherapy or counselling, and in many European countries a training in clinical psychology is considered to provide adequate evidence of competency in psychotherapy. This situation is changing in the UK and in some other European countries. In the UK, psychologists who wish to practise psychotherapy have had the opportunity to train as counselling psychologists, and can now be registered as such. In addition, the BPS is introducing a register of psychotherapists for any chartered psychologist who has additional training in psychotherapy.

The criteria for registration are not yet established, but it is likely chartered psychologists who are registered with UKCP will be eligible for 'grandparenting'. Most of the psychologists who are registered with UKCP will have completed a training in psychotherapy, additional to their training in psychology. This will make the training of psychological psychotherapists equivalent to that of medical psychotherapists: a first degree, followed by general professional training, followed by specific training in psychotherapy for four years.

Psychotherapists argue in Europe about whether psychotherapy is an independent profession. That means that an undergraduate degree and general professional training in either psychology or medicine are not essential to psychotherapy training, any more than a degree in theology and five years as a parish priest are essential. Being a priest and practising psychology will bring relevant experience. A theology and a psychology degree provide knowledge that is applicable to psychotherapy. But, or so it is argued, other degrees and other kinds of life experience should also count as a basis for psychotherapy training.

Psychologists in many countries now oppose the existence of an independent profession of counselling and psychotherapy, arguing that training in psychology *is* an essential prerequisite for a psychotherapist. This has led many countries that have introduced regulation of psychotherapy in recent years to restrict reimbursements for psychotherapy to qualified psychologists or psychiatrists (see Figure 3.1: these countries are black on the map). Finland, Hungary, and Austria are exceptions. The governments of these countries have accepted the importance of psychotherapy and have tried to make it as available as possible (see Figure 3.1: the countries with horizontal hatching). One way of doing this is to recognize several routes into the profession, not just the psychology or medical routes.

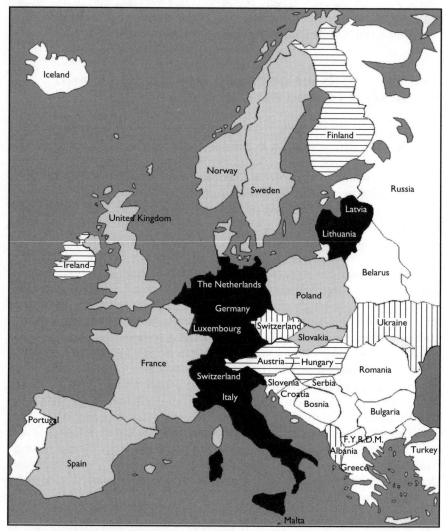

Figure 3.1 Regulation of psychotherapy in Europe. Grey = voluntary regulation, black = statutory regulation with psychotherapy restricted to medicine and psychology; horizontal hatching = statutory registration; vertical hatching = voluntary registration based on European Certificate of Psychotherapy; white = no regulation

REGULATION

The EU is active in promoting equivalence between professional training in the interests of mobility, but it has no interest in imposing standards of training or practice. In fact, the European Commission has also resisted the appointment of designated authorities for psychotherapy or counselling, although it has, as we have already noted, appointed them for psychology. One reason for this is that psychotherapists and counsellors are divided in many European countries with no one body having the authority to speak for all. The same tendency to splitting has dissuaded many European states from regulating psychotherapy. Finland, Austria and Hungary are exceptions. To use the title 'psychotherapist' or to receive reimbursement from the state and from certain insurance companies in Austria and Hungary, it is necessary to be on a government-maintained register. The criteria for registration are comparable in each of these countries, although only three years of training is required to be a practitioner in Finland but to be a trainer or supervisor requires an advanced level training of 4–6 years. No distinction is made between practitioner level and advanced level in Austria or Hungary. Psychology is also state-registered in Finland, Austria and Hungary, but by a separate procedure as these countries recognize that psychotherapy and psychology are distinct professions.

Restriction of reimbursement has been a common way to regulate psychology and psychotherapy in the many other parts of Europe. Reimbursements may be restricted to practitioners who have received state-recognized or local-government-recognized training, to those who have received particular types of training, to particular types of psychological approach, or to a combination of all of these. In some countries reimbursement is only made to psychotherapists who are also psychiatrists or psychologists. In many European countries, third parties such as the state health benefit system or insurers may only reimburse psychotherapists if psychological treatment by either a psychotherapist or a psychologist is given on the recommendation of a medical practitioner. However, insurers are increasingly specifying modalities or durations of psychological treatment, too. Voluntary regulation has developed in most European countries, with psychologists, psychotherapists and, in a few countries, counsellors having their own national organizations who maintain a register of accredited practitioners. The BPS and EFPA recognize that psychotherapy and psychology are sufficiently different that a specialist register of psychological psychotherapists is needed.

Registration is based on a tripod of training standards, ethical commitment, and continuing professional development, which, in the case of counsellors and some psychotherapy modalities, include the continuing supervision of practice even after registration.

Voluntary registration exists alongside control by reimbursement in many countries. Many practitioners hope, as they do in the UK, that these voluntary arrangements will develop into statutory registration, although there are also dissenting voices about the dangers of regulation. One of the main advantages of registration is that it provides some security to the public. Being registered therefore confers commercial advantages that may justify the paperwork and scrutiny that it involves.

TRAINING STANDARDS

One of the strengths of psychotherapy and counselling is that they attract people with a wide range of backgrounds and aims. This is also true of psychology, but the requirement that all psychologists must have a psychology first degree does make for a more homogeneous profession. However, this variety is also a weakness when it comes to agreeing a common approach, a weakness that is further complicated by the number of different psychotherapy modalities, each of them requiring something slightly different from their trainees. Cognitive-behavioural therapists, for example, do not require their trainees to have personal therapy unlike almost every other modality recognized by UKCP. A successful solution to this is for entry to the register to be determined by adherence to an overall training standard and, in addition, to specific training requirements specified by the modality.

Both the EAP and EFPA have been working towards common training standards across Europe for their respective professions. EFPA has a working document, but the EAP has already created a register based on the 'European Certificate of Psychotherapy', whose regulations were developed by a large representative working group over several years. More and more European countries are awarding the ECP, and the register therefore includes practitioners from many European countries. Two European countries, Ukraine and the Czech Republic, have also adopted the ECP as the basis for their own state registers of psychotherapy. Possessing the ECP means that a practitioner moving to another country which accepts the ECP will be eligible for inclusion on the voluntary register of her or his new country.

CONTINUING PROFESSIONAL DEVELOPMENT

Training standards were not originally devised as an assessment of competency, but as a means of acculturation – of ensuring that each practitioner of a modality had studied the same theory and acquired the same beliefs. Training is now seen more as a means of imparting essential knowledge and skill. Training standards are accordingly seen as an assurance of competency even though, in psychotherapy, studies have shown a limited correlation between a practitioner's training and the outcome of the therapy that they provide (Stein & Lambert 1995). Direct measures of competence are difficult to devise, and even more difficult to apply, but increasingly the public expects that psychologists, counsellors and psychotherapists continue to maintain their skills, long after they have been trained.

Two approaches are being taken to this. The first is to require continued training or professional development (CPD). The other is the introduction of practice guidelines, which set out what competent practice is. Psychologists, counsellors and psychotherapists in many European countries are starting to set out the requirements for CPD approval, and to link approval to continued registration. They are starting long after fellow organizations in the USA, perhaps because there is greater professional scepticism in Europe about the value of training in safeguarding competence.

Guidelines are a fairly new concept in clinical practice. They reflect a cultural shift from the notion of skill being a product of the wisdom and experience of an experienced practitioner, to the notion of it being a rule-bound activity in which evidence is selected, tested and applied. Clinical guidelines have been defined as 'systematically developed statements to assist practitioner and patient decisions about appropriate health care for specific clinical circumstances' (Field & Lohr 1990). They have been quickly subverted by the wishes of governments, insurers, and other third party payers to limit the costs of healthcare and it is probably fair to modify this definition to read, 'systematically developed statements to assist practitioner, patient, and payer decisions . . .' (Field & Lohr 1990: 39).

Guidelines exist for specific therapies, and for specific conditions. Their development has been driven by the USA, and by the power of insurance companies and health maintenance organizations in the USA to influence clinical judgement. The US National Guideline Clearinghouse currently publishes 61 for the use of psychotherapy in a range of conditions, including cardiac rehabilitation, borderline personality disorder, the misuse of drugs, and suicidal behaviour in children. A recently published UK guideline for the treatment of schizophrenia also included psychotherapy (National Collaborating Centre for Mental Health 2002). This guideline was commissioned by NICE (the National Institute for Clinical Excellence) to inform purchasing decisions by the UK National Health Service. It is likely that in the near future clinical guidelines will continue to be developed country by country, in response to local purchasing demands. Clinical guidelines are also being developed by psychotherapy organizations, particularly when faced with a rapidly growing and new area of their field. The BACP has, for example, recently developed guidelines for its members on their use of internet therapy (Goss *et al.* 2002).

Although there are no European guidelines in psychotherapy, the European Commission has funded an international collaboration of guideline developers – the AGREE collaboration, which includes partners from nine European countries and partners from Canada, New Zealand, and the USA. One of the first reviews published by the partners has shown disparities in how guidelines are disseminated and implemented.

ETHICAL GUIDELINES

The development of ethical codes has usually lagged behind the development of training regulations in the early years of psychotherapy organizations. Ethical codes are only useful if they can be backed up by adequate complaints and disciplinary procedures, and these are both time-consuming and onerous. However, registers, whether voluntary or statutory, are only useful if they not only attest to training but to ethical standards.

There is considerable similarity between ethical guidelines in Europe, and between the ethical guidelines of psychologists, psychotherapists, and counsellors. Their core is the provisions against sexual, financial, emotional, and other exploitation (Blunden 1999). These guidelines often need to be given a specific interpretation by training institutes in particular modalities. For example, touching would be considered to be a boundary violation by many analytic therapists, but is an essential element of the work of body therapists. Taking off clothing would be anathema to most cognitive-behavioural therapists, but might be acceptable for those therapists who use massage or even hydrotherapy in their work. In recent years, the dangers of 'false memory syndrome' have pointed up the potential difficulties in hypnotherapy or regressive therapies that may increase the risk of false memory (Brandon *et al.* 1998).

Recently an attempt has been made to integrate the diverse national guidelines into European principles, and both EFPA and EAP have published ethical guidelines (European Association of Psychotherapy 2003). The EAP principles are divided into specific undertakings, which give a useful introduction to the areas of ethical concern currently (see Table 3.2).

Pan-European guidelines will probably have to remain guidelines until there is greater harmonization in the legal systems of different European countries. As noted previously, most European countries have ratified the Convention of Human Rights and Fundamental Freedoms. This has only happened recently in the UK, and the implications are only beginning to permeate through UK practice. At the moment, there is considerable doubt in the UK whether proposed legislation to give courts the right to detain individuals diagnosed with a personality disorder, and require them to receive treatment, is in contravention to a person's right to protection from arbitrary detention. The treatment that is proposed is primarily psychological and will pose new ethical dilemmas for UK counsellors, psychotherapists and psychologists. The ethical codes of the BPS, the UKCP, the BACP and other organizations will have to include reference to these dilemmas that are specific to this local legislation, and will not be relevant to other European countries.

Table 3.2 Coverage of statement of principles of European Association for Psychotherapy

Heading	Areas covered
Responsibility	The transparency, honesty, and autonomy of the therapist.
Competence	Careful work. Continuing professional development. Developing the skills and ability to work with excluded or disadvantaged groups.
Moral and legal standards	Adherence to relevant laws, codes, and guidelines. Non-discriminatory practice. Respect for human rights.
Confidentiality	Maintaining confidentiality. Circumstances of disclosure. Dealing with non-consenting client.
Welfare of the client	Welfare of client comes first. Avoidance of dependence or exploitation. Relationship with client when psychotherapist employed by a third party. Avoidance of unnecessary prolongation of therapy.
Professional relationships	Respect for colleagues. Proper working with colleagues. Avoidance of harassment or sexual exploitation. Being a good employer of other professionals. Dealing with ethical violations of other professionals. Sharing authorship of publications. Obtaining institutional sanction for research.
Public statements	What can be said in advertisements, catalogues, radio broadcasts etc. (the longest list of any of the principles).
Assessment techniques	Using appropriate assessments, reporting them accurately, reporting their limitations, interpreting the results to the client, ensuring that the assessors are appropriately trained.
Research	Obtaining consent, minimizing harm, allowing participants to withdraw at any time without penalty.

A final obstacle to a unified, agreed, set of ethical guidelines for Europe is the multiplicity of existing guidelines. In the SEPT study (Tantam *et al.* 2002), we found that many psychotherapists had previous professions (Table 3.3), with 25 per cent being psychologists and 17 per cent being medically qualified. These and other professions have their own ethical guidelines, and they sometimes do not coincide.

Psychotherapists have to work in an increasingly complex ethical framework which reflects professional guidelines, perhaps more than one of these; specific guidelines which exist in the UK and other European countries for research and for consent; guidelines proposed by Europe-wide organizations, including modality-specific organizations; the guidelines of employers, which may address specific issues like discrimination, harassment, and continuing professional development; and, finally, legal requirements that cover human rights, disability access legislation, anti-racist legislation, social security law, and employment law.

Table 3.3 Competing loyalties: the professional backgrounds of European psychotherapists (N = 359)

Previous profession	Percentage psychotherapists with that profession
Teacher	30.92%
Psychologist	25.63%
Counsellor	19.55%
Other	15.17%
Social worker	15.04%
Medical doctor other than psychiatrist	9.19%
Psychiatrist	7.52%
Nurse	7.24%
Clergy	6.41%

Given this complexity, the ethical practitioner is best advised to make her or his guiding principle the best interests of the client.

IMPLICATIONS

We feel sorry for an aspiring psychotherapist who cannot make up their mind what training to pursue in the current state of flux in European psycho-therapy, psychology and counselling. Their decision will be influenced by the conditions in their own country, but even that may not be the main determin-ant of their choice if they want to have the flexibility to work in other coun-tries in the future. Let us consider how a hypothetical trainee might make their decision.

Kurt is an 18-year-old who has devoured the works of Freud and would like to be a psychotherapist. He lives in Cologne, in Westphalia. His careers master at school advises Kurt that many psychotherapy training institutes do not take candidates younger than the age of 25 as some personal maturity is required. It is also a graduate entry profession. So he is advised to choose a relevant course at university and Kurt chooses psychology. When he has completed this, he has to choose a suitable psychotherapy training. Although he knows that psychoanalysis con-tinues to have a very high status in Germany, he is drawn to the ideas of Gestalt therapy, which he has heard about on his course. So he applies to his local Gestalt training institute, but is told that he is still too young. He is also told that even as a fully qualified Gestalt therapist he will not be able to be reimbursed if he treats patients who are funded by the state's health insurance unless he is a qualified psychologist. Kurt therefore applies to do a training in clinical psychology and this gives him a valuable background in research and in the treatment of severe mental illness. But he is given less training than he expected in psychological treatment, and there is a strong cognitive-behavioural bias to what he does get. Once he obtains his professional qualification in psychology, Kurt reapplies to the training institute. However, he now has a family and cannot afford to stop working. So he wants to work part-time and do the training part-time. Unfortunately the main seminar of the week at the Gestalt institute falls on the one day that he has to be in the clinic, because it is the weekly case allocation meeting. Fortunately, he is able to find another Gestalt institute in a nearby town and undertakes his training on a part-time basis. It takes four years, but at the end of that time he is able to build up a private practice in Gestalt therapy quite quickly, and is soon able to cut down his hours working in the state-funded hospital.

REFLECTIVE QUESTIONS

1   What part do guidelines play in continuing professional development?
2   Your principal professional organization has just published guidelines for the therapy of survivors of child sexual abuse. You wrote during the consultation process, pointing out the flaws in them, but your letter was ignored. Your own practice reflects your views, and is not consistent with some of the guidelines. What should you do?
3   Your current client, a litigious sort, wants to know what the guidelines are for the therapy of his condition. What might you do and why?
4   You are a member of one professional organization but are employed by an organization, which uses the ethical guidelines and codes of practice of another professional organization, what implications might this have for you?

REFERENCES

Blunden, F. (1999) What makes a good psychotherapist, bad? Talk given to Universities Psychotherapy Association Conference, 1999.
http://www.popan.org.uk/Articles/003.htm [On-line].
Brandon, S., Boakes, J., Glaser, D. & Green, R. (1998) Recovered memories of childhood sexual abuse. Implications for clinical practice. *British Journal of Psychiatry*, 172, 296–307.
Council of Europe (2003a) Convention for the Protection of Human Rights and Fundamental Freedoms, ETS No. 005.
http://conventions.coe.int/treaty/en/WhatYouWant.asp?NT=005 [On-line].
Council of Europe (2003b) *Demographic Yearbook, 2002*.
http://www.coe.int/t/e/social%5Fcohesion/population/demographic%5Fyear%5Fbook /2002%5Fedition/ [On-line].

European Association of Psychotherapy (2003) *Statement of Ethical Principles.*
   http://www.europsyche.org/contents_suche.asp?content_id=EAP_ETHICAL_
   PRINCIPLES&bereich=eap [On-line].
Field, M. & Lohr, K. (1990) *Institute of Medicine Committee to Advise the Public
   Health Service on Clinical Practice Guidelines. Clinical Practice Guidelines: Direc-
   tions for a New Program.* Washington, DC: National Academy Press.
Goss, S., Palmer, S., Jamieson, A. & Anthony, K. (2002) *Online Counseling Guidelines.*
   Rugby, UK: BACP Publications.
National Collaborating Centre for Mental Health (2002) *Schizophrenia. Core
   Interventions in the Treatment and Management of Schizophrenia in Primary and
   Secondary Care.*
   http://www.nice.org.uk/pdf/CG1NICEguideline.pdf [On-line].
Schneider, H. (2000) *The Recognition of Diplomas in the European Community.*
   http://www.fdewb.unimaas.nl/eurecom/PDF/Papershneider.PDF [On-line].
Stein, D. M. & Lambert, M. J. (1995) Graduate training in psychotherapy: are therapy
   outcomes enhanced? [Review] [94 refs]. *Journal of Consulting & Clinical Psychology*, 63, 182–196.
Tantam, D., van Deurzen, E., McHale, E., Pritz, A., Szafran, W., Zerbetto, R. *et al.*
   (2001) The Survey of European Psychotherapy Training 1: Information provided
   in the National Reports. *International Journal of Psychotherapy*, 6(2), 141–187.
Tantam, D., van Deurzen, E. & Osterloh, K. (2002) The Survey of European Psychotherapy Training 2: questionnaire data. *European Journal of Psychotherapy, Coun-
   selling & Health*, 4, 379–396.
Tantam, D. & van Deurzen, E. (1999) The European citizen's right to ethical and
   competent psychotherapeutic care. *European Journal of Psychotherapy, Counselling
   & Health*, 2, 228–235.
World Bank Group (2003) World Development Indicators Database World Bank
   Group.
   http://devdata.worldbank.org/data-query/ [On-line].
Zerbetto, R. & Tantam, D. (2002) The Survey of European Psychotherapy Training 3:
   What psychotherapy is available in Europe? *European Journal of Psychotherapy,
   Counselling & Health*, 4, 396–406.

Further information about the ECP can be found at
http://www.europsyche.org/contents_suche.asp?content_id=EAP_ECP_HOW_
   TO_ APPLY&bereich=eap

The US National Guideline Clearinghouse is at http://www.guideline.gov/index.asp

The AGREE collaboration is at http://www.agreecollaboration.org/

Chapter 4

Psychological contracts with and within organisations

Michael Carroll

Jeremy was spitting venom. Tears of fury streamed down his face. 'How could they do this to me after all I have given them,' he shouted, 'I gave them the best 10 years of my life. I was in the office every morning at 7.30 a.m., never left once before 7.30 in the evening, lost the best years of my children's lives . . . and now they do this to me.' Jeremy had been made redundant from his Managing Director job with a large bank and I was his counsellor. 'Clearly, they were a poor employer,' I said, 'they didn't treat you well, didn't pay well, they didn't give you a deserved redundancy package.' 'Not at all, they were terrific employers.' 'Why are you so angry, then?' I probed. We worked with the anger and Jeremy came to realise, slowly, that his negative feelings were not about a company that broke its contracts or treated employees poorly. I still remember Jeremy's words: 'I will never get into that kind of a relationship with an organisation again.' Jeremy had discovered the power of the psychological contract. He had felt angry and betrayed, not because the company had broken its contract with him or treated him badly, but because he had worked out a psychological contract with them (albeit they knew nothing about it) – that if he worked dedicatedly and conscientiously the Bank would never make him redundant.

The aims of this chapter are to describe what is meant by the psychological contract, show how the psychological contract is an integral part of all contracts and how it can be applied to the work of counsellors, especially those who work within organisations. While the focus of the chapter is on trainee's awareness of the ethical and professional implications of understanding and working with the psychological contract, the ideas and applications will also be of relevance to experienced counsellors, in particular those who supervise the work of others.

CONTRACTS

Contracts (overt and covert) underpin all relationships whether these are one-to-one, team or organisational. They contain the agreements, conscious and unconscious, of all parties in the relationship and the rules and procedures that guide these relationships. Overall, contracts revolve around

- 'exchange' (what we will do for each other),
- a sense of 'reciprocity' (two-way arrangements),
- 'choice' (I or we freely enter this arrangement),
- some sense of 'predictability' (we can have some guarantees that this will happen),
- the future (we 'will' do),
- the responsibilities of parties concerned (I will take accountability for doing x if you take accountability for doing y).

While overt contracts attempt to articulate these elements, either verbally or in written form, words and gestures are always open to interpretation. It is because they are open to interpretation that the psychological contract is part of all contracts. Individuals bring to their contracts and agreements their own assumptions, beliefs and expectations, most of which will be unspoken and unnegotiated. This part of contracts is called the 'psychological contract', the subjective side that contains our hidden agendas in respect of the covert contract.

THE PSYCHOLOGICAL CONTRACT

Psychological contracts are much more prevalent than overt, negotiated, agreed contracts. In our heads we work out an agreement with someone else, a team or an organisation. Unsuspectingly, we make them mentally sign it and thereafter it has all the force or a binding agreement. There is a psychological agreement in place when you hear phases such as: 'But I had expected you to . . . I thought we would . . . I understood it to mean that . . . I hoped . . . anyone can see that is what should be done . . . I believed that . . . I assumed . . . .' Breaking the psychological contract (where someone else or an organisation does not keep the promises I have made on their behalf) often results in more pain and distress than breaking an actual contract. Sills (1997) points out that failed or discontinued treatment in therapy is largely caused by a difference in expectations between participants, i.e., differences in the psychological contract.

Contracts are like icebergs with the formal, agreed and overt contract as the part of the iceberg that is above water, while the unseen, unnegotiated psychological contract is the part beneath water (Hewson 1999). Like most icebergs, the part below water is much larger than the part above water, and much more lethal. Understanding psychological contracts, how they emerge for individuals, teams and organisations, is a key concept in fostering and enhancing healthy relationships. Not being aware of their existence and their power often leaves people confused as to why certain behaviour takes place. A client comes for counselling expecting the counsellor to provide answers as to why her relationships with men continually break down. Unaware of this psychological contract, the counsellor works to facilitate insight into the client's past that contributes to her present situation. The counsellor does not acknowledge these expectations nor work with them, resulting in frustration for the client who continually asks the counsellor what she should do. Eventually, the client terminates the sessions and tells her colleagues there is little point in going to counselling to someone who will not advise her on relationship problems.

It is not what is written or said that makes up the psychological contract but how it is 'understood' by both parties. Rousseau (1995: 9) writes 'the psychological contract is individual beliefs, shaped by the organisation, regarding terms of an exchange agreement'. The subjective side of the contract (the psychological meaning it has) does not come solely from within the individual but is shaped by outside factors. Contracts, in general, and the psychological contract, in particular, are 'promises about the future' (Rousseau 1995: xi). And like all promises, while we might want to believe and choose to believe aspects not within the written contract, others can 'lead us on', imply, hint at and even support hidden aspects of the contract. Society, culture, race, religion and a host of other sociological and environmental factors influence contracts, and the psychological contract. Rousseau and Schalk (2000: 284) define the psychological contract as 'an *individual's interpretation* of an exchange of promises that is mutually agreed on and voluntarily made between two or more parties'.

THE PSYCHOLOGICAL CONTRACT AT WORK IN COUNSELLING IN ORGANISATIONS

Let us look at the details of several interweaving psychological contracts as they pertain in a counselling arrangement within an organisational setting.

A CASE EXAMPLE

George is a professional and experienced counsellor who works as an associate for an Employee Assistance Programme (EAP). He sees employees in his own home who are referred through the EAP call line for an organisation called Avec. It is part of George's contract with the EAP that he engages in clinical supervision for his work and his supervisor provides an annual supervisor report to the EAP. There is also a case manager, an employee of the EAP who oversees counselling cases and who will contact George (or indeed, George will contact her) if there are any administrative or clinical decisions to be made regarding clients (e.g., request for more counselling sessions over and above their allocated six, where there is need for referral as in the case of alcohol or drug abuse or where there are crisis issues, e.g., where children might be at risk or where there is a suicidal client). Imagine the interconnection between psychological contracts when a client (let's call her Mandy) comes to George from the Company through the EAP for face-to-face counselling. Figure 4.1. Outlines the overt relationships and the eight conscious contracts.

In the counselling arrangements outlined below there are eight overt contracts:

1   The employment contract between George and the EAP.
2   The counselling contract between George and the individual employee.
3   The supervision contract between George and his supervisor.
4   The contract between George's supervisor and the EAP.
5   The case management contract between George and the EAP case manager.
6   The contract between the EAP case manager and the EAP.
7   The contract between the EAP and the company.
8   The employment contract between the company and the individual employee who is coming for counselling (in this instance, Mandy).

While there are eight overt and probably written contracts, there is double that amount of psychological contracts (16) present in the above set of relationships. So while George and the EAP have a written contract both have signed, each will have a very different psychological contract with one another. This counselling room in George's home is alive with unseen but active psychological contracts and awash with the implications of these 16 psychological contracts operating at different levels of the system. What might these psychological contracts look like and how might they infringe on the counselling work?

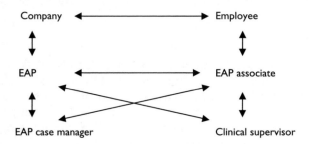

Figure 4.1 Eight contracts at work in the counselling system

THE PSYCHOLOGICAL CONTRACT IN THE SYSTEM – A CASE EXAMPLE

Mandy Jones, 35 years old, joined Avec (a fictional company) two years ago and works as Assistant Head of HR. During her induction week she read, agreed with and signed her formal contract of employment. Unknown, certainly unarticulated by her, was a psychological contract behind the written contract. This psychological contract emerged, partially, from Mandy's background and experience.

Mandy has twice had female managers whom she considers treated her unjustly, the last one (in her view) being responsible for her being made redundant. She comes from a hardworking family where her parents sacrificed for her education and told her 'that hard work and dedication were the ways ahead'. She tends to get on well with male managers and usually makes a very good No. 2 to a male boss. Married with two children, Mandy is anxious about the future, especially the economics. Some of the unarticulated expectations she brings to her new job and new company are:

- If I work hard I will be promoted (the Head of HR is due for retirement soon).
- If I make myself indispensable, when the cuts come I will not be made redundant.
- Watch out for female managers – they are out to get me.
- This new company will see my talents and use them.
- They promote those who have abilities in this company.

While the formal and overt contract says nothing about these aspects of Mandy's work, imagine her anger, hurt and disappointment when her recent annual appraisal was poor. Her boss (a woman) told her she was underperforming and that there was little hope of her taking over the HR job. It is this that brings Mandy to counselling with George where she pours out her story, amid tears of hurt and anger, about how unfairly she feels she has been treated especially, and once again let down by a female manager.

Unknown to Mandy, George has joined the EAP with high hopes that he would move from being an associate to the full-time counsellor (employed by the EAP) with Avec. He has worked hard, put himself out for demanding clients and a demanding organisation (Avec) and has even put up with what he considers excessive paperwork and interference from the EAP bureaucracy. Just before Mandy appears for her first counselling session, he has read a letter from the EAP saying they have appointed another counsellor to the Avec job but would like him to stay on as her associate.

While Mandy and George each approached work with two contracts in mind (written contract and psychological contract) so did Avec and the EAP. What Avec's contract with their employees did not specify was:

- That you are expected to lend a hand when it gets busy and that will probably mean extra hours (without pay) occasionally. No one will demand this but it is 'expected' (a hidden threat). Mandy knew this but chose to ignore it because of her home commitments with two children.
- That there are certain emotions allowed (and not allowed) within the company, especially what feelings you express to your boss and to the customers. Mandy had on several occasions got into conflict situations with her boss (HR Director and female) and publicly had disagreed with her.
- That if you come across unethical or unprofessional practice, you keep it to yourself (Mandy had questioned the professionalism and justice of the selection and promotion system and suggested it was linked to 'an old boys' club' mentality).

Avec are unhappy with the EAP provisions and have told the EAP management that the contract is up for review when it ends in two months' time. The EAP have asked the case manager to see how she can intervene to create a more positive image – this is an important and large account for the EAP. The case manager, unknown to George, is anxious that these sessions with Mandy are handled sensitively and plans to talk to George about the difficulties that would emerge if Mandy takes out a formal complaint (which she is thinking about) against the HR Director. The case manager knows Avec would be impressed if, as a result of the counselling with George, Mandy was to drop her possible complaints charge and even better if she became 'more aligned with company values' (HR Director's words which were passed to the case manager).

The hidden, sometimes unshared and even unspoken, feelings and ideas from many of these psychological contracts (not mentioning some of the other psychological contracts loose in the system) will enter the counselling room as soon as George and Mandy begin speaking. Possible professional/ethical issues that George has to face are:

- Realising that he has to keep a neutral stance between the individual employee, the organisation and the EAP. It would be very easy for him, under pressure, to make the needs of any of these paramount to the detriment of the others.
- Confidentiality: to whom does he talk about what?
- That he could be involved, by Mandy, in a complaints procedure against her boss, wanting him to come to an industrial tribunal and speak on her behalf.
- That Mandy feels he is taking the side of the organisation against her and takes out a formal complaint against him through his professional organisation.

MAKING MEANING – UNDERLYING PSYCHOLOGICAL CONTRACTS

How do people, teams and organisations as well as individuals, construct this reality called the psychological contract – mostly through their meaning-making apparatus. We do not meet reality as it is – we experience it through a series of filters (meaning-making perspectives, cognitive schemas) that interpret that reality for us. Figure 4.2 presents this in a lineal way.

We never know reality; all we know is our interpretation of it. Hence, the many differences in interpretation that exist about the same reality, e.g., five people looking at a cow can see five different realities: one a steak, one a painting, one a price, one a family pet and another a case of foot and mouth disease. A new counsellor joins the staff in a GP surgery. She offers her clients a confidential setting, assuming that the doctors understand this, while the doctor who refers patients for counselling expects her to talk to him about referred clients so that together they can provide help. The GP nurse also expects this team approach. The client has never thought about the issue. The counsellor assumes the doctor has cleared contact arrangements with the client and phones to make an appointment. She finds herself talking to the client's partner who knows nothing about this arrangement and asks 'who are you, why are you phoning my husband?' The number of different ways of interpreting the same reality (what confidentiality means) is already immense.

How we perceive is more or less determined by our meaning-making per-spectives. (We see things, not as *they* are, but as *we* are.) We fit reality into this already-existing mould, which defines the shape and texture of what is given us in reality. In that sense all contracts are psychological contracts since all are sent through our meaning-making perspectives. As these perspectives change so do our understanding and interpretations. In one sense, there are no contracts, only psychological contracts because it all depends on interpretations.

How are these filters created? Where do they come from? Some are inherited (e.g., religious beliefs and attitudes, culture, locality, race, gender) and until held up to the light for examination are never changed or adapted. We continue to interpret reality as others have taught us without critical reflection. Other filters come from our experience. There is some evidence that we cannot perceive or see what, in some way, we have no experience of before. Furthermore, we cannot see what we cannot emotionally deal with. One of Freud's major insights was that if we cannot tolerate reality or find it too painful, we change it. He named the human being's infinite capacity to change

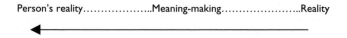

Person's reality.....................Meaning-making........................Reality

Figure 4.2 Interpreting reality

the meaning of reality as defence mechanisms. Defence mechanisms are filters (meaning-making perspectives) we have developed to help us interpret reality. Of course, they create the reality we want and not the one that is there.

Psychological contracts emerge from the way we make meaning (interpret) reality and that in turn is a result of a number of factors (Figure 4.3). Each of these elements impacts on the way in which we encounter and make sense of reality. Our own present needs influence our perception. Individual and personal needs in attending a party will largely determine what it means for different individuals: for one person who is hungry it is an opportunity to eat; for another who is looking for business, a chance to find customers; for the lonely person, an environment to make friends and so on. So with organisations, we also bring our own needs to them and through these needs we set up 'psychological contracts'. It is the same with counselling. A client may well expect that a counsellor become a friend (never articulated). She brings him presents, sends cards between sessions and asks to meet outside the counselling room. When he gently reminds her that this is a counselling relationship, she feels hurt and embarrassed, and rejected. He, on the other hand, wonders if he is being too harsh in the situation and begins to think it might be helpful for her to write down her thoughts and send them to him between sessions as part of the counselling.

Society, as mentioned above, is highly influential in helping create how we interpret reality and so set up psychological contracts. Society and cultural norms, often handed down to us from others and imbued with meaning from them, create expectations for us, give us the meaning of events and happenings and through their influence set up assumptions. Our own ability to reflect, superficially or in depth, will also influence the psychological contract. Critical reflexivity is a key to understanding our ways of making meaning and hence our level of awareness of expectations and how we interpret events. The absence of reflection in life leaves individuals and groups open to mindless

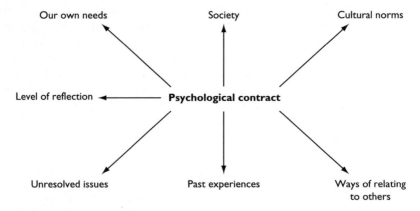

Figure 4.3 Influences on the psychological contract

routines where the underlying assumptions we bring to all our relationships are never questioned or held up to the light. Likewise, our own unresolved issues, past experiences and ways of relating to others result in perceptions and ways of seeing that create our expectations and assumptions. Psychological contracts are a result of an interweaving of these elements – hence their power and depth.

MANAGING THE PSYCHOLOGICAL CONTRACT

It is often the difficulties within the psychological contract that results in ethical charges, formal and informal complaints, legal stances and breakdowns in professional (and indeed personal) relationships. It is imperative to look at how counsellors, supervisors and others involved in helping relationships can 'manage' this side of the contract.

Hewson (1999) articulates suggestions that are helpful ways of managing the psychological contract in a healthy manner:

- All parties are involved actively in developing the contract.
- The contract provides a mental set or overall perception of what end goal is in mind for everyone.
- Contracting creates a guard against the abuse of power and all participants are aware of and patrol the boundaries of power.
- Overt contracts are designed to minimise covert agendas.
- Transparency, honesty, openness and dialogue are built into contracting.
- Contracts are often developmental (they change and need to change over time, e.g., marriage) and need to be re-negotiated. The psychological contract is part of that development.
- Contracts are emotional arenas as well as rational agreements.
- Pay heed to the social, political, organisational and professional contexts in which contracts are lived and played out.
- Pick up subtle shifts in expectations from those who are part of the contract – articulate these expectations.
- Track the relationships to see if any new needs emerge (e.g., in counselling and psychotherapy, transference issues).

From these underpinnings, I offer three ways in which the psychological contract in any relationship can be identified and addressed so that it can be a healthy part of the contract relationship.

1. Using transactional analysis

Using a very simple version of Transactional Analysis (Berne 1966) I try to get individuals to take a stand within one of the ego-states and speak their needs and expectations from within it. Training managers and working with supervisors in a large government organisation, I taught them the TA model within 10 minutes using a few principles:

- There are three positions we can speak from, communicate from or listen from. The Child state is that part of us (still alive within us) that remains the child and reacts as you would have done as a child: the Adult state is that reasonable, rational side from which we make adult decisions and the Parent state is that set of injunctions we use or our parents used on us.
- We can move through these three ego states depending on the situation and what happens to us, e.g., a manager can move into Child state and be hurt and sulk as a result of a comment made, be Parent in telling off an employee, be Adult in working with them to make the best decision about a way forward.
- Complications arise when we talk to each other across the states (e.g., Adult talks to Child, or Parent, or other Adult; Child talks to Adult, Parent or other Child etc.

After this initial introduction, I then play the role of a new employee/ supervisee coming into the organisation and having a fictional conversation with the manager or supervisor. I come to the manager from the 'child-employee' state and make statements such as:

I am thrilled to be here and know this will be great fun. I wonder if it is possible for me to be your favourite employee. In fact, it would be truly marvellous if I could be the only employee you look after. Also, until I get up to speed, could you be available for me anytime I need you. I would also like you to have all the answers so that when I am stuck you will offer me a way through.

Participants almost always laugh at this role-play. It is amusing and puts into words how a child might think as if s/he were an employee aged 3 or 4 and could put their needs into words. I make the point, of course, that the child is still alive and active within us and while none of us would put the above 'irrational needs' into words, they often are played out transactions we go through at work. Issues of envy and jealousy, favouritism, patronage as well as bullying, harassment, cliques are often child areas played out in the adult arena of work.

What would happen were they to change roles and have the Child-manager now speak to the Adult-employee? Were they honest with each other and staying solely with their roles, what kind of conversation would emerge? The Child-manager might say, 'Please don't cause me any problems. I need this to be very enjoyable for both us. I want you to love me all the time, never say anything bad about me to others. Come on, let's play . . . If you hurt me I will never talk to you again.'

This exercise is one of the most powerful ones for bringing out and articulating hidden agendas (the psychological contract) in its most startling and vivid manner. It makes explicit the hidden assumptions and expectations we bring to relationships and organisations. It can be used where there is any relationship involved, counsellor/client, supervisor/supervisee, teacher/pupil etc.

2. Using scenario planning

A second way of identifying and managing psychological contracts is through scenario planning or scenario learning. We do not know the future, nor, despite our best efforts, can we predict it – but we try:

- Income tax will not go up; interest rates will fall.
- The Northern Ireland troubles will end/won't end.
- The price of houses will increase by 12 per cent.
- We'll live happily ever after.
- I will have a job here for life.

Scenarios are not predictions – they anticipate possible futures. Scenario planning is about imagining possible futures so that we are ready for whatever happens. Shell initiated this method of planning in the 1980s and began from the premise of thinking about 'What would happen if . . . The price of oil fell? Or if USSR was dismantled, or if the Cold War finished?' Shell was the only company that had scenarios for these possibilities. Others didn't – why? Because they had predicted the future – the price of oil would not fall, USSR would not be dismantled, there was no chance of the Cold War ending. Rather than attempt to predict for ourselves it makes more sense to ask the 'What if' questions:

- What if . . . you were to get ill and couldn't work anymore?
- What if . . . you took a year's sabbatical and set off around the world?
- What if . . . you change houses?
- What if . . . your most significant relationship broke down?
- What if . . . you live to be 60, 70, 80, 90?

The 'miracle question' of de Shazer (1988) is a wonderful case of scenario learning – you wake up tomorrow morning and a miracle has happened. What would be different? We run through the events as if they were already happening – it's a simulation game. That is why armies play games: simulation games are ways of anticipating what a potential enemy might do. Pilots learn by simulation before they tackle real flying. So clients can learn by imagining and trying to live life without problems or symptoms ('You wake up tomorrow morning and your depression is gone – what would be different?' 'Imagine you and your partner are talking again and in a healthy, mature relationship – what is different from the present?')

In devising possible futures we create stories that show our contracts in the future. So scenario planning for counselling contracts at work (which put us in touch with the psychological contract hidden in the overt contract) is to consider scenes such as the following:

- What if . . . this person does not get better?
- What if . . . there is someone at serious risk?
- What if . . . as a result of counselling the person leaves the organisation?
- What if . . . I uncover cases of sexual harassment here?

Playing out such scenarios allows consideration of what is often not considered, articulated, spoken about or even allowed into individual, team or organisational consciousness, namely, the psychological contract.

3. Asking the question: 'What are we not talking about?'

A third way of managing psychological contracts is to review relationships with a particular question: 'What are we *not* talking about?' This incisive question enables participants in relationship (dyads, teams, organisations) to look at some of the difficult areas of that relationship that will contain the unspoken elements. It is often here that the psychological contract content appears. I sometimes ask individuals in team development exercises to write out the answers to three questions:

- What can I talk about in the team today that will be easy for me to discuss?
- What can I talk about, but it will be difficult?
- What can I not talk about just now?

My hope is that in answering these questions, particularly the third question, the team members will get in touch with elements of the psychological contract. Recently, on a team development day, several participants articulated one area that they could not talk about at the moment, i.e., withdrawn and sullen mood of the team leader. They talked about their collusion in not addressing or challenging the leader about this behaviour and were able to deal with it in an adult way, as was the leader. The psychological contract between them was that it would have been too painful and conflictual to manage.

CONCLUSION

This chapter has concentrated on understanding the content and process of the psychological contract (the subjective side of all contracts) as it pertains for individuals working in organisational settings. Ignoring this element of contracts and concentrating on the overt and agreed contract often results in not understanding why people feel let down, betrayed and hurt even when this overt contract has not been broken. In many ways it is the psychological contract that is the most important part of any contract for this is the 'reality' of the contract to most people, even if it is the emotional and psychological and hidden part of the overall contract. Awareness of the existence and implications of psychological contracts in counselling helps practitioners stay in touch with the unarticulated needs and requirements (often unconscious) of clients. Helping clients articulate these expectations allows both parties to deal with them in an adult manner. Much professional/ethical boundary-breaking in counselling takes place because these unsaid assumptions and hopes are not recognised, acknowledged and managed.

REFLECTIVE QUESTIONS

1   What are some of the filters (meaning-making perspectives) that influence how you see your contracts with clients?
2   Can you think of and articulate a psychological contract you have with another person, team or organisation, e.g. your clinical team?
3   How might you deal with the unreasonable demands made on you as a result of a 'psychological contract' a client has with you?
4   How might organisations help employees effectively manage their psychological contract with them?

REFERENCES

Berne, E. (1966) *Principles of Group Treatment*. New York: Grove Press (reprinted, 1994, by Shea Press, Menlo Park, CA).

Hewson, J. (1999) Training supervisors how to contract in supervision, in E. Holloway & M. Carroll (eds.), *Training Counselling Supervisor*. London: Sage.

Rousseau, D. M. (1995) *Psychological Contracts in Organisations, Understanding Written and Unwritten Agreements*. Thousand Oaks, CA: Sage.

Rousseau, D. M. & Schalk, R. (eds.) (2000) *Psychological Contracts in Employment: Cross-National Perspectives*. Thousand Oaks, CA: Sage.

de Shazer, S. (1988) *Clues: Investigating Solutions in Brief Therapy*. New York: Norton.

Sills, C. (ed.) (1997) *Contracts in Counselling*. London: Sage.

Chapter 5

The person in ethical decision-making: living with our choices

Malcolm Cross and Joanne Wood

Ethics are complex and have far-reaching implications for the practice of counselling, psychology and psychotherapy. The fit between ethical principles and our own value and moral position can lead to varying degrees of discomfort (Cross & Papadopoulos 2001). This chapter will provide an account of why conflictual feelings may arise and how we might learn and develop through these important experiences. A range of issues relevant to the experience of ethical decision-making will be discussed including the role of reflection in the development of self-awareness, the impact of core values on therapeutic work and the importance of self-censorship in the professional context. Ethical dilemmas will be viewed as a route to personal and professional development and as opportunities for growth as a therapist and a person. This chapter draws extensively on the work of George Kelly, *The Psychology of Personal Constructs* (1955/1991) as a framework for understanding the personal impact of ethical practice.

ARRIVING AT AND MANAGING THE CONSEQUENCES OF ETHICAL DECISIONS

Ethical decision-making involves choice. In the domain of professional ethics these choices are open to scrutiny and as a consequence, we as decision makers, must be prepared to be open about *what* we do and willing and able to provide an account of *why* we act as we do. We as professionals may fully endorse the principles enshrined in our professional codes of ethics; however, this does not leave us immune to potential emotional, philosophical or spiritual conflict and confusion. Conflict often arises when (i) attention to professional ethical codes in the conduct of therapy suggests two or more competing courses of action and (ii) where ethical conduct may require us to behave in a manner that is at odds with our own personal or core values.

Rowson (2001) describes three helpful classifications for understanding an individual's relationship with ethical decision-making: the consequentialist, deontological and pluralistic view. Each of these perspectives outlines a '*why*' of action and thus provides a personal and professional story that imbues a rationale and potential defence for our actions. These approaches to ethical decision-making, however coherent, cannot ensure that the professional will not feel the impact of decision-making personally.

The consequentialist perspective

This view is concerned with outcome or consequence and is sometimes referred to as the 'teleological' view, *telos* being the Greek word for 'end' or 'objective' (Rowson 2001). From this perspective:

- the end result determines the action,
- rules of conduct are likely to be seen as somewhat flexible.

CASE EXAMPLE

Paul has been working with John for some months. Despite a productive start where both client and therapist have agreed how they might work together to achieve change – progress has stalled. After recognising feelings of frustration and impotence to effect change, Paul dutifully engaged in a process of examining possible obstacles and impediments to progress took his concerns to supervision. Reviewing the case in supervision and discussing his ideas with colleagues, Paul developed confidence in the formulation that casts John as vulnerable, fearful of rejection and terrified of leaving the 'known', however painful his present circumstances are. What was clarified through consultation was the importance of avoiding reinforcing John's fear of failure that has coloured much of his life.

So when, in a pivotal session, just hours after Paul had conceded in supervision that he doubted John's capacity and willingness to change, the client asks, 'Do you ever think that I'm a lost cause? I guess that I am frustrating to work with?' Was Paul unethical to reply that he understands that change does not happen in a predictable linear way and that he sees the failure to make progress as a glitch? He goes on to say that he has every confidence in the client.

The therapist in this example was motivated by outcome. Fearful that sharing anxiety about the client's capacity to change could seriously compromise an already fragile sense of self, the therapist failed to tell the whole truth in what he believed to be the best interests of the client. As doubtful as the therapist was of the client's capacity to change, the therapist was sure that confirming the client's doubts would be wholly unhelpful. From this perspective, actions are ethically neutral and thus neither essentially good nor bad in and of themselves. It is the action in the pursuit of what is determined to be the best possible outcome for the client that exerts influence on what s/he will do.

This approach to ethical decision-making may be attractive as it gives the initial impression that decisions are made *for* the professional, on the basis of the rule of best outcome. Should this be so, the therapist could abdicate responsibility by citing outcome, not personal preference, as the determining factor in their action. Unfortunately few actions are wholly positive; as our constructivist colleagues so regularly remind us, all events are open to interpretation. What may look like an obviously good idea today may turn out to be a source of pain tomorrow.

The deontological perspective

This view gains its name from the Greek *deon*, meaning duty. From this perspective:

- particular actions are intrinsically good or bad,
- there is little room for interpretation,
- actions that are regarded as intrinsically good usually include: respecting autonomy, telling the truth, keeping promises and being just,
- actions regarded as intrinsically bad usually include taking life and inflicting harm.

The deontological position is most closely associated with a style of meaning making described by Kelly (1955/1991) as 'tight construing'. Tight construing is rigid, rule-bound and inflexible. It provides certainty where events and circumstances are perceived as unambiguous and the course of action predetermined. This style of meaning making is unquestionably the most efficient in terms of time taken to reach a decision and the conservation of emotional and intellectual energy where principles are not in conflict. Unfortunately professional practice often involves negotiating your way through ethical dilemmas where attention to one ethical principle may suggest a course of action that could be interpreted as unethical in the light of another generally accepted and equally important code of conduct.

The principle of respecting the autonomy of the client may be compromised where the therapist perceives that the client is engaging in actions that may put him/her or others at risk. Therapists are likely to forewarn clients about this possibility when they outline the caveats about confidentiality. However, the therapist's decision to take information outside the therapeutic relationship in order to ensure the safety of the client or others will inevitably lead to the compromise of the client's right to determine his/her actions.

Case example

James was referred to therapy following his discharge from hospital after a recent suicide attempt. In working with James it quickly became apparent that issues of powerlessness were central to his distress. On the morning of his subsequent session James telephones Sarah, his therapist, informing her that he would not be attending his appointment and sees no hope for the future. James then discloses that he has taken a large quantity of prescribed medication with the intention of ending his life. On establishing that James was at home and following his abrupt termination of their conversation, Sarah telephoned the ambulance service, local police and the client's GP. Sarah's actions were determined by her agency's protocol for dealing with actively suicidal clients. Although she had a responsibility to minimise harm to her client, this did not ease her discomfort in compromising James's autonomy. This discomfort was particularly significant given the nature of the case and her understanding that her actions were just one further example of where the client was powerless to exercise control over his life.

Therapists confronted with the requirement to make choices between equally important ethical principles will inevitably feel torn and 'anxious'. Anxiety here is understood as defined by Kelly (1955/1991) as a psychological state arising when one was unprepared or unable to make sense of what one perceived. That is, the therapist was caught without the capacity to see into the future and unable to know what the actual consequences of choices will be. Regardless of our preparedness to deal with ethical dilemmas in principle, in practice we cannot predict the precise set of outcomes arising from particular competing choices.

   The notion of doing no harm may at first appear unproblematic to the average therapist; however, we are reminded regularly of the pain and difficulty our clients experience when they entertain the possibility of, or attempt to implement change. It is often said in jest that therapy should come with a health warning. The discomfort so often associated with the psychotherapeutic process may be experienced as injurious in the moment and deleterious in the long term if not handled well. There are always at least two interpretations of events that take place in the therapy context. The perspectives and interpretations of the therapist and client may or may not concur and it may be long after the event that the client has the courage to disclose that s/he experienced a particular observation or interpretation of the therapist as confusing, hurtful or upsetting. In other words we may not know that we are in effect doing harm as we do therapy.

The pluralistic perspective

Ethical pluralists are those who seek to balance both generally understood ethical codes and principles (deontological position) with the most beneficial outcome for a particular client (consequentialist position). Ethical pluralists are likely to have to spend much time and resources entertaining multiple possibilities – Kelly (1955/1991) in terms of the 'Creativity Cycle' describes such processes of personal meaning. The Creativity Cycle sees the individual shifting between tight and loose construing ad infinitum until they reach the most satisfactory understanding of events and actions. This cycle of moving between imagining possibilities and testing them out leads to development of new perspectives and options for action. In the case of ethical decision-making it requires the professional to be conversant with ethical codes while at the same time maintaining a propositional stance where the challenge is to generate as many and varied ideas as possible rather than struggle to come up with the best solution on the first attempt. It is only after multiple possibilities are generated that these ideas are examined in terms of their plausibility and suitability in the particular context. The propositional phase of the creativity cycle bears much similarity with the activity of brainstorming followed by an evaluative phase.

The therapist, prepared to suspend judgement must develop mechanisms or strategies to deal with the inevitable anxiety that accompanies active 'not knowing'. We are after all dealing with real, feeling human beings where the consequences of our actions can be clear and apparent. Whether we get it 'right' or 'wrong', real damage can be done where it remains impossible to control for all contingencies. Psychotherapy is indeed a serious job of weighty consequences and resultant responsibility.

CASE EXAMPLE

Jill came for therapy to seek support for her choice to leave a long-term relationship. Over the course of therapy Jill has grown in confidence and appreciation of self, from a former position of self-subjugation and pervasive doubt. She was actively rejoicing in her new-found sense of autonomy and independence. Quite quickly, Jill sheds a number of relationships that she saw as dependent and depleting of her capacity to focus on her self-development. Unfortunately, Jill failed to distinguish between focused and unsustainable dependency on everyone for everything and the more optimal position of relying on different people for different things. The therapist, Kate, is concerned that Jill's present course of action is extreme and likely to leave her feeling alone and isolated. Concerned that the present course of action has foreseeable negative possibilities, Kate considers a range of possible actions. Jill's autonomy and self-determination might be compromised by Kate's suggestions as to what she 'should' do. A contrasting possibility of course is that by uncritically validating Jill's choices or not acting, Kate could be inadvertently causing harm. In this case, Kate struggled to mediate these competing ethical positions through the use of transparency. That is, she shared her dilemma and encouraged the client to reflect upon these life choices in view of their possible positive and negative implications.

REFLECTION AND EXPERIENTIAL LEARNING

Experiential learning is that learning that takes place through doing. Doing, however, is a necessary but not a sufficient condition for professional development. Reflection on the experience and the processes involved in doing are required in order to profit subsequently from action (Wood 2003). As we develop professionally and accumulate certainty in our practice we must take special care to observe distinctions between what Argyris and Schon (1974) referred to as espoused theories and theories-in-use. Espoused theories are often those that are taught and may be derived from published theory or empirical research. These theories hold favour in professional discourse, while theories-in-use are those that grow out of the unique practice of the individual. Theories-in-use are operationalised routinely and may become second nature to the professional and thus often unavailable to their conscious awareness. For the ethical professional, theories cannot be allowed to become tacit, as we will be at a loss to provide a rationale for our choices. With the dimming of awareness of the influences on our practice comes also an impoverished ability to teach and instruct others.

> Every situation is unique and as a consequence espoused knowledge cannot totally guide practice.
>
> (Wood 2003)

Experiential learning requires us to develop guesses or hypotheses about how and why things might turn out as they do, and if they do not, then to go on to develop better, more embracing and 'successful' accounts for the future. The theory of Personal Construct Psychology (PCP) emphasises personal inquiry and quest. 'It does not say what has or will be found, but proposes rather how we might go about looking for it' (Kelly 1970: 1). Keeping in mind that every event we encounter is unique, Kelly emphasised frameworks for interpretation rather than advocating a search for the inherent meanings imbued in events. In this way knowledge is seen as evolving, and if it is not to be reduced to a redundant bag of facts then it is to be ongoing and lifelong.

For Kelly (1970) the unit of experience was conceived of as a cycle involving five distinct phases (Figure 5.1). This cycle is, however, constantly spinning because, as we have already noted, our experience of events is unique each time we encounter them. Indeed there will always be differences, sometimes

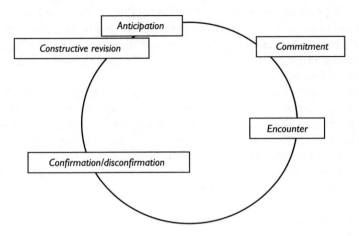

Figure 5.1 Kelly's Experience Cycle (1970)

obvious, sometimes subtle, in time, place and circumstance. Kelly's Experience Cycle can be enormously helpful in understanding the process through which we may learn about ourselves through engaging in professional practice (Cross & Papadopoulos 2001).

At the *anticipation* stage the person looks toward what is to come. Clearly some anticipatory stances are more helpful than others in terms of their utility in processes of learning, change and growth. A myopic, or dispassionate stance closes one to experience, as does certainty. Professionals who seek to take up the challenge of lifelong learning must be open and engage with the dilemmas that their practice yields. Propositionality, or an alert openness is what is called for in this phase of the cycle. Thinking about the impact of ethical dilemmas on the professional, this stage of the Experience Cycle involves noticing that a quandary has arisen. This awareness may be self-generated, where one achieves a felt, cognitive or intellectual awareness of a problem or dilemma. We may also be alerted to ethical issues arising in our work through consultation with colleagues. In each case a stance of openness and a resistance to the temptation to avoid circumstances that are difficult or uncomfortable must be maintained.

Commitment in the cycle of experience implies self-involvement. It requires us to view the dilemmas that we encounter as an opportunity, with potential to shape our subsequent practice and view of the world and ourselves. Commitment implies that we as professionals feel resilient enough to ask others and ourselves difficult questions. It is an attitude of openness and self-confidence and is characterised by an absence of defensiveness and a desire to clarify and learn to work at increasing our understanding.

The *encounter* stage suggests engagement and full participation in the process of ethical decision-making at an intellectual and emotional level.

Working through the dilemmas that will inevitably confront you, this stage of the process of personal and professional development will manifest questions such as: 'How do I genuinely feel about this at the deepest level?' 'Did I expect this outcome and what does this mean for me today, tomorrow, as a therapist and ultimately a person?'

Confirmation and *disconfirmation* refer to our evaluation of the stages of anticipation, commitment and encounter in terms of the outcome of the intervention. Did things turn out as we predicted? Has the process brought into awareness challenges, opportunities, and contradictions that had previously escaped our attention? In view of these insights what theories about others or ourselves need to be revised or fine-tuned? Or has this experience strengthened our resolve or certainty regarding a previously held perspective on particular events or sets of circumstances? The answers to such questions are likely to facilitate the resolution of the final stage of the experience cycle – constructive *revision*.

Personal and professional development is not a one-off event or activity. As the experience cycle implies experiential learning is continuous and ongoing. Within this model each revolution is both informed by the encounters of the past and in turn shapes our encounters with the future (Cross & Papadopoulos 2001). Reflection should not be something that we engage in only when confronted with an obstacle or surprised by an unexpected outcome. It is a gift of higher-order intellectual functioning and one to be exploited in the pursuit of best professional and ethical practice. Although prompts for reflection tend to arise out of conflict or dialectic (Schon 1983), professionals need to develop a discipline of reflection as second nature so that cyclical self-evaluation becomes a habit and routine.

IDENTIFYING CORE VALUES

Ethical practice may require us to act in ways, which are inconsistent and at odds with whom we believe ourselves to be. This conflict can be painful and disorientating when core values are in conflict. Through the identification of core values we can develop insight into why the most appropriate course of action may cause us discomfort and regret. Doing the right thing will not always feel right. If we are successful in knowing the origins of the impact of events on us we can begin to appreciate the way our unique nature colours our perspective on events. As our understanding of our self grows we may develop the capacity to interrupt the process of assumed causality. Causality in this context is the process of uncritically imbuing particular events or objects with meaning. For example, should we encounter a particular event and experience positive, negative or indifferent feelings the event is labelled good, bad or indifferent. The feeling becomes a quality of the event rather than the property of us, the observer. Thinking through the origins of our feelings and separating these feelings from events provides the opportunity to evaluate options with impartiality. Separating the self of the therapist from the decision-making process helps us maintain our stance of propositionality and openness that is so central to maintaining our professional practice.

In Personal Construct terms core values are referred to as superordinant constructs (Kelly 1955/1991). That is, they are important dimensions for making sense of the world and largely define who we are. In an empirical study designed to determine the validity of the Kellian assertion that some constructs are more important than others and that important constructs are most resistant to change, Hinkle (1965) developed a technique which he called 'Laddering'. This technique identifies why we think and feel the way we do about events. This relatively simple process can be extraordinarily revealing.

STEPS TO LADDERING

The laddering technique is accompanied by engaging in a series of steps as outlined below. An example is provided following this description that will help convey how to engage in the laddering process and why it can be of great personal value.

1   Identify the event or option that gives rise to personal disquiet or concern and record it on the left side of the bottom of a page.
2   Ask yourself what would be the opposite of the event identified and record it on the right-hand side of your paper adjacent to the first event you recorded. This initial process is important, as constructs are bipolar, that is they have two poles.
3   Ask yourself which option you would prefer and place a tick beside it. In the language of PCP this activity is described as identifying the preferred pole of a personal construct.
4   Having identified the preferred pole, ask yourself, 'What is the most important thing about this pole of the construct, why do I prefer it?' Record your answer directly above the preferred pole of the first construct elicited. Now ask yourself what the opposite is of this new construct. Record the opposite pole of this new construct adjacent to the construct pole elicited in step 4.
5   Repeat steps 2 and 3, identifying the preferred pole of these new superordinate constructs and again ask what makes it preferable?

This process should be repeated until you can no longer generate any new constructs. As you reach the top of your ladder of increasingly important constructs you may ultimately be left with a feeling that 'it just is important'. This feeling is likely to arise as superordinate constructs such as these are often preverbal and we may not have readily accessible verbal labels with which to describe such deep ways of seeing things.

An important note of caution offered by many Personal Construct practitioners is that much care should be exercised when working with our constructs at a superordinate level. Such constructs are at the core of who we are as a person and may never have been articulated before. What is often negotiable are the lower-order choices when we understand that the events that prompted a dilemma are more open to interpretation than the all-important superordinate constructions that loom above at the top of the ladder.

CASE EXAMPLE

Carol worked as an independent therapist who accepted referrals from the public and a number of Employee Assistance Programmes (EAP). The case in question arose when she inadvertently accepted a referral from an EAP, called Jane, whom she subsequently learned was the partner of James, an existing client. Although Jane and James lived together and worked in the same office neither knew the other was engaged in or seeking therapy. Carol had seen James for over 10 sessions and had slowly established rapport despite her client's reluctance to trust. Confidentiality and anonymity were of paramount importance to him.

The therapist in this case had observed her usual protocol in accepting Jane as a new client: discussing the presenting problem with the referrer, ensuring she had the appropriate level of competency and contacting Jane to arrange a time to meet for their initial session. During the first session with Jane it emerged that she was James's partner and that neither had knowledge that the other was engaged in counselling and nor did either wish this information to come to light. Carol felt a real sense of discomfort, recognising that she had narrowly avoided arranging Jane's and James's sessions shortly after each other. Having avoided their chance meeting on this occasion, she was acutely aware that, should she attempt to conceal that each partner was a client, this information was likely to emerge in time. She feared that this was likely to undermine her work, as her client reflected retrospectively on Carol's decision to withhold information. A further, but very real concern for Carol was that she felt a strong alliance with James. She doubted her capacity to maintain an impartial stance. Through discussions with colleagues and supervisor she clarified options. It appeared that there was a case mounting for terminating her work with Jane after one session.

Although Carol was confident that she had engaged in a rigorous, albeit frantic, process of consultation and reflection, she nonetheless remained uncomfortable with the options open to her. Having finally decided to terminate therapy with Jane after one session she communicated this by saying:

Carol: I've reflected on our session and thought about how best to help you and it concerns me that I may not have strengths in working with the kinds of challenges that you face. I have a colleague whom I believe is very well placed to provide you with what you need. I would like to encourage you to contact her, or give me permission to do so on your behalf.

Jane was surprised and clearly disappointed. Confused she asked:

Jane: Please can't I continue to see you? I have taken so long to get to this point and told you things that I don't want to tell someone else all over again.

Carol was caught somewhat off-guard and while she had time to think through a range of phrases that she might use to express her decision she was unprepared for resistance. Whilst appearing outwardly calm, Carol quickly grappled with a response that could, as sensitively and honestly as possible, convey what was to be a non-negotiable decision.

Her difficulty in responding was a consequence of her concerns that she was (justifiably) withholding information. Carol felt troubled as a consequence of not being completely honest about her rationale for not working with Jane, knowing that Jane had established a rapport with her and that she may not choose to see another therapist because of this negative experience. Carol also felt confident that she could indeed, under other circumstances, help Jane manage and resolve the issues she presented with. Although she knew what she was doing was right, Carol was personally distressed at actively withholding her capacity to help. In order for Carol to understand why doing the right thing felt so wrong she produced a ladder as a tool to further her understanding of her self.

Carol's ladder (a tick indicates those construct poles that were preferred):

No point in existence	✔	Purpose in my existence
Worthless	✔	Worthwhile
Feel bad about who I am	✔	Feel good about myself
Feel ashamed myself	✔	Sense of pride
Act hurtfully	✔	Positively contribute
Withholding capacity to help	✔	Help

Although Carol chose to 'withhold her capacity to help' in this case she would have preferred under other circumstances to 'help'. For Carol, making a positive contribution leads to a personal sense of pride and positive feelings about herself. She feels worthwhile and ultimately confident that there is a purpose in her existence. It is important to note that, although Carol's discomfort arose as a result of a particular dilemma, the superordinant construct that was invalidated related to many more issues than therapeutic practice. Indeed this core construct of purpose was defining and profound for Carol. Through reflecting on the ladder, she was able to understand the origins of her feelings and identified why it was that when confronted with the dilemma she felt like 'just giving up' and that she was an inadequate therapist and person. Carol realised that if she wanted to feel better about her decisions then she needed to find validation for those preferred constructs. In this example this would mean looking for evidence, both within and outside her role as a therapist – that she positively contributes, identifies activities and aspects of herself that she is proud of, and nurtures feelings of self-worth. Carol would be well advised to look at all the generative things in her life and recognise that there is much done and much more to do.

SELF-CENSORSHIP

Once expressed it can never be erased. This rule of therapy applies to all forms of communication and is particularly important in relation to the verbal and non-verbal actions of the therapist. In order to provide some measure of space for us to digest and reflect upon what our client brings, from time to time we will need to exercise our capacity to self-censor. Self-censorship is the capacity to suspend reaction and avoid conveying knee-jerk reactions to unprocessed disclosures. This capacity not only applies to shocking and provocative information but also information that we might find pleasing. Therapists have enormous potential to shape the discourse of therapy. Smiles and encouraging nods show our hand, as too do looks of shock, surprise and distain.

Advocating the development of the capacity to self-censor is not a plea for therapists to act incongruently or disingenuously. Rather it is a call for professionals to adopt non-judgemental practice and convey that they are robust enough to tolerate and manage all that the client has to share. Temporarily putting your values aside allows you to listen credulously with the aim of subsuming your clients' view of the world (Kelly 1955/1991). Indeed it is this exposure to the unique ways in which our clients live their lives that we are provided with the material with which to do our job and an opportunity to challenge our own preconceptions and subsequently refine our world view.

CONCLUSION

Developing through challenge, learning from reflection and coping with the discomfort of difficult choices are themes that have repeatedly surfaced in this attempt to say something of the personhood-of-the-therapist, in ethical decision-making. Doing the right thing will not always feel good; however, we should not let this dissuade us from engaging squarely with the dilemmas we face. Not only would we risk doing harm, but also lose invaluable opportunities to learn about ourselves and those we seek to assist.

REFLECTIVE QUESTIONS

1   Of the three classifications for understanding an individual's relationship with ethical decision-making (consequentialist, deontological and pluralistic view), which do you feel most comfortably disposed to and why?
2   Recall an incident where a colleague offered only lip-service to an ethical principle or guideline, highlighting the tensions that exist between what Argyris and Schon (1974) refer to as the difference between espoused theories and theories in use? What constituted the espoused theory and the contrasting theory in use in that context?
3   Identify a seemingly trivial event that caused you great personal upset? Use the laddering technique to identify what core value was invalidated by that event.
4   What value conflict, if any, can you see as arising from exercising 'self-censorship' in the therapeutic context?

REFERENCES

Argyris, C. & Schon, D. (1974) *Theory into Practice*. San Francisco: Jossey-Bass.
Cross, M. C. & Papadopoulos, L. (2001) *Becoming a Therapist: A Manual for Personal and Professional Development*. Hove, UK: Brunner-Routledge.
Hinkle, D. (1965) 'The change of personal constructs from the viewpoint of a theory of construct implications'. Unpublished PhD dissertation, The Ohio State University, Ohio, USA.
Kelly, G. A. (1955/1991) *The Psychology of Personal Constructs*, Vols 1 & 2. London: Routledge.
Kelly, G. A. (1970) A brief introduction to personal construct theory, in: D. Bannister (ed.), *Perspectives in Personal Construct Theory*. London: Academic Press.
Rowson, R. (2001) Ethical principles, in F. Palmer Barnes and L. Murdin (eds.), *Values and Ethics in the Practice of Psychotherapy and Counselling*. Buckingham: Open University Press.
Schon, D. (1983) *The Reflective Practitioner*. San Francisco: Jossey-Bass.
Wood, J. (2003) 'Mirror, mirror on the wall: considering reflection in professional counselling psychology training'. Unpublished MSc dissertation, City University, London.

Part II

Legal considerations and responsibilities

Chapter 6

Client confidentiality and data protection

Peter Jenkins

The concept of respect for client confidentiality is a value of central importance to counselling, psychology and psychotherapy practice, but it is also one which seems to be increasingly under siege. All training courses will place heavy emphasis on the crucial necessity of maintaining client confidentiality. However, the difficulties of translating this into day-to-day practice are often left to the individual therapist to negotiate for themselves, relying upon guidance of somewhat variable quality from their employing organisation. Some of the resultant problems arise from the fact that confidentiality may well be a key value informing ethical practice, but it is also one, which is heavily constrained by contextual factors. These factors can include whether the therapist is working in a statutory or voluntary agency, or in private practice. Confidentiality is at the same time a *legal* concept with many different connotations. The deceptively simple concept of keeping client information 'confidential' is often beset with challenges or constraints, which make this a highly problematic issue to work with in actual practice.

Therapists need to know about the legal protection for, and limits to, confidentiality for several reasons: firstly, in order to defend client confidential material in a robust manner from unauthorised attempts at access, for example, by managers, funding committees, partners or parents; secondly, to convey accurately to the client any limits to confidentiality imposed by the law, as well as by agency practices such as supervision; thirdly, to facilitate the client's provision of informed consent to record keeping, and their exercise of enhanced rights, such as access, under data protection law.

This chapter falls into two parts. In the first, the emphasis will be on the role of the therapist as *custodian of sensitive client personal information*, i.e. in *deciding to maintain confidentiality or to disclose client information*. It will attempt to outline some of the key features of the law relating to client confidentiality, and to identify some of the situations that may present major challenges to therapists on this issue. The notion of confidentiality will be contrasted with other legal concepts such as privilege and the public interest. Additional duties and requirements placed upon the therapist under data protection law will also be explored.

The second part of the chapter will identify routes whereby agencies *external* to the therapeutic relationship can gain access to client material, by *overriding, if necessary, the therapist's ethical duty to protect sensitive client information*. Thus the client, an employer, the police or the courts can variously seek access. Steps that therapists can take to resist these encroachments of therapeutic confidentiality will be briefly outlined.

PUBLIC INTEREST IN MAINTAINING CONFIDENTIALITY

In terms of ethical practice, maintaining client confidentiality can be framed within wider principles such as fidelity and the keeping of trust with the client (BACP 2002: 3–6). These concepts may then be translated into the specific requirements of professional codes of practice (BPS 2000: 4). At this initial point at least, there is a close correspondence between ethical and legal principles. The legal concept of confidentiality is based on the idea of equity, or fairness, insofar as a person who has received information in confidence should not then make unfair use of it. The common law duty of confidence arises out of the 'special nature' of the relationship between two parties, where it would be a reasonable expectation to keep information private. Examples here could include a relationship of trust between a doctor and patient, between friends, or between a therapist and client. Unjustifiable breach of such confidence, for example by publishing deeply private material, could result in court action by the party suffering the damaging effects of such disclosure. Confidentiality can also be protected by being written into the express terms of a contract, for example by preventing the unauthorised disclosure of innovative therapeutic techniques. However, an expectation of confidentiality will generally be assumed to apply in therapeutic work, even if not written as a specific term of a contract.

Overall, the law takes the protection of confidentiality as a serious matter, but there are clear limits to what can be kept confidential. There is no requirement to keep confidential material which is of a trivial nature, or which is already in the public domain, or where the public interest in disclosure outweighs the public interest in keeping material confidential. The 'public interest' here refers to the court's conception of what is for the 'public good', namely what is in the interest of society as a whole. While therapists are well-versed in the idea of confidentiality as part of their professional training and practice, they are often less familiar with the wider and more authoritative concept of the *public interest*. The public interest, as determined by judges with reference to past case law, may decide to *prevent* publication of confidential information, as in the case of a newspaper threatening to reveal the names of doctors who had contracted the AIDS virus. Alternatively, the public interest may be seen to lie in requiring a journalist to *reveal* the source of leaked health records relating to a convicted murderer on hunger strike.

What is absolutely clear is that therapists cannot protect client information simply by referring to a duty of confidentiality, as the public interest holds decisive authority. Consequently, the notion of *privilege* is attractive to many therapists, as this would enable therapists to protect client confidentiality, even in the face of public interest demands for disclosure. However, unlike some of their counterparts in the USA, therapists do not possess privilege in the UK. The only professional group that does possess privilege, or more accurately whose *clients* possess it, are lawyers. This is in order to facilitate the essential processes of providing legal advice and representation. Interestingly, the only area where a degree of privilege attaches to therapeutic work in the UK is in the field of marital counselling, as this may necessarily involve discussion of legal processes such as separation and divorce.

PUBLIC INTEREST IN REQUIRING DISCLOSURE

Despite the arguments of certain schools of therapy, confidentiality of client material cannot be guaranteed to be *absolute*. While the public interest is generally very protective of confidentiality, it can also *justify* or even *require* that confidential client information be disclosed, albeit in a professional and accountable manner. The situations where the therapist is faced with the need to disclose client information without consent often involve a perceived threat of harm, to the client, to the therapist or agency, or to a third party, such as to a partner or child.

With regard to threat of self-harm or suicide, any limits to confidentiality may already be part of the contract for work with the client. In other words, part of the expressed terms for therapeutic work may have specified that the client's general practitioner will be contacted in the case of threatened self-harm, a condition to which the client has already consented. Client consent to disclosure in this situation would therefore protect the therapist from any future claim for breach of confidence. It becomes more problematic, however, if the therapist is seeking to inform the GP *without* client consent, on the basis that it is in the public interest to prevent self-harm, suicide and the associated possible risk of harm to other members of the family. The courts may well favour the therapist's public interest defence for breaking confidentiality, but this cannot be known for certain without more extensive reported case law on this topic.

In England and Wales, there is the example of the *Egdell* case, where a psychiatrist breached client confidentiality in order to alert the authorities to what was perceived to be a substantial risk to the public posed by a prisoner seeking early release. The psychiatrist's ultimately successful defence against the client's legal action for breach of confidence was made on the basis of the public interest. However, breaking client confidentiality on the basis of the assumed public interest is not a risk-free enterprise, as the public interest cannot be known with absolute certainty in advance. It is, therefore, advisable for the therapist to take informed legal advice before breaking client confidentiality on a public interest basis.

The public interest generally lies in the prevention of crime, or even, as some judges have claimed, in the prevention of antisocial behaviour. The therapist, as citizen, is not legally required to report crime (outside of Northern Ireland), or the threat of crime, but can *choose* to do so in the public interest. Furthermore, therapists may report abusive practice by colleagues to their own employer as a protected disclosure under the Public Interest Disclosure Act 1998.

Reporting of allegations of child abuse can raise particularly acute dilemmas for therapists, where there may be a conflict between a duty of confidentiality to the client, and a wider public duty to protect vulnerable children from harm. It can be made more complex still where the client is a child alleging abuse by family or care-takers, but who insists that no action be taken as yet. Therapists are not under a general legal requirement to report child abuse to the authorities in England and Wales. Section 47 of the Children Act 1989 imposes a duty on the local authority to investigate situations where a child, i.e. a person under the age of 18, is suffering or is likely to suffer 'significant harm'. Therapists working for statutory organisations in health, education and social services will be bound by their contract of employment to follow child protection guidelines based on the key document Working Together (DoH *et al.* 2000; DoH, 2003). These guidelines will also apply to therapists working in voluntary organisations, which have subscribed to reporting procedures devised by the local Area Child Protection Committee (ACPC), superseded by Local Safeguarding Children's Boards set up under the Children Act 2004. However, the obligation to report abuse is based here on a therapist's *contract of employment*, rather than any more general mandatory reporting requirement, such as applies to most childcare and healthcare professionals in the USA (see 'Case example'). Hence therapists in England and Wales, who work in private practice, or for voluntary organisations outside the immediate ambit of the ACPC framework, are not bound by law to report abuse, although the ethical and moral pressures to do so may be considerable. Once again, the therapist could employ a public interest defence for breaking client confidentiality with some confidence in it being recognised as valid by the courts, in the unlikely event of ever being legally challenged by a client.

Case example

Joan was a counsellor working for student services in a College of Further Education. The college managers introduced a new child protection procedure, whereby *all* suspected child abuse had to be reported to a named person within two hours, or the employee would face disciplinary proceedings. Joan's forcefully expressed view was that this policy seriously compromised the client's right to confidentiality, as these were often mature youngsters with compelling reasons for not wanting their past abusive experiences to be reported to social services. She felt that the blanket reporting procedure was also flawed in putting her in an identical position to that of a lecturer or any other college employee, by taking no account of her ethical duty of confidentiality, or her commitment to a professional code of conduct. Following somewhat difficult discussions, the student services manager declined to renew her contract of employment at the end of the academic year.

STATUTORY DUTIES TO DISCLOSE CLIENT INFORMATION

The law generally seeks to protect client information from unauthorised disclosure without consent, as has been outlined. In rare cases, therapists can seek to use a public interest argument where they disclose information about clients presenting a risk to themselves or to third parties. In the case of child protection, therapists may be under a specific obligation of their contract of employment to follow child protection reporting guidelines, as opposed to any general mandatory requirement to report alleged abuse. There are currently two situations where therapists are under a statutory obligation to report client information to the authorities. Under s. 52 of the Drug Trafficking Act 1994, any citizen is required by law to pass on information obtained as part of their business, trade or profession about drug money laundering, with a particular relevance, presumably, for those involved in banking and financial services.

There is a further specific duty to disclose information to the authorities about terrorism, under s. 19 of the Terrorism Act 2000. Furthermore, there is a duty under s. 39 of the Act not to prejudice investigation by disclosure to any other person. A therapist would therefore be obliged *not* to inform the client that they had informed the authorities, in order to avoid being prosecuted. Terrorism is closely defined for the purposes of the Act as involving serious violence to property or persons, a risk to life or health, safety, or electronic systems. Information about actual or planned terrorist activities needs to be reported as soon as is reasonably practicable to the authorities, or where appropriate procedures exist, to the therapist's employers.

STATUTORY DUTIES TO PROTECT CLIENT CONFIDENTIALITY

More recently, there are now additional statutory requirements protecting client confidentiality to consider. The Data Protection Act 1998, considered in more detail below, puts in place very clear and specific protection for client personal data, and for the more sensitive kinds of personal data likely to be explored in therapy. (For discussion of the implications for record keeping, see Chapter 9). Unauthorised disclosure or disclosure without client consent is a criminal offence under s. 60 of the Act. Finally, Article 8 of the Human Rights Act 1998 endorses the client's right, if not to confidentiality or privacy per se, then at the very least to the right to *respect* for the citizen's 'private and family life, his home and his correspondence', and protection from any unauthorised interference by a public authority with the exercise of these rights.

The Data Protection Act 1998 represents a major shift in perspectives on a number of themes, which lie at the very heart of the therapeutic enterprise. Flowing originally from a European Directive, the Act regulates the former anarchy of a free market in personal data, and imposes statutory controls on its storage, distribution and communication. Citizens possess rights to know what forms of personal data are being processed about them, to give or withhold consent to its processing, and to gain compensation for inaccurate or damaging recording. The Act extends earlier rights of access to computerised information to most forms of manual recording, building on already established rights with regard to social work, education and health records. Taken together with the Human Rights Act 1998, and the Freedom of Information Act 2000, the Data Protection Act 1998 is designed to mark the opening of a new period of transparency and professional accountability in the handling of personal information (Information Commissioner, 2001).

The Act protects client confidentiality regarding use of personal data in a number of specific ways. Personal data refers to information relating to an identifiable living person, and, normally, data processing requires client consent. Categories of personal information deemed as 'sensitive', including information on a client's mental or physical health or sex life, require *explicit* consent for processing. Handling and communicating client information is governed by relatively clear principles of data processing – see below.

Principles of data processing: Data Protection Act 1998
Personal data is to be:

1   processed fairly and lawfully,
2   obtained only for one or more specified lawful purposes,
3   adequate, relevant and not excessive for their purpose,
4   accurate and kept up to date,
5   not kept longer than is necessary,
6   processed in accordance with the rights of data subjects,
7   protected against unauthorised use or loss,

8   not transferred outside the European Economic Area unless subject to similar levels of data protection.

However, the actual detail of day-to-day recording involves reference to increasingly complex and somewhat arcane regulations, governing the use of specific 'accessible' records such as health, education and social work files. Even the injunction to keep records 'no longer than is necessary', for example, can raise real anxieties amongst therapists and their managers in the absence of statutory requirements or established agency protocols with a clear rationale for the retention and destruction of records. (For more detailed discussion of the Act and its impact on therapeutic practice, see Jenkins and Milner 2000; Bond 2002; BPS 2002; Jenkins 2002).

The Act strengthens existing common law protection for client confidentiality outlined above. Disclosure of personal data is an offence, unless it is required by law, is necessary for the prevention of crime, or is made with the consent of the data subject, or where the consent of the latter is likely to be given. Disclosure of personal data in the public interest remains a valid ground, based on already well-established legal principles.

The major thrust of data protection law has been to extend the principles of accountability and transparency to previously unregulated forms of data handling, such as manual records kept in structured filing systems, and to electronic recording such as audio and video tapes. This change impacts on therapeutic confidentiality and recording in three ways. Firstly, whereas it was previously only an *ethical* requirement for client consent to data processing, this now becomes, in general terms, a legal requirement, particularly for the processing of sensitive data. Secondly, therapeutic records in *manual* form are now subject to regulation, control and accountability via legal processes. Thirdly, the Act throws into sharp relief the variable practice of therapists and agencies with regard to the recording, storage and use of confidential client information.

In effect, the law redefines therapeutic recording as a *public* rather than a purely *personal and private* activity. The onus is now firmly placed upon therapists and their agencies to take control of what may well have been previously multiple and often unregulated forms of records. These might well include official agency records, ongoing records of therapy, notes for supervision and allegedly *private* reflective recordings kept outside of formal agency processes. The Act therefore presents a major challenge to the former (and possibly widespread) practice of keeping confidential client notes as, in effect, a parallel system of covert and unaccountable recording. For clearly, if the client is unaware of the very existence of therapeutic process notes in addition to any more formal records retained by the agency, then he or she is not in any position to exercise their now substantial rights of consent, inspection and challenge under data protection law.

ACCESS TO CONFIDENTIAL CLIENT MATERIAL

The first part of this chapter has focused on the role of the therapist as custodian of sensitive client information, bound in this role by legal responsibilities and options available under common law and statute. This second part now turns to explore some of the situations where access to client material can be gained *without* the therapist's agreement or discretion, in effect via *legally enforced disclosure*. Access to confidential client material may be sought by the client, an employer, solicitors acting for the client, the police investigating alleged crime, and the courts in the course of legal proceedings, both civil and criminal (Jenkins 2001). Although firm evidence is lacking, it appears, at least from anecdotal evidence, that attempts to gain access to confidential therapeutic material by external agencies have definitely been on the increase in the recent period.

An employer may seek access to client records for the purposes of audit or evaluation, or to appraise risk of damage to property, or harm to other staff or to the public. In the case of audit, there should be provision for evaluation on the basis of suitably anonymised data, which does not infringe client confidentiality. Employer access to client information should be on the basis of prior client consent. Thus in employee counselling or occupational health settings, clients need to be forewarned if confidentiality is limited, on the basis of a clear contractual agreement between client, therapist, counselling agency and employer. Many counselling agencies have explicit provision for therapist disclosure of criminal activity or alcohol or drug dependency, where there is a perceived risk to other staff or to the public. Client consent or agreement to a contractual term will protect the therapist in this situation from legal challenge.

Of course, one of the possible interested parties wanting to gain access to records of therapy may well be the client him or herself, and it clearly becomes problematic to refer to the client, who is obviously a participant in the therapy, as being somehow *external* to the therapy. However, some therapists may well find a request by a current or former client for access to their records as being somehow intrusive or disruptive of the therapeutic process. It may perhaps be thought to indicate a sense of mistrust of the therapist, or a possible challenge to the therapist's competence, or represent some unspoken or unfinished business (see 'Case example'). However, putting such interpretation aside for the moment, the client has a right to access their record of therapy under ss. 7–8 of the Data Protection Act 1998, in an understandable and permanent form, within 40 days. Access to third party material on file may be restricted to protect the latter's right to confidentiality, but the law no longer provides an absolute protection for such information. In the case of specialist statutory records, such as health, education and social work files, access can be denied where it would result in 'serious harm' either to the client or to a third party. Where the agency or therapist keeps *only* manual records, and these are *not* part of a 'relevant filing system', i.e. structured to enable systematic access to personal data, then the client has access *only* to outline information rather than to the detailed contents.

CASE EXAMPLE

Paul was a troubled young man, who received counselling from a small voluntary agency for problems of low self-esteem and difficulties in forming relationships. Six weeks after abruptly ending the counselling, he asked for access to his files under the Data Protection Act. Adam, the counsellor, was initially resistant to this request. The agency's management committee took the view that the client had a legal right of access to the agency's own some-what brief records, and also to any more detailed record of the content of the therapy made by the counsellor and held in the same file. Adam arranged a session to go through the notes with Paul, in what turned into a difficult and inconclusive meeting. Paul then requested access to the notes of *supervision* relating to him as made by Adam's supervisor. After taking advice, the agency refused access to the supervisor's notes, on the grounds that all super-vision in the agency was based on the principle of client anonymity, and that these notes therefore fell outside the ambit of the Data Protection Act.

In some cases, client access may be sought in the context of preparing for a complaint to the therapist's employer or professional association. In many situations, access may be sought in the context of legal proceedings, where records of therapy are thought to be useful evidence in support of a claim for damages, or a criminal prosecution. Solicitors do not generally have legal authority to enforce disclosure of client records without a court order or a signed client consent form. Certain counselling agencies take a firm stance in responding to requests made by a solicitor for release of records, based on a policy of *only* releasing records under a court order. Of course, a client can easily circumvent this by seeking access under data protection law, rather than by going through legal processes.

The police as part of a criminal investigation, prior to court proceedings may also seek access. The law provides somewhat rare protection for records of therapy in this specific situation. Under s. 12 of the Police and Criminal Evidence Act 1984, records of therapy are classed as 'excluded material', requiring a warrant authorised by a circuit judge before the police can seize them as evidence.

ACCESS TO CONFIDENTIAL CLIENT MATERIAL BY THE COURTS

Therapists do not possess privilege, and must comply with a court order for release of records for use by the courts. This is on the public interest basis that the courts require the fullest access to material, which may be of evidential value in deciding a case. For some therapists, there is uncertainty about whether a court order necessarily applies to 'second sets of notes', namely notes which are more subjective, personal and reflective in character than the presumably more formal records kept for agency purposes. One argument frequently advanced here is that of *ownership*, in that these informal records are seen to belong to the *therapist* rather than to the agency, and are therefore not covered by a court order for disclosure. Unfortunately for this view, the courts do not accept the concept of ownership of notes as a crucial component of any argument either for or against disclosure. Any records, which are in the ownership, possession or control of the therapist, are due to be disclosed, under the penalty of contempt of court for failure to comply. Where the therapist no longer has the notes or did not keep written records, than the court may issue a witness summons for the therapist to give evidence in person.

This situation graphically illustrates the limitations of any professional training, which does not put client confidentiality in the context of the wider judicial public interest. A therapist cannot simply refuse to comply with an order for disclosure on the basis of an ethical commitment to client confidentiality, any more than a medical practitioner can. However, case law seems rather to contradict this in the instance of Dr Anne Hayman, a psychoanalyst, who declined to answer questions put to her in court, even at the risk of going to prison for contempt of court. She presented a coherent and forceful argument that any disclosure of client material would be both counter-therapeutic and a breach of client confidentiality (Hayman 2002). In this case, the judge finally accepted her arguments, and she was able to step down from the witness box, but this was on the basis of judicial discretion, rather in establishing a formal legal precedent for others to follow.

Client records released to the court are used as evidence in an adversarial process, where both sets of legal representatives have access to confidential material. Clients may not fully appreciate that their records are used in a highly selective and frequently challenging way, in order to further the interests of the case. It is not usually possible for the release of records to be controlled by the client, on the grounds that some material is too sensitive or potentially damaging to their case. Opposing solicitors will be on the lookout for material which indicates prior psychological problems, alcohol or drug dependence, previous sexual history, inconsistency in recorded narratives, or any other material, which tends to undermine the credibility of the client as witness.

While therapists need to comply with a court order for disclosure of records, there are certain limited steps that can be taken to protect client confidentiality from total breach in the public environment of the court. Disclosure of records should be limited to 'the necessity of the case' in civil proceedings, for example, rather than give solicitors a free reign in trawling through evidence of limited relevance to the case in hand. A case can be made to the judge via a formal letter or by a case put by a legal representative for records to be perused by the judge, with a view to excluding irrelevant material from disclosure. This can be successful in limiting or avoiding disclosure of client information that is highly sensitive but also not material to the case. Therapists faced with this situation need to take advice from their employer's legal department, if one exists, or their professional association or professional indemnity insurance company. In some cases, the cost of legal representation is not covered by professional indemnity insurance policies, where the therapist is technically a witness, rather than an actual party to the case.

CONCLUSION

It will be seen that therapists work in a complex matrix of countervailing legal duties regarding client confidentiality, made up of many factors. A decision to disclose client information, or *not* to disclose, needs to be based on a close consideration of specific factors such as client consent, contractual limitations to confidentiality, the therapist's own contract of employment, the strength of a public interest argument case for disclosure, and, more rarely, actual statutory obligations to disclose. There are also the assumed duties of confidence arising from the special nature of the therapeutic relationship and from the express or implied terms of any contract for such work.

Client confidentiality has additional protection under statute, such as data protection and human rights law. The therapist's role as custodian of sensitive personal information can be further challenged by rights of client access, and by the court's authority. Therapists do not possess privilege, and need to be aware of the very limited means available for defending confidentiality under the threat of enforced disclosure.

REFLECTIVE QUESTIONS

1   How might you construct an ethically based argument for *not* breaching client confidentiality in cases of potential harm by a client to self or to a third party?
2   How far should therapy be considered as a 'special case', i.e. exempt from the requirement to comply with court orders for disclosure of client records?
3   To what extent might the impact of limited confidentiality or of court access to records undermine or assist the therapeutic process?

4   Regardless of specific data protection requirements, what are the ethical arguments for and against client access to records of therapy?

REFERENCES

BACP (British Association for Counselling and Psychotherapy) (2002) *Ethical Framework for Good Practice in Counselling and Psychotherapy*. Rugby, UK: BACP.

Bond, T. (2002) The law of confidentiality – a solution or part of the problem? in P. Jenkins (ed.), *Legal Issues in Counselling and Psychotherapy*. London: Sage.

BPS (British Psychological Society) (2000) *Code of Conduct, Ethical Principles and Guidelines*. Leicester: BPS.

BPS (British Psychological Society) (2002) *Guidelines on Confidentiality and Record Keeping*. Leicester: BPS.

DoH (Department of Health), Home Office, Department for Education and Employment, National Assembly for Wales (2000) *Working Together to Safeguard Children: A Guide for Inter-Agency Working to Safeguard and Promote the Welfare of Children*. London: Stationery Office.

DoH (Department of Health) (2003) *What To do If You're Worried A Child Is Being Abused*. London: DoH.

Hayman, A. (2002) Psychoanalyst subpoenaed, in P. Jenkins (ed.), *Legal Issues in Counselling and Psychotherapy*. London: Sage.

Information Commissioner (2001) The Data Protection Act 1998: Legal Guidance. Wilmslow: IC

Jenkins, P. (2001) *Access to Records of Counselling and Psychotherapy*, BACP Information Sheet. Rugby, UK: BACP

Jenkins, P. (2002) Transparent recording: Therapists and the Data Protection Act 1998, in P. Jenkins (ed.), *Legal Issues in Counselling and Psychotherapy*. London: Sage.

Jenkins, P. & Milner, P. (2000) *Record Keeping and the Data Protection Act 1998*, BACP Information Sheet. Rugby, UK: BACP.

Legal references

W v. *Egdell* [1990] Ch 359, [1990] 1All ER 835.

Legal references: statute

Children Act 1989.

Children Act 2004.

Data Protection Act 1998.

Drug Trafficking Act 1994.

Freedom of Information Act 2000.

Human Rights Act 1998.

Police and Criminal Evidence Act 1984.

Public Interest Disclosure Act 1998.

Terrorism Act 2000.

The full text of these Acts is available for purchase from the Stationery Office. Acts of Parliament and Statutory Instruments giving additional regulations from 1988 onwards can be downloaded from http://www.parliament.uk and further policy documents and guidance on child protection can be accessed via http://www.doh.gov.uk and on data protection http://www.dataprotection.gov.uk.

Chapter 7

The legal context of therapy

Peter Jenkins

Practitioners are increasingly aware that their practice is bounded by the law, as well as by ethical and professional considerations. This may be because their work takes place within a statutory setting, such as health or social services, or via the impact of quasi-legal concepts such as contracts and confidentiality, or arising from a growing recognition of issues such as litigation, liability and negligence. Statutory changes such as the introduction of human rights and data protection law have had a major impact of therapeutic practice, which it is no longer possible to ignore (see Chapter 6). Therapists working with risk are also conscious of the interface of their practice with the law in the form of key pieces of legislation such as the Mental Health Act 1983 and the Children Act 1989. Despite the growing impact of the law on therapeutic work, the law is rarely taught to practitioners on training courses in a systematic way comparable to the way it is to other professionals such as nurses, doctors or social workers. The result is that therapists are often uncertain about the nature of their legal responsibilities and unsure about the legal parameters of their work, and may be subject to conflicting advice or guidance about their actual duties regarding compliance with the law.

This chapter attempts to set out a brief overview of the law with particular relevance to therapeutic practice (for more detailed coverage see: Jenkins 1997; Bond 2000). The term law relates to all systems of civil and criminal law, including statute, common and case law. In the UK, there are significant differences between the legal systems operating in Northern Ireland, Scotland and England and Wales. The focus here will be on the law relating to England and Wales. The legal system is based on complex patterns of law. These include statutes, i.e. Acts of Parliament, such as the Data Protection Act 1998. In turn, Acts rely upon additional guidelines in the form of Codes of Practice, secondary legislation such as Statutory Instruments and authoritative guidance and regulations. Common law, on the other hand, is the system of law built up over centuries, devised by judges on an empirical basis. This derives from legal custom and practice, rather than from the formal political process in Parliament. Principles of common law have particular relevance to therapy in areas such as confidence, contract and negligence. Case law provides key markers in the process of debate and decision-making. Specific cases embody key principles, which may then be translated into legislation, or referred to as precedents in deciding complex and contentious cases. The *Gaskin* case, for example, holds a key position in case law, as opening the doors to client access to files. Graham Gaskin, a young man formerly in care of Liverpool Social Services, brought a case against the UK government at the European Court of Human Rights. His partial success with the case then led to major changes in the law. Legislation introduced the principle of client or data subject access to files formerly considered as protected from access on the grounds of confidentiality.

STRUCTURE OF THE LEGAL SYSTEM

There is a major divide within the legal system between civil and criminal law. The criminal law operates to punish breaches of law within the wider community, and requires a correspondingly high threshold for proof of guilt. Therapists may have some contact with the criminal law, but are much more likely to need to know at least the basic features of civil law. Civil law provides remedies for resolving disputes between individuals, such as over property and in child and family proceedings, and concerning the protection of individuals' interests such as privacy and rights under contract. Cases are proven on a less exacting standard, namely 'on the balance of probabilities'.

The area of tort or negligence law has particular relevance to therapists. This is a branch of law, developed since a key case in the 1930s, concerning the limits of professional responsibility to others, including clients. (The term tort comes from the French word for 'wrong'.) Under this law, individual citizens have a responsibility to avoid harming their neighbours by any careless act or omission. In a therapeutic relationship, the practitioner has a similar duty to avoid harming the client, or may face legal action by the latter for damages. Therapists are often quite wary of the threat of being sued by clients on this basis, although the actual obstacles facing clients in bringing a case of this kind are, in fact, substantial.

A client bringing a case of negligence against a therapist needs to establish three conditions: firstly that the therapist owed a duty of care to the client; secondly, that there was a breach of that duty; thirdly, and most difficult to prove in court, that the breach *directly* caused foreseeable harm to the client as a result. Negligence law relating to therapists is an offshoot of law relating to medical negligence, presumably because the roots of therapeutic practice, such as psychoanalysis, can be traced in part to medicine. Medical negligence is a well-established and fast growing field of litigation. However, even here it is markedly difficult for patients to win cases, given the complexity of medical practice and the range of alternative viewpoints that there may be on the appropriateness of any given clinical procedure. In contrast, negligence action against therapists in the UK is almost unknown, at least in terms of successful reported cases, although an unknown number may be settled out of court (see 'Case study').

There are a number of reasons for the relative lack of reported successful cases against therapists on the grounds of negligence. The client needs to prove that the damage caused by the therapist was of a high standard, constituting a psychiatric injury such as clinical depression, rather than simple anger or dissatisfaction. The key problem, in lawyers' terminology, lies in establishing *proof of causation*. The client may be diagnosed as having depression after a course of therapy, but the court needs to be convinced that the therapist actually *caused* this to develop through serious breaches of professional conduct. The defending solicitor could well point out that the client already had a predisposition to depression, or had showed signs of depressive thinking even *before* starting therapy. This approach makes it much harder to pin responsibility for the client's worsened emotional state *solely* on the actions of the therapist. Proving causation in the case of psychological matters is not at all easy, as reference to a whole raft of unsuccessful cases brought against employers for 'workplace stress' will illustrate.

NEGLIGENCE CASE LAW

It is rare for clients to win negligence cases against therapists in England and Wales, although there is now a burgeoning case law for such actions in the USA. The key case relating to therapist negligence in England and Wales is that of *Werner* v. *Landau*. In this case, a client brought a legal action against her former therapist arising out of the latter's attempts to combine psychoanalysis with a social relationship. There were two periods of therapy, separated by a time when the therapist and client had a social relationship, including sending letters, making a visit to the client's flat, and holding discussion about a proposed holiday together. The social contact was necessary, according to the therapist, in view of the client's deep emotional attachment to him, and to avoid the client falling into an anxiety neurosis. On ending therapy for the second time, the client made a suicide attempt and was consequently unable to work. The client successfully brought an action under negligence law for breach of duty of care, which was upheld at the Court of Appeal.

This example also illustrates the process of *how* a case of this kind is heard, when the courts may well be unfamiliar with the finer points of therapeutic practice. Under the *Bolam* test adapted from medical negligence law, the therapist is judged according to the standard of care held by a body of competent professional opinion, as evidenced by expert witnesses. There was no expert who would support the therapist's practice in this instance. All the evidence pointed to a serious breach of professional norms in handling difficult transference relationships. The breach of duty of care was thus judged to have been instrumental in directly causing psychological and financial harm to the client.

In a second reported case, *Phelps* v. *Hillingdon LBC*, a woman brought a successful case against her local authority for the failure of an educational psychologist to diagnose dyslexia as the probable cause of her substantial difficulties in school. This case shows how liability for negligence has shifted to include groups of professionals such as psychologists, and also social workers, who were previously considered immune from this kind of action. However, while this may raise anxieties amongst therapists about their apparently increasing vulnerability to litigation, in reality the problems facing clients who seek to bring such cases remain almost overwhelming. Briefly, these difficulties can include providing appropriate evidence, proving causation, satisfying criteria of psychiatric injury, obtaining and funding effective legal representation (Power 2002).

These two cases illustrate another point about liability, which is important to underline. In the *Werner* case, the therapist was in private practice, and was therefore *personally* liable for his actions. In the *Phelps* case, however, the educational psychologist was employed by the local authority, which held vicarious liability, and was thus the defending party to the action. Therapists often confuse *professional and clinical responsibility* with their *legal liability*, as for example in the discussion over the contentious issue of the legal liability of supervisors. The concept of liability rests primarily on *employment* relationships. Hence freelance or self-employed therapists will carry personal liability for their practice, and employed therapists will be covered by their employer's vicarious liability. Employed therapists have a relative advantage of access to an employer's legal representation in these cases. Still, there is a strong argument for both employed and self-employed therapists to have their own legal representation via a professional indemnity insurance policy, to ensure that the individual therapist's interests are fully represented in court and in any eventual settlement of the case.

CASE STUDY

Mr Ali Said brought a legal case against a well-known relationship-counselling agency for breach of duty of care, resulting in psychiatric injury and loss of earnings. Sharon Jones, a trainee counsellor on placement from a local university, had counselled him. He claimed that the counsellor was inadequately trained and supervised by the agency, and her constant 'reflecting of feelings' only succeeded in generating an increasingly incapacitating anxiety on his part. Due to confusion between agency and the university over their respective roles, the student had not received any supervision for the six-week period of the counselling. Mr Said had been signed off work for anxiety and depression immediately following the period of counselling, and had since lost his job because of absence due to ill-health. The case was subsequently settled out of court without admission of liability by the agency, with an undisclosed payment being paid to Mr Said.

Litigation for negligence is a fast-changing field where lawyers may be quick to take up new issues for clients seeking redress. The issue of informed consent to therapy is emerging as one of significance in the context of reforms in the NHS, and this may figure in future actions. The concept of informed consent derives from medical and psychiatric practice, but also applies to those using psychological therapies. Informed consent requires that the client has the legal capacity to make a choice between alternative options, based on an understanding of their relative advantages and disadvantages, and provides freely given and continuing permission for his/her participation in therapy. The client needs therefore to be informed about the possible risks to partners and family of undergoing changes via therapy, such as the client perhaps becoming much more assertive at work or at home. Some clients need to be informed of the emotional risks of undergoing long-term dynamic psychotherapy, if their sense of self is fragile and particularly vulnerable to challenge. Another client might need to be informed about the relative benefits of using medication rather than therapy as a means of overcoming clinical depression.

The law may also be subject to change in another area, namely that of the therapist's 'duty to warn' other people put at risk by a client's behaviour or by threats made towards them. In parts of the USA, therapists are under a legal duty to warn those who are put at risk by a client who makes credible threats of harm against them. In England and Wales, the law is still unfolding on this issue. There is no clear legal obligation placed on therapists as yet to warn third parties, such as a client's partner at risk of domestic violence, unless this duty is already part of therapist's contract of employment. A therapist could pass on information about threats made by a client to the authorities by acting in the public interest, namely to prevent a crime being committed, but this is not an easy or straightforward route to take. There is case law to suggest that the law in England and Wales could expand to adopt the concept of a duty to warn third parties, if the appropriate legal case came before the courts. The law is constantly changing, and therapists need to keep up to date with significant changes affecting their day-to-day practice with clients.

CONTRACT LAW

A further aspect of civil law with direct relevance to many therapists is that of contract law. The idea of contracting with clients is current amongst many practitioners, as a necessary component of good professional practice. However, the legal concept of a contract is probably narrower and more specific than this broader professional expectation of setting out the characteristics of the therapy on offer to the client. A contract requires legal capacity of the persons involved, i.e. who are normally aged over 18. The process involves a firm offer and unequivocal acceptance, with a clear intention on both parties to create a legally binding agreement. Crucially, the contract needs to be supported by *consideration*, namely an exchange of goods or services for payment or similar. These very specific criteria would seem to exclude many therapeutic agreements as legal contracts, where clients are not required to pay for the service on offer. The therapeutic contract in many cases might therefore be more accurately described as a working agreement rather than a contract in a strict legal sense.

Where a legal contract does apply, for a therapist providing counselling to a client for payment, or a supervisor to a therapist on the same basis, or for an agency providing a service to an employer, then certain conditions will apply. The contract will include express terms, such as frequency of contact and duration and cost of sessions. Other terms may not be specified, but will be assumed or implied, such as a duty to maintain confidentiality. It is also an implied term that the therapist exercise 'reasonable care and skill' in their practice, under the Supply of Goods and Services Act 1982. Either party may take legal action for a breach of contract through a simplified and relatively straightforward process in the Small Claims Court (Cristofoli 2002). Given the relative ease of this latter process, therapists may be much more likely to encounter claims for contractual issues, rather than full-blown litigation for negligence, if legal difficulties do arise.

STATUTE LAW

Therapists will be broadly familiar with the developing raft of legislation which makes discrimination unlawful. Relevant Acts include the Sex Discrimination Acts of 1975 and 1986, the Race Relations Act 1976 and the Disability Discrimination Act 1995. The Sex Discrimination Acts of 1975 and 1986 make it unlawful for an employer to discriminate against men or women, either directly or indirectly, on grounds of sex or marital status. The Race Relations Act 1976 similarly make it unlawful for an employer to discriminate, either directly or indirectly, on the grounds of colour, race, nationality, or ethnic or national origin. Following the Stephen Lawrence Inquiry, the law has shifted to require a more pro-active stance on the part of public authorities to promote equality of opportunity and good race relations, under the Race Relations (Amendment) Act 2000. Similarly, the Special Educational Needs and Disability Act 2001 has extended the remit of earlier disability legislation to include education. Discrimination on the basis of age is covered by voluntary codes of practice for employers, rather than by actual legislation. In addition to these statutes, a substantial body of case law has been built up over the last three decades, which addresses issues of sexual harassment and, increasingly, discrimination on the basis of sexual orientation.

MENTAL HEALTH LAW

Therapists often need to have a good working knowledge of specific statutes relating to particular client groups, such as those experiencing mental health problems. The provision of psychiatric care is governed by the Mental Health Act 1983, which followed on from the previous 1959 Act. The 1983 Act endorses the shift from hospital-based to community-based provision of services, and facilitates voluntary rather than compulsory forms of treatment. As with other major statutes, the detailed procedures of the Act are spelled out in a Code of Practice that is periodically updated to take account of changes in law and practice (DoH/WO 1999). The Act sets out a series of safeguards for upholding the rights of patients, including procedures for application to Mental Health Review Tribunals, with full legal representation.

Mental illness as such is not defined by the Act, but is a condition diagnosed by clinicians such as general practitioners and psychiatrists. Mental illness provides one basis for compulsory detention under the Mental Health Act, together with additional categories of mental impairment, severe mental impairment and psychopathic disorder. (Mental impairment is now more usually described in terms of learning disability or learning difficulties.) The main principles of the Act relate to providing treatment for mental illness in the community whenever possible, rather than via compulsory admission to psychiatric care. The grounds for compulsory treatment are set out below.

Main emergency provisions of the Mental Health Act 1983

Section 2: Admission for assessment: where a patient is seen to be in need of protection from causing harm to themselves or to others, and they require detaining on the grounds of mental disorder, they can be admitted for 28 days on a compulsory basis. The 'section', as it is called, or being 'sectioned', needs to be applied for by the patient's 'nearest relative' (closely defined by the Act) or by an Approved Social Worker from the local authority social services department, and authorised by two doctors, such as a consultant psychiatrist and the GP.

Section 3: Admission for treatment: authorised on a similar basis to the above, it initially lasts six months, and is extendable for a further six months. It is thereafter renewable on an annual basis, subject to review by the Mental Health Review Tribunal.

Section 4: Emergency admission for assessment: lasting 72 hours, this to be used only where it is not possible to obtain a section 2 admission. Authorised usually by the patient's GP, the section can be applied for by the patient's 'nearest relative' or by an Approved Social Worker from the local authority social services department.

Unless working within a statutory setting such as the NHS, therapists might have little direct contact with psychiatric services and with mental health law. However, it would be useful for therapists to have a working knowledge of how to refer a client for psychiatric treatment, or how to facilitate self-referral if appropriate, for example, via the client's GP, or via contact with the local Community Mental Health Team.

Therapists may also work in the context of multidisciplinary teams, providing counselling for clients with mental health issues in the context of outpatient, community-based or aftercare services, as under section 117 of the Act. Familiarity with risk assessment protocols, the Care Programme Approach (CPA), and a willingness to work within an inclusive, team-based approach to client confidentiality are important aspects of therapeutic work in this kind of setting (see 'Case study').

CASE STUDY

Geraldine Sharp, a former social worker, was employed as a therapist in a primary care setting. She enjoyed a close working relationship with Paul Smith, a young man with a history of schizophrenia, who called in for counselling sessions on a regular, if infrequent, basis. Over a period of time, she became concerned at his deteriorating physical appearance and his growing sense of isolation from his immediate family. Relationships with the latter had become increasingly strained due to his verbally aggressive outbursts. Meanwhile, she was encouraged by her external supervisor to value the client's experience of hearing a number of different voices as a channel of communication, as an opportunity for therapeutic dialogue and as a productive arena for self-exploration by the client. In addition, Geraldine strongly valued the sense that Paul saw her as an important ally in an otherwise bleak and hostile world. Consequently, he trusted her with many of his innermost thoughts and fears, particularly about being 'taken over' by others. However, when she learned in one session that he had stopped taking his medication some time previously, she sought to persuade him to make an appointment with his GP. When he refused, on the grounds that he no longer needed medication, she informed him that she would contact the GP herself, as he was putting himself at risk by his action.

The Act is undergoing a process of review and reform, with major changes in approach under consideration. A series of homicides and suicides by former psychiatric patients released into the community with limited follow-up and support has led to pressure for changes in the law. These are intended to permit continued psychiatric treatment under close supervision for discharged patients, with provision for compulsory return to hospital on the grounds of risk of serious harm to self or others. Controversially, the White Paper focused attention on a small group of potential patients who are deemed to be 'dangerous and severely personality disordered' (DSPD), arguably a political and social description, rather than a strictly clinical diagnosis. The intention is to reduce the risk of harm to the public by the introduction of discretionary life sentences under criminal law for suitable offenders, and of indeterminate detention of individuals with DSPD under proposed mental health law (DoH 2000a; 2000b).

The need for reform is driven by the apparent need to protect the public, to adapt to the focus on community-based rather than hospital-based treatment, and to harmonise mental health law with the provisions of the Human Rights Act 1998. The use of compulsory powers to admit a person for treatment, or to require compliance with treatment in the community, will follow a similar, if more streamlined, approach to the current Act, under a proposed Care and Treatment Order. The reforms awkwardly harness together a developing professional culture of risk assessment, particularly for those diagnosed as psychopathic, with increased safeguards for patients in terms of access to independent advocacy, and recognition of their human rights.

LAW RELATING TO CHILDREN

Therapists will also be aware of the issue of child abuse, and the need for clear agency policies with regard to reporting suspected abuse to the authorities. The emphasis on reporting, and the vulnerability of young people to harm, can sometimes lead therapists to assume that there is a blanket legal responsibility for reporting in all situations. As discussed in Chapter 6, the responsibility for reporting abuse is more narrowly conceived as a contractual obligation arising from employment, rather than via a mandatory reporting duty on all citizens or even on all healthcare professionals. The local authority has a duty to investigate where a child under the age of 18 is likely to suffer significant harm. Statutory bodies and voluntary agencies, which have subscribed to the local Area Child Protection Committee procedures, are then involved in exchanging information via multidisciplinary child protection committees. This is a meeting to plan action arising from initial reports or inquiries, such as placing the child's name on a child protection register, or taking legal proceedings. This framework for responding to child abuse is now radically redrawn and strengthened by the Children Act 2004, following the recommendations of the Laming Inquiry into the death of Victoria Climbie (DoH, 2003).

Therapists may have a primary interest in the child protection aspect of the law. The Children Act 1989 is much wider in its remit than this, however. It developed out of a lengthy and comprehensive review of the previous patchwork quilt of childcare law, and marked a major attempt at translating best principles of social work and court practice into law. The Act codified responsibilities of social workers with regard to children and families, based on a conception of partnership rather than on intrusive monitoring. Resources, such as access to services provided by Family Centres, are targeted on specific groups, such as 'children in need'. This is a disparate group, made up of children who suffer disadvantage, those requiring services to avoid impaired development, and those who have a disability. Recent policy reviews have sought to shift the focus of social services provision away from a narrow child protection orientation and towards a much broader engagement with children in need and their families (DoH/DfEE/HO 2000). Rather than having a single code of practice, the Act has a series of 10 detailed sets of guidance issued by the Department of Health, including the authoritative document on child protection, *Working Together* (2000).

The Act contains a range of provision regarding children in need, of which therapists may need to be aware.

Main provisions of the Children Act 1989

Section 17: duty of the local authority to safeguard and promote the welfare of children in need.

Section 22: duty to give due consideration to the child's wishes and feelings in making decisions.

Section 26: duty to provide a complaints system for children and families.

Section 44: power to remove and retain a child in their care, on application to the court (Emergency Protection Order).

Section 46: police powers to remove and detain a child 'at risk' in police protection for 72 hours.

Section 47: duty of the local authority to investigate cases where a child is likely to suffer 'significant harm'.

The Children Act 1989 brings together aspects of public law, which regulate the activities of public authorities, with private law, in the sphere of provision for children in family and divorce proceedings. Under s. 8, courts can make orders regarding a child's residence, or can authorise or prevent specific outcomes such as undergoing medical treatment, or attending a particular school. Crucially, the Act has redefined parental rights in terms of *parental responsibility*, which can be assumed by key figures in a child's life such as a grandparent, or shared with a local authority in the case of court proceedings. Overall, the Act is imbued with a highly participative approach towards children's rights. It acknowledges the right of young people to be actively involved in discussions about their own future with the professionals charged with looking after them. Therapists might work within the framework of the Act in any number of ways. Some may be employed or contracted by social services to provide therapeutic work for children and their families. Others will work with children in other settings, such as schools, where a keen awareness of child protection issues is expected. Services such as Connexions have also been developed for young people leaving care or needing support in finding employment, where counsellors may have a role to play.

There are several areas where the therapist's role and ethical responsibilities may come into conflict with their role as defined by an agency working within the framework of the Act. One of these is where a young person may report alleged abuse, but may want this to be kept confidential. Under the *Gillick* principle, a young person has a right to confidential counselling, if judged to be of sufficient understanding. This potential conflict between the opposing principles of promoting the child's welfare or protection, and of respecting their wish for confidentiality, is recognised by the Guidelines in Working Together (DoH/DfEE/HO/NAW 2000, para. 7.32). From an ethical perspective, there is clearly a need for therapists to take into account the rights of the young person, together with the child's age, vulnerability and the perceived degree of risk in making a decision on whether to report abuse.

A further area of difficulty in the past has related to the status of therapeutic work with children who are involved in pending court proceedings, whether civil or criminal in nature. The message frequently conveyed to therapists is that *any* therapy will be seen to contaminate and undermine the effectiveness of the child's evidence in court, and should, therefore, be delayed until after the conclusion of any proceedings. This can place therapists in a very difficult position, when the child desperately needs to work with their experiences of being abused or to explore their feelings with a skilled practitioner, and moreover, one who is *not* directly involved with the process of abuse investigation. The position has been clarified by Practice Guidance, which clarifies that the Crown Prosecution Service does not, in fact, hold a veto over pre-trial therapy for child witnesses. Nevertheless, an accommodation between the therapy and the needs of the law must be carefully negotiated and respected by all parties, if the needs of the child are to be properly met (CPS/DoH/HO 2001).

CONCLUSION

Therapists inevitably work within some kind of legal context for their practice, although the exact nature of this will vary according to their work setting, client group and employment status. Broadly, therapists need to have an understanding of how civil law concepts such as contract, negligence and liability relate to their work with clients, in order to minimise the potential risk of hostile legal action against either themselves or, if relevant, their employer. The actual risk of litigation against therapists in the UK is sometimes exaggerated, as the system of peer defence against action for breach of duty of care has limited to a handful the numbers of successful reported cases. There may also be specific Acts of Parliament which are relevant to the therapist's role, such as the Mental Health Act 1983, or the Children Act 1989 and its planned successor. This will depend upon the nature of the client group and the kinds of issues, which impact, on the therapeutic work being undertaken. Therapists accordingly need to maintain a basic working knowledge of the law as related to their work, in order to best protect their clients' interests and to promote their own competent and ethical practice.

REFLECTIVE QUESTIONS

1 Which aspects of the law have the greatest potential or actual impact on your practice?
2 How do you access information on legal issues affecting your professional work?
3 To what extent does the 'legalisation of therapy' carry threats or opportunities to you as a therapist and your clients?
4 How might clients be better supported in bringing justifiable cases against therapists?

REFERENCES

Bond, T. (2000) *Standards and Ethics for Counselling in Action*, 2nd edn. London: Sage.

CPS/DoH/HO (Crown Prosecution Service, Department of Health, Home Office) (2001) Provision of Therapy for Child Witnesses Prior to a Criminal Trial: Practice Guidance. London: CPS.

Cristofoli, G. (2002) Legal pitfalls in counselling and psychotherapy practice and how to avoid them, in P. Jenkins (ed.), *Legal Issues in Counselling and Psychotherapy*. London: Sage, 24–33.

DoH (Department of Health) (2000a) *Reforming the Mental Health Act. Part 1: The New Legal Framework*, Cm 5016–1. London: Stationery Office.

DoH (Department of Health) (2000b) *Reforming the Mental Health Act. Part 2: High Risk Patients*, Cm 5016–2. London: Stationery Office.

DoH (Department of Health) (2003) *What To Do If You're Worried A Child Is Being Abused*. London: DoH.

DoH/DfEE/HO (Department of Health, Department for Education and Employment,

Home Office) (2000) *Framework for Assessment of Children in Need and their Families*. London: Stationery Office.

DoH/DfEE/HO/NAW (Department of Health, Department for Education and Employment, Home Office and the National Assembly for Wales) (2000) *Working Together to Safeguard Children: A Guide for Inter-Agency Working to Safeguard and Promote the Welfare of Children*. London: Stationery Office.

DoH/WO (Department of Health/Welsh Office) (1999) Mental Health Act 1983: Code of Practice. London: Stationery Office.

Jenkins, P. (1997) *Counselling, Psychotherapy and the Law*. London: Sage.

Power, I. (2002) Taking legal action against a therapist for professional negligence, in P. Jenkins (ed.), *Legal Issues in Counselling and Psychotherapy*. London: Sage.

Legal references: cases

Bolam v. *Friern HMC* [1957] 1 WLR 835, 2 All ER 118.

Gaskin v. *UK* [1990] 1 FLR 167.

Gillick v. *West Norfolk AHA* [1986] AC 112, [1985] 3 All ER 402, [1985] 3 WLR 830, [1986] 1 FLR 224.

Phelps v. *Hillingdon LBC* [1997] 3 FCR 621.

Werner v. *Landau* (1961) TLR 8/3/1961, 23/11/1961, Sol Jo (1961) 105, 1008.

Legal references: statute

Children Act 1989.

Data Protection Act 1998.

Disability Discrimination Act 1995.

Human Rights Act 1998.

Mental Health Act 1983.

Race Relations Act 1976.

Race Relations (Amendment) Act 2000.

Sex Discrimination Act 1975.

Special Educational Needs and Disability Act 2001.

Supply of Goods and Services Act 1982.

The full text of these Acts is available for purchase from the Stationery Office. Acts of Parliament and Statutory Instruments giving additional regulations from 1988 onwards can be downloaded from http://www.parliament.uk and further policy documents and guidance on social work and mental health law can be accessed via http://www.doh.gov.uk

Chapter 8

Writing a report for use in Court and appearing in Court as a health professional and/or expert witness

Allan Winthrop

This chapter will provide a basic introduction to the area of medico-legal report writing. Throughout the chapter a suggested template or format for the construction of a medico-legal report will be suggested. Each of the constituent areas of the report will be explored, allowing the reader to develop a feel for how a medico-legal report is constructed. The process of appearing in Court, as an expert witness will then be outlined. Whilst this chapter will help to provide an introductory overview of the area I would strongly advise any therapist intending to undertake work preparing court reports as an expert witness to undertake an appropriate training course.

There is a significant lack of available up-to-date literature/information dealing with the preparation of medico-legal reports. The British Psychological Society (BPS) has published two helpful documents relating to expert witness work. These are, *Psychologists as Expert Witnesses* (1998) and *Psychologists and the New Rules of Civil Procedure* (1999). These documents explain some of the general principles of expert witness work and provide a sound introduction for non-psychological therapists as well. At the time of writing this chapter the BACP and UKCP do not have any printed guidelines or information sheets on this matter. With reference to the latter BPS document, Lord Woolf has developed a series of reforms to the way in which civil disputes are handled within the Court system. These extensive new rules help to both clarify the role and provide guidance for the expert. While it is beyond the remit of this chapter to consider the content of these reforms, it is essential for anyone seriously considering expert work to have an awareness of them. The Civil Procedure Rules provide information about the duties and obligations of an expert witness and also highlight how the expert can seek guidance from the Court if needed.

WHO WANTS A REPORT?

Professional reports

When thinking about the area of medico-legal report writing, one of the first things to consider is why, as a therapist, may someone want a report from you? As a therapist you may be asked to provide a report that gives details of your professional involvement with someone. This sort of report stems from your involvement with the client. The requesting agency is asking you because you are the therapist the person has seen. Examples of this sort of report may include a request for a report from Social Services, who may be forming an opinion about someone's parenting abilities and they may want to know why the client is consulting you. Requests may also be received from a client's employer asking that you comment/summarise the client's reasons for consulting you and their current mental health status. In situations where a variety of professionals are involved with a client's care, each may be asked to contribute their knowledge. In the above example of parenting abilities Social Services may want reports from therapists, general practitioners, physiotherapists etc., all of whom may by virtue of their professional contact with a client have information which may help with the question being asked by Social Services. In these cases the client's consent for disclosure is needed unless you are required by a court order to release your notes, or unless there are defensible grounds for disclosure without the client's consent, i.e. child protection.

Expert witness reports

In this situation a therapist may be approached because they have a specialist interest or area of knowledge relevant to the client's situation, or because s/he is an acknowledged senior member of the profession. The most common situations are those in which a therapist is approached in order to provide an opinion as to whether someone has suffered a personal injury. The term personal injury is used in this sense to mean a psychiatric or psychological condition. Courts will not compensate people for everyday stress and upset. There must be a positive recognisable condition, for instance Post-traumatic Stress Disorder after a road traffic accident or depression after an assault. In making a diagnosis of a specific disorder, Courts often accept the evidence of a psychiatrist/psychologist as more authoritative than the evidence of counsellors or psychotherapists. The diagnosis, if made, should be supported by reference to a standard text such as the *Diagnostic and Statistical Manual of Mental Disorder*, fourth edition (DSM-IV) or the *International Classification of Diseases*, tenth edition (ICD-10).

Often, instead of direct diagnosis, psychological therapists tend to provide an overview and clinical formulation of a client's problem and may follow this up with statements such as, 'which would be consistent with a major depressive episode as defined by DSM-IV'. This allows those therapists who are comfortable with the position of diagnostician to make a diagnosis and those who have issues with the power differential in making diagnoses or with the validity of certain diagnostic categories to make a statement that behaviours are consistent with a diagnostic category. Where the therapist is approached by a solicitor to assess for psychological injury, the therapist may never have met the person that they are assessing before. The therapist is called upon as an *expert witness* (an expert within a specific field).

Although personal injury work is a large percentage of many 'expert witnesses' work, there are also those therapists who undertake specialist forensic assessments of sexual offenders, assessments of a person's ability to comprehend charges against them and advise on 'fitness to plead'. It may also include those who specialise in assessing child victims of sexual assault and those who assist the Court in family law child custody cases. The potential areas in which an expert may become involved are numerous. The therapist should ensure that they have the level of competency and experience required to comment upon the issues under question.

There are many potential parties who may request an independent psychological report. These include, the client themselves, a client's employer, solicitor, insurance company or company pension agency, social services or the criminal injuries compensation authority. If approached by an external party to provide a psychological report, it is always essential to ensure that their 'instructions' to you fall within your area of expertise. For instance, it would be wrong to agree to assist in a criminal case assessing for dangerousness or assessing for parenting skills if you do not have any experience or training in this field.

A further common request is where the therapist is asked to provide a report about a current, on-going client. These sorts of requests need to be considered carefully. The impact upon the therapeutic relationship needs to be assessed and it may be more appropriate for an independent therapist to provide a report in this instance. In some cases this will not be possible as the report requested might be specifically about the therapy undertaken with the therapist, which for obvious reasons could not be completed by a different therapist. A very difficult situation, which could arise, is the request for a report upon a current client where your professional opinion is at odds with the client's perception of the situation. If a client reads your report then this may rupture the therapeutic relationship and make it extremely difficult to continue any therapeutic work. In some cases it may destroy the therapeutic relationship altogether. It is essential that any request for a report on a current client is handled with sensitivity and the ramifications of providing the report need to be fully and honestly discussed with the client. It should be explained to the client that if a report is requested for legal usage then your overriding duty is to the Court *not* the client. The consent of the client needs to be obtained unless you have been ordered by the Court to assess the person without their agreement (more likely in forensic inpatient settings than elsewhere). You still have a duty to present your professional opinion in an honest and respectful way to the Court.

As mentioned earlier, when accepting a request to complete a report, it is essential that you are clear about the actual purpose of the report and what it is that you are expected to ascertain, and have an awareness of the issues between the parties. The 'instructions' that you receive from the requesting solicitor should always be in writing – and not merely agreed over the phone. Instructions may include requests such as:

- To assess and provide a written report as to whether or not the person is suffering from a recognisable psychiatric or psychological disorder.
- To assess the impact and effects of an incident upon a client.
- To ascertain whether they are likely to recover from a condition with or without treatment.
- Provide a full and detailed report dealing with any relevant pre-accident medical history, injuries sustained and capacity for work.

At this stage, it would be normal to agree fees and terms of payment – e.g. fees payable upon receipt of report by the instructing party or following case settlement. It is very important to ensure that both you and the instructing party are clear about this. If you agree to payment after case settlement it may take a year or more in some cases for you to receive payment. As regards fee setting for the production of reports, unlike for professional bodies like the British Medical Association there are no formal arrangements agreed. The British Psychological Society suggests that for actually appearing in Court a fee of 1 per cent of the therapist's annual earnings is charged per day of Court appearance. The BPS advises that this suggestion is not set in stone but is given as a guideline.

It is usual practice to receive copies of the client's medical notes and any other relevant reports that other specialists may have written. The medical notes are very important in that they give a source of information as to previous health difficulties and can be indicative of the client's state of health immediately prior to the accident/incident. They can also help to identify pre-existing conditions and help isolate those conditions which are a direct result of an accident/traumatic event, those which are not and those which may have been exacerbated by the event. It is preferable to receive the medical notes before interviewing the client where possible. However, this may not always be possible, it is essential therefore to review the medical notes prior to writing the report and to follow up any discrepancies if any are apparent. An example of a discrepancy could be a client stating they have never been depressed before and the medical notes indicating that they have been depressed on several occasions in the last 10 years. One of the most important things to recognise when asked to write a report for use in Court is that your overriding duty is to the Court. It is your duty to provide a true and accurate opinion; this overrides your duty to those who instructed you. This fact helps to prevent someone from being able to *buy* a specific opinion.

In order to emphasise the importance of the independence and impartiality of the expert witness, it is now more common for only one expert to be appointed to assess a client independently. This expert provides two copies of their report sent to the respective solicitors on both sides. This is known as a Single Joint Expert (SJE) and helps to minimise the number of reports which are requested and the number of experts engaged, and to reduce the legal costs of obtaining expert involvement.

When conducting an assessment appointment for the purpose of the report you should ensure that you obtain written consent from the client. This consent is often implied by the fact of their attendance at the interview. However, written consent should be obtained, as this is a further assurance that the client knows why they are here. Giving an explanation to the client that your overriding duty is to the Court also emphasises your independence and also that you cannot offer confidentiality or agree to keep certain things out of the report.

In the actual writing of a Court report, there should be an explicit initial statement at the top of the front/covering page which states, 'To the Court' or 'In the Court'. This is the first indication that you are acknowledging your duty to the Court. The covering page will normally have basic administrative details such as the client's name, address, date of birth, date of incident, date of interview, details of instructing solicitors or body. The date of the report and the name of the report writer should also be included. Most medico-legal reports follow a fairly typical format. This is true whether a psychologist, psychiatrist or physician writes the report. This similar format is because the report needs to possess certain sections, which address the issue under consideration. The suggested format below can easily be adjusted to suit specific cases.

It is usual to keep your specific opinion about the client until the appropriate section within the report as this helps to distinguish between the facts of the case as stated by the client and the opinion of the practitioner. The report should consist of numbered pages with each of the various sub-headings numbered, starting with the Introduction. Numbering the sub-headings allows ease of reference within the report.

Suggested template for a medico-legal report

Front page   – As detailed previously

Introduction   – The writer of the report
– Instructions received and from whom

— Date and place of interview
— Who was present?
— Any documents, medical notes, other professional's reports, which have been read

Upon interview — Basic description of the client
— Client's understanding of the purpose of the interview

The client's account of the issue under consideration and any subsequent developments

Personal history — Birth to present date as relevant

Previous medical history

Psychometric test results

Discussion

Opinion — Diagnosis if applicable
— Causation
— Prognosis

Signed declaration/statement of truth

Appendix — listing qualifications and positions held by the writer

This template gives you the stepping-stones with which to build up the production of your report. The template can also give you a framework for structuring the assessment interview. The sections, which follow, will attempt to highlight the type of information, which should be present in each of the sections.

Introduction

This section is made up of the elements given on the template above. The introduction should include an initial statement about the writer of the report and their professional status and field of expertise (see example).

The writer

'I am [name]. I am a Consultant Chartered Psychologist. My specialist field is the psychological impact of trauma. Full details of my qualifications entitling me to give expert opinion and evidence are set out at the end of this report.' (Include in the appendix actual degrees held, registrations, membership of professional bodies etc.)

Instructions received

This section involves a statement about the purpose of the report and includes information about what you have been asked to ascertain. It is important that, when you see the client, you make sure that they are aware that the purpose of the meeting is for the purpose of preparing a medico-legal report. The normal therapeutic confidentiality agreement is not applicable as the report will be released to the solicitor and may be used in Court. In this respect, as mentioned previously, it is worthwhile to obtain written consent from the client before preparing the report. It is also essential that adequate time be allowed for the assessment appointment, which will usually take between one and two hours for fairly straightforward cases.

The written statement of instruction should include what the solicitor has asked you to do:

> Mr Green was subjected to a violent assault at the Bank where he works. He was beaten severely by two masked men and as a result is experiencing severe psychological difficulties. I have been instructed by Smith, Smith and Bloggs Solicitors to investigate for the Court whether Mr Green has suffered a formal psychological/psychiatric condition as a result of this assault – and the effects and prognosis of this if applicable. In addition to this, I have been provided with copies of Mr Green's general practice medical notes and a copy of a physiotherapy report.

As part of the initial instructions, it is important to check whether there are any accompanying orders from the Court. These orders can stipulate a timescale for the preparation of a report. Acceptance of the instructions will usually bind you to these timescales so it is wise for you to consider whether the request is feasible for you to accept. Information as to where the interview took place and the full names of all those present should be given.

Moving on from instructions a basic description of the client may occur in a section headed 'Upon interview'.

Upon interview

For example: 'Mr Bloggs presented as a casually dressed, young man in his mid-thirties who was orientated to place and time'.

Medico-legal reports often contain reference to a client's ethnic origin. It may be relevant to specify ethnic origin only if the case has an issue which is of direct relevance to ethnic background (i.e. racially motivated crimes).

At this point, you may also include a statement to indicate whether there was any evidence of a formal thought disorder, psychosis or abnormal perception. You may also provide an opinion as to whether the client appeared anxious, irritable etc.

Client's account of the incident

This section should address the client's view as to what occurred in the road traffic accident, incident or negligence. It is often prudent to use language that further indicates that this is the client's expression of the facts as they see them, for example: 'The client reports being left for several hours in the treatment room', or 'the client states he was driving his car along Market Lane when . . .', or 'the client alleges that his car was stationary when a lorry drove into the back of it.'

Following a statement of the incident, the course of any developing symptoms and the sequence of events should be documented. 'The client continued his journey to work but stated that later that day he developed severe pains in his neck and right shoulder.'

The impact of the injury should be documented as well as any period of time off work, GP consultations, prescribed drugs, physiotherapy, time in hospital, sleep disturbance due to pain or traumatic recollections, nightmares, hobbies or interests affected, family, marital and any sexual difficulties. This section should aim to give as full a picture as possible as to the impact of the event upon the client's life.

Personal history

This section should be a summary of the client's relevant life history and development from birth to the present day. A full picture of the client may be needed, if this is relevant to the report. If so, it is usual practice to ask clients about their birth and developmental milestones. As far as they are aware, did they achieve such milestones within the expected times? This could then lead onto school: did they attend normal state schooling, special school or private education? Are there any siblings and what is the quality of their relationship with each other? Other areas of the client's life can then be detailed including employment history, relationship and/or marital history. This information is necessary as it can help to provide indications as to someone's expected level of functioning in comparison with how they present at interview.

A fairly comprehensive history can also help in the identification of other traumatic life events that may be relevant to the issue being considered. The history can also give a general impression of the sort of person the client is and help to place their current difficulties in the wider context of the rest of their life. The suggestions above are examples of areas which should be covered within this section.

Previous medical history

This section could be divided into two sub-sections: the first, medical history as presented by the client, and the second, medical history as delineated in the GP medical notes. The client should be asked about their general health and any serious conditions. They should also be specifically asked whether they have had any previous psychiatric or psychological problems and whether they have ever seen a psychiatrist/psychologist/therapist in the past. Similarly, it needs to be asked whether the client has received any treatment for the problem(s) with which they now present.

It is often the case that the client may provide some details of their previous history but upon checking the medical notes there is actually a much longer, more complex history. The dividing of the medical history into 'from client' and 'from medical notes' allows the more thorough documentation of medical history to be made. This is extremely important in cases where a client is stating that the incident caused their current problems when, in fact, the medical notes may show a lengthy previous history of consulting psychologists/counsellors in respect of the same problem. It is then perhaps more the case that the incident has exacerbated a pre-existing condition or possibly that the client is trying to falsely claim compensation for an existing condition.

At this point, it is helpful to remember that your overriding duty is to the Court. Whilst it is important to document and draw attention to such discrepancies it is the role of the Court to determine the facts of the case. It is preferable therefore to leave open the reasons for the discrepancies and simply report that the discrepancies are there. The Court will determine the relevance it attaches to the discrepancy. The situation where a significant discrepancy exists is obviously more difficult for the therapist if you already have a therapeutic relationship with the client than if s/he were a complete stranger, but if you are aware of any facts relevant to the case then you must disclose them.

Psychometric test results

If you use any specific psychometric tests within your assessment, you should ensure that you are qualified to access and use them and are competent in their administration and interpretation. It is also important to declare if anyone else administered or scored any tests on your behalf. If someone else was involved then his or her name and qualifications need to be given. You should present basic information about each test utilised and the client's result. (Save any opinion until the 'discussion' and 'opinion' section.) Typical types of tests that are used in personal injury related cases include the Beck Symptom Inventories, Impact of Events scale, Trauma questionnaires and General Health Questionnaires. Only tests that are relevant to the issues under consideration should be used. An indication should be given that the tests are not being used as a diagnostic tool, e.g. 'The Beck Depression inventory is a self-rating scale assessing severity of depression symptoms. In itself, it does not diagnose depression.'

Discussion

This section summarises the information gathered so far and explains and expands upon it. The relationship between issues are discussed; consistencies and inconsistencies are explored. Information from the client and the consistency or otherwise with other test results is examined. Discrepancies are highlighted and a discussion of potential diagnostic possibilities could occur. This section is seen as the drawing together of all sources of information. In fairly straightforward cases this section is normally easy to write, whereas in more complex cases with several sources of information it may be a lengthy section of the report.

Opinion

This section contains the writer's opinion after the relevant information has been considered. It may be helpful to include sub-headings of diagnosis, causation and prognosis. The diagnosis should be supported by relevant information and it is often helpful to make reference to the claimant fulfilling the criteria of a diagnostic manual.

> Mrs Bloggs would meet the criteria for Post Traumatic Stress Disorder as defined by the *Diagnostic and Statistical Manual of Mental Disorder*, fourth edition.

Some indication should be afforded as to the extent of the client's suffering and loss. The causation section should include your professional opinion as to the cause of the diagnosed condition and whether it is more likely than not that the client's condition was caused by or materially contributed to by the incident under consideration.

Prognosis

This section should address the likely course of the condition and whether you would predict resolution within, for example, a year without any treatment or six months with some psychological intervention. Do you think that the situation is worsening or would deteriorate without treatment? It is important to stay within your area of expertise when making your opinions and comments about causation and prognosis. Your opinion needs to remain within the psychological field and you should not comment directly upon issues such as the extent of mobility loss due to physical injury.

Declaration/statement of truth

Following the opinion section of the report, a Declaration and Statement of Truth needs to be signed and dated by the author of the report. The solicitor's instructing letter normally includes the paragraph they would like as a Statement of Truth, but the following factors are usually included:

- A statement that shows: *you understand your duty to the Court and that you have complied with that duty.*
- A statement of truth: *I believe that the facts stated within this report are true and that the opinions I have expressed are correct.*
- Signature and date at the end.

Appendix

This should include a list of all your qualifications, registrations, degrees held and any employment, publications and experience that is relevant. Locating this information in the 'appendix' saves providing all of this information within the main body of the report, which may appear too cumbersome. This also means that you can keep updating the appendix and using it for future reports.

Following completion of the report, if you are acting as an SJE, you should send one copy to each of the respective solicitors at the same time. It is also prudent to keep one copy for your own records. Upon receipt of the report, both solicitors have 28 days in which to put to you written questions about the report. These questions are usually to clarify aspects of the report. If one solicitor asks you questions it is usual practice to duplicate your response to the other solicitor so that both sides are informed.

APPEARING IN COURT

The appearance in Court as an expert witness is something that often induces anxiety in practitioners. In the advent of the new Civil Procedure Rules, the written report of the expert is emphasised. The attendance at Court to give oral evidence is now less common. However, there are cases where the Court will grant permission for the expert to be called to testify.

When appearing in Court, you should dress formally and appropriately and be prepared with copies of your report and notes used. You will be sworn in, this means you will be asked to take an oath based on your religious beliefs or to affirm your commitment to give an honest and truthful account. It is essential to remember that the Court is interested in your view as an independent expert. Courts are usually appreciative of the expert's contribution. Appearing as relaxed and confident as possible may add authority to your testimony. Before entering Court, you should seek clarification as to how the judge should be addressed. This will depend upon the status of the judge: 'Your Honour' is used in a County Court; 'My Lord' is used in a High Court.

The advice given by many on being questioned is to first listen to the question being put to you and then turn towards the judge to give your reply. The reply is addressed to the Court. This shows that you are confident and attentive in your responses. Some experts, however, prefer to stand 'side-on' to the questioner and face the Judge. These tactics have been used to deal with *aggressive questioning* and to avoid face-to-face contact with the cross-examiner. However you stand, it is important to remain calm; do not allow yourself to become obviously irritated if asked irrelevant or 'silly' questions. Most importantly, do not allow yourself to be drawn into offering opinions on areas outside of your area of expertise. If you do this, it will weaken your evidence and standing in the Court. You are there to deal specifically with your area of work. It can be daunting to enter a courtroom and it may be helpful to observe a case from a public gallery in order to familiarise yourself with Court protocol and procedures. Practitioners' levels of anxiety at testifying in Court are often tied up with fears over *saying the wrong thing*. It is important to remember that you are there to advise the Court, not to represent a client. Testifying in Court will be the same for you whether you have a previous therapeutic relationship with the client or not. The difference will be in the impact your Court appearance has upon the therapeutic relationship.

Some practitioners will have a natural flair for the expert witness role; others will resist the 'expert' tag wholeheartedly. It will be for each practitioner to individually consider whether they wish to put themselves forward to regularly get involved in the legal system and expert work, or whether they hope wherever possible to avoid it.

The areas addressed in this chapter form a starting point from which to expand and develop thinking around the role of medico-legal work within the psychological and psychotherapeutic field.

REFLECTIVE QUESTIONS

1   What might be the impact upon the therapeutic relationship of writing a report on a current client (particularly if you are writing something which contradicts the client's point of view)?
2   What are your thoughts upon accepting an *expert* role?
3   Medico-legal report is more about the investigation and interrogation of a client than empathy with the client. What are your views about this?
4   How do you feel about the use of diagnosis in medico-legal reports?

REFERENCES

As a first point of reference the reader should consult with their professional body to check for up-to-date information.

American Psychiatric Association (1994) *Diagnostic and Statistical Manual of Mental Disorders* (4th edn) (DSM IV). Washington, DC: APA.

The British Psychological Society publications listed below are the most up-to-date versions at the present time.

British Psychological Society (1998). *Psychologists as Expert Witnesses*. Leicester: BPS.
Simons, D. S. & Banks, M. H. (1999) *Psychologists and The New Rules of Civil Procedure*. Leicester: BPS.
World Health Organisation (1992) *The ICD-10 Classification of Mental and Behavioural Disorders*. Geneva: WHO.

Useful websites

Academy of Experts: http://www.academy-experts.org/defaultin.htm
This provides guidelines and updated copies of the Civil Procedure Rules.

British Psychological Society: http://www.bps.org.uk

Society of Expert Witnesses: http://www.sew.org.uk
This organisation is the only independent representative body run by experts for the benefit of experts. An information pack is available from their help line 0845 7023014.

Chapter 9

The ethics and responsibilities of record keeping and note taking

David Purves

Ethical practice is one of the most important cornerstones of clinical work. Clients trust that we, the therapist, will not be abusive, manipulative or place our own concerns above those of the client. These trusts are implicit in the therapist–client relationship, but the impetus to ensure them must come from the therapist. One of the most dangerous forms of therapist malpractice is the misuse of power. The government, over a period of years, has developed legislation to enable clients to gain greater access to material held on record about them. This serves to reduce secrecy and facilitate openness. The tide of secrecy and paternalism that has dominated the medical professions has now started to turn, at least where the keeping of records and notes is concerned.

ARE RECORDS AND NOTE TAKING NECESSARY?

For the purpose of this chapter, records are considered to be anything that is kept in the client files and notes and are a record of the content of individual sessions, which may or may not be kept together depending upon the practice of the individual therapist. Different professionals are likely to view the necessity and usefulness of note taking and record keeping differently. While there is currently no legal requirement to keep notes or even records, nevertheless there may be good reasons for doing so, for example, as a demonstration of good practice. The codes of ethics and professional guidelines of the British Psychological Society (BPS 2000, 2002) and the Ethical Framework for Good Practice in Counselling and Psychotherapy of the British Association for Counselling and Psychotherapy (BACP 2002) both advocate the keeping of records. The United Kingdom Counsel for Psychotherapy (UKCP 2000) requires member organizations to have a code of ethics by which they abide, and it is left to member organizations to specify whether keeping records is part of that code. However, Venier (1999) notes that only one of the eleven UKCP organizations mentions record keeping in their code of ethics.

Alternatively, there are arguments against keeping records and notes. The increase in litigation and claims against healthcare professionals in the United States has led some practitioners to adopt a defensive stance to records and notes. Some practitioners may feel they must keep no records at all to protect themselves, while others keep records that are mere statements of fact, so sparse that they easily pass any legal scrutiny because they contain little information – a case of going through the motions! Neither of these defensive positions would seem appropriate or indeed ethically defensible. The psychotherapeutic professions cover a wide variety of orientations and practices and it is likely that different practitioners will have different needs for clinical notes and client records. For example, it is easy to imagine a practitioner who emphasizes personal growth and development to consider that taking notes may be almost entirely peripheral to their work, as they rely upon memory and work in the 'here and now' with whatever the client brings. Alternatively, a cognitive-behavioural practitioner may often generate paper materials during the course of a therapy session, these are de facto client notes, and may be referred to from time to time during subsequent sessions.

While there may be different views about the usefulness and even the necessity of notes and records, modern practice now requires the therapist to adhere to minimum standards where note taking and record keeping are concerned and ideally to exceed these minimum standards where possible. This means that failure to keep adequate records and notes may be regarded as a failure to demonstrate adequate professionalism.

WHO BENEFITS FROM NOTE TAKING?

In cases of medical treatment, record keeping on the history of medication prescribed and/or the procedures implemented in treatment would seem an obvious professional obligation. Is the same true of the therapist–client interaction – possibly not? Of the many things clients tell their therapist, only a fraction will be written as *verbatim* accounts and for the most part, notes made during or after the meeting will be the therapist's recollection (interpretation) of the salient points, as seen from his or her subjective perspective. Therefore, such notes cannot be considered as a simple record of fact, but may be considered an interpretation of the meeting.

As an illustration, let us consider you, as a client, were to read your therapist's notes taken during and after your sessions. It may be the case that these notes are unlikely to emphasize your good points, are problem focused, and contain information that indicates misunderstanding at some fundamental level. In fact, you may even wonder at the idiosyncratic, even arbitrary, selection of material that has been included. Given these possibilities, it may be difficult to see what possible benefit you would gain from reading the notes your therapist made of the work with you. Indeed, it may be just as likely that there would be the possibility of a poor outcome from reading this material. This indicates that, in principle, client notes are taken for the benefit of the therapist in aiding the client, and not necessarily designed for the direct scrutiny of the client.

There are probably only five valuable purposes that client case notes and records can serve. First, records can act as a simple recording of facts about the client, such as date of birth, address, name and location of the GP, next of kin, and a record of dates and times of meetings. Second, records can serve as an aide-memoire of the client work. It may not represent a full account of everything that happened within a session, but it should contain enough information to enable the therapist to retain the themes and threads of the work, including salient events and other points he/she may need to remember. The aide-memoire, if used creatively, can act to enhance continuity between sessions. Third, records can demonstrate that due care and attention was given to the client should litigation occur, or if a therapist is required to explain or defend their practice, for example in the case of a client suicide. Fourth, records are a collection of clinical outcome measures, audit data and service evaluation. Finally, records can be used to explore client issues, transference and countertransference material and as a record of supervision meeting discussions about the client. The first four of these five uses of notes and records are relatively uncontentious; however, the fifth use of notes and records must be looked at more closely and cautiously (BPS 2002). It is doubtful whether it is in the best interests of the client or the clinician that speculation, personal issues and countertransference issues should be referred to in the active client notes. One must ask whether, if the client were to read this material, it would enhance their well-being? Alternatively, does this material have such a potential for misunderstanding that it may be thought of as more likely to cause problems than to give benefits? The recent current legislation on the rights of clients to see material kept on file (Data Protection Act 1998) now makes it necessary for the content of notes and records to be created with this potential access always kept in mind.

THE DATA PROTECTION ACT

The Data Protection Act (DPA 1998) covers the keeping of records in either paper or electronic form. In reality, any information kept on an individual is now subject to the DPA. The Act contains eight data protection principles that are concerned with security, accuracy, adequacy, lawfulness, the rights of the subject, and issues of transference to countries without adequate data protection legislation. Depending upon the therapist's role in an organization he/she may have to register with the Data Protection Agency. Guidance can be obtained easily on this matter by accessing the Data Protection

Agency web page at http://www.dpr.gov.uk or by contacting the information commissioner at Wycliffe House, Water Lane, Wilmslow, Cheshire, SK9 5AF. The web page will allow the therapist to rapidly determine if it is necessary to register. Failure to register, if appropriate, is an offence.

GOOD PRACTICE AND GOOD NOTE TAKING

There do exist some 'good practice' guidelines regarding what to place in records, although, it must be remembered that these are simply guidelines driven by current understandings of best practice and a need to conform to the Data Protection Act (1998) (BPS 2000; BACP 2001). There are also ethical imperatives that determine how we should take notes and keep records. These include a responsibility for the security of the data, the confidentiality of data and the rights of the client to access data pertaining to them. A clear understanding of these roles and responsibilities will be useful in avoiding poor professional practice.

It is worth thinking clearly about what is the purpose of note taking. If we, as therapists, place note taking within our professional and ethical duty, then the notes need to fulfil a clinically useful purpose. If notes simply fulfil an obligation to 'look professional' then the act of note taking is morally dubious. Therefore, such notes need to be useful. Some ways this may be achieved are – to refer to them during sessions, to use them to monitor progress and to engage the client in their creation and ongoing usefulness. When this is done, client notes have the potential to be a more relevant clinical tool.

With consideration of the DPA and ethical and professional issues, there are useful guidelines for what may constitute good note taking practice. Notes should:

1   Be factual and accurate.
2   Be contemporaneous with the events contained therein.
3   Be written in black ink or typed in such a way as to make alterations or changes evident.
4   Be dated and signed and not obscure the original entry, where any alterations or additions have been made.
5   Carry a legible date, location and signature of the therapist.
6   Refrain from the use of jargon, abbreviations, meaningless phrases, speculation, defamatory and derogatory comments.
7   Avoid stating anything that would prove counter-therapeutic should a client see the notes.
8   Avoid making statements that are speculative.
9   When hypotheses are included they should be identified as such, as they may change over time.

CONFIDENTIALITY AND CLIENT INFORMATION

Clients have a legal right to have information about them kept confidential. Indeed, confidentiality is both an important concept in the law and in the ethical practice of therapy. In practice, however, no guarantee of confidentiality can be absolute. Clients must be given an opportunity to make an informed consent for the creation of a record of their treatment. As part of the information required for consent, the client must be told potentially who might ever require access to their records and notes, and under what circumstances. Clients must be assured that, as much as is reasonably possible, confidentiality will be maintained. Unfortunately, what I call the 'circle of confidentiality' is in practice much wider than is often acknowledged. More specifically, the therapist will have a supervisor, with whom s/he will need to be candid, there may be organizational rules about disclosure of certain types of information that will need to be abided by, and occasionally, the therapist may need to share information with a GP or another member of a team, for the benefit of the client. It must also be acknowledged that we often do not do our own typing, filing or appointment making and that non-clinically-trained individuals may come into contact with information that is supposedly confidential. It is consistent with good practice to make these limitations apparent at the outset of working with a client. These same limits of confidentiality also extend to the information contained within client records and need to be incorporated into one's attitude about client note taking. It is consistent with good practice that (although informed consent has been given) a client be informed that the sharing of information is taking place.

WORKING IN TEAMS

There are many circumstances in modern practice where there is a shared responsibility for client care. This is particularly important in the NHS and other organizations. From time to time, other clinicians may require the information contained within clinical records. Therefore, the therapist has a professional responsibility to ensure records are fit for purpose.

A team may consist of numerous members of the general healthcare professions, for example, general practitioners, psychiatrists, nurses and social workers. The question arises: do all of these people need to have access to the contents of therapeutic sessions? Clearly, the answer is: no, they do not. However, they may need information relevant to their own involvement with the client. How does the therapist resolve this matter? In organizations, it is often the practice that psychotherapeutic notes are kept separate from the general client file. Only the therapist and the client have access to this restricted file, unless it can be satisfactorily demonstrated that access is in the welfare of the client and thus required for this reason. This can ensure that highly sensitive material remains, quite rightly, very restricted. In cases of on-going or long-term care, continuity of information is likely to be important and good records serve this purpose. One can easily imagine that, where client care is to be transferred completely to another service, lack of any written record of treatment could be considered negligent.

WHEN OTHERS WANT ACCESS TO NOTES AND RECORDS

At times, other agents working on behalf of clients, such as solicitors, may request to see information kept on their client. This experience will be more or less common depending upon the practice and/or organization. However, if a therapist regularly deals with clients who have suffered accidents, are involved in medical negligence complaints, or who are involved in any litigation then, at times, such requests will be made. Even though an agent of a client makes a request, formal client consent is still required, in writing. In such circumstances, it is worth remembering that the therapist must exercise appropriate duty of care towards the client. Sometimes clients may seek to use clinical notes made by the therapist for purposes other than those intended. Clients may seek, for instance, to use a clinical diagnosis to support an insurance claim. It is, however, a client's legal right to access their general medical records and any notes the therapist may have made pertaining to them, both in paper and electronic form (DPA, 1998). If the client gives consent, then the therapist must release the material requested, through the channels adopted by the governing organization.

DISCLOSURE OF NOTES AND/OR CLIENT RECORD

When a therapist receives a request for access to the notes from therapy sessions s/he can inquire for what purpose these notes are to be used. The therapist may feel that a blanket release of the notes is not in the best interest of the client. The therapist may then negotiate to release aspects of the notes that are pertinent to the issue and to withhold notes that are not relevant. Should this decision be unacceptable, and a judge orders that the whole therapy record be released then the therapist must comply with this order, or face a legal sanction. Any letters or material written by other professionals that are contained either in the general record or in the more confidential therapist record referring to other people, family members, or other third parties require the written permission of that person before disclosure. If permission has not been obtained, then such information must be removed before the records are released. Failure to do so would be in breach of confidentiality of this third party. Cases where a therapist has been placed in a position of conflict between the welfare of their client and the law are rare. However, two good reports of just such circumstances are, Hayman (2002) and Palmer (2002).

The therapist's primary duty of care to the client may, at times, include withholding aspects of their record from them. However, this may put the therapist in conflict with the law! This paradigm encapsulates the fine line of professional and ethical judgement that may be needed in some circumstances. A set of records may consist of many letters and aspects of medical, psychiatric and psychological diagnosis. The therapist may decide that the nature of some aspect of the information could be detrimental to the client if seen by them. Herein lies the dilemma: does the therapist's duty of care outweigh the client's right to see their records? This will ultimately become a personal choice, made with help from supervision and other professional colleagues. However, either way the therapist could find him/herself in the wrong. If the therapist withholds aspects of their notes from the client, then the therapist is generally in breach of the law on access to personal information as defined by the Data Protection Act 1998. However, when there are good grounds for believing that access may cause serious harm to the client, then there may be professional grounds for withholding such information.

WITHHOLDING CONSENT

When routine informed consent is sought from a client to make notes and record information, on occasion, client consent may be refused. In such cases, the therapist must seek advice and make a determination of whether the circle of confidentiality can be as small as the client is requesting. If it cannot, this must be made clear to the client, and in some circumstances, the therapeutic work may be impeded. While it may be tempting to agree with the client to avoid note taking or record keeping of particulars related to a specific subject area, it should not be considered good practice as the therapist may find him/herself in a position of conflict later. In fact, information pertaining to the possibility of harm to self or others, abuse or harm to children, or criminal activities kept out of records may constitute a breach of professional codes of ethics, and the professional standards of the organization the therapist works for, such as the National Health Service (NHS). Furthermore, in the case of some criminal acts and possible terrorism, it is illegal to fail to disclose. Without a reasonable agreement between therapist and client regarding the limits of confidentiality of the records, and an understanding on both sides that nothing in therapy can be absolutely guaranteed to be confidential, little possibility for work would exist.

DISCLOSURE WITHOUT CONSENT

There are some circumstances where information contained in client records may be shared without the client's consent, such as in cases where harm to others is considered likely, in cases of child abuse, and potentially where the therapist judges that client care may be harmed by not allowing others to see their records. Such ethical issues may override client confidentiality. However, these decisions are complex and not to be taken lightly. Supervision and consultation with senior colleagues and legal professionals would seem necessary should any action of this sort be taken.

CASES WHERE THE CLIENT CANNOT GIVE CONSENT

In cases where the client cannot give consent for the taking of notes and records, because they are too young or are considered to be of impaired judgement, the therapist still has a professional and ethical duty to treat such notes and records with care and consideration. In these cases, the possibility may arise where someone who considers themselves to be the guardian of the client wishes to see their full record. Are they able to do so simply on request? Ethically, the therapist should afford these clients the same respect of their therapeutic work as any other client. This may mean not giving automatic access to a parent or guardian simply because they wish to see what is written. However, in the case of children, if the guardian applies through the appropriate channel then the therapist may not be able to withhold this information (BACP 2002). No one can give consent on behalf of an adult (BPS 2002), therefore requests for access to the notes and records of an adult who is unable to give informed consent are not valid. In such cases, it is the responsibility of the therapist to act to safeguard the well-being of their client, while being mindful of their wider support system.

HOW LONG SHOULD NOTES AND RECORDS BE KEPT?

There is no law about the length of time the therapist should keep client records but there are good practice guidelines. The Law Society recommends that legal professionals keep records for six years, with one additional year as a precaution (Jenkins 1997). The law allows legal proceedings to be instigated for negligence or malpractice within six years from treatment and these statutes of limitation would seem a sensible guideline to follow as a bare minimum, with the addition of the extra year as a final cut-off point. However, in the NHS, records of patients defined as 'mentally disordered' need to be kept for 20 years and in the case of death eight years. It is suggested that the records of children be kept until they come of age. It is important to recognize that the DPA stipulates that data on a subject be kept for no longer than necessary. In many cases, it is difficult to know if clinical material will be needed in the future, therefore, it is prudent to be very cautious. If, for example, the therapist is requested by the client to destroy their records upon termination of therapy, the therapist may see this request as valid, and indeed such a request maximizes confidentiality. However, this request may place the therapist in an ethical dilemma, as it does not remove the therapist from the obligation to keep records for as long as necessary, as part of their professional duty. Similar issues are raised by a client's death. Does the therapist have to retain notes after the client has died? There are some circumstances where it may be considered negligent to destroy notes after a client's death, for example, a coroner may wish to see notes to help establish the cause of death. It is noteworthy that coroner's courts can sit long after a death has occurred. As a general principle it is wise to retain notes of clients who have died for as long as you retain those of living clients. It is also worth noting that death does not remove your clients' rights to confidentiality should others, such as family members, wish to view your record of work with their relative.

SECURITY OF RECORDS

Given the confidential nature of client records and notes, additional care should be taken to ensure security. In organizations, the general client file may be stored in an appropriate place to allow access to those healthcare professionals who need it. However, even general records must only yield access to those having legitimate business with them. To keep client files in a place where casual visitors could access them would be a breach of data security. The more confidential psychotherapy file should be stored separately and under more strict rules of access. In addition, the file should be identified as 'confidential and not to be copied without express permission of the author' (BPS 2002). Rules of access to this file should be established at the outset of data storage.

Private practice may offer particular difficulties. It is often considered good practice to separate any client identifiers from the confidential client information. Some practitioners keep factual client details, such as name and address, on index cards and link these with a code number to the client file. These two sources of client information are kept entirely separate.

It is especially important that these materials are kept in a secure place. The therapist must consider the likelihood that his/her house or place of business may be broken into, and what might be the consequences if such an event were to occur. If working from home or keeping files at home, then certainly there is a need to protect files from the eyes of children and other family members, preferably, under a lockable system. However, if the therapist lives in a high crime area then he/she may need to consider providing a safe for these materials. Computer materials should be secured under password, at the very least, and potentially under more sophisticated protection if this is available. Finally, what if someone stole the computer, would this person be able to gain access to the computerized records of the clients? If so, then there is a duty of care to increase security in this area.

DEATH OF A THERAPIST

What happens to client records and notes when a therapist dies? Obviously, the therapist must arrange for this eventuality before it happens. In the case of organizational work, the organization will need to specify a clinician of not less professional standing than the therapist to oversee the filing or destruction of these materials. If working in private practice, it is advisable that the therapist arranges with a colleague, or executor, to deal with these records (Traynor & Clarkson 2000). The executor will oversee the destruction of the notes and client records freeing family members from this task, and maintaining professional confidentiality.

VIDEO AND AUDIO RECORDINGS

The care taken in keeping paper and electronic records also applies to video and audio recordings. Client consent must be sought before recording and a signed client consent form obtained. It is good practice to keep this separate from the actual recording to preserve confidentiality.

CONCLUSION

The codes of ethics and guidelines on professional practice can, in general, only give best practice guidelines. It is left to the individual therapist and their professional support colleagues to determine the outcome of each ethical dilemma on a case-by-case basis. The reason for this inability to be definitive is that we, as therapists, must constantly weigh our professional duty against the law, the best interests of the client, and our own professional survival. This entails a complicated balancing act, where often the outcome will not be entirely satisfactory, but may approximate the best we can do under the circumstances. Records and notes are both a window into therapy and a record of a treatment process that can be re-interpreted out of context and for purposes other than therapeutic ones. We must be mindful of this whenever we put pen to paper.

REFLECTIVE QUESTIONS

1   A therapist considers it necessary that a fellow professional become involved in a case. In principle, the fellow professional agrees but requests to see the whole client file before making a decision. The therapist asks the client for permission to release the file, but the client refuses. The therapist believes the refusal stems more from the client's previous life experiences than any real concern for the actual material contained in the notes (as they have never seen the notes nor expressed any interest in them). What should the therapist do to resolve this dilemma?

2   Consider some of the ways a therapist can make notes relevant to their practice.

3   In your view, to what extent is it legal or ethical for a therapist to write about a client in his/her own diary intending that these writings never be revealed?

4   To what extent does your practice conform or not conform to the good practice guidelines, as laid out in this chapter.

REFERENCES

BACP (British Association for Counselling and Psychotherapy) (2001) *Access to Records of Counselling and Psychotherapy*. Rugby, UK: BACP.

BACP (British Association for Counselling and Psychotherapy) (2002) *Ethical Framework for Good Practice in Counselling and Psychotherapy*. Rugby, UK: BACP.

BPS (British Psychological Society) (2000) *Clinical Psychology and Case Notes: Guidance on Good Practice*. Leicester: BPS.

BPS (British Psychological Society) (2002) *Guidelines on Confidentiality and Record Keeping*. Leicester: BPS.

DPA (The Data Protection Act) (1998). London: Stationery Office.

Hayman, A. (2002) Psychoanalyst subpoenaed, in P. Jenkins (ed.), *Legal Issues in Counselling and Psychotherapy*. Sage: London.

Jenkins, P. (1997) *Counselling, Psychotherapy and the Law*. London: Sage.

Palmer, S. (2002) Confidentiality: A case study, in P. Jenkins (ed.), *Legal Issues in Counselling and Psychotherapy*. Sage: London.

Traynor, B. & Clarkson, P. (2000) What happens when a psychotherapist dies? in P. Clarkson (ed.), *Ethics: Working with Ethical and Moral Dilemmas in Psychotherapy*. London: Whurr.

UKCP (United Kingdom Council for Psychotherapy) (2000) *Ethical Requirements for Member Organizations*. London: UKCP.
http://www.psychotherapy.org.uk/CodeEthics.pdf

Venier, K. (1999) Confidentiality, psychotherapy's dilemma. *The Psychotherapy Review*, 1(2), 65–68.

Part III

Clinical considerations and responsibilities

Chapter 10

Referrals: clinical considerations and responsibilities

Rebecca Haworth and Tim Gallagher

To understand the sometimes complex nature and importance of referrals, the NHS is used to offer a backdrop for describing general referral routes. Different agendas influencing psychotherapeutic services are discussed, illustrating some of the dilemmas therapists face with regard to this issue. Diagnoses and problem types are often used to define referral criteria and understand issues of mental health. However, a holistic view of an individual's situation is demonstrated as essential for determining where an individual should be referred and whether a referral should be accepted or rejected. Receiving and making referrals are discussed along with other clinical responsibilities. Case illustrations are used to highlight the ethical issues therapists need to consider and suggestions are made about how to handle referrals. The terms patient and client are used in keeping with the respective terminology in different therapeutic settings.

AN OVERVIEW OF NHS MENTAL HEALTH SERVICES AND REFERRAL ROUTES

Although there are regional variations, the structure of the NHS can be broadly understood as having a number of tiers, with services organised accordingly.

Tier one: primary care services

Primary care (PC) services are often the first point of contact for people with mental health problems (Goldberg & Huxley 1992). Tier one services therefore usually comprise general practitioners (GPs), practice nurses, district nurses, midwives and health visitors. PC services and especially GPs are often seen as gatekeepers to more specialist services. Other professionals may also work in PC, such as counsellors, psychologists, physiotherapists and dieticians. However, Primary Care Trusts (PCTs) may not directly employ these professionals. PCTs are collections of GP surgeries serving a locality, where they have been given the responsibility to assess the health needs of their locality population and commission services accordingly. A PCT may therefore commission mental health services from a Mental Health Trust, to be located in GP surgeries. Some of the benefits of having mental health professionals working at the tier one level are: ease of access and referral, early interventions, brief interventions, and support to other PC staff who may have very little training in mental health issues.

Other potential initial contact services include Accident and Emergency, Social Services, the Police and more recently NHS Direct. NHS Direct provides 24-hour clinical advice, information and referrals to NHS services (Boardman & Steele 2002). Another initial contact service is Genito-Urinary Medicine, where an individual can walk in and be treated for sexual health issues without needing to provide identification.

Tier two: secondary care services

GPs will often refer patients to secondary services for more specialist care. Referrals may be to services being provided by a district General Hospital (for general physical health problems) or Mental Health and Learning Disability Trusts. It is very likely that referrals for adults with more severe mental health problems will be made to Community Mental Health Teams (CMHTs), where, social workers, psychiatrists, psychologists, community psychiatric nurses and occupational therapists work together offering community-based services. A person admitted to a general psychiatric ward either voluntarily or under the Mental Health Act would also access tier two services. CMHTs usually work closely with the local mental health hospital to arrange continuing care when a person is discharged. Other secondary mental health services may include multidisciplinary teams working with children and families, older adults and people with learning difficulties. Clinical and counselling psychologists can be based in any of these teams as well as inpatient services for people with physical health problems such as paediatrics. Referrals made to tier two services are usually more complex or chronic in nature than referrals made to tier one services.

Tier three: specialist tertiary services

Tertiary services are usually those specialist services that are not routinely provided by tier one or two services. Tier three services may therefore include: secure accommodation for people who have severe mental health issues and forensic histories, people with chronic functional/organic mental health issues who need rehabilitation, and specialist psychotherapy services for people with personality disorders or adolescents with conduct disorder. Referrals to some tier three mental health services may only be accepted from tier two services, after assessment by a mental health professional indicates more specialist care. A professional working in any of the three tiers needs to have a good understanding of the structures and availability of services in their area, as well as information about referral criteria and where services are based. All statutory services as well as voluntary services are increasingly expected to work in partnership. NHS and Social Services professionals are often not just expected to work in multidisciplinary teams, but also under the same management.

It is also useful for therapists working in private practice to have some understanding of the local structure and systems of mental health services. For example GPs may have employed their own counsellors/mental health workers and referrals are only made to tier two mental health services when necessary. You may wish to advertise your services to your local PCT and CMHT. Being aware of different service boundaries may also be useful, for making onward referrals.

SERVICE DILEMMAS AND THEIR IMPACT ON REFERRAL CRITERIA

The primary purpose of a service will ideally determine the referral criteria. However, sometimes, owing to conflicting agendas, the purpose of a service can become blurred. An adult mental health psychology service may state their primary purpose as alleviating psychological distress and promoting psychological well-being in individuals, families and the community. However, what may be actually going on is an attempt by an under-resourced service to keep waiting lists and suicide rates down so that government targets are met (DoH 1998, 2002), rather than fulfilling their primary purpose. Tightening of referral criteria to restrict referral rate and reduce waiting times for an overloaded service is one possible response to such pressure. However, this may also change the primary purpose of the service, creating a tension between 'what we say we do' and 'what we really believe we are doing' (Stokes 1994: 121). Alternatively, a service may resist pressures and not restrict referral criteria, especially if it leads to criticism from referrers. Unintentionally changing the purpose of a service often changes the task of the job and this can also lead to dissatisfaction and resistance amongst staff, as quality of services offered to clients is often perceived as being compromised.

Closing therapists' waiting lists is another means of reducing referrals and therefore waiting times; however, this has moral and ethical implications, as some people are effectively denied services. There may be a desire to shift the dilemma and quantity of referrals back to the referrers, especially if they are funding the service, since the level of demand for psychological services is dependent upon their referral behaviour. However, this could lead to conflict, as equitable services require GPs to reach a consensus in their attitudes towards people with psychological issues and how to alleviate their distress, as well as in their ability to accurately assess. GP referral rates to psychological services are very variable and this may reflect varying attitudes towards the use of therapy approaches (see Ross & Hardy 1999).

Age, locality boundaries and a history of violence may be three easily determined variables for beginning to define referral criteria. However, defining the severity and types of problems the service receives can still be complicated. This is discussed further in the next section on the medical model. However, if two teams offer similar services, but are expected to be different and still liaise with each other, issues of referral criteria and service purpose may become blurred. Blurring may occur between psychologists and counsellors taking referrals from GPs; Cape and Parham (2001) found a substantial overlap between these professional's caseloads. There may be politics influencing a team to show they are the most effective, efficient and best-value service. Professionals may become rivalrous and team leaders/managers/Heads of Department may compete for resources, status and power.

There may also be rivalry between professional groups working in a multidisciplinary team whereby certain types of referrals are sent to the different professions. For example, a child psychologist may only be given referrals for ADHD, Asperger's syndrome and behavioural problems while the nurse therapist does family therapy and the social worker's caseload primarily consists of children who have been sexually abused. The difficulties of team working are resolved, but the primary purpose of working as a multidisciplinary team (i.e. synthesising different professionals' expertise) becomes an illusion. What is actually going on in the team may be avoidance of conflict. The tensions between the primary purpose of a service (or a professional), available resources, internal politics, and government targets – which all impact upon referral criteria – are at times left with the therapists. Ideally referral criteria protect therapists from being over-burdened with referrals that are inappropriate and team leaders and service managers need to hold the tensions between the task of the therapist and other pressures highlighted above. The therapist needs protecting from such influences in order to fulfil their roles and tasks. Although defining clear referral criteria and the parameters of the service may be difficult, it is essential to inform referrers, protect the therapist and accurately reflect the purpose of the service.

THE INFLUENCE OF THE MEDICAL MODEL ON REFERRALS

Cape and Parham (2001) point out that the Department of Health is concerned that people are referred to the most effective and cost-effective service, and the Department has begun drawing up evidence-based guidelines for GPs to facilitate this process. Recommendations are given on which therapies are the most appropriate for a particular problem type. For example cognitive-behavioural therapies are recommended for people with marked symptomatic anxiety (e.g. panic disorder and obsessive compulsive disorder) and brief counselling is considered appropriate for adjustment reactions and milder cases of emotional disorders (e.g. separation and loss). Labelling a person's distress and especially using diagnostic labels is seen as important, as it enables categorisation for research purposes and for defining referral criteria.

The NHS is still dominated by the medical model. This attempts to understand physical and mental ailments as diseases that can be identified by observing a pattern of signs and symptoms that are believed to have an underlying organic cause (see Boyle 1990). Diagnoses may therefore be argued to offer an easy method of labelling people for allocation to appropriate services. Referral criteria based on diagnosis clearly help to identify who is included and excluded from a service. However, there are some problems with this approach.

A basic diagnosis says nothing about the patient's background, or the psychological and social factors mediating a person's history or current distress. A GP may therefore make a referral stating, for example, that Shamim (aged 21) has been suffering with moderate depression and that following a number of recent consultations she has now agreed to try brief-counselling and medication. As Shamim has been labelled with early onset of depression she is thought to fit tier one referral criteria. When she meets with the counsellor, however, she discloses childhood sexual abuse and recent violence from her boyfriend. She acknowledges that this is the first time she has ever disclosed this information and that she works hard to portray a sense of being strong and in control to others. The counsellor empathises and although Shamim may feel ashamed she also feels understood and has hope that the counsellor will be able to help. The therapeutic relationship has therefore started to form. It is likely, however, that longer-term counselling is required, as she will need space to begin processing the childhood sexual abuse, as well as reflecting on her current situation and life choices. Counselling may also be disrupted if she chooses to leave her boyfriend and spend time looking for new accommodation, which may result in a change of GP. She may also have to be supported during a time of being homeless if there are no sympathetic, local family or relatives.

A PC counsellor may experience a very long waiting list if all clients are offered a service according to individual needs. It may feel inappropriate to refer Shamim on to tier two services, especially if they also have a long waiting list and she has stated a wish to continue seeing the counsellor because a trusting relationship has begun to form. Alternatively tier two services (e.g. CMHTs), may only focus on adults with long-term, enduring mental health issues and the counsellor therefore may have no other services to refer on to.

Referral guidelines are important, but basing them on categories of presenting symptoms may not be enough to ensure that a person is referred to the most appropriate service. Therapists may find themselves in a dilemma where the ethos of their department or team focuses on diagnosis/problem type and recommended treatments, but with the knowledge that people do not fit neatly into categories and are likely to have other needs. It is the legwork the therapist does once they have received a referral that often equips them with the information necessary to help them decide whether to accept a referral.

RECEIVING AND MAKING REFERRALS

This section will give examples of the sort of referrals sent to therapists and the questions they need to ask when considering a referral and structuring their service.

From a straightforward referral, many questions and hypotheses can be generated about what may be going on for the client, their family, and indeed the referrer. Here are some basic questions that may be usefully asked when a referral has been received:

- Does the referral fulfil the referral criteria?
- Do I have all the necessary information regarding this referral?
- What are the possible unspoken agendas/issues connected to this referral?
- Are all parties being motivated solely by the best interest of the client?
- Do I have the skills and resources to accept this referral, taking into account issues of safety, number of sessions required and complexity of case?
- Does the patient agree with the referral?
- Has the patient been referred to counselling/psychological/mental health services before? If so where and when?
- Is there any history of the patient being abusive or violent?

Below is an illustration of a tier one referral letter and some questions a therapist might ask about the referral.

In-house referral

Dear Colleague,

Re: Robert Smith

I would be grateful if you would see this 15-year-old boy who has a 2-year history of panic attacks. These originally started at school. He says that he has never been bullied but lives in fear of being bullied. He was started on Cipramil at that point by Dr Bennett and has been on it ever since. The dose was recently increased to 20 mg daily and so far it has made little difference.

His main problems now are frequent panic attacks, which consist of pins and needles in the hands, headaches, nausea, and vomiting and obviously high levels of anxiety. When asked about precipitant factors he says that usually just worrying about having a panic attack is enough to bring one on.

He is currently revising for his GCSEs, which he is due to start at the end of May. I suspect this has a lot to do with the recent worsening of symptoms. Both his parents have a history of anxiety and depression and I suspect that the family dynamics may not be ideal as well.

I wonder if he would benefit from some cognitive therapy, and would value your opinion.

Many thanks,

GP Registrar

The therapist may consider having a conversation with the GP Registrar and/ or the family GP to gather further information on the following.

Medication

What is Cipramil? Why did the GP (Dr Bennett) initially prescribe the medication? Did he offer therapy services and if so were they declined? Did he feel that Robert would not benefit from therapy? Did he believe that the anxiety would naturally subside and that the medication would eventually be withdrawn?

Exacerbation of symptoms

What has precipitated the worsening of Robert's symptoms? Is he very anxious about his impending exams or have other events taken place?

Family functioning

What is known about the parent's psychological health and their way of relating to each other? Have there been long-term family problems? If there are other offspring have they ever presented with psychological difficulties?

Cognitive therapy

Why does the Registrar suggest cognitive therapy? On what does she base this suggestion?

Referral

Does Robert wish to be seen, or are his parents pressuring him to agree to a referral? If the panic attacks are related to exams, then does he need to be seen quickly, so that he can be supported?

These sorts of questions will facilitate thinking about whether this is an appropriate referral for tier one services or whether the referral needs to be directed to tier two services where longer-term work may be offered with a multi-professional approach. If the therapist decides to do an assessment, s/he needs to consider whether Robert attends by himself or whether the whole family are invited. A cognitive-behavioural approach could be used to facilitate his understanding and management of panic and anxiety. However, a therapist may also consider taking an alternative approach, for example more systemic – focusing on the family dynamics. The family may need to learn to relate to each other differently to enable transition and change to take place as Robert enters adulthood. Gathering further information about a referral is essential, as it can save time, inconvenience and sometimes anxiety on the therapist's part at a later date. It is important to ensure that the referral is appropriate for the service you provide and it is worth *not* assuming that the referrer has fully considered this when they made the referral.

A referrer may decide that a person needs counselling without gaining their consent. Consider a 10-year-old boy referred for counselling because the GP was concerned about how he was coping with regard to his parents' marital problems and his mother's sudden onset of a terminal illness. The GP had listened to the boy's parents' concerns, without taking the time to discuss the boy's wishes. Only during the counselling assessment does the boy clearly state that he does not wish the offer of help. Instead it became clear that the mother wanted marital counselling. The family had waited many weeks for the assessment and then the boy's parents had to wait again before being seen by the adult therapy services. Facilitating professionals' assessment of their patients/clients, for referral to therapy services, is discussed later.

Sometimes there can be a number of stakeholders involved in a person being referred for therapy. A family may scapegoat a member, and there may be a subsequent wish for that family member to be 'fixed' by the therapist. Alternatively a number of professionals may have a stake in a person being referred. It is important to be mindful of this and to liaise with family members/professionals (confidentiality allowing), to ascertain what their expectations are of clinical contact. A stressed social worker (SW) may be looking either to close the case once the referral has been accepted, or for therapy to make their client easier to relate to. The therapist may decide to initially consult with the stakeholders rather than offer therapy. A man with severe obsessive-compulsive disorder (OCD) was referred to a CMHT psychologist as other professionals were finding it increasingly difficult to gain access to this man's home and work with him. The referral asked for CBT in the hope that the OCD would decrease. On reviewing records, it became apparent that psychologists had previously been involved with minimal progress. It was therefore agreed that the psychologist would consult with the SW and support workers and offer to facilitate them to handle their client's compulsions more effectively. This improved working relationships as well as the patient's quality of life.

For the private therapist a non-client stakeholder may be paying for therapy and this may need to be clarified before the referral is accepted. Will the stakeholder (usually a member of the family) pay for missed sessions; will they terminate payment with no notice; and what expectations will they have regarding the sharing of information? These are important issues to consider before accepting a referral.

Checking on whether the referred client has used therapy services in the past is very important and often illuminating. A professional making a referral may either be unaware of previous referrals to a particular service or may overlook including such information. A GP may not be aware that a SW, school nurse, or practice nurse had made past referrals (although professionals are meant to inform each other of such decisions). Research into a referral may reveal much. Tina, referred for support and counselling, was struggling as a mother. Her NHS Trust records showed that she was engaged in intensive long-term therapy, as she had a history of self-harm and violent relationships. The therapist therefore decided to contact Tina's therapist and discuss the appropriateness of the referral, as well as contacting the referrer. Following discussions the therapist decided not to accept the referral as Tina was already engaged in therapy. The therapist wrote to the referrer explaining the situation.

Considering a referral requires time and effort and includes having relevant conversations and writing letters to facilitate understanding of the reasons for not accepting a referral, or clarifying the therapist's role with a particular client. The referral for support and counselling cited above, could have led to the therapist accepting the referral following a conversation with the therapist. As it became apparent that Tina's therapist was taking leave, she had then approached her GP with anxiety about how she would cope with her children during the therapy break and school holidays. An alternative scenario is: the therapist could have agreed with Tina's therapist that they would offer weekly sessions during the therapy break, with the clear task of focusing on present childcare issues and using solution-focused techniques to enhance Tina's coping. Once the therapist returned from leave a handover would take place and the therapist would discharge her.

Checking out a referred person's past use of services is useful for self-protection. Failure of communication has led to professionals taking referrals that have resulted in them being threatened and/or attacked. The therapist may consider questions about whether a client has had a history of violence, stalking, revengeful acts, and disputes with other professionals or a criminal record. These sorts of questions need to be borne in mind, particularly by therapists who may be assessing an individual in isolated rooms or premises with no security backup. Private practitioners will not have access to NHS Trust and medical notes and therefore might consider sending a questionnaire to the patient to try and gather further information as well as gaining their consent to contact their GP. Finally the decision of possibly assessing a client alone in premises must be considered carefully.

The issues cited above also suggest what to consider when making a referral:

- Does the client agree with the referral?
- What are the client's expectations of the service they are being referred to?
- What are the client's presenting issues?
- Provide details about the client's history, including whether the client has previously accessed mental health services and when, as well as any past violent or high-risk behaviours.
- The therapist's experience of the client (this may include process issues).
- Does the referral fulfil the criteria of the service being referred to?

Other clinical considerations and responsibilities

When a referral may not be necessary

Helping another professional (e.g. a GP, SW) understand a patient and what they may be able to do differently in a consultation may curb a need for a referral. They may not easily make sense of their patient's distress, or understand what they want. Sometimes talking with the professional about their patient's situation and the consultation process may empower the professional to deal with the situation themselves.

A GP was considering making a referral, as she was unsure of how to help a 16-year-old female patient named Sue, who frequently visited the surgery complaining of mild ailments. The GP was aware of difficulties in the family between Sue's parents, but she felt powerless to help. The GP offered her reassurance for her ailments, but this seemed to make no difference to her situation. Through discussing the patient's presentation as well as the consultation process between Sue and the GP, it became clear that perhaps Sue did not really want reassurances for her physical aliments, but wanted something else. The GP was helped to think about what Sue might be wanting. One of the issues explored was how she may perceive the GP, who had lost sight of how patients may perceive doctors. She was then able to think about how Sue may possibly perceive her as a powerful authority with the ability to make things better. The GP realised that Sue's physical complaints were expressions of her psychological distress and that she could not *fix* Sue's problems. The GP needed to have a different sort of conversation with Sue where process issues rather than content issues were talked about. The GP was able to talk about how she was not making things better for her and what Sue's physical ailments were communicating. This enabled them to go on to have a more useful conversation. Sue visited her GP less frequently and the GP did not refer Sue for therapy.

FACILITATING PROFESSIONAL'S REFERRAL DECISION-MAKING PROCESSES

Offering a presentation or workshop about your service and referral criteria is probably the best way of introducing yourself and informing colleagues of what you do, of your orientation and how you wish to work together. Any myths about counselling, psychology and psychotherapy can be dispelled and colleagues can gain clarity about the different working practices. Using examples to demonstrate appropriate and inappropriate referrals is useful, as this can help to define clearly your boundaries and expectations. Meeting with colleagues for regular referral consultations is another way of facilitating psychological thinking. Some may find it preferable to discuss all potential referrals rather than write letters or complete forms. Keeping figures on who refers and how many is also very useful. Patterns may emerge where it becomes clear that only one colleague refers men or people from different ethnic backgrounds. Feeding this sort of information back is very useful as it helps professionals to reflect on their practice and how they use the service. Ross and Hardy (1999) propose further methods for improving and evaluating referral practice of GPs to adult mental health psychological services.

CONCLUSION

This chapter has described some of the structures of the NHS and the referral routes, to show the often-complex nature of referrals. A psychologist, counsellor or psychotherapist working in the NHS will face many dilemmas with regard to referrals. The therapist needs to be aware of these dilemmas to avoid creating extra work, poor decision-making and risks to safety. Being clear about the purpose and referral criteria of the service that you are employed in is crucial. Also crucial are: clarity regarding the politics around government targets, waiting lists, lack of resources and evidence-based treatments; the implicit expectation to base referral criteria on diagnosis/problem type: the need for a holistic approach to referrals; and the importance of investigating referrals so an informed decision is made about accepting it them.

REFLECTIVE QUESTIONS

1   What criteria do you use when accepting a referral?
2   You are working in a busy team, where emphasis is on throughput of clients. How will you protect the time needed to investigate referrals thoroughly to enable you to make an informed decision about whether to accept the referral?
3   You receive a referral that is inappropriate for your service and there are no other appropriate services to refer on to. What professional/ethical dilemmas might you confront in deciding whether to accept/reject this referral?
4   How does the use of the medical model (diagnoses) influence the type of referrals you receive and or make?

REFERENCES

Boyle, M. (1990) *Schizophrenia: A scientific delusion?* Routledge: London.
Boardman, J. & Steele, C. (2002) NHS Direct – a telephone helpline for England and Wales. *Psychiatric Bulletin*, 26(2), 42–44.
Cape, J. & Parham, A. (2001) Rates casemix of general practitioner referrals to practice counsellors and clinical psychologists: a retrospective survey of a year's caseload. *British Journal of Medical Psychology*, 77, 237–246.
DoH (Department of Health) (1998) *The New NHS Modern and Dependable: A National Framework for Assessing Performance*, Consultation document, Cat. No. 97FP0148. London: NHS Executive.
DoH (Department of Health) (2002) *National Suicide Prevention Strategy for England*. London: DoH Publications.
Goldberg, D. & Huxley, P. (1992) *Common Mental Disorders: A Bio-social Model*. London: Routledge.
Ross, H. & Hardy, G. (1999) GP referrals to adult psychological services: a research agenda for promoting needs-led practice through the involvement of mental health clinicians. *British Journal of Medical Psychology*, 72, 75–91.
Stokes, J. (1994) Institutional chaos and personal stress, in A. Obholzer & V. Z. Roberts (eds.), *The Unconscious at Work: Individual and Organisational Stress in the Human Services*. London: Routledge.

Chapter 11

Complaints: professional and ethical issues

Tim Gallagher and Rebecca Haworth

This chapter reviews a complex area, which will be of concern to an increasing number of practitioners. The broad focus of the chapter concerns client-related complaints. Complaints against or by you may arouse anxiety and affect the therapeutic relationship. Yet any endeavour involving human beings produces possible error and harm; and without appropriate complaints procedures, errors might not be recognised, addressed or indeed prevented. Consider a quote overheard recently from a senior professional in a health setting: 'If nobody ever complains about you in the whole of your profession – then you're probably not doing your job.' While this may not be actually true, in an increasingly litigious society where many of us have growing expectations and are more aware of our rights, there is an increasing probability that practitioners will be involved at some level in a complaint process.

INCREASING FREQUENCY OF COMPLAINTS

Schoenfeld *et al.* (2001) suggests that in America, 11 per cent of psychologists will have to respond to a complaint during their careers. Gottlieb (1990) observed that the number of complaints of sexual misconduct against psychologists has risen dramatically in recent years. The principal focus here, however, will be the British Psychological Society (BPS). Davey (2002) (while President of The British Psychological Society and chair of the Society's Investigatory Committee) observed in his president's column, 'It is clear that the number of complaints against practising psychologists is growing' (p. 275). He indicated a need to act 'quickly and effectively', 'both to protect the public and to discipline those in violation of the Code' (p. 275). He noted an increasing complexity of complaints, as well as greater transparency in procedures, and the advent of the Human Rights Act, as relevant factors contributing to change. He reports 'very diverse' complaints, including a member 'convicted of manslaughter', those 'convicted of sexual offences', and others where members have 'blurred professional and personal boundaries with clients'. He adds (p. 275),

> the disciplinary committees are increasingly taking the view that members have a responsibility to consider their conduct away from the workplace to ensure that it does not bring the profession into disrepute. In a profession that is dealing in many cases with vulnerable client populations it is indeed important that the Society is able to protect the public – and to be seen to be doing so – in an effective way.

PROFESSIONAL BODIES DEVELOPMENT OF ETHICAL CODES (see also Chapter 2)

The BACP, BPS and UKCP have all developed codes of conduct or rules and regulations of membership, as will most major health or social service employers. Their aims include: providing practitioners with principles to guide their work, protecting clients, and so arguably minimising the risk of complaints. The guidance of these bodies has some common themes, e.g. competence and confidentiality. They may include specific rules for the management of complaints (e.g. BPS (1999) *Time and Performance Standards for the Complaints Investigatory and Disciplinary Procedures*) so that when a practitioner abuses their position they may be held to account, and if necessary restricted from practising. It is essential that there are effective, fair and transparent complaint procedures to uphold standards and protect the public and therapists, and that therapists have read, understood and adhere to them.

Joscelyne (2002), however, reviews the BPS (2000) code of conduct and suggests a 'new government emphasis on quality assurance' is 'gradually being felt within the working lives of psychologists' (pp. 176–177). Perhaps, then, government legislative pressure rather than internal self-regulation may drive construction of some rules. She argues that the code is currently 'confusing', with specificity about some issues and vagueness about others, and that it needs to be clearer about its guiding purpose and principles. While the protective aspects of codes and rules are vital, it is also worth considering Clarkson and Murdin's (1996) observations of possible conflicts, whether internally between different rules or principles (e.g. self-determinism, self-abuse, confidentiality and duty to care); or more externally with clashes between rules of professional body and rules of employer (e.g. inter-agency working versus client confidentiality or pressure to reduce waiting lists versus client need). Clarkson and Murdin (1996) also observe the need for 'protection' of therapists from such potentially abusive phenomena as 'delusional transference', or clients 'consumed by rage and a desire for revenge'. They reflect on the limitations of codes and rules and make useful observations about the centrality of the therapeutic relationship.

THE NATURE OF COMPLAINTS WITHIN THE TALKING THERAPIES

Complaints have varying forms. In a sense, anyone consulting with health practitioners inevitably comes with some complaint. Kress (1989) discusses the 'polymorphous, ubiquitous, and ambiguous nature of the patient's complaint', which may be 'expressed through a cry for help or precisely verbalised'. It may be 'rooted in a painful physiopathology or can be a manifestation of existential suffering and anxiety' (p. 305). Complaints are a crucial aspect of therapeutic process. Those approaching therapies often voice complaints of psychological distress. A client may speak of their depression, or be referred following self-injury. At times, however, the therapist may also become the subject of complaint. A client may complain that you do not really care if you take an agreed break or if you had to cancel a session due to illness.

Complaints against the therapist may be thought about from a number of aspects:

• What are the grounds for complaint?
• Who is complaining?
• To whom?
• In what context?

Grounds for complaint

Complaints will ultimately be judged as to how well grounded they are. A well-grounded complaint will concern a breach of professional codes. An ungrounded complaint may be either the result of a misunderstanding, or a deliberate attempt at harm by an aggrieved individual. Complaints will usually concern an aspect of the service that you are providing or have provided, which you may or may not have influence over. Possible complaints concern: therapist's behaviour, process in session, the relationship, or amount of therapy available. Employer or management complaints will perhaps most often concern performance measures, e.g. numbers of individual contacts made, or sessions per client. Complaints about services, or against an individual therapist may be well-grounded and will require investigation. There are poor practitioners, and professional bodies need to ensure that good practice is maintained. There are a variety of behaviours occurring for different reasons, which might justifiably generate complaints. Palmer Barnes (1998) offers four useful categories, which we illustrate:

1   Genuine mistakes or errors of judgement, e.g. sending an appointment with the wrong date.
2   Poor practice, e.g. being repeatedly late for appointments.

3   Negligence, e.g. giving inadequate advice, which places the client at risk.
4   Malpractice, e.g. knowingly doing something wrong (e.g. having sexual relations with a client).

Who is complaining?

1   Clients – this is likely to be the most problematic or distressing form of complaint for the therapist.
2   Your employing organisation.
3   Non-client purchaser or other stakeholder in process, e.g. GP, family member.
4   Yourself – (whistleblowing/grievance). This may be about the professional conduct of a colleague, or standards within a department. This is a separate, complex area, dealt with briefly at the end of the chapter.

Complainants may be further considered in terms of personality, culture and age:

- Bernhardt (1981) studied the consumer complaint characteristics of subjects over 65 years of age, finding that they complained less than the population as a whole. Many indicated believing complaints would not accomplish anything or were not worth the effort.
- Rinehart (1999) found individuals with an internal locus of control evaluated negative service encounters more favourably than their externally focused counterparts.
- Harris and Mowen (2001) found support for the possibility that a limited set of basic personality traits might underlie dispositions to bargain and to complain.
- Riboulleau (1989) reviews malpractice suits filed by patients against physicians and notes that there are different complainant profiles, including habitual complainants, those craving recognition who seek an encounter with a powerful individual, and those who seek revenge against the accused party, regarding judicial apparatus as the instrument of vengeance.
- Hui and Au (2001) found that voice (i.e., allowing customers opportunity to express dissatisfaction and listen to them) had a stronger effect on Chinese than Canadian customers, whereas compensation had a stronger effect on Canadian than Chinese customers. They suggest attributing causality to culturally bound values.
- Au et al. (2001) found that collectivists are more likely than individualists to blame service providers for errors. In addition, in some circumstances Canadians are seemingly less likely to attribute responsibility to themselves than Chinese.

To whom?

The complaint may be to yourself, your colleagues, your governing body, your employer, the police, other professionals, or perhaps a local councillor, or the press.

In what context?

Complaints may be informal or formal, verbal or in writing. A client might begin a session by complaining to you that they are no better since their previous session. They might complain to their GP that it is a slow process. Another family member might complain that their relative is not yet 'cured' of a particular difficulty. A client or relative might complain to your employer or professional body about a real or imagined breach of ethics or professionalism. Conversation about the first two might reasonably be deemed part of therapeutic process; the third is trickier, as in most circumstances confidentiality prohibits even confirming that you are working with a person. The final example, however, will usually lead to a full formal process of scrutiny and adjudication. A complaint made to your professional body will be run under procedures notified to all parties in advance of any action and the therapist may have legal representation should they choose.

PROCESS ISSUES IN THE COMPLAINTS ARENA

Therapy process

To make sense of some complaints it is worth remembering that therapy is a complex process variously understood according to theoretical orientation, training and experience. The therapeutic relationship is central, as all communication must be interpreted within its context. What a person experiences or understands from what they hear may not be what was in the speaker's mind when they articulated a thought or idea (i.e. their intention). It may be useful to bear in mind this model of intention versus experience. Supervision is vital to reflect on meaning and response in these relational encounters.

Causal processes

Notwithstanding factors already mentioned, complaints are perhaps most likely when a mismatch of expectation and experience occurs. Expectations of clients or therapists may be affected by many factors including a changing historical socio-cultural context, the eroding historical authority of medicine, increasing media coverage of new research developments (often before the peer review process is complete), changing attitudes, the culture of the self, the introduction of the Human Rights Act, an increasingly litigious contemporary Western culture, increasing patient knowledge and assertiveness, NHS complaints procedures, risk management training, and clinical governance. Beloff (2001) for example, speaks of 'many risks' of responding to journalistic enquiries, commenting on recent complaints to the BPS disciplinary board about psychologists' expressed views.

Complaint process

The process will depend on whether complaints are formal and whom they are addressed to. Each complaint process will be unique, involving a combination of unique individuals within specific organisations in a one-off interaction at a given point in time and culture. Every scenario cannot therefore be predicted. A formal complaint addressed to a governing body or an employer will effectively be governed by their rules for complaints. This is rarely a rapid process and will involve investigation, information gathering and consideration, usually by a panel of suitably qualified individuals. In the case of an employer, the NHS for instance, it may involve a panel with little experience of therapeutic process. In essence, however, a complaint must be heard and responded to. This may be a positive process. Ziegenfuss (1987) discusses the value of complaints and describes creative processes for handling them, suggesting that complaint procedures are valuable organisational development tools that aid organisation diagnosis and change, as any event that helps to 'expose structure and process problems' presents management with 'an opportunity to take corrective action'.

Choice of process – alternate dispute resolution (ADR)

There is a range of dispute or conflict resolution methods available now and it may be appropriate to consider using one of them, perhaps in consultation with the appropriate people. Mediation is frequently the method of choice; it may be particularly appealing to clients or professional organisations. It is also of some additional importance and weight that there is a culture change being driven by the courts by making adverse cost orders against a person or organisation refusing mediation.

Help with the process

Complaining may be difficult. Gottlieb (1990) notes women still report great reluctance in filing complaints for sexual misconduct. In addition to 'ambivalent feelings about themselves', 'institutional barriers within the profession lead women to complain of feeling intimidated and deterred by imposing and labyrinthine complaint procedures' (p. 455). He calls for an organisational structure within the profession to assist women and 'reach out' to 'actively offer assistance through the complaint process'. Presumably ethnic minorities may face additional potential difficulties of language or institutionalised racism if complaining.

It is not only a complainant who may need help, however. Cunningham and Dovey (2000) explored effects on GPs of receiving complaints against them that did not proceed to a formal hearing. They found short-term and long-term effects on the doctor and their views of patients, society and the disciplinary process. GPs reported sustained negative emotional responses that adversely effected doctor–patient relationships beyond the relationship with the original complainant. They reported short-term changes to practice, with reduced ability to work confidently and decisively. They also reported longer-term altered practice towards defensive medicine, by withdrawal from some services and avoidance of perceived at-risk activities, e.g. services for chaotic individuals such as active substance misusers. They suggest a need for professional support to minimise the negative personal and professional effects of complaints, even when the complaint does not proceed to a formal hearing. There may be an assumption that if a complaint is found to be ungrounded, everything will return to normal with little consideration of the impact on the practitioner. An ungrounded complaint, however, may be the start of something more serious. Mullen *et al.* (2000) observe that resentful stalking may follow from dismissed complaints in particular circumstances.

PREVENTION OF COMPLAINTS

It is impossible to protect oneself completely from complaints. However, well-grounded complaints highlight poor standards. One form of protection, therefore, is adherence to clear standards, whether of professional body or employing organisation. The therapist needs to have a clear role which is understood and supported by their organisation so they may have clear boundaries in terms of services they can and cannot offer. Greater transparency in our profession may lead to less misunderstanding and complaining. We need to state why we do what we do, how we do it and to whom. As clinicians we need to be mindful of the issues regarding power relations (which may be affected by race, sex, gender, age, and disability), offer adequate negotiation of contracts, give notice of breaks, prepare for endings, and consider and address as necessary transference issues (i.e. how the client is perceiving the therapist). Careful scrutiny of referrals before acceptance can forestall some problems (see Chapter 10). Ordered notes, clear formulations and appropriate records, contracts and behaviour will all help to protect us, especially if accompanied by careful, thoughtful action, regular supervision and, where appropriate, personal therapy. It is also important for the therapist to be alive to any possible breaches of conduct. The earlier any possible breaches are identified, the quicker they can be resolved with the least trauma to both the client and the therapist.

COMPLAINT MANAGEMENT STRATEGIES

A well-grounded complaint offers useful feedback to adjust practice accordingly. Peiffer and Walker (1958) suggest trying to develop an interview in a number of ways when confronted by someone with a wrathful complaint: providing for a catharsis phase, building an objective atmosphere, shifting from the specific to the general problem, with the recognition that complex problem solving requires shared responsibility, and the consideration of direct and rational activity. It will often be helpful to validate the experience of a complainant, however at odds their experience may be with the intention of the therapist.

Assess the complaint rationally and attempt to judge whether there are reasonable grounds. Good supervision cannot be undervalued, as a supervisor is one person with whom all aspects of the process may be spoken of. If the complaint is reasonable consider plans to redress the shortfall or make reparation. Insurance indemnity cover is vital in some instances (e.g. someone trips in your hall and badly injures themselves). However, in any event prepare your defence, and consider possible outcomes. Seek and utilise support, but be wary of the constrictions of confidentiality as they continue to relate to the therapy process. Within employed circumstances it will usually be wise to consider alerting managers, sooner rather than later. Formal complaints normally follow relevant organisational policies and protocols. Casemore's (2001) book offers many useful perspectives on thinking about and managing complaints.

ONE POSSIBLE COMPLAINT SCENARIO

A challenging client abruptly terminates a therapy session and cancels further sessions. You are told the complaint alleges abusive behaviour, and the head of department will be meeting with the complainant. Your professional body's investigatory committee advises receipt of a formal complaint relating to your professional conduct. It encloses procedural guides, time standards, a copy of the letter of complaint, and seeks your response. The complaint letter describes events you recall, but from a very different point of experience – conversations are remembered differently, with an apparent abusive theme running through them. Perhaps you question your own behaviour and explore for errors of judgement or misperception, or you try to rationalise and formulate.

You write a response outlining your sense of events, pointing out you have no access to notes, which your employer has removed for their investigation. You receive a formal letter from your head of department enclosing the client's formal complaint letter, the Trust's complaint procedure, and requiring discussion with you. Do you need representation? Who will be there? Personnel? Your head of department? The complainant? You may be asked again for an account of the therapy, your formulation, and how the current situation had developed. You receive further correspondence from your professional body advising that the investigatory committee had deemed it appropriate to appoint an investigatory panel to conduct further enquiry. You begin to consider your defence, keep a log, and review support facilities. Work suddenly now seems fraught with the risk of misperceptions. Perhaps the stress leads to illness and you are unable to attend work.

After some weeks you receive a copy of your head of department's initial response to the complaint, stating in summary that the complaints were not upheld. Your employer's letter to the complainant also reviews the different accounts of events and the difficulty of making a judgement, but indicating that any measures possible will be taken to ensure future quality of service. Your professional body's investigation process continues, however. An investigatory panel convenes, and seeks advice and clarification on very specific matters such as: assessment conclusions, formulation and nature of contract, correspondence with other professionals, theoretical model, and availability of notes. They do not ask you to appear before them on this occasion but they inform you they may write to your clinical supervisor for opinion on issues, and perhaps to your head of department.

You respond to your professional body, outlining developments at your place of work. The complainant remains dissatisfied, however, and seeks an independent review. You seek advice from your union and/or your professional insurance legal representatives. You may begin to feel increasingly stressed. The process grows more complex, with the complainant's request for further therapy, the involvement of solicitors, and the convening of the independent review. Your insurance company may provide legal advice and possibly a representative. The independent review takes place after another five months have passed and again the charges against you are not upheld. Up to 12 months or more after the complaints procedure began, your professional body and your employer are all satisfied to call the case closed. You are left trying to make sense of it.

Such an event will generate many questions for all involved. It may impact on your work, making you question your interventions to an extent that may feel paralysing. Supportive colleagues, supervisors and managers help; however, their positions require them to retain some impartiality. In this example a poor initial therapeutic alliance should make the case the subject of supervision – a source of support. Imagine also that the investigation highlights foreknown, predetermining issues of risk, which were not advised in the referral.

WHISTLEBLOWING/GRIEVANCE

Finally, brief consideration is given to situations where we may be the complainants. Berglund (1997) defines whistleblowing as 'public alert' (p. 5) by an insider of an organisation, to a practice, or concerning potential observed in the organisation. We suggest the term might also be used more loosely to describe any attempt to complain about perceived failure of organisational procedures or breach of ethics. There are obvious crossovers with grievances, the traditional term for complaints raised with management or authority.

Various potential dilemmas appear, not least of which is whether/when to complain? Loewenberg (1987) argues that social workers have a professional responsibility to deal with a colleague's ethical wrongdoings. However, consequences may vary. Codes for therapists may also place responsibility on them to act in such circumstances.

Lennane (1993) suggests that although whistleblowing is important in protecting society, the typical organisational response causes severe and long-lasting health, financial, and personal problems for whistleblowers and their families. Consequences have been so severe that in the UK 'Freedom to Care' was launched in 1992. Founded by Dr Geoffrey Hunt (1995), a university lecturer who was victimised for raising concerns about university academic malpractice; it is a charity aimed at helping to expose poor standards of practice by supporting victimised whistleblowers. Enquiries into Hunt's case included a public inquiry headed by Sir Michael Davies (1994).

Going public is fraught with institutional as well as personal pitfalls. Loss of public confidence in social institutions can bring with it further unanticipated negative effects (e.g. a community so disenchanted with services that it fails to heed important health education advice). Haddad and Dougherty (1991) suggest that it is critical that nurses contemplating whistleblowing exhaust all internal resources to resolve the wrongdoing before going outside the organisation.

According to Carlisle (1992) the Royal College of Nursing claims that some NHS Trusts have tried to impose 'gagging clauses'. However, the Public Interest Disclosure Act 1998 became law on 2 July 1999 (Taylor 1999). This offers statutory protection to employees who disclose information reasonably and responsibly in the public interest and are victimised as a result. An employee who is victimised in breach of the Act can bring a claim at an employment tribunal. Those who lose their jobs in breach of the Act can be fully compensated for their losses. There is no limit to the amount of potential awards in these circumstances. Similarly, there is no cap on awards for victimisation short of dismissal. Gagging clauses in employment contracts and severance agreements which conflict with the protection afforded by the Act will be void. The Act does not require organisations to set up a whistleblowing policy, but provides strong reasons why they should. Snell (1998), however, questions whether new legislation to protect whistleblowers will have any effect on the tendency of institutions and professions to close ranks. Therapists may wish to be aware of this possibility and to consider the possible implications for their own practice.

CONCLUSION

It is unlikely that complaining about something, or being complained about, will ever be a simple or easy process. Some complaints may occur and be resolved within the therapeutic relationship, while others will involve third parties. It is important as therapists to be aware of professional codes or rules and familiar with the principles contained therein. Prepare for the possibility of complaint by role and contract clarity, maintaining firm and clear boundaries, adherence to tasks, formulating client work, keeping good records, with adequate supervision and insurance. If complained about, it may be useful to attempt a full understanding of the reasons and context. It is essential to remain calm and rational, however hurt or affronted one may feel. Use whatever support is available. Do not expect vindication, or to be praised or thanked, but endeavour to remain within your professional role and fulfil the associated tasks to the best of your ability. Complaints procedures are there to ensure that clients receive a service of the highest standard.

REFLECTIVE QUESTIONS

1   How might you experience and respond to someone complaining to you about your practice?
2   How might you experience and respond to a formal complaint about an aspect of your practice if you believed it to be (a) well-founded, or (b) unfounded?
3   How might you manage and experience the process of complaining to a senior, or authority, figure?
4   In each scenario what would your strategies be to support yourself personally and professionally?

REFERENCES

Au, K., Hui, M. K. & Leung, K. (2001) Who should be responsible? Effects of voice and compensation on responsibility attribution, perceived justice, and post-complaint behaviours across cultures. *International Journal of Conflict Management*, 12(4), 350–364.
Beloff, H. (2001) Handle with care. *The Psychologist*, 14(12), 635.

Berglund, C. (1997) Thoughts before whistling. *Australian Health Review*, 20(4), 5–12.

Bernhardt, K. L. (1981) Consumer problems and complaint actions of older Americans: a national view. *Journal of Retailing*, 57(3), 107–123.

BPS (British Psychological Society) (1999) *Time and Performance Standards for the Complaints Investigatory and Disciplinary Procedures*. Leicester: BPS.

BPS (British Psychological Society) (2000) *Code of Conduct, Ethical Principles and Guidelines*. Leicester: BPS.

British Association for Counselling and Psychotherapy (2002) *Ethical Framework for Good Practice in Counselling and Psychotherapy*. Rugby, UK: BACP.

Carlisle, D. (1992) A clause for alarm? *Nursing Times*, 88(24), 29–30.

Casemore, R. (2001) *Surviving Complaints against Counsellors and Psychotherapists: Towards Understanding and Healing*. Ross on Wye, UK: PCCS Books.

Clarkson, P. & Murdin, L. (1996) When rules are not enough: the spirit of the law in ethical codes. *Counselling*, 7(1), 31–35.

Cunningham, W. & Dovey, S. (2000) The effect on medical practice of disciplinary complaints: potentially negative for patient care. *The New Zealand Medical Journal*, 113(1121), 464–467.

Davey, G. (2002) President's column. *The Psychologist*, 15(6), 275.

Davies, M. (1994) *The Davies Report: The Great Battle in Swansea*. Bristol: Thoemmes Press.

Gottlieb, M. C. (1990) Accusation of sexual misconduct: assisting in the complaint process. *Professional Psychology: Research and Practice*, 21(6), 455–461.

Haddad, A. M. &, Dougherty, C. J. (1991) Whistleblowing in the OR: the ethical implications. *Todays OR Nurse*, 13(3), 30–33.

Harris, E. G. & Mowen, J. C. (2001) The influence of cardinal, central, and surface-level personality traits on consumers' bargaining and complaint intentions. *Psychology and Marketing*, 18(11), 1155–1185.

Hui, M. K. & Au, K. (2001) Justice perceptions of complaint-handling: a cross-cultural comparison between PRC and Canadian customers. *Journal of Business Research*, 52(2), 161–173.

Hunt, G. (ed.) (1995) *Whistleblowing in the Health Service: Accountability, Law and Professional Practice*. London: Edward Arnold.

Joscelyne, T. (2002) Professional practice guidelines: Time for a change? *The Psychologist*, 15(4), 176–177.

Kress, J. J. (1989) L'efficacite de la plainte. (The effectiveness of the complaint.) *Psychologie Medicale*, 21(3), 305–307.

Lennane, K. J. (1993) 'Whistleblowing': a health issue. *British Medical Journal*, 307(6905), 667–670.

Loewenberg, F. M. (1987) Another look at the unethical professional conduct. *Journal of Applied Social Sciences*, 11(2), 220–229.

Mullen, P. E., Pathé, M. & Purcell, R. (2000) Resentful stalkers. *The Psychologist*, 13(9), 454–459.

Palmer Barnes, F. (1998) *Complaints and Grievances in Psychotherapy: A Handbook for Ethical Practice*. London: Routledge.

Peiffer, H. C. Jr. & Walker, D. E. (1958) Interviewing the complainant. *Personnel and Guidance Journal*, 36, 473–479.

Riboulleau, M. C. (1989) De la plainte au medecin a la plainte en justice. (From the complaints addressed to the physician to the legal complaint against the physician.) *Psychologie Medicale*, 21(3), 341–342.

Rinehart, S. M. (1999) *Locus of control and the service encounter: The impact of individual differences on perceptions of service quality, customer satisfaction and consumer complaint behaviour*. Dissertation Abstracts International Section A: Humanities and Social Sciences, 59(9-A), 3553.

Schoenfeld, L. S., Hatch, J. P. & Gonzalez, J. M. (2001) Responses of psychologists to complaints filed against them with a state licensing board. *Professional Psychology: Research and Practice*, 32(5), 491–495.

Snell, J. (1998) Blowing in the wind. *Health Service Journal*, 108(5619), 20–24.

Taylor, H. (1999) The Public Interest Disclosure Act 1998: whistleblowing in the NHS. Great Britain. Department of Health. NHS Executive. Leeds: DOH, HSC 1999/ 198: 27 August.

United Kingdom Council for Psychotherapy (UKCP) (1998) *Ethical Requirements for Member Organisations*. London: United Kingdom Council for Psychotherapy.

Ziegenfuss, J. T. (1987) Corporate complaint programs make gains from gripes. *Personnel Journal*, 66(4), 40–42.

Chapter 12

Fitness to practise

Nicola Barden

> In doing psychoanalysis I aim at: Keeping alive, Keeping well, Keeping awake. I aim at being myself and behaving myself. Having begun an analysis I expect to continue with it, to survive it, and to end it.
>
> (Winnicott 1962: 166)

Across all professions, there is an expectation that those in the business of helping others should be fit to perform this task. To a degree this is a notion common to all work, which is why there are occupational health systems and legal and medical opinions on fitness to work. It is also common to personal and unpaid aspects of life where one person is responsible for another – parents can be declared 'unfit', and systems substituted to care for children until or unless a sufficient 'fitness' returns.

Therapy (which I shall use interchangeably with counselling) is no different. Whether the therapist is a volunteer, in training or fully paid with many years experience, they must be fit for the task, so that the people they 'help' can have reasonable confidence in the 'treatment' they will receive. This is recognised by codes of ethics of all therapeutic organisations. However, for therapists seeking more detailed guidance, it can be hard to discover more precisely what is meant by 'fitness to practise'. How does one recognise when one has become unfit? What are the suitable actions one might be expected to take? Who is responsible for recognition and action? This chapter will consider first the major ethical codes relating to the subject of 'fitness to practise'. It will then discuss the responsibilities of those involved, primarily the practitioner and their supervisor. Finally, it will consider what is appropriate action, and how decisions about it are made.

FITNESS TO PRACTISE – WHAT DOES IT MEAN?

The British Psychological Society's Code of Conduct (BPS 2000) states, under the heading 'Personal conduct', that psychologists shall not behave in ways that 'damage the interest of the recipients of their services'. Specifically, they shall 'refrain from practice when their physical or psychological condition, as a result of for example alcohol, drugs, illness or personal stress, in such abilities or professional judgement are seriously impaired'. The Professional Practice Guidelines (BPS 2001) of the BPS's Division of Counselling Psychology in its 'Fitness to practise' section continues with the practitioner's responsibility to 'monitor and maintain an effective level of personal functioning, i.e. should the practitioner feel unable to work effectively, they will seek advice from the supervisor/professional consultant. If necessary, the practitioner will withdraw for a time period considered appropriate.'

The United Kingdom Council for Psychotherapy has a single Code of Ethics (UKCP 2000), which defines general ethical principles and standards of conduct. Each member organisation develops its own Codes of Ethics and Practice, which must be consistent with the UKCP statement. Each member organisation has an ethics committee, which submits its Code for approval to the Ethics Committee of the UKCP Section to which it belongs. The Section Committee in turn has its decisions approved by the overarching UKCP Ethics Committee. Thus, although there is much devolution of individual organisational Codes, there is a rigorous system that holds them all together. The UKCP Code itself makes reference to 'practitioner competence': 'Psychotherapists are required to maintain their ability to perform competently and to take necessary steps to do so.'

The British Association for Counselling and Psychotherapy has recently revised its Codes of Ethics and Practice to form a new Ethical Framework (BACP 2002a). This differs from other Codes in that it begins with an outline of the fundamental values of counselling and psychotherapy, continues with a set of ethical principles that are informed by these values, and finishes with a list of personal moral qualities which, while not prescriptive, are seen as aspirational. This complete statement of ethics is then followed by a section of 'Guidance on good practice in counselling and psychotherapy', which outlines standards of good practice that follow from ethical principles. For example, in relation to fitness to practise, the Guidance states:

> If (the practitioner's) effectiveness becomes impaired for any reason, including health or personal circumstances, they should seek the advice of their supervisor, experienced colleagues or line manager and, if necessary, withdraw from practice until their fitness to practise returns. Suitable arrangements should be made for clients who are adversely affected.
> (BACP 2002a: 8)

In this way ethical decisions are presented as complex and related to circumstantial factors as well as to values and principles. Additionally, practitioners are given responsibility for making ethical judgements rather than simply following codes of practice. Ways of applying the Ethical Framework to the issue of fitness to practise can be found in the BACP (2002b) Information Sheet, 'Am I Fit to Practise?'

All the major organisations have an ethical concept of fitness to practise, and include this in their codes and guidelines. It is seen as primarily the counsellor's task to recognise if their standard of practice should be questioned, to raise this with others as necessary, and then to take some sort of action – most usually to refrain from practising. Practice is linked with competence – both are about offering an acceptable level of service to the client. Of course, one of the immediate difficulties is then what constitutes 'acceptable'. It is interesting to note that in legal terms the position of the counsellor is not normally relevant. If a client has been offered 'counselling' (or therapy, or psychotherapy) then they have a right to receive this – regardless of the status of the practitioner in terms of experience or level of training. The standard required attaches to the post, not to the person (Bond 1993), and no allowance is made for personal difficulties in relation to the amount of care and skill that a client is entitled to expect. This creates difficulties for a profession, which places such emphasis on the relational aspect of the work. The relationship requires that the person of the therapist is available to the client, and so their emotional health is relevant to 'fitness' issues in a way that is different to many other professions. Carl Jung (1935/1954) described psychotherapy as a 'dialectical procedure', emphasising the therapist as a 'fellow participant' in the process of individual development, with the implication that the person of the therapist is involved, and not just a set of skills and intellectual knowledge.

A client is unlikely to know whether their therapist is fit to practise. Unless they have read about it, or been in therapy before, this is the only relationship of its kind that they will have experienced – whatever the therapist does is going to be experienced as 'normal'. Any doubts the client has can be overwhelmed by the effect of being in an intimate relationship with a perceived authority, and the immediate power dynamics this raises. Different modalities may interpret and use the power dynamic differently, but all acknowledge its potency, and the need for boundaries to make it safe. By including personal moral qualities in their Ethical Framework, the BACP (2002a) acknowledges that the person of the therapist is an integral part of the capacity to deliver ethical practice. While this can arguably be over-intrusive into a therapist's private life, it does support the notion that, as Bond (1993: 10) states, 'From the client's point of view, the personal ethics of the counsellor are inseparable from the standards and ethics of counselling because one is the foundation of the other.'

WHAT THEN MIGHT 'FITNESS TO PRACTISE' INCLUDE?

Fitness to practise comprises an emotional robustness and capacity to both contain and work with difficult emotional and cognitive states. Depending on theoretical model, this may include an extremely sensitive use of self in the work. It requires a continuing awareness of the emotional dynamic in the room and, moreover, the ability to experience and stand separate from this dynamic in order to think about it and make it a part of the client work. It includes a certain physical robustness – the capacity to sit comfortably for an hour, to be undistracted by aches or pains, in order for the client to experience a reliable and consistent physical presence in the counsellor. It also requires a good thinking function – to be able to reflect on what is being heard, make sense of it and consider how to use it for the client's benefit.

In more specific terms, difficulties frequently mentioned in Codes of Ethics are alcohol, drugs, physical and mental health, personal stress, and incapacity or personal circumstances.

Alcohol

Alcohol is a drug that alters physical and mental functioning. Because it has a depressive effect, initially depressing the judgement and inhibitions of the individual, it is possible that the person themself is least aware of any effect that alcohol may be having on them. The implication for therapists is that caution should be exercised over any drinking during the working day – it takes the body approximately one hour to excrete a unit of alcohol through the liver, so a pint or a couple of glasses of wine at lunchtime is still being processed while the first afternoon client is seen. This is not a question of being drunk, but of recognising the small differences that alcohol can make to perception and affect. The client may well recognise them, even if the therapist does not.

There is also an issue here about giving out home telephone numbers to clients who may be at risk and needing additional support. It helps to think through every condition that a client might find the therapist in when phoning. If an evening call could find the therapist drinking alcohol with friends, or having a party, or coming home from the pub after a few drinks, are they really fit to receive and respond to a phone call? A judicious use of answering machines, and being very clear on what response the client can expect, is important here. 'You are welcome to leave a message and I will be able to call you back within 24 hours' is very different from 'Don't hesitate to ring me anytime if you feel suicidal'.

Drugs

Two issues here are prescribed and non-prescribed drugs. Counsellors may be taking prescribed drugs such as strong analgesics while being unaware of their potential effect on psychological awareness. A more difficult issue is what to do if a therapist is taking mood-altering drugs such as antidepressants for a period of time. We are used to thinking through issues of clients using medication – whether the therapeutic work can be continued with them during this period or not, and the fact that there are very individual responses to medication that can take some time to recognise and evaluate. We might prefer to say that counsellors should never work while taking medication, and this might indeed be best practice; but perhaps other issues are relevant here – the type of client work being undertaken in particular, the length of time the medication might be used for, and its precise effects. Crucial here could be the level of external monitoring of the counsellor's work, so that there is some impartial judgement of their effectiveness, and the effect of any medication on the work.

Physical and mental health

In earlier Codes, this section often included a mention of disability. Since the 1995 Disability Discrimination Act this has thankfully become the exception rather then the rule, as disability in itself is no barrier to being a good psychotherapist. The Act describes disability as '. . . a physical or mental impairment, which has a substantial, long-term or recurring adverse effect on (a person's) ability to carry out normal day-to-day activities'. It includes clinically recognised mental illnesses and progressive as well as permanent conditions, for example muscular sclerosis, cancer or HIV – conditions understood as illnesses, but not always considered to be disabilities (Jenkins 1997). This does not mean that the effect of a disability on a person's ability to do a job should be ignored; it means that there can be no discrimination on the grounds of the disability. Judgements must be made on the way that the disability affects the task, if indeed it does.

It is challenging to think that counsellors might have a mental health difficulty and still practise, and indeed in most circumstances this would be quite inappropriate. Yet mental illness can include long-term, transitory and recurrent conditions which are not all at the extreme end of ill-health, and at some points may rest quite close to ordinary life experiences. Practitioners will be aware of the tremendous difficulties with labelling in the area of mental health, and there may be some complex decisions contingent on circumstance.

A society in which disability has been largely hushed up and kept out of sight has made the able-bodied reaction to disability the problem of the person with disabilities rather than the person without. Discussions centre on the potential impact of someone in a wheelchair on a client, who is always assumed not to be in a wheelchair, or someone with impaired vision, a speech impediment, or a different body shape. These have nothing to do with fitness to practise, but more to do with an acceptance of the norm that disability is hidden, and only hidden disability is acceptable. If people with disabilities had equal access to the public areas that we live in – physically, educationally and in employment – then there would be no concern over how things might appear to a client, but simply a concern over how to work with these appearances. A speech impediment would be a part of the process of communication between client and counsellor, not a barrier to it. The disabilities that really matter are those that affect the capacity to think and to feel and to communicate, through exhaustion or medication side effects or neurological dysfunction, and these need to be taken seriously. Many illnesses are not disabilities. Some are temporary – going in to hospital for a hysterectomy or having the flu. The effect on practice may be profound but short-lived, and this is an important difference in terms of what action should be taken.

Personal stress

This can end up as a kind of illness in terms of symptoms – tiredness, poor concentration, disturbed sleep and appetite, headaches, addictive behaviour. It can become obvious to clients, and perhaps less obvious to the practitioner, as there may be denial of the stress itself and therefore of the symptoms. Causes are often out of the person's control, but in this sort of work they may affect the capacity to be sufficiently present for the client. The individual's support mechanisms, personal characteristics, stress management techniques all come in to play when attempting to decide levels of fitness.

Incapacity or personal circumstances

Personal circumstances might include a family illness, which affects the counsellor through concern for a third party, or an unplanned pregnancy – something unexpected, which changes the ability to meet the requirements to continue practice. Incapacity is more directly about the person of the counsellor – a period in hospital, or recovering from treatment, or becoming ill. These categories are often used where other more specific ones are not, and so they naturally cross over into some of the areas already considered above. Whether the problem is predictable or unpredictable, stable or unstable, progressive or static, permanent or transient are all considerations in the judgement of an appropriate response. The position of the counsellor themself is only one part of the puzzle; the question is not just *whether* someone is fit to practise, but also *what* are they fit to practise. Work context, client profile, theoretical orientation all affect decisions about what to do if fitness to practise is in question, whose responsibility it is to act, and what ethical courses of action are open.

WHOSE RESPONSIBILITY?

All ethical codes agree that the primary responsibility resides with the practitioner, and that best practice is that concerns should be discussed with a supervisor/professional consultant. While this is unarguable, there is a problem in that the person who is most subjectively involved at that point, namely the practitioner, is being asked to make an objective assessment of his or her own position. Alert and experienced therapists who are aware that their practice is suffering will want to take steps to protect their clients. But take the case recorded by Wheeler (1996) of a trainee counsellor Jane, in therapy during her training, who had a progressive and terminal illness that nevertheless allowed her to function fairly well at the start of the training. As time passed the illness progressed more quickly than was anticipated, and the therapist became concerned for the quality of Jane's work with the clients she was seeing on her training placement. The therapist therefore was herself in an ethical dilemma, and pivotal was Jane's difficulty in admitting to herself, let alone to her supervisor, that anything was substantially wrong with her, or her client work. At a counselling session not long before her death:

> She (Jane) was carried into the room. She was painfully thin, pallid and drawn. She had however been to her training session the previous evening and was fully intending to see her clients the following day. I confronted her with her responsibility to take care of herself and not see them while she was so ill but she rejected that totally, saying, 'My clients are my life'.

One might well ask why a supervisor could not see Jane's extreme situation, and it is worth remembering how little of a person a supervisor actually sees – just the hour, with no idea how heroic the efforts might be to show a 'healthy' side during that time. The supervisor is also susceptible to their own countertransference in the supervisory situation, which can be particularly intense over precisely the issues that are affecting the supervisee – death, illness, and incapacity. This is where supervision of supervision – a requirement in the BACP – can be very useful. Jane had her life invested in her clients, and could no more admit to herself that she should not be seeing them than she could admit that she was dying, as it amounted to much the same thing. Research indicates (Webb & Wheeler 1998) that even in more favourable circumstances there are barriers in honesty between supervisee and supervisor, as the level of trust must be high before vulnerabilities can be disclosed. This is an argument that has been used against mixing the supportive and developmental with the monitoring functions of supervision.

The Division of Counselling Psychology refers to the supervisory function as 'supporting, evaluating and developing professional practice, monitoring, maintaining and extending levels of effectiveness' (BPS 2001: 2.1.1 and 2.16). Barden (2001) argued that support and monitoring must be seen as a dual role of the supervisor, two sides of the same coin, as the monitoring function keeps the counsellor as well as the client safe, and it is false to create a division between the roles. Although the forms this monitoring will take may vary with experience, it will always be integral to the task. It may be very unclear how a supervisor is meant to do this. In private practice, how can the counsellor be made to act on their advice? When working for an organisation, some contracts give clear indications of accountability, others are muddled or have no contract, particularly where counselling is not the major function of the organisation. Supervisors may be expecting managers to assess someone's capacity to work adequately; managers may assume supervisors will tell them if they have concerns. With trainees, there is the added dimension of whether the contract is between the placement, the trainee or the course – preferably a clear agreement between all three, but this does not always happen.

The new BACP Ethical Framework has reached a more definite perspective on this dilemma, and in the Guidance section (para. 27) states that supervisors must 'maintain and enhance good practice . . . (and) protect clients from poor practice'. This lays a clear responsibility on the supervisor to protect the client if they have concerns about poor practice – and so, possibly, to consider more rigorously the ways in which they would know if there were problems, and how they can build a supervisory relationship in which the truth can be told. Where other professionals are appropriately involved in the situation they too carry responsibility – experienced colleagues, line managers. The unifying link is the protection of the client, which is always paramount.

Even with a clear supervisory responsibility, and a positive supervisory relationship, the most effective monitor of fitness to practise will inevitably be the counsellor themself. This raises issues for the training and selection of counsellors, and the importance of their personal qualities. There is a particular demand on private practitioners, who work largely in isolation, and for whom ceasing to practise may have serious consequences on income and lifestyle. Practical steps like adequate insurance can be very helpful here in making ethical decisions less distressing.

WHAT CAN BE DONE?

The most frequent recommendation made across all codes is that the therapist should refrain from practising when their fitness to practise is impaired. While clearly correct, this is not as simple as it might at first appear. As has been noted, therapists work in a variety of contexts, with a range of clients and from a number of theoretical orientations. Differences in personality alone mean that judgements cannot be made simply on what has happened, but on how the therapist relates to what has happened. Whether the work they are engaged in is long-term or short-term, in an agency where alternatives can be quickly offered, or in a single-person practice where onward referrals are more complicated, whether it is behaviourally based and so less reliant on the relationship, or dynamically based so the person of the therapist is integral to the work, are all factors to be considered in deciding what is in the client's best interests.

Having recognised that each situation is different, there are some options to choose from. Practice can be stopped, restricted, reduced or adapted to fit a different capacity. Additional help can be sought, to manage the circumstance or to further monitor and support the therapeutic work. The balance sought is between what the counsellor can manage, and what the client needs. These variables are examined through two case studies.

CASE ONE

Jeffries (2000) explored the management of her clients when she was diagnosed with cancer. She worked in a university Student Affairs department, responsible for client assessments, short- and long-term work, and the supervision of trainee counsellors. Her treatment involved surgery, radiotherapy and periods of chemotherapy lasting two to four months, at unpredictable intervals depending on the progression of the illness. In explaining her absences and obvious physical changes (e.g. hair loss) to her clients, she encountered various transference reactions from distress and anxiety to guilt, anger and fear. How much she told each client depended on their reaction and what would help the most – it was done on a case-by-case basis, rather than a single script, and always directly, as she felt emotionally strong enough to do this. Her strength was aided by a positive response from colleagues, and strong personal support at home. Clients were given choices in how they wanted to go forward, for example changing counsellor, having an 'interim' counsellor, or waiting until the interruptions for treatment were over and then resuming sessions. Clients were naturally in different stages of neediness and dependency, and an individualised response respected this. Prematurely ceasing work with a dependent client may be more damaging than continuing the work, even if it is on a limited basis. The counsellor needs to be 'good enough', not perfect.

At the point at which she was cautioned by her oncologist that her life expectancy made it inadvisable to take on any long-term commitments, Jeffries restricted all new work to intake and short-term clients. In this way it was possible to complete existing contracts and ensure no new work would be left unfinished. Even with these arrangements, though, the cancer remained a part of the work that required continuing attention.

Although I have been well since my return to work . . . my prognosis has affected my practice in subtle ways. All the clients I have taken on this academic year are new to me and I have not felt that it has been appropriate or necessary to tell any of them that I have cancer. But I think I am working more actively, setting a faster pace, holding back from offering myself as available for as long as I am needed. Though overt disclosure certainly influences the way that a client can use me, my own consciousness of my mortality still affects my availability, I am sure.

(Jeffries 2000)

Jeffries' own robustness on the subject of her cancer made making these arrangements a completely different proposition from the case of Jane, cited earlier, when the counsellor's denial of her ill-health meant that her clients and colleagues were denied their chance to think about what it meant to them, and to respond accordingly. Management support can also make a difference to the ease of decision-making, and managers should consider being pro-active as well as sensitive in involving themselves in fitness to practise issues. It is perhaps well-meaning but also asking a great deal to leave it all to the counsellor.

CASE TWO

Andrea was a qualified counsellor with a small private practice at home, averaging eight clients at any one time, including both short- and long-term work. She had supervision fortnightly, and her supervisor noticed that she had lost weight and looked pale and unwell. She commented on this to Andrea, and asked if everything was all right. Andrea replied that it was, and the client work seemed unaffected, so the supervisor let it go. After some weeks the supervisor reopened the conversation – Andrea was thinner, and there appeared to be some hair loss. The supervisor was anxious that an eating disorder might be developing, and felt that the clients were bound to be noticing the physical change in their counsellor. Andrea was adamant that everything was fine, and made it clear that she thought this was her own personal business and not the remit of supervision. A tetchy conversation followed – the supervisor did not feel she could just let the discussion go as she had done before, and was puzzled by Andrea's resistance, as she was normally open to questioning and comment.

After another fortnight the supervisor said quite firmly to Andrea that her physical appearance must be causing her clients some concern, and that if she was not able to discuss this in supervision then it caused the supervisor concern too, as it seemed that the needs of the clients were being put second to Andrea's need to keep something secret. At this Andrea became extremely angry, began to cry, and left the session early.

The supervisor was now extremely concerned. Working in private practice, Andrea had no line manager who could monitor her performance, there were no health and safety guidelines to follow, and no means of stopping Andrea from seeing clients. The supervisor could have stopped seeing Andrea, in order to make it clear that she believed her to be acting unethically, but this would only leave Andrea and her clients without supervision at a time when it was more than ever a necessity. Yet the supervisor did not want to be involved, even implicitly, in condoning unethical behaviour. Reporting Andrea to her professional body seemed like a drastic step, but there seemed little option in between.

At their next session, the supervisor explained gently to Andrea that she did not mean to imply that she did not care very much for her clients, but there was clearly something very wrong, and it was impossible to help unless Andrea would talk to her about it. Andrea replied that she really had no idea what was wrong, but she had been having terrible physical symptoms for some months now, her moods were all over the place, and she was terrified that she was developing some form of mental illness. She could not bear to talk about the effect on clients because the work with them was the only thing that made her feel sane, and if she had to stop not only would she feel that she must indeed be 'going mad', but she had no idea how she would pay the bills. The supervisor listened carefully and assured Andrea that it was very positive that she had started talking about it as now they could think together about what to do. Andrea had not been to her doctor, for fear of what she might discover, and the supervisor suggested she might now think about doing this.

The supervisor's persistence and willingness to risk Andrea's rage had at least brought them into dialogue over this difficult situation. The supervisor made it clear that the clients' needs had to take priority. Concern for the counsellor was also expressed, and the whole approach supportive rather than punitive, but firm. Having faced his own difficult set of choices, the supervisor was more able to help the counsellor do likewise. In the end, Andrea was diagnosed with a thyroid disorder that affected her weight and her mood. It took about a year for this to be stabilised with medication, during which time Andrea reduced her caseload so that her limited abilities could be better used. It did cause financial hardship, but this was more bearable knowing that it would not be forever.

The West Midland Institute for Psychotherapy – a member organisation of UKCP with a large number of its membership in private practice – has written a thoughtful guideline on the role of the professional executor in relation to point 11 of its Code of Practice: 'A member has individual responsibility for ensuring that, in the event of death or incapacity, arrangements are in place with a professional colleague(s) to reduce detrimental effects on patients' (WMIP 2002). The guidelines look at good practice arrangements for dealing with patients – and supervisees – at times when the therapist is unable to manage their own affairs. Having such arrangements in place, as well as insurance against income loss, may have made Andrea's experience less traumatic, enabling her to think about it earlier rather than blocking it out through fear and anxiety. Being prepared for the unexpected, though by its nature a limited strategy, is also a good one.

CONCLUSION

It will be clear that the concept of fitness to practise is not simple to define. There may be clarity at the edges, but in the middle is a mix of levels of experience, workload, work depth, client group, practice context, personal approach and circumstance that all need considering in relation to relevant ethical principles in any decisions over fitness to practise issues. Practitioners need to realise from the beginning that being a therapist requires emotional robustness and a level of physical comfort and stamina. Over the course of a 20-year career it would be remarkable if life did not produce situations that challenged fitness to practise from time to time. Such challenges are not shameful but normal, and the simplest guideline in facing them is to make the first question, 'What is in the best interests of the client?' Most things will follow from that.

REFLECTIVE QUESTIONS

1   If your practice had to cease tomorrow, what would happen?
2   What preparations could be made beforehand to manage such an eventuality?
3   What would interfere with your ability to make sound ethical decisions in this area?
4   What can you do to maintain fitness to practise?

REFERENCES

BACP (British Association for Counselling and Psychotherapy) (2002a) *Ethical Framework for Good Practice in Counselling and Psychotherapy*. Rugby, UK: BACP.
BACP (British Association for Counselling and Psychotherapy) (2002b) Am I fit to practise?, Information Sheet 9. Rugby, UK: BACP.
Barden, N. (2001) The responsibility of the supervisor in the British Association for Counselling and Psychotherapy's Codes of Ethics and Practice, in S. Wheeler & D. King (eds.), *Supervising Counsellors: Issues of Responsibility*. London: Sage.
Bond, T. (1993) *Standards and Ethics for Counselling in Action*. London: Sage.
BPS (British Psychological Society) (2000) *Code of Conduct*. Leicester: BPS.
BPS (British Psychological Society) (2001) Division of Counselling Psychology. *Professional Practice Guidelines*. Leicester: BPS.

Jeffries, R. (2000) The disappearing counsellor. *Counselling Journal*, 11(8), 478–481.

Jenkins, P. (1997) *Counselling, Psychotherapy and the Law*. London: Sage.

Jung, C. G. (1935/1954) Principles of practical psychotherapy, in The Collected Works of C. G. Jung, Vol. 16, *The Practice of Psychotherapy*. London: Routledge & Kegan Paul.

UKCP (United Kingdom Council for Psychotherapy) (2000) *Ethical Requirements for Member Organisations*. London: UKCP.

Webb, A. & Wheeler, S. (1998) How honest do counsellors dare to be in the supervisory relationship? An exploratory study. *British Journal of Guidance and Counselling*, 26(4), 509–524.

Wheeler, S. (1996) Facing death with a client – confrontation or collusion, countertransference or compassion? *Psychodynamic Counselling Journal*, 2(2), 167–178.

Winnicott, D. W. (1962) *The Aims of Psycho-Analytical Treatment in the Maturational Process and the Facilitating Environment*. London: Hogarth Press and The Institute of Psycho-Analysis.

WMIP (West Midlands Institute for Psychotherapy) (2002) Bye Law 1: Code of Ethics; Bye Law 2: Code of Practice. Birmingham: WMIP.

Chapter 13

Suicide: professional and ethical considerations

Jane Boden

A client threatening suicide poses a whole host of dilemmas for the therapist – legal, ethical, professional and personal. Action that appears appropriate in one of these contexts may be inappropriate in another. This chapter highlights the major professional, ethical and legal considerations that need to be taken into account when working with a client expressing suicidal ideation. Such considerations may well lead therapists into actions incompatible with their own personal and ethical beliefs. It is hoped this chapter will help to crystallise those beliefs and prepare therapists working in this challenging area. The task includes assessment and management of risk and a consideration of the duty of care required by practitioners. One's own personal way of working will influence how you respond to a client's threat; therapists must be aware that professional/legal dilemmas transcend theoretical positions, i.e. you cannot use your therapeutic approach as a legal defence.

It may be useful to clarify terminology. Suicide refers to the deliberate act or instance of killing oneself. Suicidal ideation/intention refers to thoughts of a plan or intent a person has to commit suicide. Self-harm is when one inflicts physical damage on oneself. Suicidal threats are warnings that one might carry out the act of suicide. Suicidal risk is the chance or possibility that a person may commit suicide. Parasuicide is a deliberately harmful act which appears to be an attempt at suicide but may not have been intended to be successful: frequently it is the proverbial 'cry for help' (Gregory 1987).

The threat of suicide sets fundamental beliefs against one another. For example, the almost universally held view, shared by those of both a religious and a non-religious disposition, that life is sacrosanct, is placed in opposition to the basic tenet of counselling of being supportive of individual rights and choices. The finality of suicide creates a problem unlike any other in counselling. The threat may require absolute choices and immediate decisions. Suicide eliminates any options that may be available. There may be no opportunity to reconsider for either client or therapist – yet hindsight will act to judge. If there is a death, both self-assessment by the therapist and evaluation by others are bound to focus on what could or should have been done – views that could have legal consequences and implications for future employment. Thus, whatever the circumstances and no matter how justified the act, client suicide is almost inevitably seen by the therapist as a personal failure.

PERSONAL ETHICS

Can an intervention in another's life be justified? If we respect the client's autonomy, is silence about the intended course of action defensible, or do we break silence in an attempt to preserve life? 'Intervention can increase risk as well as decrease it' (Royal College of Psychiatrists 1996: 1). Potentially calamitous decisions have to be made. Whilst acknowledging that it was the client's own choice and responsibility, that responsibility 'was given' to the client, the therapist who gave it may feel a personal responsibility both for the death and its inevitable aftermath. Even when the rules of the employing agency demand that suicide threats are acted upon, the sense of personal failure may still be very real. So while it is necessary for the professional to be cognisant of the professional ramifications of a client threatening suicide, the first requirement is for the therapist to know where s/he stands on the sanctity of life in advance of working with any client. Indeed, becoming aware of your own personal beliefs, principles and values early on in training is an integral part of the inevitable and necessary part of the self-development process that trainee therapists go through. Trainees are taught how (to the best of their ability) to suspend these values in order not to contaminate the therapeutic process.

Knowing yourself and where you stand regarding the sanctity of human life is imperative when working with clients. Although the actual number of clients who do take their own lives is low (Bersoff 1999; Fairburn 1995), it is reasonable to assume that therapists will come across at least one client in their working life who expresses serious suicidal ideation. This can be an extremely difficult time for therapist and client alike. Evidence is that, if the therapist is inexperienced and his/her client commits suicide, it is likely to have a powerful and unforgettable impact (Brown 1987; Kolodny et al. 1979). The therapist needs protection as much as the client. In this regard self-knowledge is crucial. If the therapist is clear that for them life is sacrosanct, there needs to be a clause in the initial contract with clients that explains what his/her course of action will be. For no matter how skilled a therapist might be at partitioning off his or her own personal philosophy it is likely that this will influence the action pursued should the client express serious suicidal intent. For those with clear religious beliefs, and if the time-scale allows, the ideal would be to refer on to another therapist. Furthermore an awareness of the different cultural/religious attitudes towards suicide is advantageous. In some religious and ethnic groups the significance of suicide is particularly marked, therefore the counsellor needs to be alert to these nuances.

The other extreme of the continuum is to hold that the responsibility for the client's actions is totally the client's. Thus the client is free to make an unfettered choice to end his or her own life. Szasz (1973) believed that, although suicide is not desirable, it is a fundamental human right. This belief is also clearly supported by Laing (1967). Therapists who hold this view have no qualms about containing the client's confidentiality and feel no need to inform others of their client's intent. They may even be involved in ensuring that matters are 'in order', including consideration as to whether to leave a note and to make sure that unambiguous messages are left for family and friends. There are therapists who take this line, and regard it as unequivocally ethical and professional – their contract with the client being fulfilled and unbroken. But in doing so, they put themselves at risk of litigation. Although suicide is no longer illegal (Suicide Act 1961) it is an offence to aid, abet, advise, conspire, or knowingly give assistance to another attempting to commit suicide. In addition, the practice of therapists being required to give evidence in coroner's courts is increasing and bereaved relatives may strive to show that the therapist was incompetent and uncaring (Bond 2000).

JUST A THREAT?

The impact of suicide on those left behind is tremendous, the trauma of shock, anger, grief and endless 'what ifs' is devastating (Fox 1981; Glover 1977; Wertheimer 1991). 'The effects of contact with suicide are likely to last for a long time, perhaps years and maybe forever' (Fairburn 1995: 193). One could assume from the evidence of effects on others that as therapists we have a moral right to do our utmost to prevent a client from self-destruction and protect others from harm. Clearly if the method of suicide is liable to cause substantial risk of injury to others, such as driving a car deliberately at another or jumping off a balcony into a busy pedestrian area below, there is no dilemma, confidentiality must be broken to protect others. Therefore, the basic question is whether the therapist is willing to respect the autonomy of the client at all times or does the possibility of the client dying, or others being hurt, absolve them from that obligation? However, in practical terms this is not a dichotomy. If the client is clearly in no position to take responsibility – being a minor, intellectually impaired or having mental health problems, then ethically a therapist may act in a way to protect the client from self-destruction. Similarly if the threat is judged not serious and the threat of death is regarded as remote, then respecting autonomy does not create a problem for the therapist. So the basis of professional and ethical judgements with respect to a suicide threat hinges on two factors: the degree to which the client can be considered to be responsible for his/her actions and the seriousness of the intent.

If the threat of suicide is considered genuine the therapist has decisions to make and maybe actions to take, some of which cannot later be undone. Acting upon the belief that the threat is real has inevitable consequences, many of which would be detrimental to both client and therapist if the belief was unfounded. Therefore, accurate assessment of risk is a prerequisite for appropriate professional practice. Yet such assessment is universally acknowledged to be very difficult. Many threats are not genuine but are intended to bully other people into changing their decisions or behaviour (Fairburn 1995; Jamison 1999); nevertheless, some may precede a genuine attempt to end a life.

So, what is 'serious suicidal intent' and how do we as therapists measure that intent and assess the seriousness of that? As therapists, most of us at some point or another have heard clients utter phrases such as: 'I feel like doing away with it all'; 'jumping off the nearest bridge'; 'shooting myself'; 'for two pins I'd take the bloody lot' and various other euphemisms for suicide. Such phrases occur fairly frequently within everyday counselling sessions. Clients want the therapist to understand just how bad they are feeling. The therapist has a duty to check out the seriousness of such statements. For inexperienced therapists there is often a fear that simply raising the topic of suicide will encourage the client to commit self-harm. Yet it is imperative that such statements are explored. Sometimes simply reflecting how desperate the client is feeling will be sufficient to clarify whether the client is seriously considering ending their life. However, on occasions direct questions are necessary, for example, 'Is it bad enough to make you think about suicide?' 'Do you have any ideas on how you might do that?' 'Have you got any pills?'

THERAPIST'S RESPONSIBILITY

Ethically, we have a professional obligation to make a formal judgement of the seriousness of a client's intent to commit suicide. This is not easy, and therapists need to seek support for themselves at such a challenging time. One of the supports is supervision. It is hoped that all therapists would take doubts over a client's safety immediately to supervision. There is a sharing of the burden of responsibility in discussing potential self-harming clients with another professional: especially as supervisors also have ethical and professional responsibilities to clients. Extra supervision needs to be built into the therapist's schedule to help support the therapist and the client. In some organisations there may be clear procedures to follow. To a large extent, if the establishment dictates your course of action, the responsibility is taken away from you – you may not have a choice to make. Coupled with clinical supervision you may also have line management supervision, which may ensure that the protocol of the employing agency be enforced.

It is crucial to remember that as therapists we are responsible *to* clients and not *for* them. We do have professional and ethical obligations to clients but we are not responsible for what the client does outside of the therapy session. This fact is a vital assimilation early on in a therapist's working life. We have very little control over the rest of the client's life. We are not omnipotent – as I was frequently told as a trainee and inexperienced therapist. Indeed, Gorkin (1985) states that the degree of omnipotence a therapist believes they have will affect the therapist's ability to deal with the impact of suicide. However, one of a therapist's obligations is to assess the gravity of the client's intentions. In order to do this, there are a number of factors that need to be taken into account before a therapist makes the final diagnosis.

RISK FACTORS

For all clients the therapist should be aware of the previous psychiatric history of both the client and the client's family. In particular, have there been any previous attempts at self-harm? What is the client's perception of his/her self both before self-harm and at the present time? What is the client's history of previous depression and/or anxiety? How were similar problems dealt with in the past? What helped and what did not? Does the client appear to be suffering from any abnormal beliefs or experiences; severe depression can be accompanied by paranoid delusions or hallucinations, etc. Psychological disturbance would indicate the client does not have the capacity to make rational decisions and therefore intervention would seem reasonable to prevent suicide. Direct questions may be necessary if the client is uncommunicative or withdrawn. What is the history of previous and present relationships? Who is around to offer support to the client? Those who live alone are at greater risk than those living with family or friends (Fremouw *et al.* 1990).

Following on from history taking, there is no ethical dilemma as to what direction the therapist takes within a session. The therapist is duty bound to challenge the client and to check out the client's understanding of what suicide means for them. Jamison (1999) emphasises that a high degree of ambivalence is contained within the suicidal act: frequently people want to live and die, with some only wanting temporary escape from their problems. Ringel (1981) supports the view that self-preservation is the strongest human driving force, confirming the view of many professionals that the majority of those who act suicidally do so with the hope that somehow they will be saved. Frequently people do not appreciate that suicide is absolute (Jamison 1999): there is no coming back because you made a mistake; there is no coming back to see what effect your death has had upon those it was intended to hurt – death is final.

So, whilst listening to the client's perception of their reality there are also a number of variables to take into account when assessing the seriousness of the situation. These are dependent upon the client's environment, history, and psychological factors. For with suicide threats there are principles to follow rather than rules. Each case will be unique and needs to be handled with compassion. Any decision will always be very personal and may be based upon 'clinical instinct' as much as anything else. However, accurate assessment of risk is a prerequisite for appropriate professional practice. Yet how can we truly know what is going through a person's mind? It is true that most threats are just that, a cry for help rather than a plan of action. Most clients who talk of, or threaten suicide, do not carry it out. Yet it is estimated that 75 per cent of those who do commit suicide have indicated their intent in the weeks or months prior to their death (The Metanoia Institute 2002). Jamison (1999) suggests that most have communicated their intentions to others and Solomon (2001: 251) agrees, pointing out that 'those who talk about suicide are the most likely to kill themselves'.

So the dilemma: some threats could be just threats but many may not be, and all have to be taken seriously. This means carrying out a formal risk assessment. There is no single predictor; the best predictor is a previous incident of parasuicide. Solomon (2001) suggests about a third of those who kill themselves have tried before although Franchino (1999) puts it as high as 80 per cent. The next high-risk predictors are: evidence of careful planning, for example, steps to tidy up affairs, making financial provisions, recent wills; severe depression; precautions that have been made to avoid discovery; and an elaborate method (to ensure death). In addition, there are demographic factors. Young adults are particularly at risk. Most at risk are males (75 per cent; The Samaritans 2002), those living alone with little support; those who have a childhood history of physical or sexual abuse; women in the first year following childbirth; those who are suffering chronic alcohol or drug abuse; similarly, those suffering from serious physical illness, mental illness and self-harm.

Clients suffering from schizophrenia, personality disorders and depression are particularly at risk. DePaulo and Horvitz (2002) state that approximately 66 per cent of people who commit suicide suffer from major depression or bipolar disorder. The risk of suicide increases in proportion to the severity of the depression. Dexter and Wash (1997) propose that suicide is often thought of as the *only* solution to a desperate situation and is *always* an option for depressed people. Someone in the first depressive episode is more likely to commit suicide than someone who has survived a number of depressive episodes and learned how to live through it (Solomon 2001). It is important to note, a person coming out of a depression may be more at risk than one who is incapacitated by lethargy (DePaulo & Horvitz 2002).

There is a close connection between suicide and parental death. Close proximity to suicide makes the unthinkable, thinkable (Solomon 2001).

A threat may also relate to a significant life event such as bankruptcy, bereavement, or physical/emotional/sexual abuse. Loss of self, for example the loss of activities that define a person, e.g. spouse, breadwinner, parent or executive, may render them vulnerable. This may show as a cognitive dysfunction, hopelessness coupled with difficulties in problem solving. Hopelessness and helplessness can sometimes be an extremely disabling state: such despair needs to be watched out for. Indeed, Jamison states 'the most consistent warning of suicide is the sense of hopelessness and negativity about the future' (1999: 94). Undeniably, suicidal ideation is always associated with feelings of desperation, which the therapist must provide a safe climate for the client to ventilate. The therapist has to contain the expression of painful affect so neither the client *nor* the therapist feels overwhelmed by distress. Affective reactions might include impulsiveness, aggression, apathy, severe self-hatred/blame, rage, deep despair, guilt or shame.

Although one or a combination of these factors is an indication that a person is at risk, they cannot definitely predict suicidal intent. Obviously, the greater number of factors one person has, the higher risk quotient they have. A useful summary of procedures to be followed is Bond's (2000) suggestion that they consist of an assessment of the client's suicidal intent and mental state, and exploration of current difficulties, resources for coping and risk factors.

WORKING WITH CLIENTS

According to Solomon (2001) there appear to be four main groups of people who commit suicide. Firstly, there are those who are impulsive for whom the trigger appears to be a specific external event. Secondly, there are the revenge thinking, for whom the main reason is to hurt others. Thinking tends to be contaminated with the extreme desire for retribution; the fact that suicide is absolute appears on occasions to be irrelevant and imprudently considered. Thirdly, there are those who employ faulty logic reasoning in which death seems to be the only escape from intolerable problems. They usually believe that death will improve their condition but also remove a burden from those who love them. Into the fourth group fall those who commit suicide through reasonable logic, such as an incurable disease, mental instability, or a change in life circumstances. They no longer wish to experience the painfulness of life and any payoff that they might receive in pleasure is unable to combat their current pain. Jamison's (1999) book *Night Falls Fast* contains a clear example of this type of reasoning as the author relates her thinking prior to her suicide attempt.

It is useful to bear these classifications in mind when working with suicidal ideation: they may provide some framework to work from. For example, on discovering that the client's reasoning and main motivation appears to be retribution, check out what alternative options there may be to achieve revenge. Has the client explored any of these? Remind the client that s/he will not be able to have the satisfaction of seeing the other party hurting – would it not be better to stick around and watch? Perhaps as a therapist you can suggest to the client there is nothing to lose by delaying suicide – it will always remain an available option. Therefore, can you contract with the client to come back next week and finish exploring what alternative methods there may be to achieving his/her intent? As a therapist you are duty bound to challenge the client's thinking. In doing so you may also be delaying and protecting them from their immediate course of action. Ask specifically how the future is seen – does *everything* seem hopeless? Is there something here that may be worth exploring, which may help the client discover a sense of purpose or meaning within his/her life?

Fremouw *et al.* (1990) suggest that the majority of suicidal acts are impulsive, executed in response to acute stress. For those clients who are impulsive there may be an element of professional judgement, which comes into play. Without doubt, in all cases experience is invaluable in assessing the seriousness of the client's intent and refuting and challenging irrational thinking. Find out from clients who they *don't* want to hurt. Perhaps the client does not want to hurt anyone close to her/him and can be encouraged to understand that suicide will hurt the very people it was not intended to – how could s/he alleviate that hurt?

For those clients who appear to believe that their death will help others, again the therapist's job is to start to gently challenge the client's logic. This can be a difficult task, especially if the client is suffering from depression, when all thinking tends to the negative. However, it is important to remember that the therapist's own expectations about a client's chances of recovery can have a powerful impact on the outcome. The use of positive language and the fostering of hope can play a significant part in reducing the client's negative thinking.

If your perception of the 'no hopers' realism coincides with theirs, bearing in mind all the available facts, then you have to make a personal decision about whether you inform others about your client's state of mind. If the client has rational authentic reasons for wanting to be dead, not preventing his/her death may be the caring thing to do (Fairburn 1995).

LEGAL CONSIDERATIONS

When it appears clear and unambiguous that self-harm is imminent then the therapist has to decide what action s/he is going to take. By law therapists have a duty of care. Daines *et al.* (1997) suggest that there are three factors that are crucial in demonstrating you have fulfilled this duty: whether the suicide was foreseeable; whether, if the risk was known or could be inferred by the therapist, the therapist took appropriate precautionary measures; and whether the therapist offered help in a consistent and responsible manner. They further suggest that these factors are likely to play a vital role in determining negligence on the part of the therapist.

To avoid an accusation of negligence, a thorough and careful assessment of the situation must be demonstrated to have been carried out; this will form the basis of any decision. The British Psychological Society (BPS) advocates that therapists have to be able to explain and justify any decisions made (2002). Careful documentation of the procedures and measures taken must be in place. However, the definition of 'appropriate precautionary measures' is open to debate. The British Association for Counselling and Psychotherapy (BACP) are even more ambiguous. Their ethical guidelines are unclear. They suggest that therapists should 'normally make any disclosures of confidential information conditional on the consent of the person concerned' (BACP 2001: 3), here echoing the necessity of client consent to disclosure. However, there are no suggestions as to the therapist's direct course of action when this is not possible, or when confidentiality should be broken. Consider the rubric contained within the ethical principle of beneficence: 'An obligation to act in the best interests of a client may become paramount when working with clients whose capacity for autonomy is diminished because of immaturity, lack of understanding, extreme distress, serious disturbance or other significant personal constraints' (BACP 2001: 3). This places even greater onus on the practitioner's professional judgement and therapists remain in the same grey area: having to decide what is in the client's best interests.

On occasions, therapists get it wrong and this may have professional and ethical consequences. Therapists may believe they will be protected from claims for breach of confidentiality especially if his/her original agreement with the client contains the exception to confidentiality. However, this is unlikely: the English legal system has throughout a long series of medical cases protected the adult citizen's right to refuse treatment. If the therapist were to make an inappropriate disclosure, which adversely affected the client's career, the therapist may be liable for considerable damages (Bond 2000). These consequences need to be acknowledged by therapists, but not be allowed to deter the breaking of client confidentiality if it is deemed necessary. Before any disclosure by the therapist it is strongly recommended that the client's consent, preferably written, be obtained. Bond (2000) suggests that in legal terms it is unwise to break confidentiality without the client's explicit consent to do so. BACP (2001: 6) advocates 'Overriding a client's known wishes or consent is a serious matter that requires commensurate justification. Practitioners should be prepared to be readily accountable to clients and colleagues if they override a client's known wishes.' BPS (2002) makes a similar point, adding that therapists must use his/her professional judgement when deciding to break confidentiality, informing and involving the client so far as possible.

However, consent is not always forthcoming. Daines *et al.* (1997) suggest that therapists would be less likely to be at risk of legal action if their actions were to find support amongst a number of responsible practitioners. Therefore it may be necessary to seek the opinion of other experienced practitioners in the field. In addition, the client's best interests must be at the forefront of any disclosure made. Clients may have good reason for not informing their GP, perhaps suspecting them of being unsympathetic or not wanting such information on their medical records; or maybe the GP is a family friend. The disclosure needs to be limited only to information that is required by the recipient to act in the client's best interests (Bond 2000).

Therapists need to be aware of the possible loss of professional credibility. The ramifications, including legal consequences, could also be widespread if you do not inform. You may have to stand in a court of law and defend your decision to protect confidentiality and the client's right to autonomy. Relatives of the deceased are also liable to be angry and eager for someone to blame – professionals are an easy target.

CONCLUSION

For suicide threats there are principles to follow rather than rules. Each case will be unique and need to be handled with compassion. Any decision will always be very personal. Judging the seriousness of a threat is not easy and will depend as much upon the therapist's 'clinical instinct' as on formal statements that can be checked off against a risk assessment chart. Secondly, the decision puts the therapist in the position of knowing what is best for the client and their loved ones, a position at variance with counselling philosophy of belief in autonomy and personal responsibility; if the 'best' turns out not to be so, then the therapist has personally to accept the responsibility of their judgement. The Royal College of Psychiatrists suggests 'risk cannot be eliminated' (1996: 1) therefore as therapists we need to recognize that we cannot be infallible in our assessments and we may not always have the luxury of sufficient time to deliberate. The time-scale necessitated by the threat of imminent suicide means that personal beliefs and values need to be firmly in place prior to work with a client.

Respect for the client's autonomy and right to choose remains the overriding principle; this, coupled with honouring the trust the client has placed in the therapist, dictates action in the majority of cases. The law appears to support the client's autonomy even if this may prove fatal and therapists must strive to acquire the client's consent before breaking confidentiality. In doing so, the therapist must endeavour to disclose the client's intentions to someone who has the power to prevent the suicide. Remember that to override a client's explicit wish not to break confidentially may have legal consequences for the therapist. The therapist's own view regarding the value of life may also play a deciding role in the final decision; indeed this may be the deciding factor – if I do not intervene will I be able to sleep at night?

REFLECTIVE QUESTIONS

1 The therapist's own values remain an integral part of the dilemma. What are your beliefs regarding the sanctity of life?
2 Respecting the client's autonomy and right to choose should remain the overriding principle within therapy. What dilemmas might prompt this principle to be ignored and why?
3 How might the possible threat of legal proceedings from either clients or relatives dictate your course of action?
4 Ultimately a decision to act is judged as much upon rational assessment as clinical instinct. How much trust do you place in your clinical instinct and what has been the result of this in the past?

REFERENCES

BACP (British Association for Counselling and Psychotherapy) (2001) *Ethical Framework for Good Practice in Counselling and Psychotherapy*. Rugby, UK: BACP.

Bersoff, D. N. (1999) *Ethical Conflicts in Psychology, 2nd edn*. Washington, DC: American Psychological Association.

Bond, T. (2000) *Standards and Ethics for Counselling in Action, 2nd edn*. London: Sage.

BPS (British Psychological Society) (2002) *Guidelines on Confidentiality and Record Keeping*. Leicester: BPS.

Brown, H. N. (1987) The impact of suicide on therapists in training. *Comprehensive Psychiatry*, 28, 101–112.

Daines, B., Gask, L. & Usherwood, T. (1997) *Medical and Psychiatric Issues for Counsellors*. London: Sage.

DePaulo, J.R. & Horvitz, L.A. (2002) *Understanding Depression*. London: BCA.

Dexter, G. & Wash, M. (1997) *Psychiatric Nursing Skills, 2nd edn*. Cheltenham: Stanley Thornes.

Fairburn, G. J. (1995) *Contemplating Suicide*. London: Routledge.

Fox, R. (1981) Suicide, in *Dictionary of Medical Ethics*, revised and enlarged edn. London: Darton, Longman & Todd.

Franchino, L. (1999) *Grief Work*. Gwynedd: L. V. Franchino Counselling Services.

Fremouw, W. J., de Perczel, M. & Ellis, T. E. (1990) *Suicide Risk: Assessment and Response Guidelines*. New York: Pergamon Press.

Glover, J. (1977) *Causing Death and Saving Lives*. Harmondsworth, UK: Penguin.

Gorkin, M. (1985) On the suicide of one's patient. *Bulletin of the Menninger Clinic*, 49, 1–9.

Gregory, R. L. (ed.) (1987) *The Oxford Companion to the Mind*. New York: Oxford University Press.

Jamison, K. R. (1999) *Night Falls Fast*. London: Picador.

Kolodny, S., Binder, R. L., Bronstein, A. A. & Friend, R. L. (1979) The working through of patients' suicides by four therapists. *Suicide and Life Threatening Behaviour*, 9, 33–46.

Laing, R. D. (1967) *The Politics of Experience and the Bird of Paradise*. Harmondsworth, UK: Penguin.

Ringel, E. (1981) Suicide prevention and the value of human life, in M. P. Battin & D. J. Mayo (eds.), *Suicide: The Philosophical Issues*. London: Peter Owen.

Royal College of Psychiatrists (1996) Assessment and clinical management of risk of harm to other people, Council Report CR 53. London: Royal College of Psychiatrists.

Solomon, A. (2001) *The Noonday Demon*. London: Chatto & Windus.

Suicide Act (1961) London: HMSO.

Szasz, T. (1973) *The Second Sin*. New York: Anchor Press.

The Metanoia Institute (2002) *What can I do to help someone who may be suicidal?* Retrieved 13.09.02 from
http://www.metanoia.org/suicide/whattodo.htm

The Samaritans (2002) *Suicide statistics*. Retrieved 13.09.02 from
http://www.Samaritans.org.uk/know/statistics_suicide.html

Wertheimer, A. (1991) *A Special Scar: The Experiences of People Bereaved by Suicide*. London: Routledge.

Chapter 14

Working in a healthcare setting: professional and ethical challenges

Amanda Evans and Robert Bor

Ethical principles clearly should inform all therapeutic practice. However, some situations and contexts present unique and especially challenging ethical problems for the practitioner. This is especially the case in working with patients with medical problems. Here, dilemmas can be related to the nature of the medical problems encountered. For example, in infectious diseases such as viral hepatitis or HIV where there is a risk of transmission, the therapist may have to deal with issues of secrecy, denial and the risk of possible harm to others. Furthermore, in conditions where the patient's mental state may be altered, the therapist may have to assess the patient's decision-making capabilities. Other challenges to ethical practice can occur where there is a requirement to work within multidisciplinary teams and where varying definitions of confidentiality apply or where there are different philosophies of and approaches to patient care. In medical settings, therapists are therefore required to address a wide range of ethical concerns, adding considerable complexity to their work but also adding an interesting challenge to the therapeutic task. In this chapter, we describe some of the main therapeutic challenges to working with medically ill patients and in healthcare settings, and offer some guidance to the practitioner for addressing some of these issues.

THERAPISTS IN THE MEDICAL SETTING

The traditional view of psychotherapy emphasises the privileged and wholly confidential relationship between the patient and their therapist, as distinct from any other healthcare providers. This separateness has led some therapists and medical practitioners to feel a level of antipathy towards each other, with some doctors believing that therapists can be 'over-sensitive' and some therapists seeing doctors as patronising and autocratic in their dealings with patients (McDaniel & Campbell 1986). In psychological therapies, for example, confidentiality is seen to apply to the dyad of patient and therapist with few exceptions (the risk of harm to self or others is a major exception).

In medicine, confidentiality usually applies to the relationship between the patient and the wider healthcare team such that information is shared with a wider number of people. Therapists may have some difficulty in deciding what information is relevant (and ethical) to share with the colleagues who also care for the patient. It is not surprising therefore that their colleagues consider some therapists unnecessarily secretive and obstructive in medical settings in sharing information relevant to patient care.

Despite the apparent differences in the goals and approaches of doctors, nurses and therapists, the foundation of each profession's ethical decision-making lies in the field of bioethics, which originally arose from medicine (Tjeltveit 1999). Thus, many different types of health professionals use the work of Beauchamp and Childress (1989) in providing a framework for ethical decision-making. Here the four moral principles of autonomy (the individual's right to self-government), beneficence (a commitment to benefiting the client) non-maleficence (avoiding harm to the client) and justice (a fair distribution of services within society) should underpin all policy, professional behaviour as well as the analysis of ethical dilemmas. The current emphasis on patient autonomy in medical decision-making is a major achievement in bioethics as it gives rise to the notions of confidentiality and informed consent (Green 1999). Although therapists and medical practitioners may interpret ethical principles differently, they share a great deal and both embrace a patient-centred autonomy model in which the practitioner must act in the best interests of the patient. In the medical setting, the therapist accustomed to working alone and without accountability to a team will find that s/he is required to adapt to the reality of team working and accountability. In this setting, ethically sensitive decisions are most likely to occur through group discussions where there is mutual respect among the participants (Doherty & Heinrich 1996).

MULTIDISCIPLINARY TEAMS AND COLLABORATIVE WORKING

The emergence of multidisciplinary teams in the treatment of a wide range of medical problems represents a recognition that optimal patient care is best served by an integration of medical, psychological and social care. In order to maximise the efficacy of such teams, the professionals involved must be committed to the concept of collaborative working and decision-making between clinicians, mental health professionals, patients and their families (Seaburn et al. 1996). The movement towards this bio-psychosocial model of care involves a process of change that is challenging both professionally and personally for the different types of staff in hospitals. It may also be that the psychologically aware therapist is best placed to enhance and facilitate this process. In hospital care, where the medical model and the immediate physical needs of the patient rightly dominate, the therapist will need to take a sensitive and pro-active role in promoting collaborative relationships and the consideration of psychological factors in patient care.

Collaborative healthcare is a complex and challenging goal and much has been written about it in recent years. Below we have listed some guidelines that can help facilitate collaborative working (Bor *et al.* 1998; Seaburn *et al.* 1996).

- Treat doctors as customers equal to clients.
- Develop working relationships with all relevant staff, doctors, nurses, administrators etc.
- Initiate discussions about how communication will occur between different healthcare professionals. Discuss the goals of medical treatment for a particular patient and ask others for their perspective on the case. Encourage doctors to ask psychosocial questions early and involve you in potentially difficult interviews with a patient from the onset.
- When appropriate, offer to participate in joint meetings with patients in the doctor's consulting room or on the ward. If possible, it can also be useful to share office space with another healthcare provider to facilitate communication and the building of good working relationships.
- Be aware of potential 'splitting'. Encourage medical providers to let you know if they get complaints or confusing statements from patients about your work with them.
- Use a variety of modes of communication with other professionals; most health professionals favour brief concise communication in face-to-face consultations and formal letters. Responses to referrals should include initial assessment, diagnosis and treatment strategy. Information relevant to the referrer's goals should be included. In terms of language, avoid the over-use of psychotherapeutic jargon exclusive to the talking therapies; use terms that other health professionals are familiar with.
- Discuss the nature of confidentiality in your organisation early on with all patients. Patients often assume that confidentiality in the therapeutic relationship is absolute. When this is not so it should be pointed out. Have release of information forms available to facilitate liaison with other professionals outside your immediate team.
- Accept that building good relationships takes time and goodwill on all sides. Model respect and good manners. Accept that not all professionals want to work collaboratively.

PRACTITIONER COMPETENCE IN THE MEDICAL SETTING

According to the principles of beneficence and non-maleficence, therapists have a duty to ensure their own competence in a given field. Most issues of competence are covered by professional codes of conduct (e.g. BPS *Code of*

Conduct, Ethical Principles and Guidelines (2000), BACP *Ethical Framework for Good Practice in Counselling and Psychotherapy* (2002), UKCP *Ethical Requirements of Member Organisations* (1998). As therapists may be required to treat a range of patients experiencing a wide range of medical problems and psychological problems, it is crucial that they maintain good current knowledge of the conditions concerned. Therapists would do well to remember that the individual consists of physical as well as psychological and interpersonal processes (Seaburn *et al.* 1993). Medical problems can have a direct effect on behaviour and psychological functioning (e.g. Alzheimer's disease, brain tumour, and stroke) or an indirect effect (e.g. diabetes, anaemia, and hyperthyroidism). Failure to take these effects into account could result in patients blaming themselves for their difficulties (Bor *et al.* 1998). For example, a patient with vitamin B12 deficiency may experience lethargy, confusion and depressive symptoms but may attribute their difficulties to problems 'in their mind'. According to a bio-psychosocial approach to care as outlined by Engel (1980), McDaniel *et al.* (1992) and Rolland (1994), medical problems can influence the patient's physical, cognitive, emotional, behavioural and social functioning. Furthermore, the nature, severity, typology, treatment and prognosis of any condition will have profound effects on coping.

As medical colleagues often do not have extensive time to spend with patients in processing the effects of illness or in decision-making, therapists are well placed to facilitate patient adjustment. It is important, therefore, to also have a reasonable knowledge of the implications of tests, diagnoses and different approaches to treatment. It is equally important not to claim medical competence in working with patients. Where there are questions about the course of an individual's illness it is important to defer to medical practitioners (Bor *et al.* 1998).

As part of their assessment, therapists should take a detailed history of the patient's medical problem and the effects it has had on the patient in the ways described above. Good communication with medical staff during the course of therapy will keep the practitioner informed of the goals of medical treatment, significant changes and crisis points. Appropriate feedback to the medical team will also encourage them to take psychological factors into consideration in planning patient care.

The self-reflective therapist recognises the influence of personal history on practitioner competence. It is useful for therapists intending to work in this field to examine their own attitudes and beliefs about illness and health and those of their family of origin. Unacknowledged beliefs and feelings may cause a therapist to practise unethically in that they may, for example, be opposed to patients withdrawing from treatment in any circumstances or believe that it is always best that all family members know about a particular diagnosis. These issues can be explored in training, professional development and supervision.

COMMON ETHICAL DILEMMAS IN THE MEDICAL SETTING

In the medical setting there are many situations in which the therapist will need to make ethical decisions both singly and in collaboration with others in the healthcare team. With increasing complexity in the field of medicine these situations can only increase. Here we consider a few common dilemmas; our inclusions are by no means exhaustive but are chosen to illustrate certain important points and a generalised approach that can be of use in diverse situations.

Dealing with the risk of harm to others: infectious diseases

In medicine and psychotherapy there is an appropriate emphasis on the principle of autonomy in that patient confidentiality is prioritised both legally and in most codes of ethics for professionals. With rare exceptions in the case of self-harm or potential harm to others, confidentiality should be maintained within the healthcare team. In the context of infectious diseases, healthcare providers are concerned for the well-being of all those at risk and in certain circumstances the principles of autonomy and beneficence/non-maleficence may come into conflict. This is so where the patient with an infectious disease such as HIV, TB or viral hepatitis declines to inform contacts who may be at risk. In such situations the therapist should apply the principles of ethical analysis and make decisions in conjunction with a supervisor and other relevant healthcare professionals. The application of sound therapeutic techniques in the context of the counselling relationship can lead to the satisfactory resolution of apparent conflicts in ethical principles (Bor *et al.* 1998; Bond 2000).

An example that clearly illustrates the dilemmas for the therapist is that of a newly diagnosed HIV-infected patient who continues to have unprotected sex with a partner and discloses that s/he has no intention of telling them about the potential risk. Current knowledge about the transmission of HIV shows that the partner, if not already infected, is at high risk of contracting the virus. If the partner were aware of the risk they would have the opportunity to choose to protect him/herself and seek diagnostic testing and treatment (Cohen & Spieler-Cohen 1999). In this situation the therapist is presented with an ethical dilemma in that maintaining patient confidentiality in accordance with the principle of autonomy is in conflict with the duty to prevent harm to others (non-maleficence). Many codes of practice would support the action of informing the partner in this case, although in reality the need for such measures is rare as there are several strategies available to the therapist that might facilitate disclosure (Bond 2000).

Primarily, this situation is a personal and moral dilemma for the patient concerned. In keeping with the principle of beneficence, the therapist's role is to facilitate resolution through the exploration of the factors contributing to the reluctance to disclose. People with HIV and AIDS are still stigmatised in many communities and some patients would face the very real risk of rejection, prejudice or physical harm if they disclose their HIV status (Cohen & Spieler-Cohen 1999). Therapists need to be aware of this in their analysis of the case. They can help the patient to evaluate the potential costs and benefits of disclosure and the long-term consequences of a failure to do so. The process of disclosure can also be facilitated through rehearsal in the counselling session or, in some situations, the therapist can offer to be present when the patient tells their partner in order to provide a safer environment for both parties. Further strategies for reducing risk through practising safer sex or abstinence can be explored. A positive therapeutic relationship can, over time, lead to appropriate disclosure to partners. It is worth emphasising that Department of Health Guidelines (DoH 1992) stress the importance of confidentiality, indicating that pressuring people to disclose their status may result in a reluctance of people to come forward for diagnosis and treatment, a further risk to public health.

Dealing with problems arising from secrets

As discussed previously, patient confidentiality is the cornerstone of ethical practice and may only be broken in certain circumstances. Knowing that information is confidential allows patients time to adjust to a diagnosis before telling others, fosters trust in their dealings with healthcare providers and enhances a sense of control in what can be a threatening time for personal efficacy (Bor *et al.* 1998). Secrets between the next of kin, the medical team and the patient and between different healthcare professionals can present dilemmas for the therapist working in the medical setting and test the limits of confidentiality. This can happen when the therapist believes that maintaining a secret may be against the best interests of the patient or others. There are a number of examples of this which are actually quite common in hospital practice.

- A patient discloses that they are no longer taking the prescribed treatment for their condition but does not want the medical team to know. Not taking the treatment may result in deterioration in health or even death.
- A patient does not want to tell their family about their diagnosis of heart disease. Their family is then unable to provide help in rehabilitation or practical and emotional support.
- Family members ask the medical team not to tell the patient about their diagnosis of cancer in the desire to prevent distress to the patient; however, decisions about treatment have to be made with the patient.

- The family of a teenage boy with HIV does not want to tell him about his diagnosis in order to protect him from upset. The adolescent is reaching the age of sexual maturity.

The secrecy issues alluded to in each of these examples could create considerable stress for the therapist and their colleagues and can lead to a feeling of impotence in working with the case. There may be pressure to take sides, advocate for disclosure of information or even to break confidentiality, all of which could infringe the principle of patient autonomy. The presence of secrets might provide an opportunity for therapists to explore the issues that secrecy masks (Lloyd & Bor 1996). In the example of the parents not wanting to tell their son about his HIV diagnosis, they might be trying to protect him from shock or potential stigma and themselves from any guilt they might feel about how he became infected. Exploration of these issues might eventually lead to planning for how the son might deal with stigma if it occurs and how he might become sexual without passing on HIV. The following are guidelines for dealing with secrecy-related problems (Lloyd & Bor 1996):

- Establish whether a secret exists. Clarify your role in relation to it (e.g. are you being asked to share confidential information?).
- Do legal and ethical concerns apply (e.g. BPS, BACP, UKCP codes of ethics, Hippocratic oath, the Children Act 1989)?
- Clarify the dilemmas involved in keeping the secret and discuss them within the team and, where relevant, with the patient. Sometimes a general discussion is sufficient to resolve the problem.
- Weigh the advantages and disadvantages of keeping the secret. Discuss the range of possible outcomes for the patient.
- What prevents disclosure is the fear of consequences. Ask hypothetical and future-oriented questions to help people imagine the consequences, e.g. 'What might be your son's reaction if you decide not to tell him now and he finds out from someone else later on?'
- Establish with the patient who can be told what about their condition. This will reduce pressure on you and your colleagues. Talk with the patient if relatives continue to demand information. Reassure the patient that you will not breach confidentiality but that you may ask relatives to consult the patient when they next approach you.

Following these guidelines helps to foster patient autonomy as it conceptualises the dilemma and possible solutions as their responsibility. Further, future-oriented and hypothetical questions (Bor et al. 1998) can help to address patients' dreaded issues such as death, fear of dependency or the anticipated rejection of others (Penn 1985). Thus, managing secrets may have the effect of improving communication between the medical team and the patient and the patient and their family. The issues that confront therapists, patients, and healthcare workers do not remain static; we live in an era of rapid advances in biomedicine and therefore new technologies and advances in treatment raise issues that might not have been relevant previously.

Dealing with issues arising from medical advances in treatment and diagnostics

Advances in medicine and diagnostic techniques can present challenges to ethical principles and it is important to apply ethical decision making to these changes in order to maintain well-informed and ethical practice (Green 1999). The recent media attention given to fertility treatment and genetic testing affirms this.

In the field of human genetics, in common with other forms of medicine, the principle of individual patient autonomy is given primacy (Childress 1990). However, genetic information is transpersonal in nature, impacting on families, ethnic groups and groups with similar genetic features (e.g. achondroplasics). Genetic mutations have been implicated in the development of some cancers, Alzheimer's disease and even some psychiatric disorders such as depression and alcoholism. Furthermore, the range of genetic tests that can be used to detect genetic predisposition is increasing rapidly (Marteau & Coyle 1998). Information relevant to an individual may therefore also have costs and benefits for relatives such that the principle of autonomy may come into conflict with the related principles of beneficence/non-maleficence. For example, tests revealing a genetic disposition towards breast cancer in a woman may also indicate an increased risk for her sisters and daughters. Conflict over ethical principles can occur where family members do not want this information because of the psychological cost of living as if a disease already exists or is unavoidable ('asymptomatic illness') or where the index patient refuses to tell implicated family members of their increased risk and so they cannot take preventative measures. These and similar situations will challenge the normally neutral stance of the therapist or specialist counsellor. Where such conflicts occur, there is often an underlying history of family conflict (Green & Thomas 1997) and it may be possible to resolve conflict through the gentle exploration of these issues. Again, the use of future-oriented and hypothetical questions may help the index patient to consider the consequences of their decisions in a non-threatening manner. It is also highly desirable for genetic screening to be preceded and followed by accurate information and emotional support in order to reduce emotional distress and facilitate the uptake of treatments or behavioural change where appropriate (Marteau & Coyle 1998).

Autonomy may also conflict with the principle of justice in the field of prenatal testing for conditions that are not necessarily life-threatening. Some groups or healthcare workers might argue that gender determination and the early detection of achondroplasia could lead to the abortion of female and achondroplasic foetuses that would have otherwise thrived. Thus, in promoting parental autonomy in decision-making the counsellor may be infringing the principle of justice (Green 1999). Furthermore, it has been suggested that where certain disabilities are seen as avoidable, the parents who refuse genetic testing and go on to have an affected child might be viewed as culpable (Marteau & Coyle 1998). Research into individual, family and societal responses to genetic testing is needed to inform ethical decision-making and practice in this field.

While these examples illustrate the need to take a range of principles into consideration in ethical practice, it should be remembered that the principle of autonomy should remain the cornerstone of good practice. Respect for privacy engenders the trust that brings patients forward for genetic testing in the first place. Without trust and the neutrality of practitioners fewer people will come forward and the potential benefits of genetic research may not be realised. It behoves the providers of medical testing to formulate guidelines for approaching ethical dilemmas in order to avoid the dangers of working in isolation (Green 1999).

CORE GUIDELINES FOR WORKING WITH PATIENTS WITH MEDICAL PROBLEMS

1   Obtain knowledge of the medical conditions faced by your patients, how physical, cognitive and emotional functioning might be affected, how the condition might progress and the prognosis, how it might affect others either directly or indirectly, the meaning and interpretation of diagnostic tests and the costs and benefits of treatments.
2   Form good working relationships with the wider multidisciplinary team. Initiate communication both formal and informal, attend and make contributions to team meetings and ward rounds and meet with relevant colleagues when ethical dilemmas occur.
3   Be aware of the codes of ethics of each professional group and how they differ or match your own and get information about the local clinical procedures for the treatment of the medical problems you encounter.

CONCLUSION

As we have tried to demonstrate, the medical setting presents the therapist with a unique range of ethical challenges related to the nature of illness and the organisation of healthcare into multidisciplinary teams. The way in which the therapist approaches these dilemmas and construes his or her relationships with colleagues has a profound influence on the well-being of patients. In the words of Susan McDaniel, 'Counselling in healthcare settings offers opportunities for healing and growth to patients, families and healthcare providers. It gives professionals the chance to contribute to humane, comprehensive and responsible approaches to health and illness' (cited in Bor *et al.* 1998: viii).

REFLECTIVE QUESTIONS

1   What are the main ethical issues to consider in working in the medical setting as opposed to a private or mental health setting?
2   How can you improve your professional relationships with colleagues in the multidisciplinary setting?
3   How do you decide what to include and exclude from your official communications with other healthcare professionals?
4   How have you and your family of origin dealt with health problems in the past and how does this influence your attitude to the non-compliant patient?

REFERENCES

BACP (British Association for Counselling and Psychotherapy) (2002) *Ethical Framework for Good Practice in Counselling and Psychotherapy*. Rugby, UK: BACP.

Beauchamp, T. L. & Childress, J. F. (1989) *Principles of Biomedical Ethics*. New York: Oxford University Press.

Bond, T. (2000) *Standards and Ethics for Counselling in Action*. London: Sage.

Bor, R., Miller, R., Latz, M. & Salt, H. (1998) *Counselling in Health Care Settings*. London: Cassell.

BPS (British Psychological Society) (2000) *Code of Conduct, Ethical Principles and Guidelines*. Leicester: British Psychological Society.

Childress, J. F. (1990) The place of autonomy in bioethics. *Hastings Centre Report*. 20(1), 12–17.

Cohen, E. & Spieler-Cohen, G. (1999) *The Virtuous Therapist*. New York: Brooks, Cole.

DoH (Department of Health) (1992) *Department of Health Guidance: Additional Sites for HIV Antibody Testing: Offering Voluntary Named HIV Antibody Testing to Women Receiving Antenatal Care; Partner Notification for HIV Infection*. London: HMSO.

Doherty, W. J. & Heinrich, R. L. (1996) Managing the ethics of managed healthcare: a systemic approach. *Families, Systems & Health*, 14(1), 17–28.

Engel, G. L. (1980) The clinical application of the biopsychosocial model. *American Journal of Psychiatry*, 137, 535–544.

Green, R. M. (1999) Genetic medicine and the conflict of moral principles. *Families, Systems & Health*, 17(1), 63–74.

Green, R. M. & Thomas, A. M. (1997) Whose gene is it: a case discussion about familial conflict over genetic information. *The Journal of Genetic Counselling*, 6, 245–254.

Lloyd, M. & Bor, R. (1996) *Communication Skills for Medicine*. New York: Churchill Livingstone.

Marteau, T. M. & Coyle, R. T. (1998) The new genetics: psychological responses to genetic testing. *British Medical Journal*, 316, 693–696.

McDaniel, S. & Campbell, T. (1986) Physicians and family therapists: the risk of collaboration. *Family Systems Medicine*, 4, 4–10.

McDaniel, S., Hepworth, J. & Doherty, W. (1992) *Medical Family Therapy*. New York: Basic Books.

Penn, P. (1985) Feed-forward: future questions, future maps. *Family Process*, 24(3), 299–310.

Rolland, J. S. (1994) *Families, Illness and Disability: An Integrative Treatment Model*. New York: Basic Books.

Seaburn, D. B., Gawinski, B. A., Harp, J., McDaniel, S. H., Waxman, D. & Shields, C. (1993) Family systems therapy in a primary care medical setting: the Rochester experience. *Journal of Marital and Family Therapy*, 19, 177–190.

Seaburn, D. B., Lorenz, A. D., Gunn, W. B. Jr., Gawinski, B. A. & Mauksch, L. B. (1996) *Models of Collaboration: A Guide for Mental Health Professionals Working with Health Care Practitioners*. New York: Basic Books.

The Children Act (1989) Guidance and Regulations. London: HMSO.

Tjeltveit, A. (1999). *Ethics and Values in Psychotherapy*. London: Routledge.

UKCP (United Kingdom Council for Psychotherapy) (1998) *Ethical Requirements of Member Organisations*. London: UKCP.

Part IV

Working with diversity – professional practice and ethical considerations

Professional and ethical considerations when working with children and adolescents – an educational psychology perspective

Irvine S. Gersch and Gráinne Ní Dhomhnaill

A number of different professionals work with children and adolescents, such as educational psychologists, clinical and counselling psychologists, therapists, and teachers, who each have their own particular code of conduct, to reflect their distinct type of work. This chapter attempts to consider some common key strands and principles that are felt to have general applicability. In addition, we have decided to focus on some specific issues, rather than provide a comprehensive list for all situations and for all professionals. Consequently the reader is referred to detailed codes of conduct for a comprehensive review of the issues.

In recent years, there has been a growing realisation of the importance of prevention and early intervention for emotional, behavioural and educational difficulties of children and adolescents. It is argued that early intervention prevents the problems becoming entrenched with the attendant impact on the self-esteem of young people. This has resulted in increasing numbers of professionals working with young people, their parents and teachers. The nature of the work that these professionals undertake has changed too. In the past, the focus of professional attention was on the child or young person with the implicit assumption that factors which accounted for the difficulty experienced lay within the child. Nowadays, some professionals working with children and adolescents are likely to work with parents and other key individuals as they recognise that the family system and/or school may have an important impact upon the functioning of the young person.

Greater complexity therefore characterises the work of professionals working with young people: it is not unusual for some practitioners to be working simultaneously with an individual child, his/her parent(s) and teacher(s), the school authorities and other professionals working with the child, such as speech and language therapists, amongst others. Consequently ethical and professional concerns may take on greater significance. This chapter will examine two distinct topics:

- issues relating to working with children and young people,
- working in Local Education Authorities (LEAs) and schools.

This chapter will refer to the most commonly used codes by practitioners in this area (British Association for Counselling and Psychotherapy (BACP 2002); British Psychological Society (BPS 2000, 2002); and the Association of Educational Psychologists (1996)) to which further detailed reference may be made by the reader.

SOME ISSUES RELATING TO WORKING WITH CHILDREN AND YOUNG PEOPLE

Informed consent

Professionals clearly have a duty to ensure that their clients agree to their involvement, but in the case of children, parents should also consent. Children are regarded as such, up until the age of 18 for this purpose, but most codes of conduct indicate that, depending upon a child's maturity and understanding, they might be able to give their own consent for professional involvement at a younger age. However, practitioners may need to get exact clarification about this, depending upon the context and nature of their involvement.

It is also important to stress that such consent should be 'informed' meaning that before anyone can agree to involvement, they need to be fully informed about all the material facts to make that choice. In the case of psychological involvement, parents and children need to know who will be carrying out the consultation, assessment, therapy or intervention, what will actually take place, where and at what times, what they might expect to happen to the child, likely outcomes and what involvement, if any, might be expected of parents. There should be an ample opportunity for questions, not least because such detailed processes may well be unfamiliar to the parents and child. In some cases, other professionals will be explaining such processes to the parents and child and, in such cases, it is important to ensure that those professionals give accurate and clear information.

Two problematic issues may arise regarding informed consent. The first concerns the need for informed consent and the second revolves around who should give consent. In the first case, some practitioners have interpreted informed consent as referring only to direct personal contact between a child and a practitioner. On this basis, they have, for example, undertaken classroom observations prior to parental consent being obtained. They justify such conduct by ensuring that they do not converse with the child/young person and that the child is unaware that s/he is the focus of the observation. However, we are of the opinion that under no circumstances should one proceed to work with children or adolescents without the express consent of the parent(s) or those with parental responsibilities. To do otherwise is contrary to the spirit of informed consent and fails to respect the right of the parent(s) to choose what is in the best interests of their child.

Practitioners should also discuss their rules regarding confidentiality and disclosure, and answer any questions the parent(s) or young person might have about the process. Indeed, it might be helpful to invite questions of children and young people, since they might be hesitant to ask. The following scenario concerns a commonly encountered problem concerning who is entitled to provide consent and how informed one must be to consent to assessment and/or therapy.

CASE EXAMPLE

Justin is a twelve-year-old with learning difficulties attending a mainstream school. He has been upset recently as he is being bullied at school. The school authorities have been alerted to the problem by Justin's parents. However, the bullying is still continuing. Justin's parents want him to receive counselling. Yet he does not want to appear different to the other students. He is adamant that he does not wish to receive counselling. Martin, the practitioner, listened carefully to Justin's reasons for not wishing to attend for counselling. He studied a report previously written by a psychologist suggesting that Justin's performance on psychological tests of intellectual functioning indicated that he had a significant learning difficulty. On this basis, he questioned whether Justin was in a position to make an informed choice. However, equally Martin recognised that undertaking counselling with a reluctant person could be counterproductive and furthermore could serve to undermine Justin's already limited sense of control over his life. Following discussion with Justin, it was agreed that Martin and Justin would meet to discuss any issues raised by Justin as being of concern to him. Martin promised not to initiate discussion on the subject of bullying. Over a period of months, Martin and Justin built up a good relationship and eventually Justin chose to discuss the issue of bullying with Martin.

Confidentiality

Professionals are obliged to maintain confidentiality with regard to disclosures made by clients including those made by children, subject to the law of the land. There are some general exceptions to this rule, which mainly fall under the heading of child protection, for example where:

- a child or adolescent is threatening to kill or injure him/herself;
- an adult reveals that a child or adolescent entrusted to his/her care may be put at risk due to his/her conduct or negligence;
- there may be risks to third parties who are involved, e.g. threatened violence or sexual abuse;

- it is necessary to comply with legal requirements, such as when disclosure is requested in a court case.

There is therefore a continuum of confidentiality (Webster & Bond 2002). Consequently, practitioners should ensure at an early stage in their development of the professional relationship that all participants understand the limits of confidentiality. As Swain (1996) argues, confidentiality is ultimately about trust, not secrecy. Dilemmas arise when one may wish to disclose information revealed in one context to other participants working with the client(s), e.g. where a teacher may be more understanding and sympathetic to a student if s/he understands the issues with which a student has to contend at home. In such circumstances, it is good practice to negotiate with the person who revealed the information as to whether the information can be disclosed to others. However, if the child, adolescent or parent declines the request for disclosure, that view must be respected and the confidentiality maintained.

CASE EXAMPLE

Tammy, an eleven-year-old student tells Joan (the school counsellor) that she has something important to tell her, but that Joan must promise not to tell anyone. Tammy says that Joan is the only person she can really trust. She needs to speak to her today. Joan agrees to meet Tammy later that day. She explains to Tammy at the outset, the limits to confidentiality and the difference between secrecy and confidentiality. The reason why she may have to tell someone else is carefully explained to Tammy. Joan asks Tammy to consider what might happen if Joan failed to alert the authorities. Joan indicates her willingness to be of help while also highlighting for Tammy that she may have to refer her on for specialist help. Tammy agrees to these terms and discloses to Joan that she thinks that she is going to fail her exams. Joan counsels Tammy and with Tammy's agreement, she consults with Tammy's parents and her teacher.

Advocacy

Practitioners may be expected to act as advocates for children and adolescents, since young clients may not always be able to articulate their concerns effectively. Furthermore, inequalities in the power relationships between children and parents or teachers amongst others, may inhibit some young people from voicing their views. The practitioner may have a role to play in representing the child's perspective in terms of his/her dealings with other clients, stakeholders and other professionals involved with the case. This is vital in circumstances where there are conflicting rights. The paramount concern of the practitioner is for the welfare and well-being of the child or adolescent.

CASE EXAMPLE

Paula is a six-year-old with a visual impairment. She is attending a mainstream school. Helen, her teacher, is worried about catering for Paula's special educational needs and suggests that Paula should attend a special school. Paula explains to Anne, the school counsellor, that she now enjoys school, although she finds the lessons difficult sometimes. Paula experienced difficulty settling into school and was socially isolated for the first year.

Now, she and Catherine are best friends. Paula is adamant that she does not wish to attend the special school, as she wants to stay in the same class as Catherine. Paula's parents are unsure what to do. Anne recognises that Paula might benefit academically from attending the special school. However, her self-esteem may be negatively affected by such a move. Acting as an advocate for Paula, Anne represents her views to Paula's teachers, educational psychologist and parents and the LEA. Following discussion, it is agreed that Paula will remain in the mainstream school and that she will be provided with additional special resources to facilitate her learning needs. Helen agrees to work closely with the special needs coordinator in planning and catering for Paula's educational needs. This action fits happily with the LEA's policy of inclusion whereby it is working towards all children with special educational needs being educated in mainstream schools.

RELATIONSHIPS WITH CHILDREN AND YOUNG PEOPLE

It is of critical importance that one takes time to establish rapport with children and young people so that they feel at ease. The establishment of rapport may entail getting to know the client as a person and his or her interests and hopes for the future. It may be necessary to proceed slowly, especially in cases where children/young people have been exposed to negative experiences in the past. The practitioner should therefore adopt a relaxed and positive manner with the children and young people. Treating them with respect is an integral element of all aspects of work with children and young people. Deception should be avoided at all costs.

Even very young children will have insight into, and views of their situation. It is of vital importance that we seek to ascertain their perspective of the situation. Perceptions guide actions: it would be naive to ask all of the adults dealing with the child about their interpretation of the situation without also obtaining the perspective of the central player, i.e. the child. Children can provide us with reasons for their behaviour, with an indication of their level of self-esteem and with their perceptions of their emotional well-being as well as other important areas of their life. As an indication of our respect for children, giving them specified appointment cards for example, enables them to prepare effectively for meetings and to anticipate any questions/comments they may wish to make. This empowers them, while also enabling us to work effectively with them.

Although not usual practice, there may be some occasions when a home visit may be necessary, for example if the practitioner is working with a young person who is unable to leave his/her home for medical reasons. Home visits can provide the practitioner with additional information regarding family functioning and the climate of the home. With regard to home visits, it may be appropriate to ensure that one works with the child/young person in full view of others. It is inappropriate for the practitioner to work in a bedroom with the child. A parent should not leave the child unattended in the house, i.e. in the sole care of the professional.

THERAPEUTIC BOUNDARIES

In today's world, special care is needed in respect of physical contact and how actions might be construed. Whilst no simple answer can be given for all situations, it is clear that the context is key. According to Koocher and Keith-Spiegel (1998) some psychologists agree that non-erotic contact (hugging, touching) can be beneficial, particularly for emotional support or reassurance. However, they also advise that touching should be restricted to the hand, back and shoulder, and that even brief touches can provide powerful messages of reassurance. Others may hold the view that physical contact of any sort should be strictly prohibited. Practitioners working with children and adolescents are obliged to uphold the highest possible standards in their professional work. They should not exploit the relationship of trust that exists with children and young people in order to satisfy their personal desires. All codes of conduct are extremely clear in prohibiting such contact. Practitioners need to be aware of their own feelings and attractions, and not ignore them.

CASE EXAMPLE

Liam is counselling Robert, a 14-year-old boy who is experiencing relationship difficulties. He becomes increasingly inquisitive about Liam's personal life and is behaving in an over-familiar manner. Liam begins to feel uncomfortable about Robert's interest. He recognises that Robert wants this professional relationship to become a personal relationship. Liam resolves to discuss the situation with Cary, his supervisor. Following discussion with Cary, Liam appreciates that he is flattered by Robert's interest in him as a person, and as a result has engaged in sharing personal information. Both Cary and Liam explore how the professional relationship is being compromised in this situation. They explore different ways in which Liam can continue working with Robert whilst maintaining professional boundaries within the relationship.

Many children now take medication or require mildly invasive medical treatments such as the use of inhalers, insulin injections and massage for cystic fibrosis. Parents and care assistants in schools may administer such treatment. The child might ask the professional to undertake such treatment or to help. In all but a life/death emergency, unless prior written approval has been give by parents and it is part of the strict protocol agreed by medical practitioners responsible for the child's treatment, it is inappropriate and undesirable for practitioners other than medical personnel to engage in this practice. In the UK, for schools, clear guidance is offered by the Department for Education and Employment and Department of Health in their documents, *Supporting Pupils with Medical Needs: A Good Practice Guide* (DfEE & DoH 1996a) and *Supporting Pupils with Medical Needs in Schools* (DfEE & DoH 1996b) to which further reference should be made.

CARRYING OUT ASSESSMENTS

Many educational psychologists carry out a consultation process in order to consider what, if any, detailed assessment is required and appropriate. They may spend time interviewing teachers, rather than working directly with the child. All practitioners must work within the boundaries of their competence; they should ensure that their knowledge and expertise is up-to-date, and that they are providing a quality service. Jacob-Timm and Hartshorne (1998) advocate that practitioners should seek to ensure that assessments are comprehensive, fair, valid and useful. A thorough assessment, when it is decided that it is appropriate to undertake this, should seek to identify all of the significant factors and exceptional circumstances impinging upon a child's emotional well-being or behaviour, social development and educational attainment at a particular point in time. This involves gathering as much information as possible and may involve using triangulation (i.e. relying on several different data collection methods and various sources of information) to support the conclusions drawn. Gathering data from a variety of different sources, e.g., interviews, self-reports, behaviour rating scales, psychometric tests, is part of this process. Prior to using any instrument, we need to check that it is reliable and valid for the purpose intended. Cultural differences or differences apparent from the composition of the standardisation sample need to be considered at this stage too.

At times, it may be appropriate for parents to be present physically when one is administering a psychometric instrument to a young child. The practitioner should clearly explain to the parent(s) the purpose of the test and outline the importance of adhering to the administrative instructions. Care needs to be taken to ensure that the child and parents understand all technical terms deployed and their significance. Conclusions should not be based on a single observation or score, as the behaviour observed may be atypical of the child/young person. If conflicting information becomes apparent this should be reported and further investigation is usually considered. Care should be taken in assigning a child a label which could have negative consequences.

Any written report about the child or young person should be both clear and comprehensive, identifying the nature of the concerns and the precise details of the information gathered, including the perspectives of others on the situation. A detailed intervention strategy should be outlined, indicating the responsibilities of the participating individuals for the implementation of each phase or segment of the intervention strategy. Review and evaluation data is commonly included in order to assess the effectiveness (or otherwise) of the intervention. It is also helpful for the reader to know *whom* to contact in the event of any concern. When trainees write reports it is often standard practice for the supervisor to countersign them. With regard to assessment, as in all professional matters, practitioners have a duty of care to maintain the highest levels of competence, and to ensure that they undertake continuous professional development and training.

LEGAL ISSUES

It is made explicit to readers of the respective codes that professionals are expected to work within the law. However, where there is discretion between what is required legally and ethically, practitioners are advised to uphold the highest ethical standards, even if this goes beyond that which is legally required. Furthermore, in cases where the law of the land contravenes best ethical principles practitioners are responsible for initiating action designed to bring about appropriate policy and legal changes designed to safeguard the rights of children and adolescents. Francis (1999) argues that ethics are a set of value principles which enable us to resolve professional issues that are not addressed by the law. Legal issues impinging upon one's work in terms of working with children are manifold. Swain (1996) highlights the fact that clients can seek legal redress on three principal grounds, namely:

- negligence, as in failure to uphold reasonable standards of professional practice, e.g. neglecting to address client's concerns;
- malpractice, i.e. unethical conduct such as engaging in a sexual relationship with a client;
- breach of contract through failure to provide a previously agreed service, e.g. failure to provide counselling to a distressed child.

This list is not exhaustive: legal and other professional advice should be sought regarding any concerns in this area. Caution should be exercised in making any claims in reports/letters regarding the current and/or future functioning of children/adolescents; we need to be able to justify all the statements made. Practitioners are not merely the subject of legal action, they are also increasingly acting as expert witnesses, frequently in their role as advocate for the child or adolescent (see Prasse 2002; Harris 1998; Jacob-Timm & Hartshorne 1998; Scoggins *et al.* 1997; Swain 1996).

NEGLIGENCE AND MALPRACTICE

Negligence/or malpractice can arise when a professional, working with young people:

- operates outside his/her field of competence;
- undertakes a psychological assessment of a child without the informed consent of the child's parent(s) or his/her legal guardian(s);
- does not adhere to professional standards of working due to personal stress and/or illness, e.g. s/he overlooks a significant aspect of child's functioning;
- discloses confidential information to other parties without the expressed permission of the client, e.g. chats openly with a teacher about issues a parent disclosed in confidence;
- administers and/or scores a test/instrument in a careless manner;
- causes distress to children and other clients through offensive comments and/or through degrading treatment;
- fails to listen to the concerns expressed by clients;
- engages in a personal relationship with a client that serve to gratify his or her desires;
- neglects to deal with correspondence or report-writing in a prompt manner.

In any of these circumstances, a client can lodge a complaint in writing to the professional association of the practitioner. Once it is ascertained that this is a matter that warrants further investigation, a disciplinary board (comprising both professionals and others outside the profession) examines the evidence. It is usual for the findings of a disciplinary committee to be published. In both the Republic of Ireland and the UK, there are plans for the statutory registration of all psychologists and therapists, which will mean that any registered practitioner found guilty of serious negligence or malpractice could be struck of the register and debarred from such work. At the time of writing, this process is a voluntary one.

THERAPEUTIC ISSUES

It may be difficult to convey a sense of the therapeutic process to potential clients who have never experienced it and results cannot be guaranteed (Swain 1996). A concern may arise especially concerning the suggestibility of children in cases involving suspected sexual abuse. Bruck *et al.* (1998) provide an excellent overview of the influence of different interviewing techniques on the reliability and credibility of young people's reports. Since therapy may involve working with young people at a vulnerable time in their lives, it is essential to clarify one's precise role in the process. Professionals need to be clear, *in advance*, about the detailed procedures they need to implement in the event of a disclosure of child abuse, and all matters pertaining to child protection.

WORKING IN LEAs AND SCHOOLS

The next section focuses upon the specific ethical concerns that can arise when one is working with young people in an LEA or schools. Special considerations are needed for professionals working in schools and LEAs, which relate particularly to possible conflicts of interest. For example, how does the practitioner respond when key teaching staff ask about the child? What, if any, information should be shared? What if negative comments are made about a child, which suggests that the teacher does not fully understand the child's circumstances? Should the practitioner intervene in the interests of the child? These issues need to be negotiated carefully with school staff. In our experience, the headteacher is the key to negotiating appropriate channels of communication and decision-making.

CONCLUSION

Although codes of conduct are designed to guide professionals' behaviour, they cannot anticipate every contingency of professional practice. Consequently, there is an onus on each practitioner to gather as much information as possible regarding the situation in question. Reference to ethical principles may clarify one's thinking and assist in ethical decision-making. Practitioners can safeguard their clients' interests by seeking supervision and by engaging in discussion of ethical dilemmas with their supervisors and their colleagues. Reflective practice is at the core of ethical conduct. An objective analysis of one's conduct together with an acknowledgement of any occasion when ethical principles may have been challenged will assist in ensuring ongoing professional development in respect of sound ethical decision-making.

REFLECTIVE QUESTIONS

1   You are a parent about to visit a practitioner because of concerns regarding your child's behaviour. What would you need to check for yourself before being assured that you were comfortable in seeking that professional's help?
2   You have contracted to meet with Emma for 12 sessions. After the tenth session you become suspicious that her stepfather is abusing her. What might you do? With whom might you consult?
3   You are a member of a multidisciplinary team working with children and adolescent clients. Several children complain to you about the treatment that they are receiving from a colleague. What, if anything, would you do about their complaints?
4   An adolescent client discloses to you that s/he has been stealing from a local shop. What, if anything, do you do?

REFERENCES

Association of Educational Psychologists (1996) *Code of Professional Practice.* Durham, UK: Association of Educational Psychologists.

BACP (British Association for Counselling and Psychotherapy) (2002) *Ethical Framework for Good Practice in Counselling and Psychotherapy.* Available from http://www.bac.co.uk.

BPS (British Psychological Society) (2000) *Code of Conduct, Ethical Principles and Guidelines.* Leicester: British Psychological Society.

BPS (British Psychological Society) (2002) *Professional Practice Guidelines*, Division of Educational and Child Psychology. Leicester: British Psychological Society.

Bruck, M., Ceci, S. J. & Hembrooke, H. (1998) Reliability and credibility of young children's reports: from research to policy and practice. *American Psychologist*, 53(2), 136–151.

DfEE & DoH (Department for Education and Employment and Department of Health) (1996a) *Supporting Pupils with Medical Needs: A Good Practice Guide.* Suffolk: Department for Education and Employment and Department of Health Publications.

DfEE & DoH (Department for Education and Employment and Department of Health) (1996b) *Supporting Pupils with Medical Needs in Schools.* Suffolk: Department for Education and Employment and Department of Health Publications.

Francis, R. D. (1999) Why I study ethics. *The Psychologist*, 12(6), 291.

Harris, N. (1998) Negligence, liability and educational professionals. *Educational Psychology in Practice*, 14(2), 101–108.

Jacob-Timm, S. & Hartshorne, T. S. (1998) *Ethics and Law for School Psychologists.* New York: John Wiley.

Koocher, G. P. & Keith-Spiegel, P. (1998) *Ethics in Psychology: Professional Standards and Cases.* New York: Oxford University Press.

Prasse, D. P. (2002) Best practices in school psychology and the law, in A. Thomas & J. Grimes (eds.), *Best Practices in School Psychology IV*. Bethesda, MD: National Association of School Psychologists, pp. 57–75.

Scoggins, M., Litton, R. & Palmer, S. (1997) Confidentiality and the law. *Counselling: Journal of the British Association for Counselling*, 8(4), 258–262.

Swain, R. (1996) Ethical codes, confidentiality and the law. *Irish Journal of Psychology*, 17(2), 95–109.

Webster, A. & Bond, T. (2002) Structuring uncertainty: developing an ethical framework for professional practice in educational psychology. *Educational and Child Psychology*, 19(1), 16–29.

Chapter 16

Professional and ethical issues when working with older adults

Eleanor O'Leary and Nicola Barry

This chapter focuses on professional and ethical issues which emerge in therapeutic practice with people over 65 years. Ageism is discussed in reference to older adults and its possible influence on practice. Opportunities for trainees and therapists to attend to their own internal process, values and beliefs can enhance their capacity to work with the older age group, particularly when addressing the issue of loss. Boundary issues, specifically those involving confidentiality in relation to families of clients and multidisciplinary teams, are considered. Special attention is given to older adults who are ill or experiencing partial cognitive decline while the consent of older adults to research initiatives is briefly addressed.

In the Western world, we live in an ageing society in which the rate of births is falling, resulting in an increasingly ageing population. In the UK, there were 9.4 million older adults over the age of 65 in 2001, an increase of 51 per cent since 1961. It is anticipated that by 2005, older adults will outnumber those under 16 by 1.6 million (Office for National Statistics 2003). The projected increase in Wales for people over 90 years indicates a doubling from 11,900 in 1989 to 22,300 in 2006 (Slater 1995). Thus, the length of this stage covers a period of 30 years for some older adults. Bromley (1988) differentiated between the young-old (65–75 years) and the old-old (75+ years). Given these trends, a growing number of older people are likely to need help from therapists in the years ahead. Of primary concern is the readiness of professionals to deal competently with this age group.

AGEISM, PROFESSIONAL PRACTICE AND ETHICS

> Near or above the age of fifty the elasticity of mental process, on which the treatment depends, is as a rule lacking – old people are no longer educable.
>
> (Freud, 1905: 264)

Almost a century later, one would have hoped that things might have changed from Freud's pessimistic view of the value of psychotherapy for older people. However, therapy for older adults remains relatively novel. Murphy's (2000) survey of 100 UK psychotherapy departments demonstrated that psychotherapy for older people is often a scarce resource. Several reasons for low referral rates have been suggested, including ageism on the part of professionals, organisational and historical factors and insufficient resources (Hepple et al. 2002). Such issues permeate society, affecting both service provision and access to services for older adults. However, the last two decades have seen the emergence of therapy for this age group as outlined in the literature by Scrutton (1989), O'Leary (1996), Knight (1996) and Hepple et al. (2002). The American Psychological Association's 1981 Conference on 'Training Psychologists for Work in Ageing' (APA 1981) was the first initiative to focus explicitly on educating and training psychologists to work with older people (Santos & VandenBos 1982). Yet 17 years elapsed before this Association (APA 1998a) described the basic competencies needed. The authors were unable to easily locate any comparable British list of competencies. We believe that the foundation of competent practice with older adults involves an awareness of ageism.

Ageism threatens the dignity of older adults in its implication that they are somehow deficient relative to other age groups. This negation process may be internalised by older adults leading to diminution of their self-worth. Ageist attitudes stem from cultural beliefs about older adults and the ageing process (Nelson 2002). These cultural beliefs are learned and are often reinforced in the media through less than favourable presentations of older people. Ageism can reflect a fear of growing old and an inability to deal with the powerlessness and changes, which may occur, in old age. However, O'Leary (1996) writes of finding that between three-fifths and three-quarters of older adults experienced old age favourably.

A key responsibility of therapists working with older adults involves an examination of their beliefs and assumptions in relation to this population. Yarhouse (2000) argued that bias may not take the direct form of prejudice or discrimination but rather relate to assumptions about older individuals based on an inaccurate understanding of normal adult development, ageing and the specific needs of this client group. Such assumptions can result in perspectives that characterise later life as synonymous with decay and decline. For example, some people may avoid older adults since they remind them of their own mortality, ageing process and loss of youth.

Mr Brown a 70-year-old client, who was having difficulty adjusting to a progressive hearing impairment, visited his general practitioner. During the consultation, he disclosed that the most distressing aspect of his hearing loss was the sense of loneliness and isolation. He was aware that people around him found engaging in conversation with him frustrating, as they would frequently have to repeat what they were saying. He reported feeling distressed and increasingly angry. The general practitioner sought to refer him for therapy but found it difficult to find anyone willing to work with the client as those she consulted felt that the client's distress was a normal part of getting old.

Adulthood tends to be globalised into a 'being state rather than a becoming state' (Sugarman 1996: 295). The implication is that development is completed at the beginning of adulthood and maintenance is all that is required thereafter. We view development, particularly emotional, social and spiritual, as continuing up to the point of death, provided significant cognitive decline does not occur (O'Leary & Barry 1998, 2000). If practitioners are not informed by such a lifespan developmental perspective, there is a danger that the dignity and autonomy of older adults with whom they are in contact may be compromised. Furthermore, such a perspective could counter myths of ageing (Shura 1974; Dixon & Gregory 1987) and prevent the perception of ageing as a homogeneous group.

In 'cost-effective societies' where economic contribution determines worth, older adults may be viewed as a drain on the system not meriting investment of resources, medical or psychological. Particularly alarming is the finding by Uncapher and Arean (2000) that physicians reported less willingness to treat the older rather than younger suicidal patient since they were more likely to feel that suicidal ideation on the part of the former was rational and normal.

ELDER ABUSE

The most extreme expression of disrespect for older adults is that of abuse. Such abuse can take many forms ranging from involuntary institutionalisation, neglect in the home, refusal to feed older people who are unable to feed themselves, financial abuse, bullying, physical violence, over-medication, sexual assault and psychological abuse causing confusion, isolation or loss of contact with reality in older people. If clients tell therapists that they are being abused, appropriate action should be taken. This may involve liaison with health authorities or police services while addressing the need for ongoing support for the older victim.

THE ISSUE OF LOSS IN OLD AGE AND PROFESSIONAL PRACTICE

The greatest challenge facing older adults may be the loss of intimate emotional relationships through illness or death. Either of these losses can bring about an overriding sense that life has no further meaning since the absence/death of spouse/partner, siblings and friends may be more problematic for older people than lack of work roles. The availability of group therapy can provide a forum for meaningful connections in the face of such losses. An example of this is described below.

Mrs Green, an older adult who attended a support group at a community health centre, had experienced multiple losses including the death of her spouse, several friends and a relative whom she had nursed. In addition, she had a young relative who was terminally ill and died during the duration of the group. She found that the group was a context in which she could process the losses and derive support, not only for the present but also for the future.

Loss through death of someone close brings with it a realisation of the inevitability of the client's own death. Contemplation of one's mortality is deeply challenging for older adults, who may actively block processing these issues due to their own anxiety. In their study of emerging psychological issues of older adults when talking about death and dying, O'Leary and Nieuwstraten (2001) found a range of coping mechanisms were used, including deflection, prayer and humour. However, the use of both blocking and coping strategies needs to be considered, not only with reference to older adults but also in relation to professionals. Britton and Woods (1996) pointed out that there is a clear need for specific exploration of bereavement and loss in initial training and in continuing professional development. However, exposure alone is not enough. Trainees and professionals also need to identify and examine possible unresolved issues concerning their own beliefs and feelings about ageing, death and bereavement in order to work effectively with their clients and families. This can best occur through attention to their internal processes in personal development groups, personal therapy and supervision.

Mrs Black, an older client, on learning of the death of a family member, began to talk about how she felt about her own mortality. During the session, she was able to voice her wishes for her own funeral including details of the service. The therapist, however, felt uncomfortable, as she feared that the session might become morbid and upset the client unnecessarily. In supervision, she acknowledged her discomfort and her impulse to redirect the focus of the work to a 'safer' and more 'optimistic' topic. Having explored the issue in supervision, she became aware that the discomfort she experienced was rooted in her own anxiety of death in relation to her ageing parents. However, the experience of discussing this issue was empowering for the client as it allowed her to engage with this critical aspect of her life, which most people find so difficult to acknowledge – the inevitability of death.

AWARENESS OF INTERNAL PROCESS, PROFESSIONAL PRACTICE AND ETHICS

An awareness of internal process, personal values and beliefs is central to the work of therapists. The Division of Counselling Psychology of the British

Psychological Society (BPS 2001: 4) stated that the models, which provide the foundation for counselling psychology, seek 'to engage with subjectivity and inter-subjectivity, values and beliefs'. We believe that the more understanding trainees and therapists gain of these areas of their lives, the more it enhances their capacity to work ethically with older adults. Reflection on and exploration of one's own process as a trainee and practitioner is echoed in models of ethical decision-making.

A critical dimension of professional practice relates to the facilitation of empowerment by the therapist for those over 65 years, many of whom may feel increasingly powerless as they age. The right of people to make choices affecting their lives has been outlined by the American Psychological Association Council of Representatives (APA 1981), which emphasised informed consent and freedom of choice throughout the treatment process. Professionals should be alert to respecting the autonomy of older individuals, their right to be self-determining, and be wary of adopting a paternalistic stance towards them. Woolfe and Biggs (1997: 190) claimed that associating older adults with one's parents on the part of therapists may result among other things in an 'over-commitment to client change, irrational anger with a client, feeling wounded if the client questions their expertise'. These authors also speak of grandparent fantasies, which can impede counselling through generating a feeling of protection towards older people.

Following a car accident, Mrs Silver, a 68-year-old widow who had suffered extensive injuries, was transferred from hospital to a residential nursing home for respite care. The accident had been extremely traumatic for her and she had begun to exhibit symptoms of depression. Staff in the nursing home felt that she might benefit from therapy and discussed the possibility of referral with the family, who declined the offer on the grounds that they felt that talking about the accident would upset their mother. As she became increasingly withdrawn, members of the staff became concerned and approached a therapist to discuss their concerns. While understanding the family's concerns the therapist first agreed to meet Mrs Silver to assess if she wanted therapy and to gain her consent to schedule a meeting with some family members to discuss their concerns about the nature and purpose of the service. Mrs Silver chose to have some therapy and gave her consent for the meeting with her family. Although she declined the offer to attend the meeting, the session provided a forum for her family to discuss their fears in relation to their mother's distress. Having had some time to consider what therapy could offer, they subsequently accepted her decision to receive therapy. The wishes of the family were considered in a respectful way while still allowing room for the protection of the rights of the client. When the wishes of relatives become paramount, there is a danger that older adults can be infantilised and excluded from consultative processes concerning their well-being.

Empowerment is intimately linked to the principle of responsibility. This includes the duty of care that practitioners hold in relation to their clients.

According to Ritter and Watkins (1997), the most difficult ethical issue concerning the treatment of older people is to ensure that they are involved in decisions relating to that treatment. Although these authors were writing in a medical context, the principle extends to the psychotherapeutic field. Enhancing the empowerment of older clients implies ongoing consultation with them and a heightened awareness of the primacy of prizing individuality. Sometimes older people may not be consulted by their relatives or friends about the decision to transfer them to a residential home. One of the saddest experiences in our work is the oft-repeated story of some older adults in nursing homes: 'I am going home next week'. If it is the family's or next of kin's intention that their parent, relative or friend is to remain in the residential setting, the therapist may need to inform the matron/owner that the older person is unaware of the finality of the move. The issue of the most appropriate person to communicate such information needs to be discussed and subsequently implemented. Similar issues may arise when an individual is living in their own home, when family members may take over responsibility for decision-making in terms of the older person's personal affairs.

CONFIDENTIALITY BOUNDARY AND THE FAMILY

Confidentiality involves the principle of fidelity (Fitting 1984, 1986). This principle invokes the need to be wary of referrals of older adults for therapeutic intervention that are grounded primarily in the family's wishes. Families may assume that they have a right to access information on sessions without the client's permission. It could happen that an older adult's case is discussed in some detail with a son or daughter without the permission of the client. Britton and Woods (1996) considered this to be an abuse of power. Furthermore, boundary issues may arise when older individuals are resident in hospitals, in nursing homes or with their families. Blurring of boundaries serves to disempower older people and leads to the subjugation of their wishes to those of others. For example, professionals may more readily form alliances with younger family members (Knight 1996) or it may occur that the family, next of kin or nursing home owner/matron may feel that the therapist's role is to implement their wishes. In such situations, the role of the therapist may be to educate those concerned on their responsibility to respect the client's wishes.

Hughes (2001) invited professionals to reflect on the need for full disclosure of information to older clients. Drawing on the work of Pinner (2000) and Marzanski (2000), he advocated truthfulness and highlighted the practitioner's responsibility in ascertaining what the older person wishes to know. It can occur that relatives may fear that the discussion of sensitive issues with older adults could have a potentially negative impact on them. However, this age group can be more emotionally robust than society is willing to recognise.

Many have weathered difficult experiences at various stages in their lives. They often move to later life having coped and adapted to multiple losses and yet they are repeatedly and narrowly characterised within Western society as vulnerable and in need of protection. This narrow characterisation is reflected in the reluctance of some professionals to treat older adults as having the right to information about diagnosis and treatment, whether medical or psychological. In relation to truth-telling, Maguire *et al.* (1996) reported that, whilst 83 per cent of relatives of Alzheimer's disease patients did not support the idea of the client being told, 71 per cent expressed a preference for such disclosure themselves if they developed the condition! In a study of 30 people with dementia, Marzanski (2000) found that 70 per cent wished to know what the problem was or to have more information if they already knew. Hughes (2001) argues that the key point was to ascertain whether the client wants to be told.

CONFIDENTIALITY BOUNDARY, MULTIDISCIPLINARY TEAMS AND QUALITY OF CARE

Managing the boundaries of confidentiality can be particularly challenging when working in a team context; however, interdisciplinary collaboration, in conjunction with supervision, can provide a safe context in which the processing of ethical issues can be facilitated. Grappling with boundary issues and dilemmas is emotionally taxing and may leave therapists feeling disempowered. Ethical decision-making implies drawing on the support, guidance and alternative perspectives available through supervision and interaction with other team members. However, who constitutes the team should be clearly defined and known to the older adult concerned so that no breach of confidentiality occurs. It must also be borne in mind that, the larger the number in the team, the greater the possibility of inappropriate disclosure of information.

PROFESSIONAL ISSUES IN WORKING WITH OLDER ADULTS WHO ARE ILL

Working with older adults involves flexibility on the part of therapists. At times, clients may become ill or housebound for different physical reasons. In such instances the therapist may visit the client at home and the length of the session may have to be shortened, based on the client's physical well-being. Clients may also cancel sessions during periods of hospitalisation or recovery. Appointments for future sessions may need to be negotiated on a week-to-week basis. With the permission of clients, it may be necessary to consult with their doctor on the potential psychological impact of any medication or procedure. The issue of older adults somatising may require consideration and the therapist needs to remain alert to the possibility that physical symptoms might be masking depression, possibly relating to the physical losses frequently associated with ageing. Illness frequently facilitates the disclosure of critical fears on the part of older adults, for example, fear of being alone when dying.

If quite ill, older adults occasionally might wish the therapist to sit with them rather than engage in counselling. This is particularly important for the ongoing relationship as it actively demonstrates unconditional positive regard. However, this is rarely likely to occur. What is particularly important from a professional practice perspective is the flexibility required with respect to boundaries when counselling older adults. It is important that the therapeutic relationship is maintained while not allowing it to develop into friendship.

Further practical concerns relate to limitations in freedom of choice due to physical difficulties. With respect to their own practice, professionals need to ensure that their offices or meeting rooms are convenient in terms of transport, are situated on the ground floor and have access for wheelchairs. If the last is not the case, the therapist may need to meet older persons on entry to the building and accompany them to and from the office or make alternative arrangements for clients. This is particularly important where older people are experiencing physical or sight difficulties. Convenient access to toilets is also a priority. Twining (1996) highlighted the importance of taking practical issues, such as the length of sessions, into account; a maximum of ninety minutes for group therapy is advisable.

COGNITIVE DECLINE, ASSESSMENT AND ETHICAL BEHAVIOUR

Cognitive decline in older adults does not automatically mean an inability on their part to make decisions. In the case of dementia, adults over 65 years of age in the initial stages of Alzheimer's disease, have periods of lucidity which may be longer than their periods of being out of contact with reality. Hughes (2001) asserted that one of the major sources of ethical dilemmas in working with people with dementia is that of determining their cognitive capacity.

In using the evaluation of other professionals with respect to the cognitive functioning of older adults, it is important that the therapist ensures that the professional involved has a special competence in the area. Its importance was apparent to the first author when she asked a trainee how the first session with an older adult had progressed. The trainee reported that the nurse, who had an interest but no specialised training on cognitive decline, had told her that the older adult was 'out of it'. Since the supervisor had supervised another trainee's work with the particular client four months previously, she asked the trainee to visit the client on the following week. Not only was the older person lucid for the following 25 weeks but also the trainee expressed her amazement at the clarity of the client at frequent intervals throughout the supervision! Speaking in relation to psychologists, the APA (1998b) proposed that 'psychologists who propose to perform evaluations for dementia and age-related cognitive decline are aware that special competencies and knowledge are required for such evaluations' (p. 1299). This proposal is relevant to all professionals who assess, or are working with, older people.

Hughes (2001) suggested that, in order to promote autonomy in people with dementia, it is necessary to make it as easy as possible for clients to act. He identified the need for effective communication through explanation and re-explanation in an empathic manner in terms that are as simple as required. Through this approach, professionals can respect and promote the autonomy of cognitively impaired individuals. Knight (1996) warned of the dangers of assuming that those over 65 years experiencing cognitive decline are incapable of participating in treatment. He made clear that older adults with dementia could give consent up to an-as-yet undefined point in their cognitive decline.

Overall, the evidence points to the conclusion that, in general, it is possible to discern the wishes of older adults suffering from cognitive decline with respect to the disclosure of their condition, provided this decline is not too severe. Ethically, it is necessary for professionals to attempt to do so in order to respect clients' autonomy. An area for future research is to identify at what point older people with cognitive decline are no longer able to make such a decision, bearing in mind individual variability. In the area of cognitive assessments, therapists need to collaborate with appropriately trained professionals. What is important is that older adults are allowed the freedom to choose for as long as is possible. This freedom of choice should also be respected in the participation of older people in research.

RESEARCH AND ETHICAL BEHAVIOUR

Arie (1981) pointed out that the voices of older adults are heard neither often enough nor loudly enough. Participation in scientist-practitioner research can enable these voices to be heard. The principle of consent must clearly extend to the involvement of the older age group in such research. Given the physical difficulties which some older adults may experience, there is a need for procedural versatility. In the case of visual impairment, it may be possible to tape record their consent. Alternatively, if they suffer from a hearing deficit, a written agreement should be sought. Ideally, both written and audio-taped consent should be obtained. If ratings or reports are requested from other professionals on any aspect of the older adults' functioning by the researcher, it is important that the consent of these older individuals be obtained. Attention to such practical concerns in research with older adults demonstrates an understanding of and respect for their needs.

CONCLUSION

Unfortunately psychotherapeutic intervention with people over 65 years remains a relatively new endeavour. In this chapter, we have considered a number of professional and ethical issues that need to be considered when working with this client group. Professionals should examine possible latent ageist attitudes which, if left undetected, may hinder the demonstration of respect for the personhood of older adults, and hinder effective therapeutic practice. Empowerment of older individuals is a key aspect in such practice and implies the active participation of clients in the use of psychological therapies. Failure to do so may mean that little will change in the years ahead.

REFLECTIVE QUESTIONS

1   What is your own internal process (beliefs, fears) in relation to working with older adults?
2   What aspects of ageism are particularly salient for you in working with older clients?
3   How could you enhance the individuality and dignity of older adults with whom you work?
4   What boundary issues might you encounter in your work with older adults?

REFERENCES

APA (American Psychological Association Council of Representatives) (1981) Ethical principles of psychologists. *American Psychologist*, 36(6), 633–638.
APA (American Psychological Association Working Group on the Older Adult) (1998a) What practitioners should know about working with older adults. *Professional Psychology: Research and Practice*, 29(5), 413–427.
APA Presidential Taskforce on the Assessment of Age Consistent Memory Decline and Dementia (1998b) Guidelines for the evaluation of dementia and age-related cognitive decline. *American Psychologist*, 53(12), 1298–1303.
Arie, T. (1981) *Health Care of the Elderly*. London: Croom Helm.
BPS (British Psychological Society) (2001) *Professional Practice Guidelines*, Division of Counselling Psychology.
   http://www.bps.org.uk
Britton, P. G. & Woods, R. T. (1996) Introduction, in: R. T. Woods (ed.), *Handbook of the Clinical Psychology of Ageing*. Chichester, UK: John Wiley.

Bromley, D. B. (1988) *Human Ageing*, 3rd edn. Harmondsworth, UK: Penguin Books.

Dixon, J. & Gregory, L. (1987) Ageism. *Action Baseline*, 21–23.

Fitting, M. D. (1984) Professional and ethical responsibilities for psychologists working with the elderly. *Counselling Psychologist*, 12, 69–78.

Fitting, M. D. (1986) Ethical dilemmas in counselling elderly adults. *Journal of Counselling and Development*, 64, 325–327.

Freud, S. (1905) On psychotherapy, in the Standard Edition of the Complete Works of Sigmund Freud (1935). London: Hogarth Press.

Hepple, J. Pearce, J. & Wilkinson, P. (eds.) (2002) *Psychological Therapies with Older People: Developing Treatment for Effective Practice*. Hove, UK: Brunner-Routledge.

Hughes, J. C. (2001) Ethics and the psychiatry of old age, in R. Jacoby & C. Oppenheimer (eds.), *Psychiatry in the Elderly*. Oxford: Oxford University Press.

Knight, B. G. (1996) *Psychotherapy with Older Adults*, 2nd edn. Thousand Oaks, CA: Sage.

Maguire, C. P., Kirby, M., Coen, R., Coakley, D., Lawlor, B.A. & O'Neill, D. (1996) Family members' attitudes toward telling the patient with Alzheimer's disease their diagnosis. *British Medical Journal*, 313, 529–530.

Marzanski, M. (2000) Would you like to know what is wrong with you? On telling the truth to patients with dementia. *Journal of Medical Ethics*, 26, 108–113.

Murphy, S. (2000) Provision of psychotherapy services for older people. *Psychiatric Bulletin*, 24(5), 181–184.

Nelson, T. D. (Ed.) (2002) *Ageism: Stereotyping and Prejudice against the Older Person*. California: MIT Press.

Office for National Statistics, Government Actuary's Department, General Register Office for Scotland, Northern Ireland, England and Wales Statistics and Research Agency (2003).
http://www.statistics.gov.uk/CC1 [accessed 14 May 2003].

O'Leary, E. (1996) *Counselling Older Adults: Perspectives, Approaches and Research*. London: Chapman & Hall.

O'Leary, E. & Barry, N. (1998) Reminiscence therapy with older adults. *Journal of Social Work Practice*, 12(2), 159–165.

O'Leary, E. & Barry, N. (2000) Counselling older adults, in I. Horton & C. Feltham (eds.), *Handbook of Counselling and Psychotherapy*. London: Sage.

O'Leary, E. & Nieuwstraten, I. (2001) Emerging psychological issues in talking about death and dying: a discourse analytic study. *International Journal for the Advancement of Counselling*, 23, 179–199.

Pinner, G. (2000) Truth telling and the diagnosis of dementia. *British Journal of Psychiatry*, 176, 514–515.

Ritter, S. & Watkins, M. (1997) Assessment of older people, in I. J. Norman & S. J. Redfern (eds.), *Mental Health Care for Elderly People*. New York: Churchill Livingstone.

Santos, J. & VandenBos, G. (eds.) (1982) *Psychology and the Older Adult: Challenges for Training in the 1980s*. Washington, DC: American Psychological Association.

Scrutton, S. (1989) *Counselling Older People: A Creative Response to Ageing*. London: Edward Arnold.

Shura, S. (1974). *Ageing: An Album of People Growing Old*. New York: John Wiley.

Slater, R. (1995) *The Psychology of Growing Old: Looking Forward*. Buckingham, UK: Open University Press.

Sugarman, L. (1996) Narratives of theory and practice: the psychology of life span development, in R. Woolfe & W. Dryden (eds.), *Handbook of Counselling Psychology*. London: Sage.

Twining, C. (1996) Psychological counselling with older adults, in R. Woolfe & W. Dryden (eds.), *Handbook of Counselling Psychology*. Thousand Oaks, CA: Sage.

Uncapher, H. & Arean, P. (2000) Physicians are less willing to treat suicidal ideation in older adults. *Journal of the American Geriatrics Society*, 48(2), 188–192.

Woolfe, R. & Biggs, S. (1997) Counselling older adults: issues and awareness. *Counselling Psychology Quarterly*, 10(2), 189–194.

Yarhouse, M. A. (2000) Review of social cognition research on stereotyping: application to psychologists working with older adults. *Journal of Clinical Geropsychology*, 6(2), 121–131.

Chapter 17

Professional and ethical practice in the consulting room with lesbians and gay men

Lyndsey Moon

A starting point for this chapter will be the way good professional and ethical practice can be encouraged within the consulting room for lesbians and gay men. This will be considered in light of their role as either client or therapist. As a backdrop to this chapter it is important to recognise the psychological history that has been negatively constructed with the 'help' of therapeutic discourses for lesbian and gay populations. Such discourses incorporate 'sexuality scripts' (Simon & Gagnon 1986) which told us how to behave 'appropriately' meaning heterosexually. This pathologising discourse held that lesbian and gay people were in need of treatment to make them become heterosexual and 'well'. Consequently, this chapter will consider the use of counselling scripts and sexual scripts and how these may be used when working with lesbians and gay men in the consulting room. A major shift in thinking has been introduced over the past decade through the concept of Gay Affirmative Therapy, which has tried to bring about a more positive image and understanding in the way we work with these client populations (Davies 1996; Milton 1998; Milton and Coyle 2003). The central principle of Gay Affirmative Therapy is that 'it affirms a lesbian, gay or bisexual identity as an equally positive human experience and expression to heterosexual identity' (Davies 1996: 25). This will be referred to within this chapter as an example of a good practice model.

The American Psychological Association's (APA) (2000) 16 guidelines for psychotherapy with lesbians, gay men and bisexual clients will also be presented. These were introduced to encourage and enhance good ethical and professional practice for both client and therapist and may be consulted by all practitioners. The overall intention of this chapter is to discuss the challenges and opportunities concerning lesbian and gay issues within the lesbian and gay client and lesbian, gay, bisexual and heterosexual therapist matrix.

PROFESSIONAL AND ETHICAL ISSUES IN THE CONSULTING ROOM WITH LESBIANS AND GAY MEN

Developing professions are constantly reviewing their standards, codes and principles to accommodate changing socio-political conditions and circumstances. The increasing presence of the lesbian and gay community is likely to influence such standards. For example, the lesbian and gay social movement, including lesbian and gay mental health professionals, undoubtedly influenced the removal of homosexuality from the American Psychiatric Association's *Diagnostic and Statistical Manual of Mental Health Disorders* (DSM) in 1970 (Greene 1994). As mentioned earlier, this also resulted in the APA guidelines, which act as a frame of reference for the treatment of lesbian, gay and bisexual clients. These guidelines aim to improve practice and overcome prejudice within the consulting room by providing a set of principles that aim to govern 'good practice'. For example, it is expected that therapists will increase their knowledge and understanding of lesbian, gay and bisexual lives through continuing professional development, training and consultation. Also, professional ethics presented through codes of practice, establish ways of the therapist understanding behaviour and obligations in the practitioner–client relationship.

In Britain similar guidelines have not yet been developed which would help in developing therapeutic practice in relation to the various sexualities. Society and therefore the BACP, BPS, and UKCP have established 'professional norms' (Pilgrim 1991) which are based on particular formulations of psychological knowledge that privilege heterosexual ideologies, in relation to the social world. As Clarkson (1998: 6) explains: 'The drive for acceptability to the status quo, commonly agreed standards and consensually developed criteria becomes a repository of conformity, uniformity and people who are like us. The unusual, the challenging, questioning of the basic assumptions underlying the hard won professional status (or similar) is often experienced as threatening, untrustworthy and therefore excluded or marginalized.'

Given that professionals may carry these assumptions into the consulting room, it is important that practitioners question meanings surrounding their beliefs in relation to lesbians and gay men. Therapists may use the following questions to identify/reflect on their sexual and subsequent related social script beliefs.

SEXUAL SCRIPT EXERCISE

Consider where you draw your knowledge from about the various sexualities (heterosexual, lesbian, gay, bisexual, etc.). Imagine yourself in each of these roles and consider what your script would say. Start your example by saying,

'My name is . . . and I am a gay man/lesbian/heterosexual female' etc. and spend a few minutes answering the following questions:

- How do you feel?
- How do you imagine you will behave?
- What will your future be like and how will everyday life be constructed?

By doing this you can begin to broaden your understanding of sexual scripts, and by imagining other social and sexual worlds.

DOMINANT THERAPEUTIC SCRIPTS AND THERAPEUTIC PRACTICE WITH LESBIAN AND GAY CLIENTS

Perhaps initial training as a therapist is when issues relating to working with lesbians and gay men first begin to emerge. Prior to training, access to knowledge about lesbians, gay men, bisexual or transgender clients is usually through societal scripts, which, in the main, are heterosexually ordered. For example, the mass media may have been the therapist's only encounter with information about lesbian and gay male people. Thus, the heterosexual therapist who begins training and is faced with lesbian and gay issues may have very little understanding of what it was like to designate the self as non-heterosexual or what it is like to live as a lesbian or gay male in society. The consulting room may be the first occasion to both meet and work with a lesbian or gay man. This can be a very close and intimate relationship and for this reason it is important to really think about your code of ethics.

Variations in training about lesbian and gay issues are widespread. Over ten years ago, as part of a research project, a small sample of counselling psychologists reported that, although they would be prepared to work with lesbian and gay clients, they had received inadequate training in working with these client groups (Moon 1992). In a more recent study (Moon 2002), conducted with 30 counsellors, counselling psychologists and psychotherapists, similar results were found. This means that it is likely that a frame of reference for the application of therapeutic knowledge in relation to lesbian and gay issues will be missing.

Taking this into account, I am introducing Peter, a heterosexual male counsellor who is a fully accredited counsellor and trainer who stated that he enjoyed his work with gay men who were described as one of the main populations he worked with. Peter expressed views, which were in common with other heterosexual counsellors interviewed:

> I mean it's just me getting a bit frustrated with them I suppose . . . and the movement will swing back against them, I'm sure, if it's not already.

And that's me, and I'm the most tolerant person going. I mean some-times I just don't know what to say. They [gay men] want me to help them, but they just don't seem to know what they want. I try and stay calm but I find myself getting really irritated and wanting them to just get it together . . . to just stop messing around and try and find someone and settle down. And really, I love working with them, they're just so easy to get along with.

Perhaps the most worrying aspect of this statement is how Peter is completely removed from self-understanding and fails to see his own prejudice while at the same time assessing himself as 'tolerant and forming relationships with gay men therapeutically'. In referring back to the list of personal moral qualities such as empathy, wisdom, humility and respect we would be right in questioning how Peter aspires to these in his response. Also, the way Peter shapes his own moral authority is likely to determine his understanding of 'ethical principles' and how he teaches these to students of counselling. Should Peter be working with gay men? Is he acting within an ethical frame-work? Who monitors the way Peter will supervise or teach counselling trainees? The quote from Peter only serves to illustrate how important it is to challenge and confront attitudes towards lesbian and gay issues before meet-ing these populations in the consulting room. Excluding lesbian and gay perspectives may mean that issues presented within counselling theory and practice, e.g. bereavement, abuse, and separation, are not 'seen' equally from heterosexual and non-heterosexual viewpoints. In fact, sexuality itself is incorrectly translated into an issue. What needs to happen is that all 'issues' are informed through all perspectives so that an issue of abuse for example, is considered from the perspective of the lesbian, the gay man, the bisexual, the transgender person and the heterosexual – not the heterosexual alone.

If we consider counselling and sexuality as a set of scripts then we may begin to challenge the scripts we shape in response to questions about sexual-ity. In the above, Peter could learn from the overarching heterosexual script he adheres to by really questioning the implicitly organised meanings for gay men. Through this, he can begin to challenge his own dominant scripts and begin to introduce new meanings about non-heterosexuality and begin to read their scripts as well as tolerate new meanings. Taking this further, this can be used as one way of tackling prejudice within training and beginning to rewrite therapeutic scripts so they become less discriminatory towards lesbian and gay men. This will increase the knowledge of all therapists when working with their lesbian and gay male clients.

Training and continuing professional development activities are ways of transmitting professional standards and guidelines, and how these may be shaped within the consulting room. Likewise their formulation requires that professional bodies, such as BACP, BPS or UKCP, have considered the mean-ing of these codes/guidelines for working with lesbians and gay men and have made them available. For example, let us consider the following scenario in relation to professional guidelines:

> Peter, a gay man, is in the first year of a counselling training course. He is the only non-heterosexual student on the course. When the tutor begins to introduce the various approaches to counselling, Peter asks the tutor how these would differ if the client were a lesbian or a gay man or a bisexual client. The tutor is unable to answer the question and tells Peter that lesbian and gay issues will be addressed next term under the heading of 'Diversity' and invites Peter to bring his questions to the class at that point. None of Peter's colleagues support him and the tutor continues to present the approaches to counselling without regard to non-heterosexuality.

In relation to British guidelines there is very little in place to support the trainee at this stage. The Lesbian and Gay Section of the BPS is actively involved in trying to establish these along a similar route as the APA. This will lead to guidelines for good practice with lesbians and gay men and may encourage reflection and help remove discrimination and prejudice in therapeutic practice.

Ethical principles have been outlined by all the major organisations in relation to valuing difference and diversity. According to Francis (1999), ethical principles help the practitioner to 'keep our sense of balance and fairness' (p. 14) and it is imperative therefore that trainees seriously contemplate what they mean by ethical practice in relation to lesbian and gay male clients. For example, the BACP combines professional values with ethical principles and personal moral qualities in their statement of 'Ethics for Counselling and Psychotherapy'. The various principles include those of fidelity; autonomy, beneficence, non-maleficence, justice and self-respect (BACP 2002). These act as a framework for client and counsellor safety. Additionally, these operate through the 'personal moral qualities' of the counsellor. Personal moral qualities, which BACP suggests should be encouraged, include those of empathy, sincerity, integrity, resilience, respect, humility, competence, fairness, wisdom and courage. The BPS has also incorporated autonomy, beneficence, non-maleficence, justice and fidelity into a framework for the protection of clients. As Shillitoe-Clarke (2003: 618) remarks 'each principle is binding unless, in a given situation, there is a more significant principle that overrides it'. Brenda Almond, commenting on professional ethics and diverse values, questions the need for ethical values and concludes that these provide the search for moral unity in a context of diversity (Almond 2001: 9). With this in mind, let us consider the following situation:

> As a female heterosexual trainee therapist, you begin working with a gay man who, after telling you he feels he can be open about himself for the

first time, begins to share with you that he quite often visits sex bars where he enjoys anonymous sex. He now wants to have a more settled relationship although he also wishes to continue enjoying sex at the bars he visits. He wishes to explore what this means in relation to his ideas of a relationship. You acknowledge to yourself that you are anxious about what this will mean as it is the first time you have worked with a gay man and are unaware of the gay male community.

Although the therapist has a good working relationship with her client, was she aware of feeling uncomfortable when he spoke about his beliefs about sexual behaviour? Supervision is particularly relevant at this point as the therapist needs to know that she has a space where she can safely explore her own script and feelings about sexuality. In this example, the counsellor used supervision to explore and consider a number of factors in relation to the work she will conduct with the client. She asked her supervisor if she was adequately protecting the client if she continues to work with him without knowledge or possibly even a positive regard for her client? She asked how would she show respect for the client's autonomy? She also questioned if she was able to work 'doing the least harm' to her client by continuing the relationship? She also wished to explore openly if she was the most appropriate person to counsel this client. This scenario highlights how important it is for therapists to really question their belief system, their own personal scripts and how they feel when establishing a therapeutic relationship with someone of the same or opposite sexuality.

Additionally, a client who wishes to change their sexual orientation from lesbian or gay to heterosexual may face some counsellors. This poses quite a serious ethical dilemma. As Davies (1996: 37) asks, is it ethical to 'treat a condition which is not an illness, but which society condemns? And do sexual orientation conversion therapies question the legitimacy of non-heterosexuality?' There is no doubt that lesbians and gay men questioning the acceptability of being gay are likely to be experiencing low self-esteem and negative beliefs about their sexuality (Ritter and Terndrup 2002). At a point when people may be experiencing strong feelings about their sense of self, including their sexual self, and are at a particularly vulnerable stage in this development, the therapist must consider their motivation for offering therapy to the person who expresses a strong desire to be converted to heterosexuality. Again, the therapist is more likely to have been prepared for these issues if they have been discussed openly in a professional forum, if a Code of Practice is in place and if these issues have been considered in training or continuing professional development activities.

DUAL RELATIONSHIPS

Davies and Gabriel (2000) discuss ethical practice when lesbian or gay practitioners are working with lesbian and/or gay clients, due to the complexity of their possible 'dual relationships'. These types of relationships are defined as 'those relationships where a client–therapist relationship extends intentionally or unintentionally, to include encounters, activities or relationships outside the therapeutic relationship' (p. 35). Imagine the following:

> Helen, a lesbian therapist, has been invited by her girlfriend to a party being held in a well-known lesbian bar. Helen soon realises that her client is in the crowd and has been drinking heavily. As soon as she sees Helen she waves and later, taking Helen by surprise, takes her a drink over and introduces her girlfriend to Helen. Helen is not sure if she should stay, tell her partner about the situation or simply leave.

This scenario is not that unusual for lesbian and gay male therapists because of the limitations imposed socially on the lesbian and gay male communities in terms of meeting places. It may help to address these issues in the early stages of the therapeutic relationship rather than simply waiting for it to take place. Davies and Gabriel (2000), introduce a number of 'moral principles' which, if considered in relation to 'dual relationships', will help guide practitioners who are lesbian or gay when working with lesbian or gay clients. They also recommend the usefulness of exploring with the client how s/he might manage *duality* and how it might affect the therapeutic relationship. They present an overview of three possible stages that lesbian and gay therapists may be faced with when they meet their lesbian/gay client in a social setting and how the therapist may set boundaries to overcome these problems.

Working with dilemmas in dual relationships and overlapping connections model (Davies & Gabriel 2000: 42):

Stage 1: Impact and containment

Immediate actions   Contain shock and impact of situation
Invoke stress/crisis management techniques.
Contain any immediate 'fallout'/acting-out impulses
Invoke an 'internal supervisor'
Make contact with client, acknowledge situation
Seek agreement to discuss situation at the next therapy session
Model healthy, appropriate behaviour

Stage 2: Containment and processing

Intermediate actions and interventions	Acknowledge situation at next therapy session
	Discuss with client issues of confidentiality, boundaries
	Overlapping connections and possible rehearsal of agreed actions should other situations arise
	Address client's reactions/responses to the situation
	Address transference issues
	Provide ongoing containment
	Redeem the therapeutic alliance
	Discuss countertransference reactions in supervision and personal therapy

Stage 3: Ongoing processing

Longer-term	Explore transference and countertransference in personal therapy and supervision
	Work with issues triggered by or linked to dual or multiple roles and relationships

CODES OF PRACTICE FOR WORKING AFFIRMATIVELY WITH LESBIANS AND GAY MEN

Perhaps it is time for all therapists, regardless of their sexual label, to consider professional standards in relation to lesbian and gay male clients in the UK. As Rudolph (1988: 166) remarked, 'Counsellors should not choose to treat gay clients by simple whim or default, complacent in the deceptive reassurance that they are relatively tolerant or basically open-minded about an issue decidedly more complicated and elusive than is immediately apparent.'

This may mean incorporating a variety of texts from various sources, e.g. sociological, anthropological, cultural studies etc., which challenge or add to those already shaped through psychological formulations. By taking this sort of responsibility, all therapists and psychologists can then contribute to professional practice by quoting from a multitude of available resources. The following outline from the APA indicates their commitment to setting standards for work with lesbian, gay and bisexual clients. Following on from this are guidelines established by Davies and Gabriel (2000), which are useful for lesbian and gay therapists to consider when working with lesbian and gay clients. Although these are useful for heterosexual therapists in dual relationships, they were originally intended for lesbian and gay therapists, as they are likely to meet clients more frequently outside the consulting room.

The American Psychological Association (APA 2000) has adopted a set of 16 guidelines which aim to provide practitioners with a frame of reference for their work with lesbian, gay, and bisexual clients as well as a point of reference for 'assessment, intervention, identity, relationships and the education and training of psychologists' (Ritter and Terndrup 2002). These are intended to have an impact on professional practice and inspire research. They are divided into four major sections and comprise a list of recommendations for specific professional behaviour, endeavour, or conduct for psychologists (Ritter and Terndrup 2002) and are listed below.

- Attitudes toward homosexuality and bisexuality

  – *Guideline 1*. Psychologists understand that homosexuality and bisexuality are not indicative of mental illness.
  – *Guideline 2*. Psychologists are encouraged to recognise how their attitudes and knowledge about lesbian, gay, and bisexual issues may be relevant to assessment and treatment and seek consultation or make appropriate referrals when indicated.
  – *Guideline 3*. Psychologists strive to understand the ways in which social stigmatisation (i.e. prejudice, discrimination, and violence) poses risks to the mental health and well-being of lesbian, gay and bisexual clients.
  – *Guideline 4*. Psychologists strive to understand how inaccurate or prejudicial views of homosexuality or bisexuality may affect the client's presentation in treatment and the therapeutic process.

- Relationships and families

  – *Guideline 5*. Psychologists strive to be knowledgeable about and respect the importance of lesbian, gay and bisexual relationships.
  – *Guideline 6*. Psychologists strive to understand the particular circumstances and challenges facing lesbian, gay, and bisexual parents.
  – *Guideline 7*. Psychologists recognise that the families of lesbian, gay and bisexual people may include people who are not legally or biologically related.
  – *Guideline 8*. Psychologists strive to understand how a person's homosexual or bisexual orientation may have an impact on his or her family of origin and the relationship to that family of origin.

- Issues of diversity

  – *Guideline 9*. Psychologists are encouraged to recognise the particular life issues or challenges experienced by lesbian, gay, and bisexual members of racial and ethnic minorities that are related to multiple and often conflicting cultural norms, values and beliefs.
  – *Guideline 10*. Psychologists are encouraged to recognise the particular challenges experienced by bisexual individuals.

- *Guideline 11.* Psychologists strive to understand the special problems and risks that exist for lesbian, gay and bisexual youth.
- *Guideline 12.* Psychologists consider generational differences within lesbian, gay and bisexual populations and the particular challenges that may be experienced by lesbian, gay, and bisexual older adults.
- *Guideline 13.* Psychologists are encouraged to recognise the particular challenges experienced by lesbian, gay, and bisexual individuals with physical, sensory, and/or cognitive/emotional disabilities.

- Education

  - *Guideline 14.* Psychologists support the provision of professional education and training on lesbian, gay and bisexual issues.
  - *Guideline 15.* Psychologists are encouraged to increase their knowledge and understanding of homosexuality and bisexuality through continuing education, training, supervision and consultation.
  - *Guideline 16.* Psychologists make reasonable efforts to familiarise themselves with relevant mental health, educational and community resources for lesbian, gay and bisexual people.

Additionally, all the above guidelines could be used to show that therapists are working towards equality on behalf of lesbians and gay men through their training and continuing professional development.

ETHICAL DILEMMAS IN THE CONSULTING ROOM

We need to take the above and consider the way this may shape the work that takes place in the consulting room. Imagine the following scenario:

> You have been working with John, a gay man who brings to the session that he and his partner are intending to try and start a family with a lesbian couple who want a donor for their child. John has decided with his partner that he will father the child. He wants to explore this with you and questions if you know of any books he could read or how to find out about donor insemination. You take the issue to supervision where your supervisor clearly states he is against the idea of gay men and lesbians creating families in this way. He verbalises that he is unable to provide you with any support although you may bring it to supervision.

In relation to your understanding of ethical principles, which must be applied to your supervisor as well as yourself, then what is your next course of action? Regardless of how you perceive the issues posed, how would you show professional competence in this issue, especially if you are fairly new to training in counselling? How will you address questions of 'good practice' and how will you address the personal qualities of the supervisor? This scenario is not uncommon and is likely to be much more common in the future. Without a solid understanding of ethical standards and a thorough grounding in lesbian and gay lifestyles and issues, then the work we carry out with lesbian and gay clients will fall below the standards expected for heterosexual clients. This alone poses questions of professional competence and ethics because, by following such a route, a disadvantaged group is unlikely to be understood through a heterosexually ordered moral authority.

CONCLUSION

This chapter has outlined professional and ethical considerations for working with lesbians and gay men in the consulting room. The chapter indicates that personal value systems are often developed in relation to societal expect-ations. As therapists are part of society, then they may also find themselves in ethical and moral dilemmas when faced with clients from minority groups who have been discriminated against because they stand outside of conventional 'social systems'. It is imperative that counselling organisations constantly review their professional standards, taking minority group con-siderations into account, when establishing professional guidelines. The adoption and incorporation of the American Psychological Association's guidelines on psychotherapy with lesbians, gay men and bisexual clients would be good practice by leading national organisations.

REFLECTIVE QUESTIONS

1   What are your own beliefs about lesbians? Gay men? Bisexuals?
2   If your supervisor or trainer dismisses lesbian and gay issues, what course of action would you take?
3   What are your thoughts about lesbian and gay clients only working with lesbian and gay therapists?
4   Do you believe you have received adequate training in working as a therapist with lesbian and gay clients? If not, how will you go about getting this information/training?

REFERENCES

Almond, B. (2001) Professional ethics and diverse values. *Counselling and Psychotherapy Journal*, 12(8).
APA (American Psychological Association) (2000). *Guidelines for Psychotherapy with Lesbians, Gay Men and Bisexual Clients.*

http://www.apa.org/pi/lgbc/guidelines.html or
http://www.apa.org/division/div44/guidelines.html [accessed 27th May 2003].

BACP (British Association for Counselling and Psychotherapy) (2002) *Ethical Framework for Good Practice in Counselling and Psychotherapy*. Rugby, UK: BACP.

Clarkson, P. (1998) *Counselling Psychology: Integrating Theory, Research and Supervised Practice*. London: Routledge.

Davies, D. (1996) Homophobia and heterosexism, in D. Davies & C. Neal (eds.), *Pink Therapy 1: A Guide for Counsellors Working with Lesbian, Gay and Bisexual Clients*. Buckingham: Open University Press.

Davies, D. & Gabriel, L. (2000) The management of ethical dilemmas, in D. Davies & C. Neal (eds.), *Issues in Therapy with Lesbian, Gay, Bisexual and Transgender Clients*. Buckingham: Open University Press, pp. 35–54.

Francis, R. D. (1999) *Ethics for Psychologists: A Handbook*. Leicester: BPS Books.

Gabriel, L. & Davies, D. (1996) The management of ethical dilemmas, in D. Davies & C. Neal (eds.), *Pink Therapy 3: Issues in Therapy with Lesbian, Gay, Bisexual and Transgender Clients*. Buckingham: Open University Press.

Greene, B. (1994) Lesbian and gay sexual orientations: implications for clinical training, practice and research, in B. Greene & G. M. Herek (eds.), *Lesbian and Gay Psychology: Theory, Research and Clinical Applications*. London: Sage.

Milton, M. (1998) *Issues in Psychotherapy with Lesbians and Gay Men: A Survey of British Psychologists*, Vol. 4, British Psychological Society Division of Counselling Psychology Occasional Papers. BPS: Leicester.

Milton, M. & Coyle, A. (2003) Sexual identity: affirmative practice with lesbian, and gay clients, in R. Woolfe, W. Dryden & S. Strawbridge (eds.), *Handbook of Counselling and Psychotherapy*. London: Sage, pp. 481–499.

Moon, L. (1992) 'Lesbian identity formation during the process of coming out: Is counselling a useful intervention?' Unpublished dissertation, University of London, Goldsmiths College.

Moon, L. (2002) 'The heterosexualisation of emotion: a case study in counselling with lesbians and gay men'. Unpublished PhD, University of Essex.

Pilgrim, D. (1991) Psychotherapy and social blinkers. *The Psychologist*, 2, 52–55.

Ritter, K. Y. & Terndrup, A. I. (2002) *Handbook of Affirmative Psychotherapy with Lesbians and Gay Men*. London: Guilford Press.

Rudolph, J. (1988) Counselors' attitudes toward homosexuality: a selective review of the literature. *Journal of Counseling and Development*, 67, 165–167.

Shillitoe-Clarke, C. (2003) Ethical issues in counselling psychology, in R. Woolfe, W. Dryden & S. Strawbridge (eds.), *Handbook of Counselling and Psychotherapy*. London: Sage, pp. 615–636.

Simon, W. & Gagnon, J. H. (1986) Sexual scripts: permanence and change. *Archives of Sexual Behaviour*, 15(2), 97–12.

Chapter 18

Professional and ethical issues when working with learning disabled clients

Peter Forster and Rachel Tribe

The Department of Health in England and Wales now use the phrase 'people with learning disabilities'. In the UK most professionals and service providers also refer to 'learning disabilities'; however, some self-advocacy organisations such as People First, prefer the term 'learning difficulties' (The Foundation for People with Learning Disabilities 2003). As a result some professionals, particularly in child services, use this term. Research and user group surveys have made clear that other terms, which in some cases are still in common currency, such as mental retardation, mental handicap and mental subnormality, have become terms of abuse, are offensive and have contributed to social marginalisation and stigmatisation.

Research conducted in Europe, America and Australia suggests the prevalence of mild learning disability is between three and six people per thousand of the general population. In the UK there are an estimated 23,000–350,000 people with severe learning disabilities and 580,000–1,750,000 people with mild learning disabilities (The Foundation for People with Learning Disabilities 2003). The International Classification System of Diseases (ICD) (WHO 1992) and the *Diagnostic and Statistical Manual* (DSM) (APA 1994) classifications still refer to the term mental retardation. The treatment of the learning disabled throughout history has been poor (Sperlinger 1997). Throughout the nineteenth and early twentieth century, alongside efforts to provide institutional care and training, people with learning disabilities were subject to humiliation, exhibited as freaks, threatened with eradication or put at risk for the 'good of others', as with early testing of the measles vaccine (O'Hara 2003). We would argue that some of these ideas are still represented in present-day ethical and moral value systems. The Department of Health (DoH 2001) guidelines entitled *Valuing People: A New Strategy for Learning Disability for the 21st Century*, which place the individual at the heart of decision-making, are part of a move to encourage good practice and reflection on value systems and good professional and ethical practice among clinicians.

In addition to policy initiatives the value system of a therapist is likely to be reflected in their way of working and being with clients. For example, therapeutic integrity might be undermined if a therapist believes people with a learning disability do not have the capacity, or should not have the opportunity, to have fulfilling sex lives, or if a client has a genetic disorder/ syndrome and the therapist believes such people should not procreate.

WHAT IS A LEARNING DISABILITY?

The ICD-10 definition of mental retardation refers to a condition of arrested or incomplete development of the mind. This is characterised specifically by impairment of skills manifested during the developmental period up to eighteen years which contribute to the overall level of intelligence, including significant impairment of cognitive, language and motor skills, and social functioning. To be eligible for services from a specialist learning disability service, all of the above conditions need to be met. However, an 'IQ' score that falls at least two standard deviations below the mean is still a crucial element in the determination of learning disability, and is routinely requested as evidence. This means that for the purpose of classification, for a person to fall within the range of what is termed a mild learning disability, psycho-metric testing would need to produce a combined score of between 55 and 69. Other terms in current use are: moderate learning disability, with a combined score of between 40 and 55, and severe/profound learning disability, which demands a combined score of below 40.

The Department of Health document mentioned earlier (DoH 2001) is based on 'person-centred planning'. This places client autonomy and informed consent at the apex of decisions about their future, and is the favoured model for Learning Disabilities services. In the past, learning dis-abled clients were often excluded from meetings about their future, as it was believed they would be unable to understand or make important decisions about their future. As is the case with other health professionals, the work of Beauchamp and Childress (1989) and Kitchener (1984) is used in conjunction with the appropriate professional and ethical codes for ethical evaluation and decision-making.

CONSENT AND CONFIDENTIALITY

Informed consent is particularly difficult in learning disabilities, especially if clients have had little previous opportunity to make choices or have their wishes taken into account (Fiddell 2000). Clients have often had decisions about their lives made by others, with parental views and sensibilities being given primacy to the detriment of client autonomy. Additionally, capacity to understand complex concepts like consent might be diminished by learning disability itself, which may significantly impair cognitive processing and recall (Lindsay 1999). Practitioners need to be mindful of any obstacles to understanding for clients and seek to maximise opportunities to develop autonomy and exercise choice. Attention to and awareness of the danger of becoming too directive, not paying attention to issues of competence, power and control, is central to therapeutic work in learning disabilities. In Learning Disabilities more than any other specialism, work may involve carers, family members or other people within the client's system or network. Complex dilemmas may arise which require consultation with supervisors, careful thought and reference to codes of ethics.

> Let us imagine the case of Joe, who has a mild learning disability and discloses to his social worker an allegation of sexual abuse that morning by an old acquaintance who was visiting the town for a friend's wedding. In accordance with local and national guidelines (DoH 2000) regarding vulnerable adults, social services would call a strategy meeting (which involves calling together various professionals involved in Joe's care, including social services and, given the nature of the allegation in this instance, the police). Joe, let us suppose, is in therapy with a member of the Learning Disabilities team which you manage, and it was decided that you would attend the strategy meeting.

At the strategy meeting Joe expressed the wish not to involve his parents. Although those attending the meeting agreed that involving the family might substantially reduce the risk of further assault and help provide a supportive environment for Joe, it was accepted that he was an adult and had made his wishes clear. Joe thought that if his parents heard about the abuse they would be devastated, and might remove him from independent activities. Although technically Joe's parents would have no right to do this, it is common practice for parents of adults with learning disabilities to act in this way. The alleged abuser had left the town and returned to his home town; this seemed to suggest Joe was in no immediate risk within the home. To remove him from any risk outside the home, or to enable him to remain living in the borough, without his parents' express support would require Social Services to obtain a guardianship order (DoH 2000). All present at the meeting agreed that this would be draconian at this stage and in conflict with the primacy of client autonomy. Additionally, it would be a decision that might need to be defended in court. Although an agreement not to involve Joe's parents would hamper the efforts of the police to gather sufficient evidence and make a case, it was agreed that the client's expressed wishes should be respected.

Although many codes of practice would seem to give guidance for complex circumstances, they are not and cannot be prescriptive. Ethical dilemmas by their very nature suggest alternative courses of action, and the key ethical concepts such as beneficence and non-maleficence must be used as guiding principles. The British Association for Counselling and Psychotherapy

(BACP 2002) refers to the obligation of a therapist to act in the best interest of a client when there is evidence of reduced capacity either because of immaturity, a lack of understanding, extreme distress or other significant restraint. The role of the clinical supervisor and line managers may be important here.

APPROPRIATE REFERRALS TO A LEARNING DISABILITIES TEAM?

It is usually someone other than the client in cases of learning disability who makes the referral to the team, and so it comes from their perspective not that of their client. This is often a parent or health professional. Although it is a necessary requirement of the referral process that a client is made aware of the referral, it could be argued, within the Learning Disabilities context that it should be part of the assessment process, to meet with the referrer. A therapist needs to be mindful of the possibilities of difficulties associated with meeting with people other than the client and engaging in an exploration of their view of the situation and network.

In a therapeutic assessment, clients should be given the opportunity to describe their life and problems. This is particularly necessary as recent studies have shown the gulf that can exist between the referrer and the client's conceptualisation of the problem and its significance to them (Nadarajah *et al.* 1995). A second focus of an assessment should be the development of a therapeutic alliance, the creation of an atmosphere of trust, in which clients feel valued and heard, as well as ensuring they understand the therapeutic process. Finally, a goal should be to develop a conceptual understanding of how the client uses language to describe their problem. In this way, the therapist and client may reposition the focus of their meeting.

There can be circumstances when it might not be in the best interest of a person to have a label of learning disability. Let us imagine Sarah, a 47-year-old woman who has successfully attended mainstream education, brought up children and held down a job. Her husband has recently left her, and is now living in a different town with a new partner. Sarah is distressed and her GP felt she could not cope without specialist support from the Learning Disabilities team. Sarah has good social and independent living skills and has previously successfully accessed generic services, albeit with support from her husband. However, she appears depressed and lacking in confidence, and is grieving the loss of her husband. Would it be ethical or helpful to this woman to re-label her as learning disabled? Best practice might suggest not, and that a Learning Disabilities team might better direct their support to facilitate her access to mainstream services with the recommendation that she receive additional home support until her confidence in her capacity is restored. Instances like this frequently occur in Learning Disabilities, and may require considerable thought, discussion with the client and possibly involvement of the multidisciplinary team and the client's network if the client is to receive optimal service from the NHS and associated services.

Psychiatric problems are at least as common in the learning disabled as in the general population (Bernal & Hollins 1995). The presence of a learning disability can alter presentation and psychiatric diagnosis. Dilemmas can occur when there appears to be uncertainty over the main factors in a client's distress. Is it their learning disability or their mental health status? And can the two be separated? Until recently, a learning disabled client with psychological symptoms might not have received support from mental health services, as lack of communication, detachment and withdrawal may have been construed by family or staff at a day centre or in a residential setting as a product of a learning disability. Symptoms like talking aloud to oneself, head banging, repetitive/ritualised behaviours and/or other behaviours, such as aggression, self-harm, eating or sleeping problems, were either ignored or described as challenging behaviours that needed to be modified (Bernal & Hollins 1995).

> Let us imagine a client we can call Derek referred with a dual diagnosis of psychopathic disorder and a mild learning disability. Adult mental health services believe he could benefit from specialist LD therapeutic support, as they had been unable to engage effectively with him. A meeting with the referrer from mental health services describes their perception of Derek as non-compliant, chronically ill, subject to outbursts of anger and aggression and dependent on the ambivalent support of his family. The dilemmas for the therapist within the Learning Disabilities team include whether to engage in a therapeutic encounter with a person who has a history of violence, whether to try to open a dialogue with him and his wider system to engage in the co-creation of a network of support, or whether to assess him with the intention of re-referring to mental health, on the grounds that Derek's mental health status was the main factor in his distress. His family appears unresponsive and does not wish to be involved, and mental health services have not managed to improve his quality of life. Given Derek's paucity of complex language and cognitive strategies for coping with complex demands, the therapist could have developed a behavioural strategy that might have been supported by allocated care workers. However, Derek did not have any additional support.

As with many people with a learning disability, Derek has been brought up in relatively protected environments and has spent a significant period of his life in an institutional environment. As a result, he may not have had exposure to the same opportunities as others in the general population to develop coping skills for dealing with complex emotions (Lindsay 1999). Arguably this has led to the development of sets of distorted cognitions which seemed to militate against adaptive coping. Previously it has been assumed that his poor cognitive and linguistic skills would rule out the use of self-report to investigate emotional experience. However, recent research and developments in practice indicate stability of cognitive processes and that, by employing simplified language and concepts, respondents may use assessment tools with a high degree of reliability (Lindsay 1999; Nadarajah *et al.* 1995; Black & Novaco 1993). Other studies have suggested that words, role rehearsal, use of pictures and objects and relaxation techniques can help develop adaptive cognitions and coping strategies (Lindsay 1999). It was judged that if the therapist emphasised the importance of relationship-building, trust and understanding, then a useful and therapeutic assessment of the thoughts and feelings of Derek might be possible.

One way in which we might have worked with Derek would be to consider with him alternative strategies for coping and addressing restraints to change as well as perhaps introducing the notion of problem-solving. We might have used role-play and homework tasks in auditory form and attempted to generate solutions to issues in his life as well as develop a therapeutic alliance.

COMMON ETHICAL DILEMMAS IN LEARNING DISABILITIES

Ethical dilemmas can arise from stereotypical beliefs about learning disabilities and related syndromes. For example, there persists a common belief that people with Down's syndrome are happy and gentle. If a person with Down's syndrome subverts that notion by showing anger or other behaviours that challenge the system, this can often lead to a referral for specialist services to change the behaviour. Discussions with a referrer can highlight phrases such as, '. . . it's just not like him/her . . . not the boy/girl we used to know'. If, like the referrer, the therapist has unacknowledged beliefs about how a person with Down's syndrome should present, this might influence the nature of the intervention. The dilemma for the therapist is whether to focus on the referred problem, which might include the development of an anger management programme, with perhaps limited value, or to attend to issues of client autonomy and beneficence. The latter would appear to be in line with the 'valuing people/person-centred' perspective advocated by the DoH (2001). The following imaginary scenario illustrates this point.

> Jenny, a young woman with Down's syndrome, revealed she was afraid '. . . to reveal my dark side'. Hesitatingly, she described anger she felt '. . . I'm not normal . . . damaged . . . different'. Jenny referred to the effort she had made to deny this aspect of self over many years. It emerged that

denial of this 'different-self' was at the centre of her difficulties. It could be argued that the energy Jenny expended in trying to disguise from others, as well as herself, pain, anger and disgust with herself, had become increasingly demanding, and it seemed that even minor irritations challenged her capacity to cope. In a society that values success and has a particular view of beauty, is it so hard to accept that a person such as Jenny might fight hard to disguise her sense of loss? It might be that Jenny had colluded with her parents to deny her disability and their loss of the so-called 'traditional child'.

FAMILY ISSUES AND RELATIONSHIPS

The gradual process of separation between mother and baby encourages learning and development for the infant. When a baby is born with a syndrome/disability this process can be disturbed and arguably 'normal' functional separation might not occur (Sinason 1992). The disability is not curable; therefore parents and even staff groups might feel guilty that they cannot cure the disability, so that they become 'co-dependent', and devote their lives to the well-being of the disabled person. It could be argued that this does not always allow the client to develop a sense of their own well-being, separateness or identity, and could lead to fear of new experiences, stifling of curiosity and possibly the formation of a false identity to disguise the pain of disability. A therapist needs to reflect on their own familial history and how this might influence their thinking when working with these issues. This is especially true with issues concerning a client's freedom to explore their sexuality. How can an undifferentiated part of the parent be a sexual being?

The learning disabled can suffer enormous stress and frustration because of lack of choice, privacy and respect, as well as lack of opportunity to express their sexuality. Efforts to maintain an identity as asexual with parents and or carers might prove intolerable. However, referral by parents or health professionals can involve a request to change aspects of the person's behaviour, rather than work with the client and/or system to address the underlying denial of an individual's right to pursue a sex life. For example, clients might be afraid to talk about their sexuality or orientation and might therefore be referred for inappropriate touching, of self or others. They might also exhibit outbursts of aggression or tearfulness without explanation. All such behaviour may be exacerbated by, and mask, past sexual abuse. The therapist needs to be mindful of the possible vulnerability of this client group, from family as well as professional carers.

Additionally, families may have specific ideas about the nature of death and whether their sons/daughters should be included in family rituals. Often a client is excluded from the funeral and given misleading information about their loved ones' absence. Referrals may be made as a result of a complex grieving reaction, which it is clear on assessment has not been understood or tolerated by the family or wider network. Clients can be confused by well-meaning but misguided efforts to rush them through a process the network believe should be easily resolved, '... *well she didn't really understand... we thought he would get too upset if he went to the funeral... he should be over it now... it was five years ago... there must be something wrong in his head he keeps asking where his dad is...*'. A client's powerlessness and detachment from decision-making can be further exacerbated by communication problems, especially when using interpreters (Newland 2003).

A dilemma for the therapist can be whether to discuss with the client the costs and benefits of disclosing their inner world to parents/carers when this might include the real possibility of destabilising a complex system of personal relationships. The client could be further isolated from family and friends. As previously stated, families have no legal rights unless they have been awarded guardianship. However, they may impede access to their sons/daughters, and so effectively sabotage the working relationship between client and therapist. Therapists need to be mindful of the above issues. While therapy can help empower people with learning disabilities, work with the wider network, including collaborating with other clinicians in the multidisciplinary team, can overcome some of these difficulties.

FORMS OF LEARNING DISABILITY

Failure to attend to the complex interaction of psychological, biological and interpersonal processes may lead to further confusion, raised levels of anxiety, a decrease in self-efficacy and increased self-blame. For example, a referral might be made for a person described as obese and an 'over-eater'. At their first meeting, a therapist may believe the client is comfort eating. There might be indicators of depression, anxiety, low self-esteem and poor body image, as well as feelings of worthlessness, and intervention focused on these issues might be beneficial. However, people born with the syndrome Prader-Willi (for further details please see Beitman *et al.* 2003) tend toward obesity, and the therapist needs be mindful of the complex mind–brain link and consider how the effect of chemical and psychotherapeutic interventions can be maximised (Beitman *et al.* 2003). The focus of therapy might shift toward establishing a non-judgemental support network that would help the client adopt a healthier lifestyle and eating pattern, as well as promote self-efficacy.

People with Down's syndrome have significantly higher risk of dementia than the population as a whole, with as many as 60 per cent of those over the age of 50 having detectable traits. This can lead to confusion. Carers and staff can misconstrue behaviours that might otherwise indicate depression or anxiety, such as forgetfulness and confusion, and believe the client is showing symptoms of dementia. The converse can also be true. A dilemma for the clinician is whether to conduct a psychotherapeutic intervention or to consider the possibility of dementia screening, which would be intrusive, would need regular repetition and might produce anxiety in the client. Possibly, a psychotherapeutic intervention should be undertaken while a colleague carries out the screening procedure.

Dilemmas can arise when a person has damage to the frontal lobe region of the brain, which can result in impulsivity and lowering of inhibitions. In epilepsy a client may suffer a number of absences, which can also confuse presentation. A client might be labelled as difficult, challenging, distractible, withdrawn or confused. Other disorders that might confuse presentation include diabetes, anaemia and hyperthyroidism. The therapist needs to consider what type of intervention would be in the best interest of the client, as well as who should be told and how will this affect the client, their carers and network. In this context, good communications and support from other members of the multidisciplinary team, especially medical advisers are crucial. The therapist may also need to undertake additional reading or attend specialist lectures or training.

CULTURE AND FAMILY

Another important aspect of the challenges to a therapist working in this field is the interaction of the client, their family and the wider community. Families may have belief systems that are influenced by cultural background, or they may be highly individual. It is essential that a therapist determine what the client and/or family understand about their son or daughter's disability. They may consider the client to be possessed or 'mad'; they may believe that the birth of a disabled child is a judgement from God, a punishment, or a test, or that the child is 'special'. A family may believe a child should grow out of their disability, or that with the right care or treatment, there will be a cure. It might be important that a therapist does not confuse notions of improved emotional well-being and the possibility of more adaptive social functioning with what the family and client regard as a cure from the learning disability. Conversely, if the disability is perceived as a judgement from God, then for the family, it is possible that, no matter what is offered, nothing will change.

Finally, the Bengali parent often perceives it to be their prime responsibility to ensure their sons and daughters marry, and apparently some services struggle with the ethical implications this might pose (O'Hara & Martin 2003). If the therapist, for example, believes arranged marriages to be wrong and does not reflect on considerations other than notions of autonomy and informed consent, then he/she could be in conflict with cultural and parental mores.

CONCLUSION

In this chapter we have drawn attention to some of the main ethical and professional challenges that face a therapist working in the field of learning disabilities. These are confounded by the nature of the related syndromes and medical problems, as well as by the complex interaction of biological and psychological processes. The therapist needs to ensure good communication with colleagues and to be aware of the roles and boundaries appropriate to a multidisciplinary healthcare setting. While client autonomy and informed consent have primacy, the therapist needs to be mindful of the personal beliefs and values that can influence notions of the helping relationship. It might sometimes be in the client's best interests to work with people other than the client to enhance the prospect of creating change. However, the therapist needs to ensure the client understands and consents fully. In such instances there can be a fine line between the therapeutic desire to do the most good and being overly directive.

REFLECTIVE QUESTIONS

1   How might a therapist's moral and ethical values influence choice of intervention?
2   Does the role of a therapist conflict with the demands of multidisciplinary working within a learning disabilities service? If so, how can this be avoided?
3   In learning disabilities, what might be the boundaries of confidentiality?
4   Why is it necessary that a therapist attends to the medical as well as the psychological aspects of the client's presentation?

REFERENCES

APA (American Psychiatric Association) (1994) *Diagnostic and Statistical Manual*, 4th edn. Washington, DC: American Psychiatric Association.
BACP (British Association for Counselling & Psychotherapy) (2002) *Ethical Framework for Good Practice in Counselling and Psychotherapy*. Rugby UK: BACP. http://www.bacp.co.uk/ethical_framework/
Beauchamp, T. L. and Childress, J. F. (1989) *Principles of Biomedical Ethics*, 3rd edn. New York: Oxford University Press.
Beitman, B. D., Blinder, B. J., Thase, M. E. & Safer, D. L. (2003) *Integrating Psychotherapy and Pharmacology: Dissolving the Mind–Brain Barrier*. New York: Norton.
Bernal, J. & Hollins, S. (1995) Psychiatric illness and learning disability: a dual diagnosis. *Advances in Psychiatric Treatment*, 1, 138–145.
Black, L. & Novaco, R. W. (1993) Treatment of anger with the developmentally

handicapped man, in R. A. Well & V. J. Giannetti (eds.), *Textbook of the Brief Psychotherapies*. New York: Plenum Press.

DoH (Department of Health) (2000) *No Secrets: Guidance on Developing and Implementing Multi-agency Policies and Procedures to Protect Vulnerable Adults from Abuse*.
http://www.doh.gov.uk/scg/nosecrets.htm

DoH (Department of Health) (2001) *Valuing People: A New Strategy for Learning Disability for the 21st Century*. London: Department of Health.

Fiddell, B. (2000) Exploring the use of family therapy with adults with a learning disability. *Journal of Family Therapy*, 22, 308–323.

Kitchener, K. S. (1984) Intuition, critical evaluation and ethical principles. *The Counselling Psychologist*, 21(3), 43–45.

Lindsay, W. R. (1999) Cognitive therapy. *The Psychologist*, 12, 238–242.

Nadarajah, J., Rot, A., Harris, T. O. & Corbett, J. A. (1995) Methodological aspects of life events research in people with learning disabilities; a review and initial findings. *Journal of Intellectual Disability Research*, 39, 45–56.

Newland, J. (2003) Working with interpreters within services for people with learning disabilities, in R. Tribe & H. Ravel (eds.), *Working with Interpreters in Mental Health*. London: Routledge.

O'Hara, J. (2003) Learning disabilities and ethnicity: achieving cultural competence. *Advances in Psychiatric Treatment*, 9, 166–176.

O'Hara, J. & Martin, H. (2003) Parents with learning disabilities: a study of Gender and cultural perspectives from East London. *British Journal of Learning Disabilities*, 31, 18–24.

Sinason, V. (1992) *Mental Handicap and the Human Condition*. New York: Free Association Books.

Sperlinger, A. (1997) Introduction, in J. O'Hara & A. Sperlinger (eds.), *Adults with Learning Disabilities: A Practical Approach for Health Professionals*. Chichester, UK: John Wiley.

The Foundation for People with Learning Disabilities (2003) Learning disabilities: the fundamental facts.
http.//www.fpld.org.uk [retrieved 14.6.03 and 11.7.03].

WHO (World Health Organisation) (1992) *The ICD-10 Classification of Mental and Behavioural Disorders*. Geneva: WHO.

Chapter 19

Professional and ethical practice in multicultural and multiethnic society

John Newland and Nimisha Patel

The theory and practice of psychological therapy is often presented as if it is somehow insulated from the social context in which it operates. Psychology and therapeutic theories have not found it easy to embrace the challenges encapsulated in the criticisms of its inherent Eurocentricity and often biased and racist practice. This chapter outlines some of the issues that need to be discussed in relation to professional and ethical practice within a multiethnic society. The main theme of this chapter is that professional and ethical practice should be such that it avoids racism and is based on developing understanding and skills in working with a diverse, multiethnic population. Merely reading about diversity or about racism is about as likely to improve one's behaviour, as reading about sport is to make one into an athlete. This chapter therefore aims to engage the reader in considering the significance of the topic. This should promote good practice and allow for attitudinal change by professionals delivering therapeutic services. While there will be examples from clinical psychology within the chapter, the main elements of the discussion apply to all forms of talking therapies within Britain.

MULTICULTURAL COMPETENCIES

The term 'multicultural competencies' has emerged as a way of enabling social context to be acknowledged and addressed. As with many terms it is not entirely adequate. In part the term is an attempt to highlight the awareness required in working with people of many cultures. However, awareness is likely to be misconstrued as implying merely that the therapist needs to be sensitized and knowledgeable about difference. As ever the issues are far more complex. The term also assumes that there are similarities between individuals that also need consideration hence the 'competencies'. The therapeutic endeavour is to discern the path between similarity and difference from the perspective of the person in distress. Accordingly the term 'multicultural competencies' will evolve over time and inevitably will be replaced. For the present purposes, the term can be viewed as a signpost along the way to a more complete understanding of the therapy process.

Multicultural competencies have been developed to span the range of clinical activity, including assessments, formulations and interventions, research activities, service design and delivery. They are not prescriptions for practice, rather guidelines on areas in which we can all improve in our efforts to offer professional and ethical therapeutic services in a multiethnic society. The use of competencies is not an end in itself but part of a process that will lead to more competent practice. Incorporating them into professional codes and continuing professional development requirements assists compliance with these competencies. If there is no genuine alignment between these codes and therapists' attitudes, then the statement of competencies, codes and continuing professional development are in vain. Many ways can be found to demonstrate perceived compliance but still allow racist outcomes to prevail. Ideally racist behaviour is minimized within psychological and therapeutic practice and there is genuine respect for and understanding of diversity within our society. However, it is likely that attitudinal change will be harder to achieve.

In the American psychological literature the American Psychological Association Division of Counseling Psychology has developed a series of attitudinal, cognitive and behavioural competencies (Sue *et al.* 1992). It is significant to note that relative to the history of the APA (the APA was founded in July 1892) only in the last 14 years has thinking about a psychology for all Americans become formally addressed. The position in respect of the British Psychological Society is that it is behind the APA in formally addressing diversity in the United Kingdom. However, it is still unclear as to how far these multicultural competencies have been fully incorporated into practice in America (Pedersen 1995). Similarly, in Britain, clinical psychologists have attempted to outline some of the key competencies in relation to clinical psychological practice in our multiethnic society (Patel *et al.* 2000) though there is little evidence to suggest that these competencies are integral to professional training and practice. In examining the social context of psychological and therapeutic practice in Britain it is important to acknowledge that we live in a racist society where institutional racism is embedded in all institutional structures, not excepting health services and professional bodies. Within the United Kingdom the police force has been deemed to be racist as an organization. The extension of racism to the police force in a public and visible way has also demonstrated the unconscious nature of racism reported by MacPherson (1999: 28, para. 6.34):

> The collective failure of an organisation to provide an appropriate and professional service to people because of their colour, culture or ethnic origin can be seen or detected in processes, attitudes and behaviour which amount to discrimination through unwitting prejudice, ignorance, thoughtlessness and racist stereotyping which disadvantages ethnic

minority people. [Racism] persists because of the failure of the organisation openly and adequately to recognise and address its existence and causes by policy, example and leadership. Without recognition and action to eliminate such racism it can prevail as part of the ethos or culture of the organisation. It is a corrosive disease.

Similarly within the National Health Service a report (Alexander 1999) was being prepared almost contemporaneously that echoed some of the similar issues raised by MacPherson (1999: 94). In the concluding paragraph it states:

It will take many years to eradicate racism as defined in the MacPherson Report. New ways of resourcing organisations and different working arrangements will have to be introduced to ensure that change actually happens as well as innovations in delivering culturally competent services. With the support of the political leadership, there is some indication that, this time round, institutional racism will be successfully addressed.

The above examples are given as evidence of the chapter's central thesis that perhaps racism cannot be eliminated but at best contained. Therapeutic practice is frequently embedded within these institutional structures, i.e. the health service, and is unlikely to have escaped from these influences. Thus psychology and therapeutic activities within the UK as professional activities cannot be considered without reference to the social context in which they operate. The population with whom psychological therapists engage is increasingly diverse with respect to 'race' and cultural issues (Modood & Berthoud 1997) and therapists are required to develop the competence to meet the expectations and the rights of a diverse population to quality health services. The following case example highlights the necessity of developing interventions that are context-specific and dependent on the personal stance of the practitioner.

CLINICAL EXAMPLE

An Iranian family visits their general practitioner, presenting with a range of problems. The stated primary focus is a concern about their fathers' increasing social withdrawal and outbursts of anger. These changes had become more marked following a burglary at their home. The family, comprising father, mother and two children aged five and ten, were present when three men broke their door down, threatened them with racist language, severely assaulted the father and escaped with some valuables. Following the burglary the youngest child started to wet the bed and the eldest child refused to go to school. In the consultation with the GP, as only the eldest child spoke English, he was asked to interpret for the family. The GP referred the father to a counselling psychologist in the GP practice, but no interpreter was arranged. The eldest child was referred to a child and family guidance clinic. The mother and youngest child are not seen by anyone other than the GP, but with the interpreting help of the elder child.

In this example, the practitioner is confronted with various dilemmas. These dilemmas are posed in the following questions. Who in the family should be the focus of the intervention? Should the family members be seen together or separately? Who should be interpreting for whom? (For further information on good practice when working with interpreters within mental health the interested reader is referred to Tribe and Raval (2003).) What are the reasons for the current situation? What might be an appropriate and ethical approach in this situation? What do health professionals have to say about such violence and racist behaviour? What are our own responsibilities in this situation and how do we act?

Psychology and therapeutic services may be delivered by individuals who themselves are biased. There is evidence that individuals experience everyday racism (Clark *et al.* 1999; Essed 1991) so for individuals to experience direct or indirect, intentional or unintentional racism within the therapeutic encounter is clearly unethical. The responsibility and motivation for ensuring that racism is absent in the therapeutic encounter requires little explanation. The Division of Clinical Psychology (DCP) issued a statement declaring that the core purpose of the profession was to 'reduce psychological distress and to enhance and promote psychological well-being by the systematic application of knowledge derived from psychological theory and data' (DCP 2001a). The reference to all British citizens is not explicitly stated but implied. In attempting to ensure that the core purpose is being enacted, the DCP have engaged in developing the various components of a strategy. The development of competencies begins in the professional training that clinical psychologists experience. As part of the course accreditation process by the British Psychological Society (BPS), attention is focused on ensuring that clinical psychology courses have adequate teaching on 'race' and culture. Without direct teaching and clinical experience, as well as good supervision in working with Black and minority ethnic (BME) people, there may be an unhelpful concentration on a predominantly Western conception of the self that may preclude intervention with many British citizens. For example, it is likely that misunderstandings will occur in analysing the response to the question, 'How do you feel?' Ely and Denney (1987: 176) note that 'many Asian patients may be less concerned with what is going on in their heads, and more concerned with their roles and positions in society. If you can fulfil your obligations and your role, you are well; if you cannot you are ill.' The therapist can also make basic errors at the beginning of the therapeutic interaction. Through lack of verbal fluency or exposure of individual and family naming systems, mistakes in using appropriate names is likely. The client is likely to have encountered similar lack of respect in other areas, but it is still poor practice to call someone by an inappropriate name.

Similarly, seeking consent to offer psychological therapy is an empty gesture when no efforts have been made to adequately inform BME people what exactly is on offer, how it might differ from their expectations, how relevant and appropriate it might be in light of the person/family's cultural background, and what the inherent biases are within the Western psychological or the therapeutic technology being recommended.

Within the DCP the 'Race' and Culture Special Interest Group has been pro-active in supporting the training of clinical psychologists, in particular through publishing a text (Patel *et al.* 2000), which covers the various specialties of the profession outlining the competencies that are expected. In part the activity mirrors that of the American literature. However, the dilemma with a competency-based approach is still the need to identify and select the most salient competencies that are required. Hansen *et al.* (2000) detail 12 minimal multicultural competencies for practice. Broadly these competencies fall into four categories: Personal Awareness; Knowledge Base; Formulation Skills and Clinical Practice. Interestingly one competence within the category of knowledge base deals with the history of oppression, prejudice and discrimination in the United States. It is unclear as to the extent of teaching about similar issues in the UK curriculum of professional training for psychologists or therapists. The fact that there is considerable benefit in knowing about the historical context of psychology within the UK is unquestionable (Richards 1997).

EMIC AND ETIC PERSPECTIVES

With respect to formulation skills, the multicultural competency is the 'ability to accurately evaluate emic (culture specific) and etic (universal) hypotheses related to clients from identified groups and to develop accurate clinical conceptualizations, including awareness of when clinical issues involve cultural dimensions and when theoretical orientation needs to be adapted for more effective work with members of identified groups' (Hansen *et al.* 2000).

The approach engendered by the multicultural competency is in contrast to the normative position ('etic') that assumes that all clinical practice is applicable to all individuals except in some exceptional cases. The 'etic' position is often called 'the colour blind' approach within public services. When considering culture from this approach the basic assumption is that there exists a descriptive system that is equally valid for all cultures. The cultural phenomenon is the factor that can be used to explain divergence from the majority position. For example, consider the following clinical example.

CLINICAL EXAMPLE

An Indian woman (Sunita) presents to her general practitioner with a very low mood. Her husband complains that she is increasingly being withdrawn, becoming uninterested in everything and not fulfilling her duties at home. She is refusing to meet socially with anybody and has recently stopped speaking. She is referred to a psychiatrist who eventually diagnoses psychotic depression and asserts that her refusal to speak should be understood as a cultural variation of depression. Sunita is offered antidepressant medication with supportive counselling from the community mental health nurse. No explanation is given about the sequence of events that had led to this behaviour, what the families' understanding is of her difficulties and what she and her family might see as viable culturally meaningful explanations and possible ways forward. In this example the contrast between explanations based on cross-cultural and cultural psychology perspectives is clearly identifiable. In many instances drawing distinctions between 'etic' and 'emic' conceptualizations is harder to achieve. The predominantly powerful 'etic' position is perceived as 'self-evident' and the most 'obvious' explanatory method.

A broad definition of cross-cultural psychology is given by Berry *et al.* (1992: 2) as:

> the study of similarities and differences in individual psychological functioning in various cultural and ethnic groups; of the relationships between psychological variables and sociocultural, ecological, and biological variables; and of current changes in these variables.

In contrast cultural psychology ('emic') understands psychological processes as culturally constituted meaning systems. The significance of adopting a cultural psychological perspective is that it rejects the dichotomy between psychological processes and structures as being 'universal' and the cultural context and content as the 'variable'. While not necessarily made explicit, or even understood, such is the unquestioned pervasiveness of cross-cultural influence, these underlying assumptions are manifested in the literature of clinical practice within the UK. From an emic perspective, culture is not an external factor whose effects on the individual must be examined but rather is integral to the behaviour. The individual is acting according to reasons that are in part under the control of the acting person rather than determined by causal events.

In the above case example a more ethical and appropriate response might have been to engage with the whole family and Sunita to better understand the context of her presenting difficulties. To elicit what they all see as important issues and to understand the family's historical and cultural background. Again the questions arise about what constitutes being well for Sunita and her family members? What does not fulfilling her duties at home mean to all family members? What might Sunita be trying to communicate to her family members and health professionals by not speaking? What does not speaking mean to them all? What would need to change for her and her family members in order that she becomes her 'usual' self again? What and who else might help in that process from Sunita's and the family's viewpoint?

Similarly, when one conducts an assessment of a person from a minority ethnic background, we might assume the primacy of the individual and ask all the questions we might usually ask, and then consider, 'What are the relevant cultural factors . . . for example in the family?' We assume that individual experience can be understood devoid of the multiple contexts, such as the person's linguistic, cultural, historical and familial contexts, and that simply taking 'account of family or environmental factors' is sufficient. Culture is relegated to the ranks of 'a factor' rather than being seen as constitutive of the very concept and experience of 'the self'.

The development of psychological theories can also be cast in terms of 'etic' and 'emic' conceptualizations and doing so serves to raise awareness that psychological knowledge has a political function. For example, when individual intellectual assessments are made, the underlying assumption is that intelligence is a universal psychological process. Variation is considered in terms of the cultural content, that is, by changing some of the information items to reflect different historical events, introducing pictures that show people from BME populations. However, the core assumption is that intelligence is a universal construct that can be measured by a Western statistical methodology. Currently it is difficult to conceive that the concept of intelligence was never a universal psychological process waiting to be discovered by psychologists. There is no question that intelligence, as a construct exists. The central issue is whether intelligence is a constructed reality or a natural phenomenon. The decision to adopt either position (illustrated in an abbreviated form here as there are other positions) is a political decision based on personal circumstances and experiences. Thus, the work of the psychologist cannot be free from the personal values and beliefs at the individual level. The constraints on those values and beliefs may be imposed by the service systems that employ psychologists, but ultimately there is a personal decision to be made about what position they take as a professional. It is perhaps helpful to state that the current discussion is not about ascribing prominence to one position but rather to rehearsing the assumptions that often are hidden in the frenetic delivery of services, and in so doing reaffirming that psychological or therapeutic practice is not a value-free occupational activity. The usefulness of the multicultural competence is in prompting the psychologist to discover other conceptual positions and then to make decisions about clinical action.

PSYCHOLOGICAL AND THERAPEUTIC ACTIVITIES AS BIASED

What the therapist reads is critical in the development of the capacity to consider alternative perspectives. Access to reading material that does not necessarily reinforce a personal worldview is important. For example, with respect to the children of Black Americans, Cress-Welsing (1991: 204) writes:

> Any established social system has assigned social roles for every child born into the system, inasmuch as children are born to parents who already are occupying 'their place' in the structured social system. True power is the key factor in the determination of 'identity', which is the individual's relationship to actual power. In an oppressive social system, one's identity is either that of the oppressor or that of the oppressed.

Such a view held by Black parents of children who are in 'family therapy' clearly will result in outcomes that are different from the outcomes for parents who do not hold this view. The point is not whether one position is tenable or not (or even that there may be multiple positions), but the awareness that the position exists. Access to reading material that highlights other ways of construing the world is a critical feature of therapist development. This is in contrast to the increasingly 'specialist' reading that reinforces an existing worldview.

Given that the knowledge base of psychology and therapy is not value-free, alternative accounts are not necessarily easily accessible. Zuckerman (1988) has argued that the reporting of scientific activity is an institutionally structured social process. Within this process there are two institutional gatekeepers, funding and publishing organizations. There is a complex relationship within psychology/therapeutic practice and between research-grant-making institutions and the research that is undertaken. In part the research funding may come from organizations that have arisen because of specific individual experiences of some families (e.g., autism spectrum disorders) and therefore have their own political agenda for the construction of research activity. There are also very clear political reasons for publishing in a particular journal and for the creation of new journals for perspectives that cannot be admitted into existing ones. The point remains that none of the professional psychological or therapeutic practices are bias-free and again are sources of values and beliefs which continue to influence the training of new staff. The significance of acknowledging the literature sources is that it invariably determines which service systems are developed. The service systems then determine access to psychotherapeutic services and ultimately at the client level on whether trained and supported interpreters are available to engage in the therapeutic process. A cursory examination of many leaflets offering psychotherapeutic services will establish the saliency of the underlying therapeutic model and its ability to offer services to BME people.

OBTAINING RELEVANT CLINICAL EXPERIENCE

In developing multicultural competencies, personal clinical experience is essential. When the availability of working with BME people is not an option, then it is clearly difficult, though not impossible, to develop the necessary thinking and practice skills. One competency not mentioned by Hansen *et al.* (2000) though potentially implied is that of having access to quality supervision. The opportunity to reflect on both etic and emic perspectives within a supervisory relationship is also likely to enhance professional competence. It is unclear as to how many psychologists or other therapists have ever had experience of being supervised by a BME peer or even having supervision where issues of 'race' and culture are integral to the development of knowledge and practice within supervision. These issues and tasks for culturally competent supervisors are described more fully elsewhere (see Patel 2004).

EXPERIENCES OF THE CLIENT AND THE THERAPIST

Both therapist and client(s) bring to the interaction their own values and beliefs, and their historical, political and cultural experiences of privilege and disadvantage. All these ingredients form the basis of an intercultural interaction, even where there may be no overt signs of difference between therapist and client, for example in cultural terms, but enormous differences in terms of class or other privileges. Patel (1998) reports on the experiences of BME clinicians who themselves experienced racism from their clients. This too requires skill in understanding and practice in a way that does not condone and reinforce racist behaviour. For example, what would constitute an ethical and culturally competent response in a therapeutic encounter where a client was overtly racist to a therapist? What might be the responsibilities of not just the individual therapist, but also of their organization?

The BME client brings into the therapeutic space his or her own experiences of a world that may not accord with the experiences of the psychologist or therapist. The experience of 'everyday racism' (Essed 1991) is a common one and needs evaluation into any formulation about the stress that is being experienced by the client. Clark *et al.* (1999) give one model of including 'everyday racism' in problem formulation. In the UK there is continuing evidence that mental health services are providing differential services to BME people (Raleigh 2000). One clearly documented response in the literature is that of the 'over pathologizing bias' (Lopez 1989). BME people are more likely to be perceived as more disturbed or as requiring more treatment by mental health professionals when compared with their White counterparts. The bias is also directional in nature, for example, Jones (1982) found that White therapists gave more severe diagnoses to Black clients than to White clients. Lopez (1989) provides a comprehensive review of client variable biases and clinical judgements, including the further perceptual bias of underestimating disturbance.

Another aspect of client and therapist experiences which influences the therapeutic process is what has been described as racial identity schemas by Helms and Cook (1999) who define this as people's styles of expressing their internalized reactions to racism. They suggest that the content of these reactions differ according to whether their group was victimized by or benefited from racism and racial oppression. Thus, in the therapeutic space the therapist needs to be aware of and reflect on the impact and significance of the potentially differing reactions and related racial identities of both the therapist and the client.

COMPETENCY DEVELOPMENT AND CONCEPTUAL CONFUSION

The main dilemma faced with developing a competency-based approach is that there is no 'expert' position to determine what constitutes good practice. Many psychologists and therapists work within organizations that do not have effective ethnic monitoring of service users or staff. Many do not have adequate monitoring of complaints or even translations of the complaints procedures for clients that would inform good practice. Many do not even acknowledge the reality and impact of institutional racism. There are many levels and areas where we could readily develop multicultural competencies, for example at the level of establishing a diverse and competent workforce, developing effective policies in relation to healthcare and professional training, conducting more ethical and competent research, and radically revising the basic education and training given to psychologists and therapists at all levels.

However, the current focus is on the difficulties that are faced in thinking about competency-based approaches in clinical practice even though, as discussed earlier, these organizational issues are critical in delivering clinical practice. Conceptual changes are necessary before progress can be achieved. An example of a fundamental conceptual error is evident in the DCP's document on 'Continuing professional development', first published in 1998, by the 'Race' and Culture Special Interest Group who developed and provided the first section on core competencies (DCP 1998). In 2001, a revised version was produced (DCP 2001b) in which broadly the same text was reissued but located at the end of the document. Thus the apparently emic competencies provided by the 'Race' and Culture Special Interest Group were placed after the seemingly broad, etic competencies had been articulated. The juxtaposition of the two sets of competencies reflected the views of both etic and emic perspectives. Even when we subscribe to the view that the competency-based approach is a way forward for more ethical and competent practice within a multiethnic and multicultural population, there is much to be learned about how and where we position ourselves and what we define as ethical and professional practice in this context.

In this regard several examples of difficult situations are given below, with a question to the reader about *what constitutes a just, ethical and professional response* in the following scenarios?

- A client who has been a victim of racist violence in his neighbourhood and has had racist threats pushed and shouted through his letterbox is terrified of going outside and becomes increasingly housebound. He is referred for cognitive-behavioural therapy or any therapy which would 'increase his confidence and his ability to go outside' in the same environment where he has been assaulted several times.
- In your service all African and African-Caribbean clients are referred by the team to the only Black member of the team, who is a psychology assistant trying to obtain relevant clinical experience before applying for postgraduate psychology training.
- In your service colleagues routinely discourage or reject referrals of minority ethnic people who do not speak English on the grounds that there is no evidence that therapeutic activity is beneficial when working with an interpreter, or that interpreters are costly and working with them is frustrating, time-consuming and unsatisfying for the clinicians.
- A colleague is overheard as saying that 'all this cross-cultural stuff is getting so boring and it's irrelevant, it's political correctness gone mad, we should just treat every client as an individual'.
- A service manager and your clinical supervisor are heard saying that 'we need to deal with the waiting list that we have got and get the service delivered to those people who are in real need, who are motivated to come for therapy and have been referred, before we start thinking about all those minorities whom we are supposedly not reaching'.

CONCLUSION

Within clinical psychology itself there has been support for change in professional practice (DCP) and the BPS (2000) has issued its own code of practice. Nonetheless, the challenge remains that therapeutic professions have yet to develop a consensus on the way that they view working in a multicultural and multiethnic environment. The lack of consensus means that the competencies espoused will potentially themselves be seen as irrelevant to working practice unless there is a very clear population that is requiring services. Correspondingly the BME people may themselves understandably determine that psychology and psychological approaches are not relevant to their needs. Such a situation is clearly not sustainable in the longer term. Significant and decisive action is now required from the leadership within all psychological and therapeutic professions.

REFLECTIVE QUESTIONS

1   What cultural/ethnic biases might you bring into the consulting room?
2   One of your clients makes an offensive racist remark towards a colleague of yours in the waiting room, before starting a therapeutic session with you. How would you respond (*or not*) to this?
3   If you thought that one of your colleagues was practising in a racist manner, what might you do?
4   What happens when a client says they want to be seen by another therapist from a different ethnic background to you?

REFERENCES

Alexander, Z. (1999) *Department of Health: Study of Black, Asian and Ethnic Minority Issues*. London: Department of Health.
Berry, J. W., Poortinga, Y. H., Segall, M. H. & Dasen, P. R. (1992) *Cross-cultural Psychology: Research and Applications*. Cambridge: Cambridge University Press.
BPS (British Psychological Society) (2000) *A Code of Conduct for Psychologists*. Leicester: BPS.
Clark, R., Anderson, N. B., Clark, V. R. & Williams, D. R. (1999) Racism as a stressor for African Americans: a biopsychosocial model. *American Psychologist*, 54(10), 805–816.
Cress-Welsing, F. (1991) *The Isis Papers*. Chicago: Third World Press.
DCP (Division of Clinical Psychology) (1998) *Services to Black and Minority Ethnic People. A Guide for Commissioners of Clinical Psychology Services*. Leicester: BPS.
DCP (Division of Clinical Psychology) (2001a) *The Core Purpose and Philosophy of the Profession*. Leicester: BPS.
DCP (Division of Clinical Psychology) (2001b) *Guidelines for Continuing Professional Development*. Leicester: BCP.
Ely, P. & Denney, D. (1987) *Social Work in a Multiracial Society*. London: Gower.
Essed, P. (1991) *Understanding Everyday Racism*. Newbury Park, CA: Sage.
Hansen, N. D., Pepitone-Arreola-Rockwell, F. & Greene, A. F. (2000) Multicultural competence: criteria and case examples. *Professional Psychology: Research and Practice*, 31(6), 652–660.
Helms, J. & Cook, D. A. (1999) *Using Race and Culture in Counseling and Psychotherapy: Theory and Process*. Needham Heights, MA: Allyn & Bacon.

Jones, E. E. (1982) Psychotherapists' impressions of treatment outcomes as a function of race. *Journal of Clinical Psychology*, 38, 722–731.

Lopez, S. (1989) Patient variable biases in clinical judgment: conceptual overview and methodological considerations. *Psychological Bulletin*, 106, 184–203.

MacPherson, W. (1999) *The Stephen Lawrence Inquiry: Report of an Inquiry*. London: Home Office.

Modood, T. & Berthoud, R. (1997) *Ethnic Minorities in Britain: Diversity and Disadvantage*. London: Policy Studies Institute.

Patel, M. (1998) Black therapists/white clients: an exploration of experiences in cross-cultural therapy. *Clinical Psychology Forum*, 118, 18–23.

Patel, N. (2004) Difference and power in supervision: the case of culture and racism, in I. Fleming and L. Steen (eds.), *Supervision and Clinical Psychology: Theory, Practice and Perspective*. Hove, UK: Brunner-Routledge.

Patel, N., Bennett, E., Dennis, M., Dosanjh, N., Mahtani, A., Miller, A. & Nadirshaw, Z. (2000) *Clinical Psychology: 'Race' and Culture: A Training Manual*. Leicester: BPS Books.

Pedersen, P. (1995) Culture-centered ethical guidelines for counselors, in J. Ponterotto (ed.), *Handbook of Multicultural Counseling and Therapy*. Newbury Park, CA: Sage, pp. 34–49.

Raleigh, V. S. (2000) Mental health in black and ethnic minorities: an epidemiological perspective, in C. Kaye & T. Lingiah (eds.), *Race, Culture and Ethnicity in Secure Psychiatric Practice*. London: Jessica Kingsley.

Richards, G. (1997). *'Race', Racism and Psychology: Towards a Reflexive History*. London: Routledge.

Sue, D. W., Arredondo, P. & McDavis, R. J. (1992) Multicultural counseling competencies and standards: a call to the profession. *Journal of Counseling and Development*, 70, 477–486.

Tribe, R. & Raval, H. (2003) *Working with Interpreters in Mental Health*. Hove, UK: Brunner-Routledge.

Zuckerman, H. (1988) The sociology of science, in N. J. Smelser (ed.), *The Handbook of Sociology*. Newbury Park, CA: Sage, pp. 511–574.

Part V

Research, supervision and training

Chapter 20

Research in therapeutic practice settings: ethical considerations

Adrian Coyle and Camilla Olsen

In this era of evidence-based practice, a pressing concern is to determine which psychotherapies work for which clients and under which conditions (see Chapter 21). Research on issues relevant to therapeutic practice and conducted in practice settings has thus become more vital than ever. However, the need for research, which can provide an evidence base for and inform therapeutic practice, can never justify overlooking or downplaying concerns about the welfare and well-being of those who participate in such research. The ethical issues raised by therapeutic research must always be accorded the most serious consideration. This chapter examines some of these issues.

First, it is worth saying something about the principal formal contexts in which ethical issues in therapy-relevant research are considered. National Health Service (NHS) trusts and other organisations or bodies which host or undertake research studies (such as social services departments and universities) have research ethics committees consisting of both 'expert' and 'lay' members. These scrutinise all proposals for studies that plan to collect data from or about providers or users of services (including relatives and carers of service users) within the trust or organisation and also for studies that are housed within the trust or organisation.[1] If a study falls into these categories, data cannot be collected until formal ethical approval has been obtained.

PRINCIPLES UNDERLYING ETHICAL RESEARCH: BENEFICENCE AND NON-MALEFICENCE

How do researchers and ethics committees evaluate the ethical soundness of research proposals?[2] Clearly, proposals must be examined to ensure that they

---

1 Note that different arrangements apply in the case of studies, which intend to collect data from more than one NHS trust; see DoH (2001a).

2 For a comprehensive list of the criteria currently used by NHS research ethics committees in the process of ethical review, see DoH (2001a: 23–27).

conform to relevant legislation concerning matters such as the protection of any personal data that participants provide. However, it is necessary to consider the moral principles that underlie ethical practice in therapy and research. Although there is a long philosophical tradition underlying whatever moral principles we might point to, for our purposes it is sufficient to highlight two basic and commonly invoked principles: beneficence (achieving the greatest good) and non-maleficence (causing the least harm) (Emanuel *et al.* 2000). Of course other principles are relevant such as a concern with justice (i.e. a concern that the benefits and burdens of research be distributed fairly among all groups and classes in society) and a respect for autonomy (DoH 2001b; Palmer Barnes 1998), as are the values of therapy (such as integrity and respect). These tend to be the core principles which ethics committees invoke in their assessment of research proposals: e.g., research ethics committees within the NHS are required to prioritise the dignity, rights, safety and well-being of participants (DoH 2001b). These principles should also be readily discernible in the following consideration of common ethical issues in research.

The application of the beneficence principle to research contexts can occur in many ways. At its most basic level, it raises the question of whether it is worth having would-be participants invest time and energy in a particular study. If the proposed research stands little chance of producing useful findings (however we define 'useful'), it will fail the beneficence test. If it also presents a serious risk of causing emotional or physical discomfort or distress to participants, it additionally fails the non-maleficence test.

RESEARCH DESIGN

Ethics committees give careful consideration to the nature and design of a proposed study because a poorly conceptualised and/or badly designed study is unlikely to contribute to the greater good. So what constitutes good research design? Good design in specific terms can be quite difficult owing to researchers' sometimes passionately held convictions concerning what actually constitutes good design. Psychological research has been dominated by the positivist-empiricist paradigm (and the related hypothetico-deductive approach), which assumes that the phenomena under investigation have an objective reality independent of the researcher, and can be accessed and accurately measured through systematic observation (including experiments) by applying appropriate scientific procedures. Within this paradigm, the goal of research is to produce objective, impartial and unbiased knowledge of the phenomena being studied. This perspective is generally (although not exclusively) associated with quantitative research methods. Although relatively few scientists would today espouse the tenets of this paradigm without at least some caveats, its influence can still be discerned in much psychological research. Criteria derived from the positivist-empiricist paradigm, e.g. reliability and validity, are routinely used to evaluate research quality and thereby to assess whether research that requires the involvement of human participants is likely to yield credible and useful findings.

One research design which is located within the positivist-empiricist paradigm and which deserves specific attention – as it tends to be regarded as the 'gold standard' design for evaluating therapeutic interventions – is the randomised controlled trial (RCT). This approach investigates the comparative benefits of two or more treatments and involves randomly allocating participants to different treatment conditions including 'no treatment' interventions, which allows a study to ascertain whether a particular form of treatment is better or worse than others and better or worse than no treatment. Although RCTs have been criticised (e.g., on the grounds that they require very structured, prescribed approaches to therapeutic interventions in order to ensure that all participants in a particular condition receive the 'same' input) (Mace *et al.* 2001), they have nevertheless been described as a source of research evidence on the effectiveness of therapies which brings maximum benefit to clients (Roth & Fonagy 1996). The ethics of RCTs have also been the subject of specific attention (Edwards *et al.* 1998).

More recently, however, mainstream psychology has rediscovered the value of qualitative research, which has a long and distinguished tradition within psychotherapy, especially in the form of clinical case studies. Although there is a variety of qualitative methods with differing assumptions and emphases, most qualitative research can be said to be concerned with meaning and process – how people make sense of the world and experience events (Willig 2001). Most qualitative approaches do not subscribe to the assumptions of the positivist-empiricist paradigm but instead hold that an 'objective' account of the 'known' independent of the 'knower' is impossible: the researcher is seen as inescapably implicated in the research process and product. Indeed, some approaches (e.g., social constructionist approaches such as discourse analysis) go further and are agnostic on whether any independent 'reality' can be said to exist (Potter 1996). Given these differences, qualitative researchers tend to adopt very different criteria from quantitative researchers when evaluating research quality (Elliott *et al.* 1999). With such diverse ideas concerning what makes for good research design, it is easy to imagine a situation arising where a study located within and consistent with one research approach may be seen as deficient and therefore as failing the beneficence test by an evaluator who is familiar with and committed to a different research approach.

This may be a source of major difficulty for researchers working in therapeutic practice contexts that are characterised by a consensual but limited view of what constitutes good research design. This may be particularly likely to occur in NHS settings where those who wish to conduct qualitative client- and/or service-related research may find themselves having to convince other professionals whose research socialisation did not include an in-depth consideration of the potential value of qualitative approaches. Nevertheless, it is worth noting that qualitative research has begun to attract concerted attention in many professional domains that might be thought of as resistant, including medicine and healthcare (Pope *et al.* 2000) and evidence-based practice (Murphy & Dingwall 2001) and also that official guidelines for NHS research ethics committees stipulate that committees should include members who have expertise in qualitative methods (DoH 2001a). Equally, it is possible to imagine a situation where researchers who wish to conduct quantitative research might experience resistance from some professionals who might see such research as inevitably overwriting participants' (i.e. clients' or service providers') subjectivities with predetermined questionnaire categories, and therefore being of limited value. It is important not to lapse into what Reicher (2000) terms 'methodolatry' but to see different research paradigms and methods as fulfilling different but equally valuable roles in therapy-relevant research and to remain open to the possibility that different methods might be fruitfully combined. The use of one approach rather than another does not automatically confer utility and ethical soundness on a research study. Instead, one must first consider whether the stated research aims and questions are appropriate, potentially useful and feasible and only then consider whether the chosen methods will enable these aims to be fulfilled.

RESEARCH UTILITY

This entails asking the 'so what' question of the research aims, which sometimes sinks interesting research ideas. This question arises from the assertion that 'The best psychological research should inform, amongst other things . . . professional practice [and] the delivery of public services' (Bruce 2002: 620). Hence, in assessing the value and ethics of a proposed study, we need to consider its potential implications for practice and whether its findings will be of benefit to practitioners, clients and/or services in any way. If a convincing case cannot be made for a proposed study's potential utility, the research aims and questions may need to be amended or even abandoned. One way of increasing the likelihood of achieving utility is to ensure that the research questions and any research instruments that are developed take account of the views of 'key informants' (i.e. people who have special knowledge of the research topic or of the group(s) to be studied that is not otherwise available to the researcher) (Gilchrist 1992). Key informant interviews may therefore constitute a useful preliminary stage before the research proposal is developed or before the main study begins. The application of the beneficence principle then continues by considering the appropriateness of the research methods to be used and whether the researcher has formulated feasible plans for disseminating their research findings so that they can shape policy and practice. Too little attention is paid to dissemination in many research proposals, and yet it is a vital aspect of the research process (Cowie & Glachan 2000). Much research has been conducted which could benefit service provision if only its findings were brought to the attention of audiences that could implement them.

ASSESSING, REDUCING AND MANAGING RISK

Perhaps the most salient concerns in assessing the ethical soundness of proposed research in therapeutic settings relates to the risk of the study interfering with service provision or causing or exacerbating discomfort or distress among participants. This represents the application of the principle of non-maleficence. According to this principle, any research, which might interfere in a detrimental way with the provision of therapeutic services to participants, is ethically questionable (Saks *et al.* 2002). Clearly research that seeks to evaluate therapies (such as RCTs) may require that therapy take particular forms. However, this is ethically acceptable as the researchers do not know in advance which of the forms of therapy being evaluated are most effective and so it is not the case that obviously effective forms are being withheld from some participants. Although RCTs usually include a 'no treatment' condition, participants in this condition are usually people who are awaiting therapeutic services anyway and who, if they were not taking part in the study, would simply remain on a waiting list. Concerns that research should not interfere negatively with or compromise service provision more usually apply to situations where the evaluation of therapy services requires clients to complete potentially onerous questionnaires at the start and/or end of individual sessions or where clients are interviewed regularly about their therapy experience. In the former, what might be a challenging therapeutic experience anyway may become too burdensome for clients and they may cease attending therapy. In the latter, being required to reflect upon their therapy in a structured way may change clients' understanding of it and may undermine some of the work that the therapist is doing with them. The collection of evaluative data is less risky in this sense when the client is no longer receiving therapeutic sessions. One research situation that is rarely acceptable, though, is where the researcher who evaluates therapy is also the therapist who provides it. Clients/participants may be disinclined to respond honestly in these situations, which may also lead to tensions in the therapeutic relationship.

Although concerns about causing participant discomfort or distress arise primarily in research with potential or actual therapy clients, they can also be relevant in research on sensitive topics[3] with service providers. For example, this would be a consideration in a study, which proposed to interview therapists who worked with clients with terminal illnesses and which aimed to investigate these therapists' views about their own mortality and about how they saw these views as influencing their therapeutic practice. Although one would hope that therapists working with this client group would have accorded substantial consideration to this issue in training and/or in supervision, the risk remains that, during the interview, a therapist could find that some aspect of this issue, which they had not previously considered, might prove distressing to them. Alternatively, they might think that they have reached a satisfactory accommodation with this issue only to find that their current or recent life circumstances (such as deaths or serious illnesses in their family) may have unsettled this accommodation to an extent that they had not fully appreciated.

OBTAINING INFORMED CONSENT FOR PARTICIPATION

The process of assessing the risks associated with research participation is not straightforward as it can sometimes be difficult to predict the likelihood of a particular study evoking or restimulating psychological distress among participants. Although researchers and ethics committees are expected to take primary responsibility for this risk assessment, potential research participants are also invited to engage in an informed risk assessment for themselves and to reach an informed decision about whether or not they should take part in any particular study (which could be seen as part of a process of respecting participants' autonomy). It is this consideration which underlies the principle that all researchers should obtain informed consent to participate from all who take part in a study.

In practice, this means that, before data collection occurs, all participants should be made aware of what the research topic is (at least in general terms); what exactly participation will involve (including, if relevant, where data collection will occur and who will collect the data; the approximate length of time it will take to complete the study's questionnaires or interviews; and which issues will be addressed by the questions that will be asked); the potential value of the research and the potential risks to participants; what will

---

3 A research topic may be considered sensitive if it 'potentially poses for those involved a substantial threat, the emergence of which renders problematic for the researcher and/or the researched the collection, holding and/or dissemination of research data' (Lee & Renzetti 1993: 5).

happen to the data;[4] how confidentiality or anonymity will be assured and any limits to confidentiality; participants' right to withdraw from the study at any point without incurring any sort of penalty; and how participants might obtain information about the study's findings. Potential participants should be provided with this information in writing using accessible language. In the case of studies using self-completion questionnaires, it could appear in a covering letter that accompanies the questionnaires so that recipients can reflect on this information before deciding whether or not to participate. For face-to-face interviews, potential participants should receive this information well before the interview occurs. It is not acceptable to provide this information for the first time just before the interview begins, as the person will not have sufficient time to consider it and reach an informed decision about participation. Before the interview starts, participants should also be given a consent form to sign. This should reiterate what participants have agreed to and should state that they have been informed about what the research involves, about what will happen to the data and that they have had their queries about the research answered to their satisfaction; this should be countersigned by the researcher. Studies that use self-completion questionnaires do not usually use consent forms as it is assumed that participants have consented by virtue of having completed and returned the questionnaire.

However, therapy-related research may sometimes involve the collection of data from individuals whose ability to provide informed consent to participate may be open to question. In this case, a concern with respecting participants' autonomy may conflict with a concern for participants' safety. These situations often involve children and young people aged under 16 years, for whom the consent of a parent or guardian is usually required instead of or in addition to the consent of the child or young person. However, in therapy-related research, these concerns are more likely to be centred on people with (severe) mental health problems whose cognitive, social and emotional functioning may be impaired by their condition (Roberts 2002).

In this situation, the question arises how the suitability of people who volunteer to take part is assessed. Researchers may rely on mental health professionals or workers in voluntary organisations to act as filtering agents and issue invitations only to clients with whom they have been working, who meet the study's inclusion criteria and whom they judge to be capable of making informed decisions about participation. Yet the question remains how these 'gatekeepers' assess clients' abilities to make informed decisions. Researchers may have to provide clear and specific criteria for evaluating this

---

4 Note that this requirement means that recordings of therapy sessions that were originally made for training or other non-research purposes cannot be used as research data unless clients have provided consent for the recordings to be used in research.

– e.g., by referring to clients' proven ability to have reached informed decisions about other issues of similar complexity in the recent past.

Additionally, there may also be concerns about the possibility of people with mental health problems being subjected to some forms of coercion (of varying degrees of subtlety) in order to enlist them to a study. For inpatients especially, there may be fears of some form of retaliation from service providers if they decline to participate or if they withdraw from a study. Researchers may need to think carefully about how they might minimise the possibility of individuals feeling coerced to participate in any way. For example, in her study of the relationship between the social skill levels of 17 clients with schizophrenia and the quality of the therapeutic relationships that they established with their therapists, Olsen (2000) was concerned that if clients were invited to participate by their therapists, they might feel obligated to take part. She therefore arranged for clients to be invited via their key workers once the therapists had agreed to participate. This also meant that therapists (who were working with more than one client with schizophrenia) did not know the identity of any clients who declined to take part and so there was no risk of therapeutic relationships being adversely affected.

Also, with the increasing provision of therapeutic services to people with learning disabilities, we are now starting to see research being undertaken which aims to explore these service users' viewpoints (Maynard 1999). Researchers will have to consider the extent to which potential participants can make an informed judgement about whether or not to take part. People with mild learning disabilities may be able to provide informed consent themselves if they have received information about the research in a sufficiently accessible form and if checks have been made to ensure that they have understood exactly what they are consenting to do. Sometimes when endeavouring to obtain informed consent from people with severe mental health problems or learning disabilities, it may be necessary to liaise with key workers, advocates, family members or friends of potential participants who may be able to ease communication. This can also be a useful safeguard for the researcher in case any doubts should subsequently be raised concerning whether the person was misled about the research or coerced into taking part (Saks *et al.* 2002).

AVOIDING, MINIMISING AND MANAGING PARTICIPANT DISTRESS

Some research studies on sensitive topics carry obvious risks of eliciting or restimulating distress in participants. This does not mean that such studies are necessarily ethically dubious because the beneficence principle comes into play here. The research may be deemed ethically acceptable if it could make such a significant contribution to therapeutic practice that it is worth running some risks *and* if the researchers have given careful thought to what they might do to reduce the likelihood of distress occurring and to deal responsibly with any distress that might occur. Researchers should at least be able to demonstrate that all those who will be involved in data collection have sufficient training and experience to enable them to respond effectively to these concerns (Roberts 2002). To gain insight into the practical steps that researchers might take to address ethical concerns in research that has an obvious risk of eliciting participant distress, see Bowen and John (2001).

There are various specific ways in which researchers might satisfy the concern about minimising participant distress, e.g., by posing gentle, introductory questions at the start of the interview or questionnaire, by ensuring that a non-intrusive line of questioning is followed and, where possible, by finishing the data collection process on a hopeful note if the interview or questionnaire has been exploring the participants' experiences of possibly traumatic life events. One strategy that has been advocated for achieving a gentle and potentially insight-generating line of questioning and for managing any distress, which might arise within qualitative research interviews on sensitive topics, is to locate the data collection process within the framework of the basic counselling interaction (Coyle 1998; Sen Gupta 1998). The proposal is that researchers should use basic counselling skills while fostering counselling attributes of empathy, genuineness and unconditional positive regard (to the extent that this might be possible) within research interviews in order to fulfil the dual purpose of obtaining rich data and helping to contain any distress that participants might experience. However, although this proposal has been taken up in some qualitative therapy relevant research (e.g. Wright & Coyle 1996), it needs to be implemented with care, the main risk being that the research interview is transformed into a therapy session where roles and responsibilities have not been agreed beforehand, with the research focus being lost. Regardless of whether researchers adopt this strategy in interviews, they should at the very least invite participants who become upset during the interview to take a break, continue another day or opt out of the study altogether. Indeed, they should have clear criteria by which they can decide whether or not to suspend an interview (and, in the case of very sensitive research, criteria for suspending or terminating the whole project).

It is not sufficient for researchers to attend to the minimisation or management of distress only within the actual interview. Having revisited what might have been distressing and difficult experiences in the interview, research participants may find themselves continuing to ruminate on these experiences in the hours and days afterwards. Hence, as a matter of routine, researchers who are investigating potentially sensitive topics should provide participants with information about where they might turn for help (e.g., helplines and self-help groups that deal with those issues raised by the research) if they find themselves in need of ongoing support to deal with any distress that is re-ignited. However, researchers should not include details of any organisations or resources in this information without contacting these organisations or resources first to explain the nature of the research and obtain their permission to direct distressed participants to them. Otherwise, small support bodies could find themselves overwhelmed by demand for their services without having had a chance to prepare. Of course, if participants are currently receiving therapy or are familiar with and know how to access therapeutic services, they will be able to receive support through that route. Once again, though, researchers should approach those professionals involved in participants' care (after obtaining participants' permission) and inform them about the research. Researchers may also wish to telephone participants after the interview to see whether they have been affected by participating in the research and to check on their well-being. Generally researchers should not offer to see distressed participants again for a (quasi-) therapeutic session unless the researchers are qualified therapists and this session can be accommodated within their standard framework for supervised practice (Saks *et al.* 2002). Even then, the transition in role from researcher to therapist may prove difficult to manage.

Researchers who are also therapists can experience discomfort and harbour ethical qualms about not using their therapeutic training to intervene when research participants become distressed, especially if they genuinely feel that their therapeutic interventions could make a positive difference. For example, here are some reflections on this situation from a trainee counselling psychologist who had been working therapeutically in the eating disorders field and who conducted semi-structured research interviews with daughters of mothers with eating disorders:

> When I work therapeutically with clients, we have agreed on a contract that states the number of sessions, how often and when. Difficult experiences can (hopefully) be worked through and, more often than not, the client is less distressed at the end of the therapeutic work. During the interviews, all of the participants disclosed some painful childhood experiences and conflicting feelings about their mothers. I felt extremely inadequate in that I desperately wanted to help them but was, of course, unable to intervene in an explicitly therapeutic way in my role as a researcher. Although I had dealt with similar distress previously, it has been in my capacity as a therapist where there was a clear framework from which to work. I felt myself getting very confused and unsure of how to respond.
>
> (Ahlenius 2003: 127–128)

These reflections call to mind Lee's (1993: 106) observation that 'if the interview can be distressing to the respondent, it can also be stressful for the interviewer'. The well-being of the researcher tends to be under-emphasised in considerations of the ethics of research, even though it is something that NHS research ethics committees are expected to consider (DoH 2001a). A comprehensive ethical analysis of any research study must include this issue, especially when researchers are collecting data on sensitive topics from participants in face-to-face settings. In these situations, it may be beneficial for research supervision to incorporate elements from therapeutic practice supervision to allow researchers space to reflect upon how they have responded emotionally and practically to the research topic and to the demands of the data collection process.

In terms of responding constructively to participant distress, self-completion questionnaires that are filled out by participants in the absence of the researcher pose greater challenges than interviews in some respects. However, all that researchers can do to reduce the likelihood of distress occurring is to adhere to the same recruitment procedures that should be followed by researchers who intend to collect data from participants face-to-face. That is, they should develop careful inclusion and exclusion criteria for sampling so that invitations to participate are not sent to people who are likely to be deeply embedded within any possibly traumatic issues. They should also ensure that potential participants receive sufficient information about the study and about where they might turn for support if necessary.

It may be worth noting that, from our own experience, it often seems that participant distress, which is difficult for the researcher to handle, tends to occur in studies on apparently innocuous topics where it is least expected. This may be because researchers who are studying topics that are clearly sensitive in nature and/or who are collecting data from vulnerable groups are likely to give serious consideration to the possibility that the research could cause distress to participants and will attend carefully how this might best be avoided, minimised or managed. Researchers who believe they are studying relatively uncontentious issues may not pay such close attention to these matters and so, if participant distress does occur, they may be ill-prepared to respond effectively. One particular form of research, which can carry unanticipated risks, is the evaluation of therapeutic services from service users' perspectives. Participants who were dissatisfied for some reason with the services they received may express considerable frustration, disappointment and anger and may also become vividly reconnected with the issues for which they sought help and which they feel were not satisfactorily resolved. Researchers may assume that obtaining users' views in service evaluation is in some ways akin to market research and so may underestimate the potential for generating distress; it is important to remember that asking for users' views about mental health services is very different from asking for product users' views about a brand of washing powder. Finally, given the possibility of research evoking participant distress and thereby leading participants to be dissatisfied with their research experience, it is important that researchers give careful consideration to the provisions they will make for receiving and responding to complaints from research participants or their representatives during the course of the project.

CONCLUSION

This chapter has examined a number of the main ethical considerations when planning and undertaking research in therapeutic practice settings, viewed in terms of the basic ethical principles of beneficence and non-maleficence. There are, however, additional and more specific ethical questions relevant to therapy-related research that readers may wish to consider, using (where appropriate) the various ethical principles outlined at the start of the chapter.

Note that on March 1st 2004 the system for gaining ethical approval for research that intends to collect data from NHS staff or patients (or former patients who are being asked about their experiences as patients) was changed. Previously these proposals were considered by individual NHS Trusts, now it all has to go through the Central Office for Research Ethics Committees (COREC), from where the proposal is sent out to a local committee (if the proposal is for work in one Trust) or to another body (if the proposal is for research in several Trusts).

REFLECTIVE QUESTIONS

1   What might be the main ethical issues in the use of RCTs to evaluate therapeutic effectiveness?
2   Imagine that you are devising an interview schedule for research, which aims to explore a sensitive topic. What general principles would you use to help you frame/word the questions in order to increase the likelihood that participants will experience their interviews as gentle and non-intrusive?
3   How might we ensure that, in our research, we represent our participants and their experiences in an accurate and responsible way?
4   How might we assess the ethics of discourse analytic research (see Willig 2001), in which participants may assume that the data they provide will be treated either as 'truth' or as 'views' and instead find their accounts deconstructed to expose the assumptions and ideologies upon which they rest?

REFERENCES

Ahlenius, N. (2003) 'A portfolio of academic, therapeutic practice and research work including an investigation of "Maternal eating disorders: adult daughters' reported experiences"'. Unpublished PsychD (Psychotherapeutic & Counselling Psychology) Portfolio: University of Surrey.

Bowen, A. C. L. & John, M. H. (2001) Ethical issues encountered in qualitative research: reflections on interviewing adolescent in-patients engaging in self-injurious behaviours. *Counselling Psychology Review*, 16(2), 19–23.

Bruce, V. (2002) Changing research horizons. *The Psychologist*, 15, 620–622.

Cowie, H. & Glachan, M. (2000) Designing and disseminating research in counselling psychology. *Counselling Psychology Review*, 15(3), 27–30.

Coyle, A. (1998) Qualitative research in counselling psychology: using the counselling interview as a research instrument, in P. Clarkson (ed.), *Counselling Psychology: Integrating Theory, Research and Supervised Practice*. London: Routledge, pp. 56–73.

DoH (Department of Health) (2001a) *Governance Arrangements for NHS Research Ethics Committees*. London: Department of Health.

DoH (Department of Health) (2001b) *Research Governance Framework for Health and Social Care*. Retrieved December 10, 2002, from http://www.doh.gov.uk/research

Edwards, S. J. L., Lilford, R. J., Braunholtz, D. A., Jackson, J. C., Hewison, J. & Thornton, J. (1998) Ethical issues in the design and conduct of randomised controlled trials. *Health Technology Assessment*, 2, 15.

Elliott, R., Fisher, C. T. & Rennie, D.L. (1999) Evolving guidelines for publication of qualitative research studies in psychology and related fields. *British Journal of Clinical Psychology*, 38, 215–229

Emanuel, E. J., Wendler, D. & Grady, C. (2000) What makes clinical research ethical? *Journal of the American Medical Association*, 283, 2701–2711.

Gilchrist, V. J. (1992) Key informant interviews, in B. F. Crabtree & W. L. Miller (eds.), *Doing Qualitative Research*. Newbury Park, CA: Sage, pp. 70–89.

Lee, R. M. (1993) *Doing Research on Sensitive Topics*. London: Sage.

Lee, R. M. & Renzetti, C. M. (1993) The problems of researching sensitive topics: an overview and introduction, in C. M. Renzetti & R. M. Lee (eds.), *Researching Sensitive Topics*. Newbury Park, CA: Sage, pp. 3–13.

Mace, C., Moorey, S. & Roberts, B. (2001) *Evidence in the Psychological Therapies: A Critical Guide for Practitioners*. Hove, UK: Brunner-Routledge.

Maynard, S. (1999) 'A portfolio of academic, therapeutic practice and research work, including an investigation of psychologists' views and experiences of the working alliance with people with learning disabilities'. Unpublished PsychD (Psycho-therapeutic & Counselling Psychology) Portfolio: University of Surrey.

Murphy, E. & Dingwall, R. (2001) Qualitative methods in health technology assessment, in A. Stevens, K. Abrams, J. Brazier, R. Fitzpatrick & R. Lilford (eds.), *The Advanced Handbook of Methods in Evidence Based Healthcare*. London: Sage, pp. 166–178.

Olsen, C. C. (2000) 'A portfolio of academic, therapeutic practice and research work, including an observational pilot study into the effects of ego consolidation therapy on symptomatology and the therapeutic relationship in hospitalized schizophrenic clients over a period of four weeks'. Unpublished PsychD (Psychotherapeutic & Counselling Psychology) Portfolio: University of Surrey.

Palmer Barnes, F. (1998) *Complaints and Grievances in Psychotherapy: A Handbook of Ethical Practice*. London: Routledge.

Pope, C., Ziebland, S. & Mays, N. (2000) Qualitative research in health care: analysing qualitative data. *British Medical Journal*, 320, 114–116.

Potter, J. (1996) *Representing Reality: Discourse, Rhetoric and Social Construction*. London: Sage.

Reicher, S. (2000) Against methodolatry: some comments on Elliott, Fischer, and Rennie. *British Journal of Clinical Psychology*, 39, 1–6.

Roberts, L. W. (2002) Ethics and mental illness research. *Psychiatric Clinics of North America*, 25, 525–545.

Roth, A. & Fonagy, P. (1996) *What Works for Whom? A Critical Review of Psychotherapy Research*. New York: Guilford Press.

Saks, E. R., Jeste, D. V., Granholm, E., Palmer, B. W. & Schneiderman, L. (2002) Ethical issues in psychosocial interventions research involving controls. *Ethics and Behavior*, 12, 87–101.

Sen Gupta, A. (1998) Training in the use of the 'counselling style' interview in qualitative research. *Counselling Psychology Review*, 13(3): 13–19.

Willig, C. (2001) *Introducing Qualitative Research in Psychology: Adventures in Theory and Method*. Buckingham: Open University Press.

Wright, C. & Coyle, A. (1996) Experiences of AIDS-related bereavement among gay men: implications for care. *Mortality*, 1, 267–282.

Chapter 21

The ethics (or not) of evidence-based practice

Martin Milton

As so many psychologists, psychotherapists and counsellors are employed in the National Health Service, a text such as this would not be complete without a look at ethics in relation to one of the important contemporary debates in the public sector delivery of healthcare. In this sector, the notion of evidence-based practice (EBP) is increasingly used to think about psychological therapies,[1] plan psychological services and commission such services. This chapter therefore looks at the main ethical principles that therapists use to guide their practice and considers the ethical issues that may arise in practice guided by the notion of 'evidence'. A question informing the chapter will be whether EBP facilitates or hinders ethical thinking and practice in the delivery of psychological therapies.

DEFINITIONS

Ethics is often understood in terms of a number of broad principles that guide practitioners in making specific, individual decisions about the manner in which they intervene with their clients. Palmer Barnes (1998: 11) suggests that therapists would probably all accept that the following four principles are fundamental to our work:

1   maximising benefit and minimising harm,
2   achieving the greatest good,
3   acting justly,
4   respecting autonomy.

---

1   In line with the current discourse of EBP, the term psychological therapies will be used in this
     chapter to denote therapeutic practice in clinical and counselling psychology, psychotherapy
     and counselling.

EBP has been conceptualised as a process of five steps. These include:

1   formulation of clinical questions in such a way that they can be answered;
2   search for the best external evidence (which often does not consist of the results of randomised clinical trials or systematic reviews);
3   appraisal of that evidence for validity and importance;
4   application in clinical practice (integration of individual clinical expertise with the best available evidence external clinical evidence;
5   evaluation or performance (Baker & Kleijnen 2000: 18)

Thus, we need to keep in mind that EBP is a process rather than a simplistic one-off recognition that a particular therapy is effective. EBP has clear links to the scientist-practitioner models of practice, as well as calls to account-ability in that (as is self-evident) it calls for practice to be based in evidence that it is doing good, rather than relying on the baseless whims of individual practitioners. This means that, in essence, where there is research evidence for a given therapy this approach should be used first (DoH 2001a). Without a doubt, therefore, EBP is inevitably and always synonymous with ethical practice. Or is it?

FIRST IMPRESSIONS

Many psychological therapists will have sympathy for the abovementioned view and will feel that this ethos is embedded within their everyday practice and their attempts to offer therapy that is ethical. However, it is in the attempts to operationalise this term, in calls to develop 'lists' of empirically validated or supported therapies, that some psychological therapists experience the greatest anxiety – and some of this is in relation to what is ethical.

Science, medicine and Health Service policy frequently engage in dis-courses suggestive of achievable certainties (cure, control of symptoms and the like) and EBP is just one example of this. It is important to recognise that these discourses have wide-ranging effects – impacting upon clients' hopes for therapy, the manner in which therapists try to work and of course the ways in which psychological services are commissioned and run. This wish for cer-tainty is therefore wider than the therapeutic disciplines themselves and seems to be a current socio-cultural preoccupation pervading all aspects of our lives. This is at times useful (and potentially a clearly ethical stance) in clarifying routes of action, expected responses and outcomes to life's chal-lenges. However, at times this is completely at odds with the awareness that the therapist has from the day-to-day, moment-to-moment experience of the fluid, moving nature of personal meaning in the therapeutic encounter. The juxtaposition of these two perspectives draws our attention to the chasm that still exists between human reality and our desire for empirical certainty, between research on a population level and that of the individual and meaning. In this regard it is clear that complexities exist and that the ethics of EBP may be more complicated than appears on first reading.

One of the complexities relates to the different constituencies of EBP – individual clients or the population at large, individual therapists or health service systems. While health service documents outline the usefulness of a hierarchy of evidence with the randomised-controlled trial (RCT) as the 'gold standard' with and 'expert opinion' at the lowest level (DoH 1996, 2001a, 2001b; Roth and Fonagy 1996) when thinking at a populations level, the psychological therapist has a different focus. Ours is the consideration of what this 'evidence' means for the client we sit with session after session and the psychotherapeutic project that has been engaged with. As well as an ethical discourse about appropriate therapy for particular patients, this chasm also results in dilemmas with regard to organising services that meet the demands of EBP yet are still relevant to the unique and very personal therapeutic journeys that are undertaken by 'mere' individuals.

The ethics of EBP are not just an issue for those therapists who deliver psychological therapies, of course. There are ethical issues at the level of research and service development as EBP requires service commissioners to consider the available 'evidence' and researchers to consider which research methodologies are relevant and appropriate to the task (DoH 1996; Milton 2001; Sandler et al. 2000). It is true that research at the level of populations may be useful in thinking ethically as RCTs enlighten psychotherapy with respect to epidemiology and a degree of response to 'treatment'. However, it is also important to consider the predominance that such an approach should have, as it cannot account for individual experience and the evolving and ongoing co-construction of meaning. Indeed, despite the best efforts of some of our technocrats we may never be able to technologise existence and develop as much certainty as we might wish for (Heaton 2001; Milton & Corrie 2002; Taylor 2000).

Another interesting and related question is the relationship that traditional, quantitative methodologies based on modernist assumptions can have to other research findings – formal research such as that undertaken by qualitative researchers (Dennis et al. 1994; Howe 1996) as well as those other forms of informal yet highly educative 'evidence' (Milton & Corrie 2002; Newnes 2001), for example biography and literature. EBP has not traditionally attended to these so there is a question as to whether this means that ethical therapists should ignore this knowledge base or use it without the traditional 'evidence'. This raises the question of what these other forms of research look like, the sort of evidence they generate and the manner in which we assess the ethical issues that may arise. These questions have resulted in a very active debate in the psychological professions (see Heaton 2001; Mace et al. 2001; Milton & Corrie 2002; Newnes 2001; Rowland & Goss 2000).

ETHICS AND METHODOLOGY

In terms of psychological therapy, the appropriateness of research and the evidence it generates is dependent upon an understanding of the nature of the relevant discipline and the aim of the research. Thus, psychological therapists are right to be cautious about adopting research methodologies directly from medicine or elsewhere before critically evaluating their ability to remain true to the psychotherapeutic aim and ethos and the ethics that govern such practice. One of the particular concerns is the difficulty in developing models of research and human science that recognise an appropriately attuned exploration of individual experience (Spinelli 2001).

This is, of course, a complex undertaking as different psychological therapies are based on different assumptions and practices and may therefore require different approaches to research. A definition of psychological therapy limited to the intrapsychic – for example some representations of psychoanalysis (Green 2000) – will offer different views on the nature of appropriate research as opposed to another understanding that might privilege the external or intersubjective, for example behavioural therapy. Yet both of course are relevant to the work of most psychological therapists when engaged in therapeutic work with the complex personalities humans are blessed (or burdened) by.

Another way of thinking about this is to examine current DoH policy (DoH 1996, 2001a, 2001b). Practitioners often recognise the difficulties in finding appropriate methodologies with which to explore the effects of interpretative and insight-oriented approaches to therapy. Indeed this difficulty has led to accusations of a lack of research in some areas – especially the insight-oriented psychotherapies. Despite the fact that this is a difficulty for psychoanalytic and systemic therapies in particular, it should not be taken to suggest that there is evidence against the usefulness of these psychological therapies. The Department of Health recognises this and its publications are littered with comments such as 'Other psychotherapeutic approaches have not been systematically reviewed/evaluated' (DoH 2001b: 24). In this context it is important to consider how free the psychological therapist is to engage with the knowledge that these models contribute to a rich understanding of individuals and systems without the permission from the EBP discourse? 'Free' in both legal and psychological terms.

Readers will be aware that the issues raised so far have implications for our stance to evidence and requires us to be cautious about the definitions of science, research and evidence that we adopt. It also requires us to think long and hard about the ethical implications of our knowledge bases and practices. While recognising that, for pragmatic reasons, much 'local' research undertaken in the health service is seen to be 'quick and dirty' in order to speedily explore a question or offer information to stakeholders, ethical issues arise when the psychological therapist feels that such research may sometimes do a disservice to science and to psychological therapy. This is not to suggest that psychological therapists and local services should not undertake small-scale and manageable research because, of course, as in therapy itself, a question may not need an extensive analysis when a concise, time-limited response will suffice. The issue of deciding which approach to take requires consideration of the question posed, the anticipated outcome, contextual realities and the impact on those being researched.

In terms of contextual realities, EBP is often silent – and this lack of attention to wider factors is problematic. Fonagy addresses the complexity of relationship between research and the application of research to practice when he notes the place of clinical work in psychoanalysis. He suggests that clinical work *is* research. The same argument seems valid for the broader field of the psychological therapies.

> The empirical basis of psychoanalysis is the clinical situation. The laboratory does not provide its empirical base and as the theory is not based on laboratory findings it cannot be either disproved or validated by them.
>
> (Fonagy 1982)

Fonagy's point is important as it again notes the chasm that can occur between academic research and clinical practice. This chasm leads to difficulties in making ethical decisions about practice due to the apparent reluctance to see the reality that psychological theory and practice cannot be based on as much certainty as we might hope for. If these two highly important domains (research and practice) are to usefully inform each other and generate fruitful dialogue (rather than deny or attack) we need some kind of bridging potential. Wallerstein outlines the qualities of what such a bridge might look like when he states:

> Research that is simultaneously faithful both to the highly subjectivistic and complex data of the psychoanalytic consulting-room and the so-called objective canons of the empirical scientific enquiry [. . .] should be, after all, the heart of what we call psychoanalytic research. (Wallerstein 2000: 28)

The notion of 'psychoanalytic research' is important here as by invoking such terms and working to include these in the EBP debate we may be in a position to clarify questions that will enlighten our therapeutic practices, and to give thought to the methods we might develop to explore them – without having to limit ourselves to the narrow confines of traditional and rather static quantitative methodologies. The advantages, of course, are that by having both a research and practice eye, both endeavours may be enriched.

These thoughts bring us to a crucial issue: if the psychological therapies recognise the limitations of some of the more orthodox approaches to research (or at least their inability to provide the answers that we would wish for within an EBP), what alternatives can it suggest to allow the field to develop greater clarity and therefore greater ability to undertake ethical research and provide ethical services and therapies? Some responses to this question seem to have argued the case for alternative methods to be used. Other responses have challenged the focus of the whole EBP debate and suggested alternative foci.

Alternative methodologies suggested are often qualitative[2] in nature and include that mainstay of psychoanalytic and psychotherapeutic research: case study methodologies (see Sandler *et al.* 2000). In some respect these already have a clear place in official EBP as a manifestation of innovative practice and case study evaluation (DoH 1996; see figure 21.1 for a diagrammatic representation of official EBP).

Recognition of the individualised, qualitative aspects of the EBP debate may free psychological therapists from the constraints they often report (see Milton 2001). It is important to note that as well as health targets on a population level, Health Service policies do support the psychological therapist in a personalised approach to practice through the activities of personalised assessment and decision-making on the specifics of each individual's need (DoH 2001a, 2001b). As case studies are so individually responsive to particular therapies, they have the potential to be used to illuminate factors in the therapeutic process as well as client characteristics. As with RCT methodologies they also have limitations – one being that by taking a case study approach the psychological therapist is not able to take a stance that their findings are generalisable at a population level and, of course, the presence of the author's subjectivity has both great advantages and its own difficulties. Each gives rise to a greater need to consider the ethics of the individual encounter.

In addition to their legitimacy as a research enterprise in their own right, case studies can also be used in other qualitative methodologies as the data for further and alternative analyses (Mitchell & Brownescombe Heller 1999; Milton 2001). Methodologies such as Discourse Analysis (DA), Grounded Theory, Thematic Content Analysis and Interpretive Phenomenological Analysis can all use a single case study or series of case studies to explore issues relevant to psychotherapy and the questions that EBP asks us to consider. Researchers have used DA on transcripts of therapy to review the 'to-and-fro' of therapeutic sessions in order to explore the manner in which unconscious mechanisms manifest themselves in psychodynamic work and

---

2 Developments in quantitative research methodologies are also possible; see, for example, single case design studies focused around the individual undertaken.

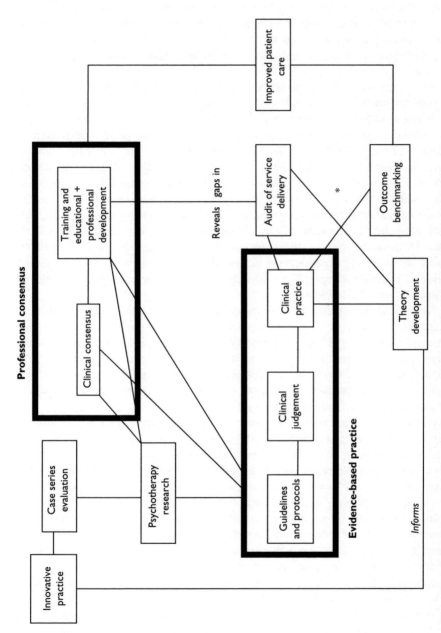

Figure 21.1 Representation of official evidence-based practice. (Reproduced from DoH (1996).)

the issues that this raises for therapeutic practice and provision (Diamond 2002; Lewis 2002). Other methodologies can, of course, be used independently of case study work. And of course the methods outlined above will all be able to offer interesting and unique perspectives on the question of useful and ethical practice and can be tailored to consider particular models of psychotherapy, specific population groups and issues related to therapist practices.

As mentioned above, those involved in the EBP debate have often thought critically and creatively about the issues involved and complementary positions have been recognised. One that is worth considering from an ethical position is that of practice-based evidence (PBE) (Barkham & Mellor Clark 2000; Carroll & Tholstrup 2001). As well as EBP making demands on those in the clinic, PBE attends to how research might be tailored to explicitly meet the agenda of those involved in the psychotherapeutic enterprise. This approach has only recently been invoked in the psychological therapy literature and therefore requires further development, including the development of guidelines and criteria for what PBE will look like. In principle it uses the evidence of the therapeutic process itself to assist clinicians and service providers to evaluate services. Such a stance values local and idiographic evidence as well as the nomothetic evidence available from RCT research.

As well as recognising the efforts of those in the clinic and those in academic contexts, it is very useful – and ethically important – when those charged with policy development collaborate in the EBP debate. While clinicians and researchers are aware of what Target calls 'feasible research' (1998: 79) it is important for this to be discussed with all those involved so that the value of what is possible is recognised and the desire for unrealistic answers is recognised and worked through by all involved.

It is also important to locate research within systems that have the required support. It is not possible for most NHS psychological therapy services to undertake research of the RCT type, and therefore it is appropriate to leave such large-scale research within government-sponsored academic departments with access to multi-site samples. This type of research needs well-resourced posts with adequate support. It would also be appropriate to consider the type of work that can occur in single-handed practices, community mental health teams and poorly resourced psychotherapy services. In these contexts psychological therapists often undertake their own literature reviews (for in-house consumption or to add to published literature in more accessible journals and newsletters). Of course, case studies are obviously relatively easy to undertake and to discuss as a way of promoting awareness of practice strategies as well as providing invaluable support to therapists. In addition, trainee therapists very often need to undertake service-related research for their training. Trust requirements for audit can also be useful in examining the relationship between practice and the literature. It may only be through effective dissemination and discussion of all these findings that truly ethical decisions can be made at all levels.

THE FOUR ETHICAL PRINCIPLES: ARE THEY ACHIEVABLE IN EBP?

While developments are occurring in the philosophy of science, it remains difficult for many to protect (or limit) the psychological therapies from the problems of the rational/traditional empiricist assumptions of a knowable truth. If it is possible to enrich science with a respect for what the psychological therapies can do, what do the stakeholders of the psychological therapies gain? What are the benefits that clients, therapists, health services and, of course, our society more broadly, might gain?

In this respect, the arguments are many and varied. Some have suggested that properly targeted and executed research has the potential to enrich our therapeutic work and in particular make the therapeutic enterprise more relevant to contemporary existence. In addition, where psychological therapy takes advantage of a range of research methodologies we are able to ensure that we explore questions from a range of perspectives and may thereby avoid some of the 'false causal connections, which may be read into a case history, or the story of a therapeutic intervention' (Target 1998: 81). As well as the 'in-session' benefits that may accrue when we undertake and use appropriately targeted research, there are also advantages to be gained for the relationship between those within the psychological therapies and those on the outside.

One benefit that is immediately apparent is to confirm to others – service commissioners and, of course, patients – that our efforts to assist people result in benefit rather than harm. There is already a body of evidence that we can draw upon to assert this; but the greater our body of evidence the more useful it can become (DoH 2001a; Fonagy 1999; Milton 1996; Roth & Fonagy 1996).

As well as a broad recognition of the benefits of the psychological therapies, there is also evidence of the nature of the benefit experienced by patients in psychotherapy. Authors in the field note that there are broad benefits taking the form of:

> reduced somatic symptoms or problems, more satisfying and loving relationships, greater capacity to cope with life and its problems, less use of medication, fewer GP visits, fewer episodes of violence or self-harm, less offending behaviour and more time spent in employment and fewer difficulties at work.
>
> (Mitchell & Brownescombe Heller 1999: 40)

It is interesting that the EBP debate also draws our attention to economic benefits in the form of fewer trips to Accident and Emergency departments, lower reliance on medication and visits to GPs, etc. (Mitchell & Brownescombe Heller 1999). While it is not possible to unpack all the ethical issues associated with finances and power, it is important that therapists note the importance given to this dimension in the debate and think more broadly about how this assists or compromises ethical thought and practice.

PROFESSIONAL RESPONSES TO EBP

Many psychological therapists are (at best) sceptical about the role of formal research in informing therapy. In fact, despite the pervasive nature of EBP rhetoric, there seems to be a reluctance to undertake research once core training is completed (Milton 2001) and even to regularly read up-to-date research reports. In this climate of research awareness it might be interesting to consider why this aspect is avoided.

Where therapists do engage in the EBP debate there is often a degree of anxiety evident about it (Milton 2001). Some have gone further and construct the call to EBP as an attack on themselves and their profession:

> Overvaluation of 'Research' often goes together with an undervaluation, or devaluation, of the research with which we engage in our psycho-analytic work. And if this Research (with a capital R) is privileged within psychoanalysis, we will, in order to placate and propitiate our enemies from without, succeed in destroying psychoanalysis from within. I believe this to be a 'real' (not just a fantasized) danger!
>
> (Brenman Pick 2000: 109)

These anxieties may develop for a number of reasons but some initial possibilities include a lack of familiarity with research and its potential and a lack of research training (Milton 2001; Target 1998). The limitations of research methodologies that confine their attention to symptom checklists and the 'manualisation of treatment' may also influence this (Target 1998). As indicated by Brenman Pick above, it may also be related to a realistic appraisal of the power and function of what Foucault termed the 'psy-complex' (Foucault 1995). In Foucauldian terms, the mental health systems and professions such as psychiatry, psychology and psychotherapy function as regulators of social interactions and thus he draws our attention to their joint powers. The EBP agenda is just one manifestation of this system with benefits and dangers – to all involved, clients and carers, therapists and managers. Clients may be 'sold' a more certain outcome than is realistically possible, therapists may have unrealistic demands on them and service providers may structure their services in ways to appease this agenda regardless of the impact on the client. In the midst of all the discussion of EBP 'a mental health service user made an apt observation: "So when are we going to talk about what works for me?" ' (Bond 2002). This is (or should be) the core ethical issue for all those involved in public sector healthcare.

As well as an 'objective' reading of the EBP literature it is interesting to note a tone of moral superiority that is woven through it. This tone attempts to discredit the therapeutic project and/or individual practitioners who are not able to quote indices of behavioural change. This is evident in the Government rhetoric about 'unqualified/bad practitioners', 'bad apples' and 'do-gooders with no training' (Parry 2001). It is interesting that a tone such as this seems to ignore the high quality of work that does occur, the level of skill that exists and also the goodwill that the NHS relies on. This will, of course, have an impact on the already vulnerable people that approach such services – as well as the well-being of those involved in the provision of services.

Left unattended, these dynamics threaten to spoil the potential for creative thought that originally drew so many psychotherapists into the field. Where this happens we must accept that rather than maximising benefit we might be limiting it. Rather than minimise harm we might ignore or contribute to it (for both clients and therapists). Rather than achieving the greatest good we might be limiting our attention to what can be afforded, and there are, of course, many questions to be asked about how just this would be?

Reflection on this issue is not just a task for psychological therapists on their own – it needs to be an inclusive debate. Without this, there is potential for misunderstandings at all sorts of levels – between those involved in research and those in practice and between commissioners and providers and users, with all the disruptive and destructive potential that this has. If we were to allow this to occur without due care, consideration and potentially correct-ive action it is unlikely that we would be seen to be exercising our ethical duties.

CONCLUSION

Hopefully this chapter has reminded all readers of the well-known but often-ignored reality, that psychological therapy, 'evidence' and EBP are all filled with uncertainty and lower limits of knowability than may be the case in other areas. The challenge we face is to engage with what we do know and what we do not know in a thoughtful and ethical manner with the best interests of our clients in mind. This aim may infuse our stances to the practice of psychological therapy as well as research and service develop-ment. The challenge also requires us to generalise what we know from the psychological therapies (e.g. about staying with uncertainty and aiming for collaborative, engaged and attuned discussions) to our relationships outside of the consulting room with colleagues at all levels of service organisation.

It may be important to consider the ways in which we can bridge the gaps in an effort to respond to the complex ethical issues that arise in EBP. A stance that facilitates the curiosity and interest that often motivates therapists is something that can easily be turned to the research endeavour. The most feasible (and interesting) approaches to research are those that draw on the well-honed skills used by psychological therapists every day – collaborative, qualitative approaches that value the attunement to the client's world of meaning. Grounded theory research of clients' understanding of characterological change through long-term insight-oriented therapy or DA research as to the presence of socio-political material in clients' narratives and its relationship to distress and recovery are two projects that come to mind and may be feasible within most psychological therapy services with nothing more than some time for continuing professional development.

REFLECTIVE QUESTIONS

1   If the evidence suggests that a form of therapy is useful for the majority of clients, how ethical is it to structure our services so that this is available but other approaches are not (e.g. short-term therapies in primary care settings or cognitive-behavioural models in secondary care services)?

2   As much of the EBP is researched with a view to behavioural change, how ethical is it to engage clients in therapy when their expressed wish is to review and reflect on their life without (at that point in time) an explicit goal?

3   If so much of the psychotherapy literature notes the importance of interpersonal factors in successful therapy, what are the ethics involved in training therapists to excel in the application of 'manualised treatments'?

4   How does the EBP debate facilitate the gathering of broad nomothetic information as well as local, individual experience?

REFERENCES

Baker, M. & Kleijnen, J. (2000) The drive towards evidence-based health care, in N. Rowland & S. Goss (eds.), *Evidence-based Counselling and Psychological Therapies: Research and Applications*. London: Routledge.

Barkham, M. & Mellor-Clark, J. (2000) Rigour and relevance: the role of practice-based evidence in the psychological therapies, in N. Rowland and S. Goss (eds.), *Evidence-based Counselling and Psychological Therapies: Research and Applications*. London: Routledge.

Bond, S. (2002) PPA Secretary's report: verbal rugby? *The Journal of Critical Psychology, Counselling and Psychotherapy*, 2(3), 200.

Brenman Pick, I. (2000) Discussion (III), in J. Sandler, A. M. Sandler & R. Davies (eds.), *Clinical and Observational Psychoanalytic Research: Roots of a Controversy: Andre Green and Daniel Stern*. London: Monograph Series of the Psychoanalysis Unit of University College London and the Anna Freud Centre London.

Carroll, M. & Tholstrup, M. (2001) *Integrative Approaches to Supervision*. London: Jessica Kingsley.

Dennis, M., Fetterman, D. M. & Sechrest, L. (1994) Integrating qualitative and quantitative evaluation methods in substance abuse research. *Evaluation and Program Planning*, 17, 419–427.

Diamond, D (2002) 'How rude can you get? The dialogic unconscious in therapy'. Unpublished PsychD Portfolio, University of Surrey.

DoH (Department of Health) (1996) *NHS Psychotherapy Services in England: Review of Strategic Policy*. Wetherby, UK: NHS Wetherby Executive.

DoH (Department of Health) (2001a) *Treatment Choice in Psychological Therapies and Counselling Evidence Based Clinical Practice Guidelines – Brief Version*. Wetherby, UK: NHS Executive.

DoH (Department of Health) (2001b) *Treatment Choice in Psychological Therapies and Counselling Evidence Based Clinical Practice Guidelines*. Wetherby, UK: NHS Executive.

Fonagy, P. (1982) The integration of psychoanalysis and experimental science: a review. *International Journal of Psycho-Analysis*, 9, 125–145.

Fonagy, P. (1999) *An Open Door Review of Outcome Studies in Psychoanalysis. Report of the Research Committee of the Institute of Psycho-Analysis*. London: University College/Institute of Psycho-Analysis.

Foucault, M. (1995) *Madness and Civilization: A History of Insanity in the Age of Reason*. London: Routledge.

Green, A. (2000) Science and science fiction in infant research, in J. Sandler, A. M. Sandler & R. Davies (eds.), *Clinical and Observational Psychoanalytic Research: Roots of a Controversy: Andre Green and Daniel Stern*. London: Monograph Series of the Psychoanalysis Unit of University College London and the Anna Freud Centre London.

Heaton, J. (2001) Evidence and psychotherapy. *European Journal of Psychotherapy, Counselling and Health*, 4(2), 237–248.

Howe, D. (1996) Client experiences of counselling and treatment interventions: a qualitative study of family views of family therapy. *British Journal of Guidance and Counselling*, 24, 367–376.

Lewis, Y. (2002) 'A discourse analysis of clients' self-blame in psychotherapy sessions'. Unpublished PsychD Portfolio, University of Surrey.

Mace, C., Moorey, S. & Roberts, B. (2001) *Evidence in the Psychological Therapies: A Critical Guide for Practitioners*. Boston, MA: Brunner-Routledge.

Milton, J. (1996) *Presenting the Case for Psychoanalytic Psychotherapy Services: An Annotated Bibliography* (3rd edn.). Jointly sponsored by The Association for Psychoanalytic Psychotherapy in the NHS and The Tavistock Clinic, supported by the Psychotherapy Section of the Royal College of Psychiatrists.

Milton, M. (2001) Supervision: researching therapeutic practice, in M. Carroll and M. Tholstrup (eds.), *Integrative Approaches to Supervision*. London: Jessica Kingsley.

Milton, M. & Corrie, S. (2002) Exploring the place of technical and implicit knowledge in therapy. *The Journal of Critical Psychology, Counselling and Psychotherapy*, 2(3), 188–197.

Mitchell, S. & Brownescombe Heller, M. (1999) Why purchase psychoanalytic psycho-therapy on the NHS? A set of guidelines. *Clinical Psychology Forum*, 134, 36–40.

Newnes, C. (2001) On evidence. *Clinical Psychology*, 1, 6–12.

Palmer Barnes, F. (1998) *Complaints and Grievances in Psychotherapy: A Handbook of Ethical Practice*. London: Routledge.

Parry, G. (2001) *Evidence Based Psychotherapy: What Really Matters?* Keynote speech to the UKCP NHS Forum Conference Psychotherapy and Evidenced Based Practice for the NHS, Regents College, London, July 11th.

Roth, A. & Fonagy, P. (1996) *What Works for Whom: A Critical Review of the Psychotherapy Outcome Literature*. London: Guilford Press.

Rowland, N. and Goss, S. (eds.) (2000) *Evidence-based Counselling and Psychological Therapies: Research and Applications*. London: Routledge.

Sandler, J., Sandler, A. M. & Davie, R. (2000) *Clinical and Observational Psycho-analytic Research: Roots of a Controversy: Andre Green and Daniel Stern*. London: Monograph Series of the Psychoanalysis Unit of University College London and the Anna Freud Centre London.

Spinelli, E. (2001) Turning the obvious into the problematic: the issue of evidence from a human science perspective. Presentation to the Round Table Discussion Evidence Based Research, 'Qualitative or Quantitative: Pros and Cons'. UKCP NHS Forum Conference Psychotherapy and Evidenced Based Practice for the NHS, Regents College, London, July 11th.

Target, M. (1998) Approaches to evaluation. *European Journal of Psychotherapy, Counselling and Health*, 1(1), 79–92.

Taylor, M. (2000) Wendy's dread: a case study. *European Journal of Psychotherapy, Counselling and Health*, 3(2), 169–180.

Wallerstein, R. S. (2000) Psychoanalytic research: where do we disagree?, in J. Sandler, A. M. Sandler & R. Davies (eds.), *Clinical and Observational Psychoanalytic Research: Roots of a Controversy: Andre Green and Daniel Stern*. London: Monograph Series of the Psychoanalysis Unit of University College London and the Anna Freud Centre London.

Chapter 22

Mandatory personal therapy for therapists: professional and ethical issues

Andrew Grimmer

> But where and how is the poor wretch to acquire the ideal qualification which he will need in this profession? The answer is in an analysis of himself, with which his preparation for his future activity begins.
>
> (Freud 1937/1943)

In order to become a registered practitioner in most forms of therapeutic training in the UK it is now a requirement to have had personal therapy. The great majority of member organisations of the UK Council for Psychotherapy require their members to have had personal therapy, although at least three from both cognitive-behavioural and systemic orientations do not require it. For counselling psychologists to be eligible for Chartered Psychologist status with the British Psychological Society (BPS) they must have at least 40 hours of personal therapy during training BPS (2003). Since October 1998 the British Association for Counselling and Psychotherapy (BACP) has required applicants for Individual Counsellor Accreditation to complete a minimum of 40 hours of personal counselling, or demonstrate that they have had an equivalent experience of being a client, consistent with their core theoretical model, although not necessarily during training (BACP 2003a). Applicants must describe how therapy has contributed to their development as a counsellor and how it benefits their work with clients (BACP 2003b). Currently there is no requirement for trainee clinical or educational psychologists to have any personal therapy. For the purpose of this chapter the term 'therapy' is used interchangeably with counselling. The term 'therapist' is used to refer to psychotherapists, counsellors and psychologists.

A historical context and current rationales for the requirement for personal therapy will be given to help in understanding the current situation, the professional and ethical context and the differing views surrounding this requirement. It is a topic that raises strong feelings. The change in rules leading to the BACP's 40-hour requirement generated much discussion and debate within the therapeutic profession from the assertion that 'prospective entrants to the profession might be excused the impression that this is a financial scam designed to provide work for private practitioners' (Mearns *et al.* 1998) to remarks such as 'I find it astonishing that any practising counsellor/psychotherapist would not, at some point, have been in personal therapy' (Rosen 1997).

The idea that personal therapy is a desirable prerequisite for clinical work is described as 'one of the most firmly held and cherished beliefs among psychotherapists' (Norcross *et al.* 1988). It can be traced back as far as the biblical adage 'Physician, heal thyself' (Luke 4:23, cited in Sinason (1999)) and possibly more distantly to the injunction inscribed on the temple of Apollo at Delphi to 'Know thyself', or to Socrates' dictum that the unexamined life is not worth living (paraphrased in Thorne & Dryden (1991)). In contemporary psychotherapy the important position that personal therapy holds in the training of psychoanalysts and psychodynamic psychotherapists (Rawn (1991) *inter alia*) can be traced to Freud who saw the purpose of the trainee's analysis as giving the learner a firm conviction of the existence of the unconscious in order to lend credibility through personal experience to the emergence of repressed material which would otherwise 'be incredible to him' (Freud 1937/1943). Within the psychoanalytic tradition a substantial personal therapy, known as the 'training analysis', is regarded as a prerequisite for developing professional competence. The therapy should start well before the individual presents themselves as a candidate for training and the therapist is usually required to give the training committee an opinion on the individual's readiness to train as well as to state when they think the individual is ready to take their first training patient. Personal analysis on a three to five times weekly basis forms the core of most psychoanalytic training and is viewed as an essential foundation for trainee therapists and an integral component of their training as therapists. In other therapeutic trainings it is more common for trainees to be required to have personal therapy of a type, duration and frequency that is consistent with the therapy they are intending to practise.

RATIONALE FOR PERSONAL THERAPY FOR TRAINEES

Several rationales supporting personal therapy for trainees recur throughout the literature (Fleischer & Wissler 1985; Guy 1987). Norcross *et al.* (1988) summarise them as:

- Improved emotional and mental functioning of the psychotherapist. There is a suggestion that 'healthier' or less disturbed therapists secure greater positive change in their clients (Fromm-Reichmann 1950; Garfield & Bergin 1971).
- Providing the therapist-patient with a more complete understanding of

personal dynamics, interpersonal elicitations, use of self and conflictual issues (Woolfe 1996; McLeod 1993).

• Alleviating the emotional stresses and burdens inherent in this 'impossible profession' (Freud 1937/1943).
• By serving as a profound socialisation experience.
• By placing therapists in the role of client and thus sensitising them to the interpersonal reactions and needs of their own clients.
• By providing a first-hand, intensive opportunity to observe clinical methods.

Whilst personal therapy is sometimes seen as a controversial component of training, Macran and Shapiro (1998) note that there have been relatively few empirical investigations of the efficacy of personal therapy in the training of therapists, despite the general acceptance of its usefulness amongst therapists. They note that the issue needs clarification and further research. Some of the research that has been conducted to date will be briefly reviewed.

RESEARCH STUDIES

Two major reviews of the subject (Macaskill 1988; Macran & Shapiro 1998) group the literature into four main types of study. Each type of study will be briefly examined in the next sections of this chapter.

1   Surveys of therapists' evaluations of personal therapy.
2   Experimental studies, evaluating therapist responses in situations analogous to real therapy.
3   Outcome studies, comparing therapy outcome for therapists who have received personal therapy and those who have not received therapy.
4   Process studies, examining the within-session interactions between therapists and clients for therapists who have received personal therapy and those who have not.

1. Surveys of therapists' evaluations of personal therapy

The majority of therapists in a study reported by Macran and Shapiro (1998) felt positive about their time in therapy and reported it as being valuable to them professionally in facilitating clinical effectiveness and preventing burnout. Some believed it was the single most important part of their training in psychotherapy, and recommended it as an essential training experience for all future therapists. Henry *et al.* (1971) found 33 per cent of therapists rated personal therapy a major influence on their personal life compared to 14 per cent on their professional life, with 45 per cent rating influence on professional life as low or nil; 32 per cent rated influence on personal life as nil. A decade later, Buckley *et al.* (1981) noted that specific outcomes included: improvements in self-esteem (94 per cent); improvements in work function (86 per cent); improvements in social/sex life (86 per cent); characterological changes (89 per cent), and symptomatic improvements (73 per cent).

Unsatisfactory outcomes are also reported, again to varying degrees. In a study of approximately 2,700 psychotherapists, 33 per cent of respondents cited some of the following areas of dissatisfaction: lack of therapist skill, that insufficient problems were resolved and, frequently, a feeling that further therapy beyond the time-limited training analysis was indicated (Henry *et al.* 1971). In a smaller study of 122 analysts, 15 per cent felt dissatisfied with 13 respondents citing major difficulties with their training analyst and 6 having a further analysis with a different therapist. Several were still enraged years later (Shapiro 1976).

In a survey of the careers of 52 psychotherapists, Goldberg (1992) found that although some greatly valued personal therapy, others were disappointed or even bitter about their experiences. In Shapiro's (1976) study many respondents noted that the training analysis and the training setting imposed substantial, and at times insurmountable, emotional burdens. It is a sad irony that personal therapy, which is seen as (among other things) a remedy for the occupational stress of practising therapy, can become a significant emotional burden for the trainee. There is also evidence that therapeutic skills suffer when inexperienced therapists are in therapy and treating others at the same time, perhaps because therapists become preoccupied by conflicts aroused by their own therapy (Garfield & Bergin 1971; Greenberg & Staller 1981; Strupp 1958a, 1973). Macran and Shapiro (1998) note that the kinds of problems reported by trainees are not dissimilar to those experienced by therapy clients in general, including depression, marital and relationship difficulties and 'becoming too reflective'.

In Dublin, 38 out of 40 clinical and counselling psychology graduates reported that personal therapy should be included as a part of training, the view of the 20 counselling psychology participants being unanimously in favour (Rothery 1992). However, this finding should be treated with caution, as the survey does not report actual levels of take-up of personal therapy during training. The 25 per cent of clinical psychology graduate student respondents to Holzman *et al.* (1996) who had never been in therapy cited two main reasons: having no need for it (56 per cent), and finances (53 per cent).

Several studies have examined the impact of personal therapy on opinions as to the validity of therapy itself. MacDevitt (1987) found that 82 per cent of his sample of therapists felt that personal therapy was valuable, a view that was supported by Macaskill and Macaskill (1992) who reported that 83 per cent of respondents maintained or increased their levels of enthusiasm for therapy as a treatment following their own therapy. Even amongst respondents who reported negative effects, the utility of therapy was not necessarily invalidated, with many respondents rationalising the experience with comments of the 'no pain, no gain' variety (Macaskill 1999). Macaskill (1999) also points out that trainees invest a lot of time, energy and finance in their personal therapy so that it is not surprising that it was felt to offer significant benefits.

A survey of British counselling psychologists found that, as in North American studies, most respondents rated outcome and process as positive, whilst 27 per cent also reported some negative effects (Williams *et al.* 1999). Factor analysis identified three factors: learning about therapy; issues arising out of training; and personal issues. The degree of motivation seemed to be related to personal issues, whereas learning about therapy was related to a greater number of sessions.

2. Experimental studies, evaluating therapist responses in situations analogous to real therapy

Also known as analogue studies, these are laboratory-based studies of therapist's responses to situations supposedly analogous to real-life therapy. Strupp has carried out most experimental studies. His original study (Strupp 1955) found little difference between analysed and non-analysed therapists, except that analysed therapists tended to make fewer silent responses and more active ones. That result was contradicted by his 1958 study in which he found that analysed therapists gave a larger number of silent responses (1958a).

In another study Strupp (1958b) found that inexperienced therapists who had been in analysis obtained worse empathy ratings than those who had no personal therapy, but at higher levels of experience it was the analysed therapists who were seen as significantly more empathic, regardless of attitude to the client, whether positive or negative. Although a majority in both groups admitted a negative attitude towards clients, non-analysed therapists were more likely to communicate a negative attitude. As Macaskill (1999) points out, this finding could be interpreted as suggesting that, at least with certain clients, analysed therapists are less effective clinically if therapist genuineness is a significant factor in therapeutic outcome. However, Strupp's studies are weakened by small sample size in some studies and low levels of statistical significance in others, making it difficult to draw firm conclusions from his work (Macaskill 1988). It is also unclear to what extent the therapists' responses reflected their real-life behaviour (Macran & Shapiro 1998).

A study by MacDevitt (1987) found that the number of personal therapy hours, rather than the receipt of therapy per se, was significantly positively correlated with the use of countertransference awareness (CA), i.e. the use of self-examination in order to understand clients, independent of whether the therapist's background was psychoanalytic. It was also positively correlated with reports of personal therapy being of professional value, although it is unclear what relationship exists, if any, between the use of CA and client outcome.

3. Outcome studies, comparing therapy outcome for therapists who have received personal therapy and those who have not received therapy

According to Macran and Shapiro (1998), three major reviews of the outcome literature (Macaskill 1988; Clark 1986; Greenberg & Staller 1981) all conclude that 'there is no evidence that either receipt of personal therapy or length of personal therapy is positively related to various measures of client outcome' (p. 19). Kernberg (1973) found a positive relationship between personal therapy and client improvement, but did not factor out therapist experience. Guild (1969) found that experienced analysed psychotherapists had a more effective therapeutic relationship with clients than did non-analysed therapists. Because previous studies had found the relationship qualities of warmth, empathy and genuineness led to better outcomes it was assumed, although not directly tested, that the results supported the hypothesis that therapy for therapists benefited clients (Greenberg & Staller 1981).

Katz et al. (1958) found ratings of patient improvement had no relationship with personal therapy for the therapist, although they did find outcome was more related to therapist experience. McNair et al. (1963) found there was no significant difference in dropout rates for clients of therapists who had had, or had not had, personal therapy. However Greenspan and Kulish (1985) found that therapists who had received personal therapy had significantly lower premature termination rates than those who had not. Four other studies found no significant difference (Derner 1960; Holt & Luborsky 1958; McNair et al. 1964; Strupp et al. 1969) and one found a negative effect (Garfield & Bergin 1971), although small sample size makes this last finding tentative at best.

4. Process studies

A number of studies have attempted to look at the relationship between personal therapy for therapists, and clients' and therapists' ratings of within-session experience. As previously presented, Strupp's analogue studies (1958b: 1973) rated empathy levels, although the results were contradictory. Wogan and Norcross (1985) found that therapists who had received personal therapy placed greater emphasis on their personal relationship with clients whereas those with no therapy tended to be more technique orientated. Peebles (1980) found that the number of hours of therapy experienced as a client to be significantly related ($p < 0.5$) to therapists' ability to display empathy and genuineness as rated by independent observers, although not to the presence or absence of personal therapy.

OTHER RELEVANT RESEARCH

One thing that all studies seem to agree on is the need for further research. However, it has been argued that it may be more fruitful to pursue process, rather than outcome, issues because of methodological problems and because receipt of personal therapy may be confounded with other therapist characteristics, such as motivation (Macran & Shapiro 1998). It may therefore be more useful to ask therapists to describe the ways in which they believe their personal therapy helps them to deal with particular therapeutic situations or clients by collecting qualitative accounts of therapists' experiences of their own therapy and how they think it has affected their work with clients.

There are at present relatively few such qualitative studies in print. However, there are three such studies on the experience of personal therapy for experienced and trainee Clinical Social Workers (Mackey & Mackey 1993, 1994; Mackey *et al.* 1993). In addition Grimmer and Tribe (2001) sought accounts of personal therapy from British counselling psychologists and counselling psychology trainees. Participants in the various studies by Mackey and Mackey had sought therapy voluntarily in order to ameliorate personal conflict, as opposed to those in the study by Grimmer and Tribe, where therapy was a requirement of training. Whilst results are similar to previous quantitative studies on the perceived impact of personal therapy on professional development, the qualitative studies include fuller accounts of the process from the trainee's perspective. Both Mackey and Mackey (1993) and Grimmer and Tribe (2001) found that the therapist became a potent role model. Paradoxically, both sets of studies found instances when trainees adopted therapist behaviours that they had experienced negatively because they saw them of being to the benefit of the client in the longer term, such as the ability to tolerate silence.

HOW RELIABLE IS THE RESEARCH TO DATE?

Although widespread therapist satisfaction with personal therapy is frequently reported, the literature is problematic. Most research has been conducted in the USA and been based on studies of psychiatrists, psychologists and social workers. It almost invariably refers to psychodynamic psychotherapy (Macran & Shapiro 1998) and there is a paucity of research that specifically addresses the experience of mandatory personal therapy.

The absence of a clear relationship between personal therapy and therapist efficacy can be attributed to a number of factors, including diverse reasons for entering therapy (Beutler *et al.* 1994; Macran & Shapiro 1998). Macran and Shapiro (1998) note that whilst evidence for a direct effect of personal therapy on client outcome is 'inconclusive' it should be understood that research has also failed to demonstrate evidence for professional training having a consistently good effect on outcome for clients (Christensen & Jacobsen 1994).

Macran and Shapiro (1998) provide a thorough critique of the methodological and conceptual shortcomings of much of the research. These include:

- Sample size: survey-based research suffers from low response rates (40–50 per cent) leading to a bias towards positive experiences of personal therapy. In addition, most samples have consisted solely of psychodynamic therapists. Process studies have usually involved only small numbers and their failure to find any effect may be due to lack of sensitivity.
- Lack of control: most studies do not include a control group. For example, level of experience as a therapist and receipt of personal therapy are usually confounded yet many studies fail to control for it. There is also a general failure to control for the diverse reasons for entering therapy (Beutler *et al.* 1994).
- Outcome measures: different studies have used various measures of outcome (see Peebles 1980).

In addition some of the research is now rather old and further studies are required to enhance our understanding of this complex area at a time when the profession is undergoing considerable changes in the light of potential compulsory registration and the drive towards empirically sound, evidence-based practice. It should also be borne in mind that regulations regarding the requirements of trainees to undertake a particular amount of personal therapy over a particular period of time may vary as training organisations change their regulations and thus the research may not always reflect the latest situation.

Having said that, the sheer diversity of training institutions with differing underlying philosophies and theoretical models means that personal therapy will be seen as having a very different role to play in the professional development of practitioners. And whilst the efficacy of personal therapy has not been validated empirically it is believed to be efficacious by many therapists and relevant training committees, although not unanimously. Also each sub-group of professionals (counsellors, therapists, different types of psychologists and analysts) will find their personal therapy located in a different matrix of other training, theoretical models, organisational and professional values, varied curricula and other requirements. These are likely to reflect the culture and values of the chosen training organisation, and might influence the individual trainee's perceptions of personal therapy and the values ascribed to it.

ARGUMENTS FOR AND AGAINST PERSONAL THERAPY AS A COMPULSORY COMPONENT OF TRAINING

Whilst voluntarily undertaken personal therapy in training is strongly supported (Thorne & Dryden 1991) the link is less clear when the therapy is viewed as an unwanted obligation and does not appear to fit with the philosophy or theoretical model of the trainees. McLeod (1993) lists five possible reasons for this;

1   The lack of choice militates against the potential efficacy of the therapy.
2   The uncovering of difficult emotional material can reduce the effective participation of the student in other areas of the course.
3   The trainee may persist with unsatisfactory therapy to comply with course requirements.
4   It may be difficult to justify the allocation of counselling as a scarce resource to trainees rather than to people in crisis.
5   The cost may place counsellor training even further out of the reach of people from socially disadvantaged groups.

McLeod (1993) does not regard the arguments against mandatory therapy as conclusive, suggesting that it could be argued that, if therapy results in a personal crisis, it is better that it happens in this arena rather than in their work with clients. A strong argument for the continuation of personal therapy in training, he adds, is that it helps to ensure the centrality of acceptance of the client role. He also includes the necessity of counsellors being aware of when they need help and to feel all right about seeking it, and says that the completion of personal therapy can represent a '*rite de passage*' into a professional role. However, Thorne and Dryden (1991) point out that without an obligation to undergo personal therapy, the trainee may avoid dealing with personal issues properly.

While brief mandatory therapy offers no guarantee that the trainee will make use of the opportunity to examine personal issues, it would ensure that a trainee who develops difficulties in response to personal issues triggered by participation in training has a pre-existing relationship in which they can be resolved. However, concerns have been expressed that some trainees might see personal therapy as 'the' arena for self-development and will therefore not fully engage with other parts of the training programme (Thorne & Dryden 1991).

The above arguments take a very different stance to the training requirements of psychodynamic psychotherapists or analysts where, as we have seen, personal therapy must begin some time, often years, before the potential trainee can be considered for training, and being an approved member of that training institution is seen as proving the quality of the therapy being offered. It is claimed that therapy in these cases is to ensure that the trainee has worked, or has begun to work through any personal issues which might prevent them practising as safe and effective therapists. The therapy is part of the assessment procedure and it is assumed, and in fact desired, that this is where personal development would occur. Those advocating different positions are likely to continue to hold different views as these stances reflect wider differences between the theoretical models within the generic profession of therapy.

CONCLUSION

In summary, it appears that ranges of views on the effectiveness of mandatory personal therapy for therapists are held. The majority of therapists and training institutions are in favour of it and believe it not only works but also contributes significantly to the work of therapists. Others believe that, because the evidence for personal therapy having a positive impact on clinical effectiveness is inconclusive, it cannot be justified as a requirement of training, given the financial and emotional costs involved.

Undoubtedly, the issue of mandatory personal therapy is complex and the debate reflected in this chapter in some part illustrates the wider philosophical and cultural differences advocated and represented by the different theoretical orientations and their proponents. Research findings are contradictory and are hindered by a number of methodological difficulties inherent in measuring the 'success' or otherwise of mandatory personal therapy.

Clearly those from the varying training organisations and therapeutic models view the purpose of mandatory personal therapy differently. It could be argued that it may not ultimately be a case of proving one or the other is right but recognising and understanding the different theoretical and philosophical traditions held by each and deciding one's own position. That would be likely to determine which type of training institution and theoretical model one wishes to train in, which in turn will determine the related personal therapy requirements. However, the number of options to train as a therapist without mandatory personal therapy is now few, whatever modality one chooses to specialise in.

One thing that is clear is that the subject is considered very important by practitioners and raises very strong feelings. Indeed Norcross *et al.* (1988) observe that the topic has been 'shrouded in mystique, defensiveness and anxiety sometimes bordering on the irrational' (p. 37). On the one hand are those practitioners who believe that to practise therapy without having experienced it oneself is incredibly irresponsible and dangerous to both client and practitioner. On the other there are those practitioners who do not see it as essential and argue that, for many, personal development can be achieved in less taxing ways and that personal therapy is only indicated when the clinician's psychological conflicts significantly impair their ability to practise safely and effectively.

REFLECTIVE QUESTIONS

1   What impact, if any, has personal therapy had on your personal and professional development?
2   What are your views on therapists practising who have never had personal therapy?
3   Would you accept a client (trainee) who says that s/he is only having therapy because it is part of the course requirements? If so, how would you go about the therapy?
4   Under what circumstances would you have personal therapy?

REFERENCES

BACP (2003a) Accreditation of individuals. http://www.bacp.co.uk [retrieved 14.3.03].

BACP (2003b) Accreditation forms. http://www.bacp.co.uk/forms/accred_pack_form.html [retrieved 14.3.03].

Beutler, L., Machado, P. & Neufelt, S. (1994) Therapist variables, in A. E. Bergin & S. L. Garfield (eds.), *Handbook of Psychotherapy and Behavior Change*, 4th edn. New York: John Wiley.

BPS (2003) Chartered Counselling Psychologists' training and areas of competence. http://www.bps.org.uk/su-syst/dcop/competence.cfm [retrieved 14/3/03].

Buckley, P., Karasu, T.B. & Charles, E. (1981) Psychotherapists view their personal therapy. *Psychotherapy: Theory, Research and Practice*, 18, 299–305.

Christensen, A. & Jacobsen, N.S. (1994) Who (or what) can psychotherapy do: the status and challenge of non-professional therapists. *Psychological Science*, 5, 8–14.

Clark, M. (1986) Personal therapy: A review of empirical research. *Professional Psychology: Research and Practice*, 17, 541–543.

Derner, G. F. (1960) An interpersonal approach to training in psychotherapy, in N. P. Dellis & H. K. Stone (eds.), *The Training of Psychotherapists*. Baton Rouge, LA: Louisiana State University Press.

Fleischer, J. A. & Wissler, A. (1985) The therapist as patient: special problems and considerations. *Psychotherapy*, 22, 587–594.

Freud, S. (1937/1943) Analysis terminable and interminable, in J. Strachey (ed.), Complete Psychological Works of Sigmund Freud. Hogarth Press: London.

Fromm-Reichmann, F. (1950) *Principles of Intensive Psychotherapy*. Chicago: University of Chicago Press.

Garfield, S. & Bergin, A. (1971) Personal therapy outcome and some therapist variables. *Psychotherapy: Theory, Research and Practice*, 8(3), 251–253.

Goldberg, C. (1992) *The Seasoned Psychotherapist*. New York: Norton.

Greenberg, R. & Staller, J. (1981) Personal therapy for therapists. *American Journal of Psychiatry*, 138, 1467–1471.

Greenspan, M. & Kulish, N. (1985) Factors in premature termination in long-term psychotherapy. *Psychotherapy*, 22, 75–82.

Grimmer, A. G. & Tribe, R. (2001) Counselling psychologists' perceptions of the impact of mandatory personal therapy on professional development – an exploratory study. *Counselling Psychology Quarterly*, 14(4), 287–301.

Guild, M. (1969) 'Therapeutic effectiveness of analysed and nonanalysed therapists'. Doctoral dissertation, St. John's University, New York.

Guy, J. (1987) *The Personal Life of the Psychotherapist*. New York: John Wiley.

Henry, W. E., Sims, J. H. & Spray, S. L. (1971) *The Fifth Profession*. San Francisco: Jossey-Bass.

Holt, R. R. & Luborsky, L. (1958) *Personality Patterns of Psychiatrists: A Study of Selection Techniques*, Vol. 1. New York: Basic Books.

Holzman, L. A., Searight, H. R. & Hughes, H. M. (1996) Clinical psychology graduate students and personal psychotherapy: results of an exploratory survey. *Professional Psychology: Research and Practice*, 27(1), 98–101.

Katz, M. M., Lorr, M. & Rubinstein, E. A. (1958) Remainer patient attributes and their relation to subsequent improvement in psychotherapy. *Journal of Consultative Psychology*, 22, 411–414.

Kernberg, O. F. (1973) Summary and conclusions of 'Psychotherapy and Psychoanalysis, Final Report of the Menninger Foundation's Psychotherapy Research Project'. *International Journal of Psychiatry and Medicine*, 11, 62–67.

Macaskill, A. (1999) Personal therapy as a training requirement: the lack of supporting evidence, in C. Feltham (ed.), *Controversies in Psychotherapy and Counselling*. London: Sage.

Macaskill, N. (1988) Personal therapy in the training of the psychotherapist: is it effective? *British Journal of Psychotherapy*, 4(3), 199–226.

Macaskill, N. D. & Macaskill, A. (1992) Psychotherapists-in-training evaluate their personal therapy: results of a UK survey. *British Journal of Psychotherapy*, 9, 133–138.

MacDevitt, J. (1987) Therapists' personal therapy and professional self-awareness. *Psychotherapy*, 24, 693–703.

Mackey, R. & Mackey, E. (1993) The value of personal psychotherapy to clinical practice. *The Clinical Social Work Journal*, 21(1), 97–109.

Mackey, R. & Mackey, E. (1994) Personal psychotherapy and the development of a professional self. *Families in Society: The Journal of Contemporary Human Services*, 75(8), 490–498.

Mackey, R., Mackey, E. & O'Brien, B. (1993) Personal psychotherapy and the social work student. *Journal of Teaching in Social Work*, 7(2), 129–146.

Macran, S. & Shapiro, D.A. (1998) The role of personal therapy for therapists: a review. *British Journal of Medical Psychology*, 71, 13–25.

McLeod, J. (1993) *An Introduction to Counselling*. Buckingham: Open University Press.

McNair, D. M., Lorr, M. & Callahan, D. M. (1963) Patient and therapist influences on quitting psychotherapy. *Journal of Consulting Psychology*, 27, 10–17.

McNair, D. M., Lorr, M., Young, H., Roth, I. & Boyd, R. (1964) A three-year follow-up of psychotherapy patients. *Journal of Clinical Psychology*, 20, 258–264.

Mearns, D., Dryden, W., McLeod, J. & Thorne, B. (1998) Letter to the editor, *Counselling: The Journal of the British Association for Counselling*, 9(2), 83.

Norcross, J., Strausser-Kirtland, D. & Missar, C. (1988) The processes and outcomes of psychotherapists' personal treatment experiences. *Psychotherapy*, 25(1), 36–43.

Peebles, M. J. (1980) Personal therapy and ability to display empathy, warmth and genuineness in psychotherapy. *Psychotherapy: Theory, Research and Practice*, 17, 258–262.

Rawn, M. (1991) Training analysis and training psychotherapy. *Psychoanalytic Psychology*, 8(1), 43–57.

Rosen, J. (1997) Letter to the editor. *Counselling: The Journal of the British Association for Counselling*, 8(4), 246.

Rothery, N. (1992) Personal growth work in the training of counselling and clinical psychologists in Ireland. *Irish Journal of Psychology*, 13(2), 168–175.

Shapiro, D. (1976) The analyst's analysis. *Journal of the American Psychoanalytical Association*, 24, 5–42.

Sinason, V. (1999) In defence of therapy for training, in C. Feltham (ed.), *Controversies in Psychotherapy and Counselling*. London: Sage.

Strupp, H. (1955) The effect of the psychotherapist's personal analysis upon his techniques. *Journal of Consulting Psychology*, 19, 197–204.

Strupp, H. (1958a) The psychotherapist's contribution to the treatment process. *Behavioural Science*, 5, 34–67.

Strupp, H. (1958b) The performance of psychiatrists and psychologists in a therapeutic interview. *Journal of Clinical Psychology*, 14, 219–226.

Strupp, H. (1973) The therapists' performance: A comparison of two professional groups. In H. Strupp (ed.), *Psychotherapy: Clinical, Research and Theoretical Issues*. New York: Jason Aronson.

Strupp, H., Fox, R. & Lessler, K. (1969) *Patients View their Psychotherapy*. Baltimore, MD: Johns Hopkins University Press.

Thorne, B. & Dryden, W. (1991) Key issues in the training of counsellors, in W. Dryden & B. Thorne (eds.), *Training and Supervision for Counselling in Action*. London: Sage.

Williams, F., Coyle, A. & Lyons, E. (1999) How counselling psychologists view their personal therapy. *British Journal of Medical Psychology*, 72, 545–555.

Wogan, M. & Norcross, J. (1985) Dimensions of therapeutic skills and techniques: empirical identification, therapist correlates and predictive utility. *Psychotherapy*, 22, 63–74.

Woolfe, R. (1996) Counselling psychology in Britain: past, present and future. *Counselling Psychology Review*, 11, 7–18.

Chapter 23

Teaching ethics for professional practice

Shirley Morrissey

One of the hallmarks of a professional discipline is the status of its ethical code. It is each individual's responsibility to know and understand the particular standards for the professional group one is a member of. The British Association of Counsellors and Psychotherapists (BACP), the British Psychological Society (BPS) and the United Kingdom Council for Psychotherapy (UKCP) each have professional standards which are described in their respective codes and that counsellors, psychologists and psychotherapists, are professionally bound to comply with. Similarly, in other countries, professional societies also subscribe to professional codes of conduct and ethical practice, for example, the American Psychological Association (APA), and the Australian Psychological Society (APS). While professional societies may differ in their approach to advising members of their particular professional standards, there is an expectation that the codes have and achieve similar purposes. These include, the protection of the public, the promotion of sound professional practice or optimal behaviour, the regulation of inappropriate behaviour with the authority to police and discipline members of the profession, and to protect the integrity of the profession.

This chapter identifies a number of issues relating to adherence to or compliance with professional codes of practice, explores the need for teaching or training therapists in ethics, and attempts to address three key issues in the teaching and training of ethical behaviour:

1   When should ethical instruction be introduced and what should it include?
2   What are the 'best practice' or preferred teaching methods for developing ethical practice?
3   How is knowledge and ethical behaviour best monitored and assessed?

The Counselling and Clinical Division of the BPS (2001, 2003) and the APS (2002) supplement their respective ethical codes with Guidelines for Ethical Practice. These guidelines describe the 'high standards of practice to which psychologists should aspire' (Lindsay & Colley 1995: 448). The BACP replaced its Code of Ethics and Practice for Counsellors (1990) with the 2001 document *Ethical Framework for Good Practice in Counselling and Psychotherapy* (updated in 2002), which is intended to unify and replace all the codes for BACP counsellors, trainers and supervisors.

The extent to which counsellors, psychologists and psychotherapists are aware of and comply with such ethical codes or guidelines for practice, however, varies across profession, country and practitioners. Research addressing ethical dilemmas and unethical behaviour which has been undertaken in the United States of America, Australia and the United Kingdom has investigated problems associated with counsellors, psychotherapists or psychologists complying with codes of ethics (Bernard & Jara 1986; Bernard *et al.* 1987; Goodman 2000; Haas *et al.* 1988; Lindsay & Colley 1995; Smith *et al.* 1991; Sullivan 2002; Wilkins *et al.* 1990). These investigations reflect widely varying practices and a spectrum of monitoring and reporting procedures.

In the UK, BPS Ethics Committee reports that complaints about unethical behaviour comprise less than 0.1 per cent of its members. However, these are often highly publicised cases, which leads to a misperception of the frequency of unethical behaviour of counsellors, psychotherapists and psychologists. A survey of psychologists by Lindsay and Colley (1995: 449) found that 172 respondents out of a sample of 284 reported ethically 'troubling incidents'. The largest percentage of troubling incidents (17 per cent) was related to breaches of confidentiality. This finding was consistent with a similar study conducted by Pope and Vetter (1992) in the USA. A later study by Lindsay and Clarkson (1999) of 213 psychotherapists found that 156 psychotherapists reported having had at least one ethical dilemma. Again, breaches of confidentiality were reported most frequently (31 per cent). The researchers in each of these studies recognised the inadequacy of the current Codes of Conduct/Codes of Ethics in providing sufficient professional guidance for practitioners.

Recent research by Goodman (2000) investigated the discrepancy between psychologists' understanding and implementation of ethical principles in psychological practice. Psychologists in Queensland, Australia, were asked to nominate the actions they thought they *should* take, and the actions they actually *would* take in response to four hypothetical vignettes depicting breaches of the Australian Psychological Society Code of Ethics (APS 1997). Results indicated that one-third of these psychologists *would* do less than they understood they *should* do as prescribed by the Code of Ethics. The finding that so many participants nominated their most restrictive *should* course of action as less than what the Code stipulates, indicates that they either do not understand this provision of the Code of Ethics, or they disagree with it.

The results of these studies have implications for the training of counsellors and psychologists, and for the teaching of ethics in professional programmes. In particular, there is a need to develop ethics training programmes that focus on a reflective understanding of why these codes of practice exist, and what they are attempting to achieve, in addition to communicating the provisions of the specific professional code of conduct to counsellors, psychologists and psychotherapists.

THE NEED FOR TRAINING IN ETHICS

Since the 1970s instruction or training in ethics has been a requirement of the American Psychological Association (Bersoff 1995). Professional psychology programmes at the graduate level have needed to include such instruction in order to gain accreditation. In Australia, instruction in ethics and professional practice is also required both at the fourth year (undergraduate level) and in postgraduate professional psychology programmes. In the UK, while the BPS requires training in professional ethics at the postgraduate level, there is no such requirement in undergraduate psychology programmes. Similarly, in accrediting counsellors and/or counselling training courses, the BACP require that training in ethics be undertaken. While a number of surveys into the training of therapists have been conducted in the USA since the mid-1970s (e.g. Tymchuck *et al.* 1982; Handelsman 1986; Vanek 1990), no comprehensive survey of training in ethics has been undertaken in the UK. A survey of UKCP member organisations was conducted in 2001 (Kent 2002). The purpose of the survey was to identify the type, format and content of ethics training that was currently required by those member organisations responsible for training courses. Fifty member organizations were sent a questionnaire, which yielded only 13 responses (a response rate of 26 per cent) providing limited information. However, this report indicated similar findings to the research mentioned above – that professional standards assume that therapists do need to be taught about ethics and trained in ethical behaviour consistent with their particular professional codes and expectations.

It appears that there is broad agreement with respect to the need for training for therapists in ethics. There is, however, little if any consensus as to what the content or duration of such training might be. Furthermore, there is no consistent view on when the most appropriate time is to introduce such training, on what a specific curriculum should consist of, on how to assess ethical competencies, or on how to examine ethical knowledge.

WHEN SHOULD TRAINING IN ETHICS BEGIN, AND WHAT SHOULD IT INCLUDE?

In undergraduate psychology programmes in the UK, introduction to ethics with respect to research begins very early in the curriculum. However, there is no requirement for undergraduate students in psychology to be instructed in ethics for professional practice in their undergraduate degree. The scientist-practitioner model is widely accepted by psychology programmes in the UK, and it is the model by which the BPS accredits courses, arguing that the undergraduate degree is largely an academic and scientific exploration of the discipline of psychology, with practitioner training occurring at the postgraduate level.

Notwithstanding this, many universities offer introductory courses in counselling within their undergraduate psychology programmes. These are not usually considered as 'core courses' in psychology, but rather as an 'elective course'. These introductory courses are often offered in the last year of the programme, and many include at least one session (1–2 hours) on ethics in professional practice. However, many psychology graduates may complete their psychology degree without taking such a course. Furthermore, graduates from psychology programmes may be employed in a variety of positions, some of which may include utilising counselling skills, or requiring the employee to conduct 'counselling'. Graduates, therefore, may begin to practise with very little, if any, training in ethics. 'On the job' supervision may be available to help the new employee to develop the skills required for the particular position. While there are BPS guidelines for the postgraduate training for counselling psychologists, which require some instruction in ethics, there is no prescribed content, even at the postgraduate training level.

Similarly, many counselling skills courses offer one or two hours on ethics for counselling, but not all do so. Counselling skills courses are often seen as a prerequisite for further training in counselling. However, in the absence of any national curriculum in counselling, the development of ethical practice has largely been left to course directors to determine, and in many cases the supervisors of professional counselling practice. The dilemma, then, both for generic counselling skills courses, and introductory counselling courses in universities that may be taught to a multidisciplinary audience at the under-graduate level, is that these skills-based courses provide little opportunity or justification for promulgating or discussing profession-specific codes of prac-tice. The first time graduates may then be faced with learning about ethical practices in their first employment setting, and/or their initial supervision sessions.

Handelsman in 1986 argued that learning ethics by 'osmosis', that is, dur-ing a discussion of cases in the context of supervision, was a dangerous practice. He argued that training centres could not assume that adequate supervision was being attained, and that students' learning of ethical practice was limited by supervisor awareness of ethical dilemmas, and supervisor competency in ethics. He argued that postgraduate professional training pro-grammes in psychology should make room for at least one course in ethics training. This argument appears to have been taken up in the USA and Canada, in Australia and in the UK in postgraduate professional psychology programmes and, as mentioned above, ethics training is required for BACP accredited courses. However, it is still the case that in the UK, in the absence of statutory registration, there are practitioners (counsellors, therapists) who may not be accredited with the BACP, or chartered with the BPS, and for whom there has been little, if any, mandatory training in ethical practice.

In the POPAN survey (Prevention of Professional Abuse Network) reported in *The Psychotherapist* (Kent 2002) course directors were asked a number of questions regarding elements of ethical practice that were taught on the courses of UKCP member organisations. These questions related to the following:

- Ethics theories.
- Code of ethics/guidelines for practice.
- Setting up initial contracts for therapy.
- Informed consent.
- Boundaries and dual relationships.
- Confidentiality, anonymity and privacy.
- Ethical dilemmas and ethical problem-solving/decision-making.
- Supervision.
- Personal functioning.
- Understanding of harmful professional practice.
- Touch and sexual feeling in therapy.
- How to handle negative feedback and/or complaints.

These topics, according to the author of the survey are 'germane to preventing unethical practice and abuse in psychotherapy' (Kent 2002: 36). Respondents were asked whether trainees received at least one hour on each of the topics listed above. Very few respondents provided information regarding the number of hours spent teaching this material, and a number of comments received implied that ethics training largely took place in supervision.

It is troubling that counselling training programmes/counselling psychology programmes have not developed uniform or national curricula with respect to teaching professional ethics. During the last decade a number of books and resources on ethics and professional practice have become available to assist instructors in teaching ethics (for example, Bond 2000; Bor & Watts 1998; Corey *et al.* 1998; Cotton & Tarvydas 1998; Francis 1999; Koocher & Keith-Spiegel 1998; Pryzwansky & Wendt 1999; Steinmann *et al.* 1998). An instructor's manual and test bank to accompany Corey *et al.*'s text is also available. These resources, however, were produced for an American audience, and there is a need to adapt some sections for a UK audience. The US health system and the US codes of practice are different from the UK systems, and reference to the UK codes of professional standards is required.

What is 'best practice' or the preferred model(s) of training in professional ethics?

In the absence of any nationally agreed criteria, or an approved curriculum for training in ethics, trainers usually base what they teach on their own training; they can look to a number of ethics considerations in professional practice texts to identify the core areas that appear to characterise the discourse; they can liaise with each other to ascertain what works in the training setting; and they can search the world wide web, where several sites can be found that provide description of ethics units taught at universities. The author of this chapter undertook a 12-week course in Ethics for Clinical Psychologists in the USA in 1992. She subsequently developed a unit in ethics that drew substantially on a 'core set' of issues presented in that course, in addition to source material that is shared by those teaching in this area across North America, adapting this material for both Australian and British audiences. The example below describes an introductory 18 hours (six three-hour sessions) of postgraduate study in ethics for counsellors and counselling psychologists.

AN INTRODUCTORY PROGRAMME IN ETHICAL PRACTICE FOR POSTGRADUATE STUDENTS IN COUNSELLING AND COUNSELLING PSYCHOLOGY

The aim of the ethics training was to introduce the BPS Code of Conduct (BPS 2000) and the BAC Code of Ethics and Practice for Counsellors (BAC 1990); to acquaint trainees with ethical theories, ethical principles and rules; introduce trainees to the key concepts of consent, competency, confidentiality, boundaries and dual relationships; and to teach the trainees how to recognise ethical dilemmas, and to provide them with a method for working through ethical dilemmas.

An objective of this programme was to provide students/trainees with an overview of the ethical, legal and professional issues facing the professional counsellor/counselling psychologist. The programme was designed to develop an awareness of the BPS's Code of Conduct and the BAC's Code of Ethics, to teach a process of ethical decision-making and to increase awareness of the complexities in practice. Furthermore, this introductory training in ethics was intended to foster the development of 'ethical mindfulness' as Bond (2000) recommends (see also Chapter 2). Learning outcomes for the trainees were:

1   To develop an understanding of ethical theories, ethical principles, ethical issues and dilemmas, and to develop a sound model for ethical decision-making.

2   To explore the major ethical issues related to sound and professional practice as a counsellor and counselling psychologist.
3   To become familiar with the ethical codes of counsellors and psychologists and to apply these ethical principles to a variety of problem situations.

Table 23.1 provides a brief overview of the content and resources that were considered to be helpful to the students/trainees at this stage of their development as counsellors/counselling psychologists.

The initial session involved trainees completing a number of reflective activities that helped them to identify their own values systems, their ideas on morality, and ethics, and the community standards that they were familiar with, and to consider these with respect to the professional standards and codes of the BAC and the BPS. In addition trainees were encouraged to identify and explore the differences among values, morals, ethical and professional conduct, and law. The aims and purposes of the different codes of ethics/codes of conduct were also discussed in the initial session, highlighting similarities and differences among the various codes.

The second session of the subject explored moral and ethical reasoning, identifying the underlying ethical principles which serve to guide psychological and/or counselling practice. The research findings of a number of well-established studies of ethical conduct were examined, and trainees were invited to indicate how they too would rate each of the situations (see, for example, Pope & Vetter 1992).

This session also considered a number of questions for the trainees including:

1   Are there particular types of psychologists/counsellors who behave unethically?
2   What are the ethical issues that arise for the individual counsellor?
3   What are some of the ethical issues that arise in the counselling relationship?

The second half of this session provided training in ethical decision-making. This included an identification of the ethical traps (Steinmann *et al.* 1998)

Table 23.1 Content for the Ethics and Professional Practice unit

Session 1	What are ethics; differences between values, morals, ethics, ethical theories, ethical standards, codes of conduct
Session 2	Ethical decision-making
Session 3	Informed consent, competency
Session 4	Confidentiality
Session 5	Boundary transgressions, dual relationships
Session 6	Self-care, personal therapy and supervision

that counsellors can fall into, and a strategy for working through ethical dilemmas and ethical decision making. Table 23.2 provides an adaptation of an ethical decision-making procedure (Handelsman 2001; Steinmann *et al.* 1998) that has been found to be useful in encouraging trainees to work through dilemmas systematically.

Subsequent sessions involved a consideration of research and practice with respect to the concepts of informed consent, confidentiality, competence and dual relationships in counselling and psychotherapy. A number of key readings were assigned for each topic and trainees were provided with a number of ethical issues and dilemmas relating to the concept under consideration. They worked in pairs to solve the dilemmas using the ethical decision-making framework presented in the previous class, and with due reference to the specific codes of conduct, legislation etc.

These sessions usually led to lively and well-informed discussion of the difficulty in resolving ethical dilemmas as trainees identified the particular traps they were likely to fall into. These sessions also provided an opportunity for trainees to reflect on their own values and ethical standards, comparing and contrasting these personal reference points with the prevailing professional standards of their particular discipline. This approach to learning is consistent with Kolb's (1984) experiential learning model, which acknowledges that learners need to develop four abilities – concrete experience, reflective observation, abstract conceptualisation and active experimentation.

Table 23.2 An ethical decision-making procedure

PROBLEM IDENTIFICATION
Is this an ethical problem?

What are the relevant facts?	What might not be relevant?	What else do we need to know?
To whom are we obligated?	What sources are available to us?	Consult with peers/ supervisor

WHAT ETHICAL PRINCIPLES OR STANDARDS ARE INVOKED?
DETERMINE ETHICAL TRAP POSSIBILITIES
FRAME PRELIMINARY RESPONSE
CONSIDER CONSEQUENCES IF PRELIMINARY RESPONSE IS ADOPTED
HOW MIGHT OUR VALUES BE INFLUENCING OUR DELIBERATIONS?
PREPARE ETHICAL RESOLUTION
GET FEEDBACK FROM PEERS OR SUPERVISORS
TAKE ACTION AND FOLLOW UP

Adapted from Handelsman (2001) and Steinmann *et al.* (1998).

Modelling appropriate ethical practice is very important when teaching professional ethics. The educational context, however, is somewhat different from the normal professional practice setting where ethical dilemmas have a more traditional practitioner–client character. The educational institution context itself provides innumerable dilemmas that the author has observed (e.g., a counsellor at the university who also teaches the counselling skills subject where a student is also her client; university lecturing staff members who form relationships with their students, etc.). The dilemma presented below has been chosen because of its somewhat innocuous and 'everyday' flavour. It pertains to the many ethical dilemmas that are more subtly intertwined with everyday life, encounters and multifaceted relationships.

> The circumstance was that the tutor of the ethics unit lived in a village approximately 10 miles from the university. The tutor regularly caught a bus to and from the university. The buses back to the village in the evening were at 8.05 p.m. and then the next not until 9.30 p.m. While the class was scheduled to run from 5.00 to 8.00 p.m., by the time the tutor had finished the class and returned to her office, she always was too late for the 8.05 p.m. bus. A mature-aged trainee lived in the same village, and offered to provide a lift home for the tutor.

The 'dilemma' had to do with whether the tutor could accept the lift. The trainees and the tutor discussed this situation, noting that the dilemma involved the principle of respect and autonomy on the part of the trainee, and the possible transgression of professional boundaries, and the potential for a dual relationship to develop between the tutor and the trainee providing the lift. Clearly both the tutor's values and her position on dual relationships were at issue and under scrutiny. Most of the trainees and another tutor on the counselling programme felt that it was acceptable for the trainee to provide the tutor with a lift in these circumstances, a lift the tutor, however, declined. Her argument was that the relationship between herself and the trainee would inevitably become more personal, and this could transgress professional boundaries, and her preference was to maintain in this instance the stricter professional boundary. This situation highlighted one of the challenges of ethical *dilemmas* – that is that there is often no correct response, and that personal and professional codes of conduct both co-exist and at times are at odds with circumstance and easy resolution. Ultimately the discussion, debate and management of these sorts of boundary issues help to develop further the sense of ethical mindedness.

The final session in this series of workshops provided an opportunity for trainees to reflect on their own self-care, factors that contribute to burnout, the importance of ongoing supervision, and their responsibility to develop, and maintain sound ethical practice. Furthermore, while the topics covered involved a critical review of the academic and research literature, the sessions were also designed to give trainees the opportunity to reflect on their own value stances, to engender professional ethical behaviour, and to provide trainees with 'permission' to discuss issues surrounding breaches of ethical behaviour.

HOW IS KNOWLEDGE AND ETHICAL BEHAVIOUR BEST ASSESSED?

As mentioned earlier, there is no national curriculum for ethics training and therefore the question as to how ethical knowledge and ethical behaviour might best be tested remains unanswered. Ethics knowledge has been tested with quizzes, correct-answer multiple-choice tests, and casebook dilemmas for students to describe their reasoning (Eberlein 1987). Since this series of workshops was adapted to be presented in the first semester of a postgraduate course, prior to first contact with clients, trainees' knowledge was assessed prior to the series of workshops and again at the end of the series. Trainees were invited to complete a self-assessment of professional ethics prior to the unit commencing (Steinmann *et al.* 1998), and again at the end of the six sessions. The main piece of assessment for this ethics training component was a written examination covering ethical theories, principles, and practice. This written examination consisted of three components, a multiple-choice section with 20 questions, an ethical dilemma, in which they were asked to demonstrate their ethical decision-making, and two short essays from a choice of three dealing with either competence, confidentiality or boundaries. Trainees were required to pass this examination prior to their first counselling placement. While monitoring ethical practice is probably better than assessment, and indeed is expected once trainees are engaging in supervised practice, assessment by written examination is appropriate to university teaching, and perhaps for registration or licensing (for example, as in North America).

CONCLUSION

Is an introductory course in ethics enough? While introductory training is critical for trainee therapists, it is the author's considered view that introductory training is not enough, and that ongoing professional development and continued education in ethical practice is necessary, and should be encouraged. The research mentioned earlier in this chapter indicated that it is not *only* novice counsellors and psychologists who breach codes of practice, and that personal and collective practice cultures can drift rather wide of the mark with respect to reflective and responsible professional ethics. Ethical dilemmas are not a hypothetical in professional practice. It is *inevitable* that counselling professionals will encounter such issues. It is therefore imperative, that counsellors, psychotherapists and psychologists are regularly updating their skills and knowledge with respect to evolving codes of practice, and professional standards. Undoubtedly, this will be one of the issues on future agendas when addressing statutory regulation of counsellors and psychotherapists.

REFLECTIVE QUESTIONS

1 When should ethical instruction be introduced?
2 What are the 'best practice' or preferred teaching methods for developing ethical practice?
3 How is knowledge and ethical behaviour best assessed?
4 What are your views about continued professional development in ethics and ethical practice being a mandatory requirement for continued registration/licensing as a therapist?

REFERENCES

APS (Australian Psychological Society) (1997) *Code of Ethics*. Melbourne: APS.
APS (Australian Psychological Society) (2002) *Ethical Guidelines*. Melbourne: APS.
BAC (British Association for Counselling) (1990) *Code of Ethics and Practice for Counsellors*. Rugby, UK: BAC.
BACP (British Association for Counselling and Psychotherapy) (2001) *Ethical Framework for Good Practice in Counselling and Psychotherapy*. Rugby, UK: BACP.
Bernard, J. L. & Jara, C. S. (1986) The failure of clinical psychology graduate students to apply understood ethical principles. *Professional Psychology: Research and Practice*, 77, 313–315.
Bernard, J. L., Murphy, M. & Little, M. (1987) The failure of clinical psychologists to apply understood ethical principles. *Professional Psychology: Research and Practice*, 78, 489–491.
Bersoff, D. (1995) *Ethical Conflicts in Psychology*. Washington: American Psychological Association.
Bond. T. (2000) *Standards and Ethics for Counselling in Action*. London: Sage.
Bor, R. & Watts, M. (1998) *The Trainee Handbook: A Guide for Counselling and Psychotherapy Trainees*. London: Sage.
BPS (British Psychological Society) (2000) *Code of Conduct, Ethical Principles and Guidelines*. Leicester: BPS.
BPS (The British Psychological Society – Division of Counselling Psychology) (2001) *Professional Practice Guidelines*. Leicester: BPS.
BPS (The British Psychological Society – Division of Clinical Psychology) (2003) *Policy Guidelines on Supervision in the Practice of Clinical Psychology*. Leicester: BPS.

Corey, G., Corey, M. S. & Callanan, P. (1998) *Issues and Ethics in the Helping Professions*, 5th edn. Pacific Grove: Brooks/Cole.

Cotton, R. & Tarvydas, V. (1998) *Ethical and Professional Issues in Counselling*. Englewood Cliffs, NJ: Prentice Hall.

Eberlein, L. (1987) Introducing ethics to beginning psychologists: a problem-solving approach. *Professional Psychology: Research and Practice*, 18, 353–389.

Francis, R. (1999) *Ethics for Psychologists*. Melbourne: ACER Press.

Goodman, D. (2000) 'Ethical dilemmas in psychological practice: a study of Registered Psychologists in Queensland'. Unpublished dissertation, James Cook University, Queensland, Australia.

Haas, L. J., Malouf, J. L. & Meyerson, N. H. (1988) Personal and professional characteristics as factors in psychologists' ethical decision making. *Professional Psychology: Research and Practice*, 17, 316–321.

Handelsman, M. (1986) Problems of learning ethics by 'osmosis'. *Professional Psychology: Research and Practice*, 17, 371–372.

Handelsman, M. (2001) Learning to become ethical, in S. Walfish & A.K. Hess (eds.), *Succeeding in Graduate School: The Career Guide for Psychology Students*. Mahwah, NJ: Lawrence Erlbaum Associates.

Kent, R. (2002) Ethical practice and psychotherapy training. *The Psychotherapist*, 19, 34–36.

Kolb, B. (1984) *Experience as a Source of Learning and Development*. Englewood Cliffs, NJ: Prentice Hall.

Koocher, G. & Keith-Spiegel, P. (1998) *Ethics in Psychology*, 2nd edn. New York: Oxford Textbooks.

Lindsay, G. & Clarkson, P. (1999) Ethical dilemmas of psychotherapists. *The Psychologist*, April, 182–185.

Lindsay, G. & Colley, A. (1995) Ethical dilemmas of members of the society. *The Psychologist*, October, 448–451.

Pope, K. & Vetter, V. (1992) Ethical dilemmas encountered by members of the American Psychological Society: a national survey. *American Psychologist*, 47, 497–511.

Pryzwansky, W. & Wendt, R. (1999) *Professional and Ethical Issues in Psychology*. New York: Norton.

Smith, T. S., McGuire, J. M., Abbott, D. W. & Blau, B. I. (1991) Clinical ethical decision making: an investigation of the rationales used to justify doing less than one believes one should. *Professional Psychology: Research and Practice*, 22, 235–239.

Steinmann, S., Richardson, N. & McEnroe, T. (1998) *The Ethical Decision Making Manual for Helping Professionals*. New York: Brooks/Cole.

Sullivan, K. (2002) Ethical beliefs and behaviours among Australian psychologists. *Australian Psychologist*, 37, 135–141. (The Australian Psychological Society Ltd.)

Tymchuk, A. J., Drapkin, R., Major-Kingsley, S., Ackerman, A. B., Coffman, E. W. & Baum, M. S. (1982) Ethical decision making and psychologists' attitudes toward training in ethics. *Professional Psychology, Research and Practice*, 13, 412–421.

Vanek, C. A. (1990) Survey of ethics education in clinical and counseling psychology. Dissertation Abstracts International, 52, 5797B (University Microfilms, No. 91–14, 449).

Wilkins, M., McGuire, J., Abbott, D. & Blau, B. (1990) Willingness to apply understood ethical principles. *Journal of Clinical Psychology*, 46, 539–544.

Chapter 24

Training supervision: professional and ethical considerations

Jean Morrissey

Clinical supervision is a central component in the process of becoming a counsellor, psychologist or psychotherapist as well as a recommended or required contributory element of continuing professional development. The knowledge, skills and modelling that a supervisor conveys are important aspects of helping the supervisee assist the client by promoting best practice in both the therapeutic and supervisory relationships. However, the nature of supervision and particularly training supervision engenders several important professional and ethical considerations for both participants of the supervisory dyad. Such considerations must always be given serious attention in terms of their impact on the welfare of the client and the process of learning. This chapter examines some of these issues and their potential to influence the supervisory experience. It will also discuss some of the responsibilities of those involved, primarily the supervisee, supervisor and training organisation. Although the chapter focuses on training supervision, the ideas and application will also be of relevance to qualified therapists in their role of either supervisor or supervisee, or both. Throughout the chapter, the term supervision will refer to clinical supervision.

SUPERVISION – WHAT DOES IT MEAN?

From the outset, it is important to clarify what is meant by supervision. At its simplest, supervision is primarily a learning process whereby a supervisee (or trainee) meets regularly with a more experienced practitioner – a supervisor – to discuss clinical and professional issues relating to the supervisee's ongoing learning and practice. Its purpose is twofold – to promote and protect 'the welfare of the client and the development of the supervisee' (Carroll 1996: 45). This dualistic role incorporates the functions of supervision – educating, supporting and monitoring the supervisee's clinical role and, where supervision is part of a formal training, the additional function of assessing and evaluating the supervisee. The role of supervision in supporting, developing and evaluating professional practice is supported by all the major professional codes and guidelines (British Association for Counselling and Psychotherapy (BACP 2002); British Psychological Society (BPS 2001, 2003a, 2003b) and United Kingdom Central Council (UKCP 2000)).

Throughout the literature numerous models of supervision have been described concerning different aspects of supervision including: supervision tasks, formats and styles, stages of supervisee and supervisor development and the supervisory alliance tasks (Carroll 1996; Hawkins & Shohet 2000; Page & Wosket 1994; Stoltenberg & Delworth 1987). These theoretical concepts inform and guide how supervision is currently understood and applied. As might be expected, there are differences as to how the generally agreed aims of supervision might be best applied and achieved. Such differences can sometimes lead to misunderstandings and misconceptions about the meaning of supervision and more importantly its usage in practice. Therefore, establishing a shared understanding and agreement, between all participants involved in the supervision contract, about its purpose and practice is essential from the outset. Failure to do so may result in its potential efficacy being undermined and undervalued. Contracting issues will be discussed later in the chapter.

SUPERVISION – CONSULTATIVE AND TRAINING

Supervision is increasingly described as either consultative or training supervision. 'Consultative supervision refers to the process whereby an experienced and qualified practitioner seeks consultation with a peer or a more experienced therapist concerning their clinical work whereas training supervision describes the process of supervision for therapists during training' (Gilbert & Evans 2000: 3). For the supervisor, the latter involves a position of authority and power, and almost invariably a responsibility to formally assess the trainee's ongoing professional development and competence. Although the supervisor's responsibility will differ considerably between the two types of supervision, the responsibility to ensure ethical standards are maintained throughout the therapeutic process applies to both.

THE FREQUENCY OF SUPERVISION

All the major professional bodies recognise supervision as a core element of training. Guidance about the frequency of supervision, qualifications of the supervisor and format, i.e. individual or group supervision, vary across the different therapeutic approaches, training organisations and accrediting professional bodies. For example, the current requirement for a BACP accredited course is one hour of presenting in supervision to eight hours of practice, the frequency of which should be not less than fortnightly. Supervision, however, does not end post training. The BACP, clinical and counselling psychology divisions of the BPS and some sections of the UKCP regard supervision as a basic ethical requirement and therefore require all members (in training and qualified) to receive regular ongoing supervision from a suitably appropriate person throughout their working career. For qualified BACP and BPS members, the minimum requirement is one-and-a-half hours of supervision per month for a minimal, uncomplicated caseload. Nevertheless, recognising that quantity itself cannot either ensure the quality of the supervision received or meet the needs of all supervisees, the expectation is that the amount of supervision will increase proportionately with the demands or complexities of each supervisee's caseload and with the level of experience and training. Yet as Mearns (1998: 2) points out, 'there is a danger in even stating such a baseline as it could be regarded as sufficient even in unfavourable circumstances'. The BACP requires all practising supervisors to have regular ongoing supervision for their supervised work.

The obligatory nature of regular ongoing supervision post qualifying has raised debates within the profession about its necessity and role. One argument that challenges the role of mandatory supervision is the paucity of empirical evidence about its impact on the outcome of clinical practice. While there is ample anecdotal evidence about the efficacy of supervision, the lack of empirical data about how or whether supervision works raises questions for all involved, as well as for the profession at large. For further coverage of these debates see Feltham (2001, 2002); McLennan (1999); Connor (1999).

THE MODE OF SUPERVISION

Whereas individual (one-to-one) supervision is the most frequently used modality, group supervision is a close second; training organisations commonly use both. Each mode presents different learning opportunities and challenges that are often interchangeable and context-dependent (Carroll 1996). Exposure to both can provide a good learning opportunity for supervisees – whereby they can experience both the intensive attention of individual supervision and the opportunity to contribute to and learn with others in a group. This in turn can help supervisees to identify which format might best meet their learning needs at the different stages of their professional development. Similarly, it is important for supervisors to be aware of their preferred format and areas of development. In practice, however, constraints of time, finance or expertise often dictate the supervision format for both supervisees and supervisors, which in turn can influence the quality of the supervisory experience. For example, Jones's (2000) study of potentially destructive experiences of group supervision reported that several participants identified the lack of choice about being a participant of group supervision as one of the contributing factors to a potentially negative experience.

Ideally, the best use of group or individual supervision should start from a positive choice for all participants, yet compromises are likely to be a reality. Given this, it is then important that supervisees, and particularly those who have minimal experience of supervision, are prepared to make the best use of supervision, either as individuals or in a group.

According to Carroll (1996) it is the supervisor's responsibility to educate the trainee about the role of supervision and how to prepare for it, whereas Inskipp and Proctor (1995) argue that this responsibility lies with the training organisation. Reflecting on my own experience as a supervisor – while most trainees increasingly receive some preparation about the use of supervision, the extent of the preparation can and does vary between different training organisations. However varied the preparation, the supervisor needs to establish the supervisee's prior understanding and experience of supervision from the outset and facilitate their learning accordingly. The latter is also important when working with beginning trainees who understandably may find it difficult to distinguish the boundaries between supervision and therapy, particularly as both share several situational and behavioural similarities. For example, both are helping processes, comprise an authority-dependency relationship and use, albeit differently, similar skills (Page & Wosket 1994). However, they are not the same; each is a separate activity with different aims: 'the aim of supervision is to help supervisees become better therapeutic workers whereas the aim in counselling stresses becoming a better person' (Carroll 1996: 59). Nevertheless, the centrality of the working alliance is essential for both.

THE SUPERVISORY RELATIONSHIP

There is overall agreement that the supervisory relationship, whether it comprises a dyad or a group, plays a crucial role in the learning and acquisition of knowledge and skills. Central to this process of learning is the quality of the supervisory relationship (McNeill & Worthen 1996; Webb & Wheeler 1998). Supervising trainees is a complex interpersonal process and usually involves a number of potentially conflicting relationships and interrelationships. These comprise the client and supervisee's placement/agency, personal therapist and training organisation, together with the anxieties and particular learning needs of the trainee, and the requirement of a formal assessment. The supervisor must consider all issues, especially in terms of their effect upon the learning alliance. While codes of ethics can and do provide boundaries and determine some aspects of the supervisory relationship (Barden 2001: 45), they cannot determine how the relationship is translated into practice or indeed its quality. Furthermore, codes on their own cannot cover all supervisory eventualities or the contexts in which they occur – each supervisory situation is different and therefore requires individual professional judgement, which at times can be both complex and challenging.

SUPERVISION AND BOUNDARIES

Similar to the therapeutic relationship, supervision is characterised by certain codes of practice and boundaries. As Bond (2000: 192) points out 'a sound ethic within the supervisory relationship is considered equally as essential for the supervisee as it is for the client in the counselling relationship'. In training supervision, however, one of the most fundamental challenges is whether it is possible, and if so how, to provide safety and containment that encourages risk-taking and non-defensive behaviour while simultaneously having an assessment role. Undoubtedly, occupying and managing the dual relationship of supervisor and assessor presents several professional and ethical challenges for both participants of the supervisory dyad, particularly given the power differential that exists between the supervisor and supervisee. These issues will be discussed further in the chapter.

Dual relationships of any sort in supervision are potentially problematic, including the loss of objectivity and a compromising of confidentiality, and as a result can interfere with the supervisor's capacity to carry out his/her role effectively. Supervisors, therefore, have a responsibility to establish and maintain appropriate boundaries that are clearly distinguished from other significant relationships, such as with a spouse or a business partner, or other relationships that would cause a potential conflict of interest. Whenever possible conflicts of interest should be avoided, but if they do occur, 'the protection of the client's interest and maintaining the trust in the practitioner (*supervisor*) should be paramount in determining how to respond' (BACP 2002: 9). Sexual relationships between the supervisor and supervisee are prohibited by all professional codes of conduct and ethics, and the general expectation is that the supervisory relationship will be kept clearly separate from any managerial role.

CONTRACTING – BILATERAL AGREEMENT

Contracting in supervision as in therapy plays a vital function in underpinning the entire supervisory process and relationship, that is to contain, support, and direct the agreed working alliance and goals for supervision. In creating the working agreement both parties clarify and negotiate the boundaries, expectations, learning styles, roles, responsibilities, and the purpose and tasks of supervision, which then guides and outlines the agreed working alliance and goals for supervision (Morrissey 1998; Page & Wosket 1994; Proctor 1997). In training supervision, negotiation of the contract should also include information and discussion about the assessment process, procedures and requirements. Although the contracting process usually takes place at the outset, it is an ongoing process, subject to regular reviews and re-contracting as and when the supervisee's learning needs change. The way in which the supervisor conducts the negotiation process will vary depending on the supervisor's theoretical orientation, style of facilitation and experience as a supervisor. The formality with which such agreements are made may also vary from formal and written to informal and unrecorded. Lawton's (2000) study of supervisory relationships found the majority of participants reported a very varied experience of contracting and that there was a strong relationship between the attention given to the contracting process at the outset and the overall quality of the supervisory alliance.

The contracting process itself also helps supervisees to begin to think about their learning needs and preferred learning styles, as well as how they might make the best use of their supervision time. However, for many novice and even some experienced supervisees, expressing their learning needs and goals to a person in a position of authority and power, i.e. the supervisor, and where supervision comprises a group of other supervisees or peers, can often be an unfamiliar and anxiety-provoking experience. Scaife (2001: 57) suggests one way of minimising such anxieties is 'to normalise the expectation of anxiety as a feature of the process of learning new skills'. Acknowledging and encouraging openness from the outset while at the same time ensuring that the needs of the supervisee and client can best be met, can also help reduce supervisees' fear of disclosure. This of course is dependent on the supervisor's judgement and skill in knowing how best to assist each supervisee in engaging in the contracting process. Nevertheless, it is essentially the supervisees' responsibility to make use of, the opportunities made available to them, or at least begin to.

CONTRACTING – MULTILATERAL AGREEMENT

Supervising trainees may also involve the same person in a series of many different interrelated contracts; for example, the supervisor may also be employed by the training organisation or placement agency in the role of a trainer or consultant. Alternatively, the supervisor may work independently and have no direct relationship with either of the above, other than through the supervisee. Working with and within such complexity highlights the importance of a shared understanding and agreement between all parties, particularly about clinical responsibility and confidentiality issues. This then raises the question of responsibility for establishing a clear working agreement – the placement agency, training organisation or the supervisor? As part of good practice for the management of clinical placements, training courses may initiate the supervisory agreement; however, this is not always the case nor should it be relied upon. The BACP (2002: 7) states that 'practitioners (supervisors) are responsible for clarifying who holds responsibility for the work with the client', and preferably this should occur before the supervisor agrees to supervise the trainee. Failure to clarify in this way may result in each assuming that the other is clinically responsible for the work undertaken by the trainee, or alternatively the supervisor may find him/herself in a situation where s/he may be left carrying the responsibility. Both outcomes place the client, trainee and supervisor in a vulnerable position. Best practice requires that there should be an explicit working agreement between all parties – supervisor, training organisation and placement agency – made at best prior to the trainee commencing clinical practice. Failure to achieve this increases the possibility for misunderstanding and miscommunication, both within and beyond the bilateral agreement. While the details of each contract will vary, clarification and agreement of the requirements, expectations and responsibilities will always need to include the following, as outlined by Izzard (2001: 89)

- expected caseload for a trainee,
- need for suitable clients to be allocated,
- lines of accountability for the trainee's clinical work,
- the complaints procedure which should be followed by clients,
- lines of communication for routine feedback and in case of concern,
- evaluation process, including criteria of assessment,
- code of ethics and practice within which each party practises.

CLINICAL RESPONSIBILITY

From a legal perspective, lines of accountability for clinical practice differ between the USA and Britain. In the USA, supervisors have been legally held accountable for the work of their supervisees, whereas in the UK there is no line of responsibility between the client and supervisor, although case law remains to be tested. Nonetheless, supervisors cannot abdicate responsibility – professionally and ethically they have a responsibility to anticipate (within reason) and minimise the possibility of negligence to the client and supervisee. If negligence does occur, then 'legally it probably is the case that the trainee carries responsibility and if successfully claimed against might have a secondary claim against the supervisor' (Bond 2000: 191). Clearly several issues would need to be examined before the supervisor could be held responsible for any harm caused by the supervisee's actions. However, if the supervisor was aware of or anticipated a potential problem between the supervisee and client and failed to act promptly and appropriately, the supervisor could to some degree be held responsible for any harm caused to the client. The fiduciary role of the supervisor, therefore, carries not only a responsibility for taking an ethical approach to conducting supervision but also the responsibility to ensure that the supervisee's practice is both safe and ethical (Scaife 2001). Accordingly, having access to legal representation via professional indemnity insurance is essential for both supervisors and supervisees.

CONFIDENTIALITY

The duty of confidentiality in supervision is twofold – it applies to both clients and supervisees. Legally and ethically the emphasis is on protecting all personal identifiable information, including tapes and client details. Best practice, therefore, requires all case material in supervision to be anonymous. For supervisees, it is essential to inform clients that confidential communication will be shared with the supervisor and to obtain their consent. Clients also need to be informed of the limits of confidentiality where supervision comprises a group. Similarly, supervisees need to be informed of the parameters of confidentiality, such as where information is shared with the supervisor's supervisor and whether information (if any) is shared with the training organisation or clinical placement, as well as how this might restrict the use of supervision. Maintaining confidentiality requires the supervisor to be mindful of any potential situations in which the supervisee might unknowingly be at risk of breaching confidentiality and to take appropriate action. Essentially, the supervisory relationship must be confidential, yet given the different circumstances of each case it is difficult, if not impossible, to provide absolutes. Clearly any breach of confidentiality by the supervisor is never an easy decision and requires careful consideration about the needs of the client and supervisee, although fundamentally the client's welfare must take precedence. Such decisions also require collegial and supervisory support and discussion about the presenting professional, ethical, and legal issues of the case, along with the consequences of taking action (or not), rather than simply responding to a code of ethics. See Chapter 6 for further discussion on confidentiality.

DUAL-ROLE RELATIONSHIPS WITHIN SUPERVISION

As previously mentioned, the nature of training supervision often involves the supervisor occupying a dual role – supervisor and assessor – suitable to enhancing the trainee's learning and professional development. These roles are integrated into the tasks of supervision and include the role of educator with that of providing support, monitoring and in most situations assessing and evaluating the trainee's professional and clinical competence. Managing these roles can be challenging since the expectations and responsibilities often appear to contradict or compete with each other and as a result may compromise the role of the supervisor as well as the quality of the supervisory relationship (Kitchener 1988), for example, where the supervisor facilitates the learning process by offering support, encouragement and guidance and yet at the same time has a responsibility to monitor, challenge and evaluate the trainee's professional learning and competence. These roles are further compounded by the unequal relationship inherent in training supervision.

This raises the question whether the role of the supervisor and assessor should be kept clearly separate. Even if such roles were separate, Barden (2001) argues that supporting and monitoring must be viewed as a dual role of the supervisor, as the monitoring functions aims to keep the counsellor and the client safe and therefore the 'complete absence of a monitoring role is neither possible or desirable' (p. 53). Furthermore, failure to provide evaluative feedback raises serious ethical concern because the supervisor fails to perform one of the most essential tasks of supervision. For the supervisor, being able to effectively handle these roles is of critical importance to ensure the welfare of the client and that the tasks of supervision are carried out to the highest possible standard. Even so, in practice this is sometimes easier said than done.

Supervisors have a responsibility for monitoring and assessing supervisees' performance consistently, carefully and constructively. As previously mentioned, in training supervision issues concerning the process and procedure of the assessment should be discussed at the outset of the supervisory relationship. In order to make a judgement about the trainee's performance, the supervisor must have sufficient knowledge about the trainee's professional and clinical competence, particularly when acting in the role of gatekeeper to the profession (Scaife 2001). The responsibility to evaluate the trainee is anxiety-provoking for both members of the supervisory dyad. No matter what efforts are made to minimise it, both are aware that the supervisor's judgement may affect the supervisory relationship and in some instances the trainee's professional career. Occasionally supervisors will encounter a trainee who is either unwilling or unable to learn the skills necessary for effective therapy, or who might be considered 'unfit' to practise. In such instances the supervisor has a responsibility to fail the trainee or recommend that the supervisee temporarily withdraw from clinical practice. Such actions are never an easy task and are only carried out after much consideration and discussion with the trainee and the training organisation and after various remedial strategies to assist the trainee in his/her difficulties have been explored and implemented. As always such actions are guided by the supervisor's primary responsibility to the client, to the public and to the profession.

When confronted with ethical dilemmas, supervisees have a choice whether to deal with the dilemma alone or bring it to supervision. However, supervision can be a threatening experience, often involving the trainee in feeling under scrutiny and experiencing uncomfortable feelings of *shame* or not being *good enough*, and as a result s/he may find it difficult to disclose particular difficulties or mistakes to the supervisor (Webb & Wheeler 1998; Yourman 2003). Therefore, not unlike the therapeutic relationship, change can be both desired and simultaneously feared, and in seeking help the trainee may therefore defend the ways in which s/he has previously learned. Clearly such responses will vary with each trainee and depend on his/her prior experience of supervision and level of professional and personal development, as well as on the nature of the supervisory relationship. In addition, the responses of both the supervisee and supervisor are likely to be laden with transferential reactions, which are bound to influence the supervisory relationship and the process of learning. The presence of other factors both within and outside the supervisory context are also likely to influence the extent of the supervisee's *honesty* in supervision; however, the quality of the supervisory relationship plays a significant influencing role. Essential to this experience is the supervisor's ability to assist the supervisee to overcome his/her fears by creating and maintaining a safe and supportive learning environment, in which the supervisee may feel safe to openly share difficult issues, while at the same time providing constructive feedback to enhance the supervisee's personal and professional development as a practitioner. This, of course, cannot be prescribed and like everything else in the supervisory experience is context-dependent and grounded in supervisory skill and judgement rather than being a product of chronology.

THE SUPPORTIVE ROLE IN SUPERVISION

The supportive role involves offering supervisees a forum to reflect on their personal reactions arising from working with clients, or indeed with supervisors. This function includes the use of counselling skills, although in supervision the central task is to focus on the work between supervisee and client. Based upon the arguments of dual relationships, the supervisor should not become, intentionally or unintentionally, the supervisee's therapist, yet sometimes there may be instances where it is difficult or unethical not to be, for example, when the trainee's personal issues are affecting the work with the client. Frankham (1987), however, argues that the most objectionable stance taken by supervisors (as reported by supervisees) is when the supervisor becomes or tries to become their therapist. As with many ethical dilemmas, determining the boundaries between counselling as personal therapy and counselling as a role within supervision is rarely clear-cut. The following case illustrates a situation where the supervisor used counselling as a role in supervision.

CASE EXAMPLE

Louise is an external supervisor to Niamh a trainee counsellor in her second year of a diploma-level course. She has been attending supervision for about eight months, on a fortnightly basis. During one meeting, Louise noticed that Niamh was unusually unfocused and distant when presenting her work, and commented on this. At this point Niamh began to cry uncontrollably. After a while she told her supervisor that her marriage of 10 years had ended and she did not know how to tell her two young sons. Louise asked Niamh if she wished to use the remaining time to talk about this further or to continue with her clinical work. She chose to use her supervision time primarily to talk about her feelings of loss. Louise listened empathetically and explored Niamh's support structures. In this situation the supervisor used counselling to understand how the supervisee's personal problem was affecting the trainee's performance while at the same time giving her the responsibility to find ways to help her during this difficult time.

CONCLUSION

Supervision clearly plays a central role in promoting and maintaining best practice within the therapeutic profession. However, the demand for a shared understanding and agreement of the tasks and responsibilities by all participants is essential if safe ethical practice and learning is to take place. The importance of the supervisory relationship is central to determining the quality of the learning alliance and accordingly the supervisor is required to conduct the various complex tasks professionally and ethically. The role of supervision carries a responsibility to the needs of the client, the supervisee and the public, as well as to the profession at large. Given the complexity of such relationships and responsibilities and the power differential involved, many ethical dilemmas can arise, including issues of confidentiality, competency, dual relationships and clinical accountability. As with all ethical dilemmas there are no absolutes and therefore each situation must be given careful professional judgement to ensure best practice. While professional codes and guidelines provide some guidance and support, they are by no means conclusive or intended to be prescriptive. This being the case, supervisors must have the capacity to be ethically minded in undertaking their challenging but important role.

REFLECTIVE QUESTIONS

1   How does supervision differ from therapy?
2   In what way does supervision enhance your professional learning and competence? Give examples.
3   What issues relating to your clinical work have you withheld from your supervisor and for what reasons?
4   What aspects of the supervisory experience has helped or hindered your professional learning and development? Give examples.

REFERENCES

BACP (British Association for Counselling and Psychotherapy) (2002) *Ethical Framework for Good Practice in Counselling and Psychotherapy*. Rugby, UK: BACP.

Barden, N. (2001) The responsibility of the supervisor in the British Association for Counselling and Psychotherapy's Codes of Ethics and Practice, in S. Wheeler and D. King (eds.), *Supervising Counsellors: Issues of Responsibility*. London: Sage.

Bond, T. (2000) *Standards and Ethics for Counselling in Action*, 2nd edn. London: Sage.

BPS (The British Psychological Society – Division of Counselling Psychology) (2001) *Professional Practice Guidelines*. Leicester: BPS.

BPS (The British Psychological Society – Division of Clinical Psychology) (2003a) *Policy Guidelines on Supervision in the Practice of Clinical Psychology*. Leicester: BPS.

BPS (The British Psychological Society Membership and Professional Training Board – Training Committee in Counselling Psychology) (2003b) *Criteria for the Accreditation of Postgraduate Training Programmes in Counselling Psychology*. Leicester: BPS.

Carroll, M. (1996) *Counselling Supervision Theory, Skills and Practice*. London: Cassell.

Connor, M. (1999) Training and supervision make a difference, in C. Feltham (ed.), *Controversies in Psychotherapy and Counselling*. London: Sage.

Feltham, C. (2001) Supervision: critical issues to be faced from the beginning, in M. Mahon & W. Patton (eds.), *Supervision in the Helping Professions*. Australia: Pearson Education.

Feltham, C. (2002) A surveillance culture? *Counselling Psychotherapy Journal*, 13(1), 26–27.

Frankham, H. (1987) 'Aspects of supervision: counsellor satisfaction, utility and defensiveness and the tasks of supervision'. MSc thesis, Roehampton Institute, London.

Gilbert, M. & Evans, K. (2000) *Psychotherapy Supervision: An Integrative Relational Approach to Psychotherapy Supervision*. Buckingham: Open University Press.

Hawkins, P. & Shohet, R. (2000) *Supervision in the Helping Professions*, 2nd edn. Buckingham: Open University Press.

Inskipp, F. & Proctor, B. (1995) *Becoming a Supervisor*. Twickenham, UK: Cascade Publications.

Izzard S. (2001) The responsibility of the supervisor supervising trainees, in S. Wheeler & D. King (eds.), *Supervising Counsellors: Issues of Responsibility*. London: Sage.

Jones, G. (2000) Group supervision: what can go wrong? *Counselling Psychotherapy Journal*, 11(10), 648–649.

Kitchener, K. S. (1988) Dual role relationships: what makes them so problematic? *Journal of Counseling and Development*, 67, 217–221.

Lawton, B. (2000) A very exposing affair: explorations in counsellors' supervisory relationships, in B. Lawton & C. Feltham (eds.), *Taking Supervision Forward: Enquiries and Trends in Counselling and Psychotherapy*. London: Sage.

McLennan, J. (1999) Becoming an effective psychotherapist or counsellor: are training and supervision necessary?, in C. Feltham (ed.), *Controversies in Psychotherapy and Counselling*. London: Sage.

McNeill, B. W. & Worthen, V. (1996) A phenomenological investigation of 'good' supervision events. *Journal of Counselling Psychology*, 43, 25–34.

Mearns, D. (1998) 'How much supervision should you have?' Information Sheet 3. Rugby, UK: BACP.

Morrissey, J. (1998) Contracting and supervision. *Counselling Psychology Review*, 13(1), 13–17.

Page, S. & Wosket, V. (1994) *Supervising the Counsellor: A Cyclical Approach*. London: Routledge.

Proctor, B. (1997) Contracting in Supervision, in C. Sills (ed.), *Contracts in Counselling*. London: Sage.

Scaife, J. (2001) *Supervision in the Mental Health Professions: A Practitioner's Guide*. Hove UK: Brunner-Routledge.

Stoltenberg, C. D. & Delworth, U. (1987) *Supervising Counselors and Therapists: A Developmental Approach*. San Francisco: Jossey-Bass.

UKCP (United Kingdom Council for Psychotherapy) (2000) *Ethical Requirements for Member Organisations*. London: UKCP.

Webb, A. & Wheeler, S. (1998) How honest do counsellors dare to be in the supervisory relationship? An exploratory study. *British Journal of Guidance and Counselling*, 26, 509–524.

Yourman, D.B. (2003) Trainee disclosure in psychotherapy supervision: the impact of shame. *Journal of Clinical Psychology/In Session*, 59(5), 601–609.

Chapter 25

Trainee perspectives on professional and ethical practice

Rachel Tribe

This chapter is based on research undertaken among a range of trainee therapists, psychologists and counsellors. It discusses the issues trainees recorded as important to their own professional and ethical practice and development. The chapter does not attempt to be definitive or comprehensive, to include all aspects of professional and ethical practice or to dictate which areas are most important. It merely focuses attention on those dilemmas which were considered important to this particular sample group. Seventy-two trainees participated in the research from a range of training institutions and courses. The nature of the chapter means that each issue is dealt with concisely, and the interested reader may wish to engage in further reading or reflection on the issues raised.

Throughout the chapter, scenarios or reflective questions based on trainee responses are interspersed (in boxes) with the text to assist thinking about some ethical and professional practice dilemmas. Examples or quotes given by the trainees are used as examples throughout to illustrate a theme raised by a number of trainees.

LENGTH AND SCOPE OF TRAINING

An issue relevant to this chapter is the scope and length of training different therapeutic practitioners receive. This can vary considerably. Some practitioners receive many years of formal training with a range of client issues and groups, regular clinical supervision, a variety of personal therapy development requirements plus regular assessment of their work; others may only receive some of these. Consequently, different groups of trainees may approach professional and ethical practice issues from different training backgrounds. This may have implications for trainees' perspectives on professional and ethical practice issues. Without compulsory regulation of the various professions working as therapists, professional and ethical standards may be less easy to uphold than in professions that are subject to compulsory regulation, such as medicine. There is no doubt that the BACP, BCP, BPS and

UKCP have a range of mechanisms to ensure that their members comply with rigorous practice and ethical guidelines; but there are people practising who do not belong to any of these bodies. As one trainee noted:

> I've come across counsellors who have attained certificates or diplomas in counselling without doing supervised client work and with no personal therapy at all, I think such qualifications should be differently labelled.

The Health Professions Council (HPC) approved the British Psychological Society's case for regulation of applied psychologists in June 2003. This will improve the situation regarding psychologists, as it should uphold standards and restrict those who may legally use this description/title. (Further details can be found on http://www.bps.org.uk/statreg/index.cfm.) Different countries deal with the issue of who is allowed to offer 'psychological services' in a range of ways. Thus the terms psychotherapist, psychologist and counsellor may be regulated in different ways around the world.

THE ROLE OF PROFESSIONAL AND ETHICAL ISSUES IN TRAINING

The importance of professional and ethical practice issues in training was noted and described positively by the majority of trainees. Eighty-five per cent reporting that this provided containment and support, and helped to uphold standards and professionalism in addition to drawing attention to potential pitfalls or dilemmas in clinical practice. Bond (1993) aptly refers to an ethical framework as being like metaphorical scaffolding, which enables work to safely take place on the building located within the scaffolding. However, other trainees expressed considerable ambivalence about the role of professional and ethical issues in training, as detailed below.

Professional and ethical issues in therapeutic practice have sometimes been seen by trainees and tutors as rather boring, over-legalistic or merely 'common sense'. Tutors, clinical supervisors and placement managers may therefore need to be innovative in the way they address these issues, especially at the beginning of training, where the trainee has little experience of direct clinical work and may understandably be anxious about the therapeutic enterprise. Morrissey (2004), in reviewing practice in a number of countries, notes a lack of consistency and argues that there should be regular input throughout clinical training on professional and ethical issues as well as these becoming a mandatory part of continuing professional development requirements. Fifty-five per cent of trainees reported additional concerns about litigation and complaints being made against them, therefore sensitive treatment and open discussion of these issues by tutors may be helpful to trainees. Schoenfeld *et al.* (2001) claim that in the USA 11 per cent of psychologists will have complaints made about them. Bond (2000) notes that it is difficult to obtain accurate information about complaints made against therapists/counsellors in the UK as some may be made at the organisational or agency level rather than at national level. He suggests that some agencies may not wish to disclose this information, as they may wish to try and protect their agency's reputation and possibly funding. Feelings of anxiety about complaints and litigation may be compounded if a trainee is starting again after having a career in another field, and believes themself to have high personal ethical standards. One trainee expressed their ambivalent feelings succinctly

> Whilst ethics provides some structure and security for trainee practitioners, it strikes me that as a subject/topic it is the least interesting, which I see as a 'brake' on our work . . . As an analogy it is a bit like studying safety issues/learning about equipment before being allowed to go flying/mountaineering/sailing etc. I can see the need, but it is really legalistic.

Aside from ensuring their relevance to practise is clear, it may be important to acknowledge that there may be ambivalence towards learning about ethical and professional practice issues. (The author has found that the use of vignettes and imaginary dilemmas is helpful in bringing professional and ethical issues into training.) Trainees in the early part of training often want to be told what to do in any given circumstance without realising the subtle differences within the therapeutic process, agency context, and other relevant variables. The desire for a containing frame or set of 'perfect' guidelines in a new and complex field seems entirely understandable. While ambivalence may exist, ethical and practice guidelines may also be thought by some trainees to have a totally prescriptive value and the significance of a talisman. The wish for trainees in *therapeutic* work to aspire to perfectionism is noted by Cross and Papadopoulos (2001). Two trainees give their views below:

> Professional and ethical guidelines provide some guidance on what is accepted and their role in training and working. In a world and profession that is fast becoming 'very unsafe' in regards of the risk of being sued or suspended etc. The professional and ethical guidelines can be a 'safe haven' to work under.

> Awareness that there are different courses of action can be disabling, this can lead to overly rigid adherence to 'rules' to avoid dilemmas and 'get it right'.

What is your worst fear about professional and ethical practice issues? If you found yourself confronted with a potential dilemma, what would you do? Who would you consult?

The theme of professional or ethical guidelines and support or guidance is continued here. Sixty per cent of trainees reported finding it hard to ask for advice and help at the beginning of their training/placements, particularly when they felt that there might be an element of judgement involved. Clarkson and Pokorny (1994) noted a similar finding. Cooper (1992) draws our attention to the fact that there may be unconscious processes which may clash with the ethical values expressed. Two trainees described it thus:

> At times it makes you feel inadequate, not knowing where to go, what to do, who to talk to. We think we 'should' know it all, prevents us from asking. In a busy part of the NHS where I am based, everyone seems to be working so hard and have so little time.

> Some ethical and professional dilemmas impact upon the therapeutic process and these may cause a lot of anxiety and affect your confidence about your work, however they are important aspects of the learning process and personal and professional development and if dealt with appropriately and discussed in seminars and supervision can have a positive impact on therapeutic process.

These findings appear to offer some challenges to the way professional practice and ethical considerations are presented to trainees and integrated into courses, placements and clinical supervision at the start of training, and the need to demonstrate to ensure that the subject is made lively and relevant. Morrissey (2004) warns against assuming that ethics will be learned merely through modelling or osmosis/passive observation. A number of professional bodies have recently reviewed their codes of practice and ethical guidelines to ensure that they are suitable and clear for therapists and clients (BACP and UKCP). The nature of the subject may well necessitate constant development of guidelines and codes of practice. Some therapists with BACP are talking about rethinking ethics for the talking therapies from rules to 'ethical mindfulness'.

If you were asked to consider designing professional and ethical guidelines, what principles might motivate or guide you? These might be personal, societal, familial, philosophical or other.

WHAT ARE ETHICAL DILEMMAS?

> (Ethical dilemmas) . . . these exist whenever there are 'good' but contradictory reasons to take conflicting and incompatible courses of action.
>
> (Kitchener 1984: 43)

Some trainees reported that they found the guidelines vague, but guidelines cannot cover all eventualities and should not be merely prescriptive. Every instance is different, and complex situations may require independent professional judgement and discussion with supervisors or line managers. Guidelines are structured to provide a framework against which dilemmas can be considered, and by their very nature must evolve as society changes (Koocher & Keith-Spiegel 1998; Kitchener 1984; Gottleib 1994). There is also a range of views about the underlying moral philosophy underpinning ethics, with the utilitarians and deontologists taking differing stances (Shillito-Clarke 1996). Reference to the debates within the differing professional bodies about the updating and positioning of ethical codes illustrates the complexities of the task. Several ethical dilemmas presented by trainees are given below to illustrate this complexity.

> I had a patient whose son (9 years of age) was witnessing her partner's violent and abusive behaviour. I was in a dilemma whether to report the matter as the son could have been in danger. I took it to supervision and sought 'hypothetical' advice from the local mental health crisis team. I also advised the patient of our initial contract and suggested she took action to end this relationship (she had already planned to do this), as I would have to report the situation. I would behave in the same way in the future.

> A client told me they were being very rough, possibly physically abusive to their child – by the time I had checked this out any trust/rapport between myself and my client was lost and therapy ended prematurely.

What would you do in these situations? (You might find it helpful to refer to Chapters 5 and 7 after having considered your first response.)

Different agencies, therapeutic models and even professional trainings may position ways of dealing with complex ethical issues slightly differently (Spinelli 1994; Bond 2000; Koocher & Keith-Spiegel 1998). Inevitably ethical and practice issues are often not clear-cut and by their very nature may be challenging and require a lot of thought and discussion, as described next.

A patient had an addiction to sex – he would expose himself to women in public – my dilemma was, do I contain this or do I report him or do I refer him to our forensic team? I have contained his behaviour and he does not expose himself any longer but he is still addicted to extra-marital affairs – we are working on this now.

What do you think you would do in this situation? What would guide your thinking? Who might you consult? How would your personal views/beliefs have influenced you?

As trainees moved through their training, they appeared to perceive the value of professional and ethical guidelines and practice at national and agency level somewhat differently, finding that as well as providing containment, they help integrate and reinforce other areas of learning.

In my first year of training I found it really helpful to be able to say that I could not do certain things, such as requests to continue the therapy on a private basis after finishing the NHS contract because the agency guidelines did not allow this. I now feel able to say this myself for therapeutic reasons.

MAJOR THEMES RAISED BY TRAINEES

One of the major findings of our research was the importance of good clinical supervision (98 per cent of the trainee participants) and personal therapy (61 per cent).

I have learnt so much from being in therapy and to a lesser degree in clinical supervision, I was not sure at the beginning; it was expensive and time-consuming, and I rather resented it. But I think these provide, and continue to provide, some of the best training experiences there are, for me anyway.

The importance of these two cornerstones is recognised by most training organisations, although there is some variation among training institutions, professional bodies and therapeutic models about their importance. Although the empirical evidence on the importance of personal therapy is not unequivocal, and a range of views are held by practitioners, the author views it as having a key role in equipping trainees to work as therapists. The interested reader is referred to Halewood and Tribe (2003).

PERSONAL THERAPY

The many different strands of training often provide overlapping experiences, which inform and build upon one another. In addition to the strands of university or training institution-based seminars, lectures and supervision, trainees' experience of personal therapy before and during training has also proved a fertile training ground for experience of bad and good professional and ethical practice. Guy and Liaboe (1986) suggest that more attention should be drawn to the benefits of personal therapy, as they claim it will not only enhance therapeutic skills but may also minimise any harmful effects of therapeutic practice. Individual therapeutic schools regard the place of personal therapy differently. For example, many years of experience of therapy may be viewed as a prerequisite to training and a part of the basic suitability procedure for some training, while other training institutions may have a loose guideline about number of hours or outcomes.

Make a list of the criteria you think are important in selecting a personal therapist? Having made the list, you might want to reflect on why the criteria you chose were important to you. Did professional and ethical practice feature in your list?

Trainees report a disturbing number of examples of unethical practice when they first sought a therapist. Before starting their own preparation for training, they may have little experience of finding a therapist, and often select on the basis of geographical locality or cost. Nevertheless, the trainees in general found personal therapy an invaluable source of learning about professional and ethical practice, apart from its other important functions. The interested reader is referred to Palmer Barnes (1998) and the Prevention of Professional Abuse Network (POPAN) for further information.

> My therapist kept leaving the room to check on their baby, I didn't feel able to say that I thought this inappropriate, so I just left after a couple of sessions.

> Having negotiated a fee before starting counselling, the counsellor informed me that he had decided to raise the fee, there appeared to be no room for negotiation and I felt trapped.

If you believed your therapist was engaging in unethical professional practice what would you do? What factors might influence your decision-making?

The issue of personal belief systems in how we view professional and ethical practice was also mentioned by many trainees (59 per cent). This issue is discussed at more length in Chapter 5 in this volume but requires mention here. The interested reader is referred to Bond 2000; Jenkins 1996; Cross 2004. Some interesting work is being done in considering whether it may be possible to develop a Universal Declaration of Ethical Principles that would be acceptable across various countries and cultures (Pettifor 2002; Leach 2002; Aljunied 2002; Tribe *et al.* 2004). Many trainees reported that although they were aware of a theoretical/academic perspective of various issues or beliefs which they viewed as having personal significance and which a proportion had discussed in their own therapy, they were still surprised at how their own views and material sometimes mediated in their clinical work. Trainees gave a range of examples, but one is used below to illustrate this point.

> When I was working with a woman who suffered from domestic violence, I was struggling with my role as a therapist and woman who needed to protect the client. I struggle to work with clients who have strong views against women, although such clients are referred to me.

Issues of power and trust in work with clients and in personal therapy were raised as challenging by a number of trainees. This is an issue, which may have particular resonance when issues of difference and diversity form part of the work. These issues need to be integrated into training and practice if high professional and ethical standards are to be maintained. It is not possible to do these issues justice here, so the reader is referred to Part II of this book for a more comprehensive account.

GIFTS

Being given gifts by clients/patients was mentioned as a difficult issue by a high percentage of trainees (43 per cent) and caused much concern about 'doing the right thing' and maintaining professional and ethical practice and 'manners'. The advice of supervisors, colleagues, tutors and organisational guidelines were said to be helpful. This issue seems to become increasingly complex when cultural values and context are considered. The author of this chapter holds the view that gifts should not be accepted by therapists, and that if they are offered in therapy, the issue needs to be dealt with in the therapeutic process. There is not scope to discuss this complex issue at length here, but it is one that merits reflection and discussion. The issue of different cultures, belief systems and explanatory health beliefs has been discussed by a number of writers, including d'Ardenne and Mahtani (1999) and Patel *et al.* (2000). Seymour (2002) has discussed how the 2002 version of the New

Zealand Psychology Society code of ethics has attempted to respect the 'bicultural values of Maori and non-Maori, especially with regard to respect for peoples, social justice, and the acceptance of a collectivist philosophy in addition to the Euro-North American emphasis on individualism'. The following extracts show how two trainees described their dilemmas.

> In my culture, it would be extremely bad manners not to accept a gift. It is a mark of respect, and one would almost expect it.

> A patient gave me a present in the middle of a therapeutic process, I didn't know what to do, I refused the gift, but the client insisted on me taking it. The client thought I was rude to refuse it and later became rather 'distant' in sessions. . . . Now I would deal with it differently, probably would use the gift to explore what made the client bring it, and use this gift as a metaphor within the therapeutic process.

What would you do if a client brought you a present of some sweets/cakes which they said they had 'baked especially for you' to mark a cultural/religious festival in session four of therapy? What factors would influence your thinking? Would the monetary value of the gift influence you?

WHISTLEBLOWING

The issue of whistleblowing has received increasing attention in recent years. It appears that as society gets increasingly litigious everyone feels more anxious about the possibility of being sued or of having complaints proceedings taken against him or her. Palmer Barnes (1998) categorised most complaints as relating to inadequate contracting or conflicting expectations, and issues relating to confidentiality, mistakes or malpractice. Apart from ensuring that their own practice was ethical, the issue of whistleblowing or of believing that colleagues were guilty of unethical practice was mentioned by a number of trainees. Koocher and Keith-Spiegel (1998) cite a number of cases of 'whistleblowers' or 'ethical resisters' within psychology in the USA; they unfortunately do not paint a positive picture of the prospects of the whistleblowers in their sample, though. As one trainee stated:

> I believed a colleague was 'over familiar' with clients, this raised real issues for me, I was only a trainee and there appeared to be a culture of collusion which accepted this person's 'foibles'.

If you believed a colleague might be engaged in unethical practice, what would you do? Who might you raise the issue with? Are you familiar with your organisation's code of practice and any guidelines on this issue?

LEVELS OF COMPETENCE

Being asked to work at the edge of professional competence was a theme mentioned by a number of trainees, as was working with complex client issues. Tangential to this was the importance of being honest about one's level of difficulties and concerns about not being seen in a negative light by the trainee's supervisor or clinical placement manager (this was noted by a number of trainees). Universities and training institutions/placements also have responsibilities to monitor and consider such instances in a coherent manner (Koocher & Keith-Spiegel 1998). Inappropriate referrals were another issue raised by trainees. Trainees feeling they were lucky to have been given a placement, which are increasingly competitive and difficult to find, sometimes complicated this. These issues may be exacerbated when the trainee's supervisor is also their line manager.

> At times it is difficult to know who we can talk to and trust, as trainees we feel vulnerable if we open too much or contradict our managers/ supervisors.

> Once I took a client who I would describe as 'difficult' and beyond my competence, but the same client was on 'top of the waiting list' and my line manager told me I should work with her. I wasn't sure if I should continue working with this client or if we terminate – would that impact on the client?

> Anxiety about these issues can damage the patient/therapist relationship but not dealing with these issues properly can leave the clients vulnerable and open to abuse . . . Clients may decide to withhold information (about their violent tendencies for example) which would really block the therapy.

DUAL ROLES/RELATIONSHIPS

Dilemmas associated with dual roles and relationships were raised by a number of trainees. (Dual roles and relationships refer to having other roles/ relationships with a client, for example being involved in counselling and then being asked to write a report that would be used in legal proceedings, or being asked to sort out housing or welfare issues, key working or undertaking advocate duties.) Whenever possible, dual roles should be avoided, but there may be occasions when they are unavoidable (Bond 2000). Herlihy and Corey (1992) offer a useful decision-making model for considering and managing dual relationships. Different organisations have different policies on this. It is important to realise that if a legal report is to be written (frequently associated with access to resources or compensation), this is likely to affect the dynamics of the therapy and the decision to engage with legal report writing needs to be considered from the start.

> I found myself doing a case report for court with my client's consent but of course the client became less disclosing of their underlying issues as their children who are in care are being considered for return, if I was asked again I think I would refuse the task, it confused the boundaries for both of us.

> My experience of being asked to undertake a so-called dual role was that my client decided to opt out of therapy ... It may affect other patients so much that they would not return to therapy.

Where there are custody or domestic violence issues, a client may present for counselling knowing that this will reflect well on them in legal proceedings but with no intention of really engaging in the therapeutic process. How we position ourselves in relation to dual roles and relationships is likely to be determined by the therapeutic model we practise, agency tasks and policies, personality and personal belief systems. The more thought that is put into considering these issues in advance the better.

You have been seeing Ms V for therapy for one and a half months in a large agency working with addiction issues. Although she has attended regularly, you feel that she has not really engaged in the therapeutic process, but is merely 'going through the motions'. Your manager tells you to write a report for Ms V's forthcoming court case where her addiction issues/mitigating circumstances may be relevant.

What are your initial thoughts about the issues which dual roles/relationships might precipitate? How do these relate to your therapeutic model, the agency employing you, personal issues or belief systems? Do you think your decision-making might be different if you were working in private practice? If so for what reasons?

BEING A TRAINEE

Trainees reported believing that professional and ethical dilemmas may be further complicated by the fact that they are trainees, in that clients may project feelings of being given someone not fully qualified and may have anxieties about this. This study found that trainees themselves may have anxieties about the work and their level of competence, and may feel they 'should' know it all. This may prevent them from seeking help as soon as a problem arises, particularly when their line manager or clinical supervisor appears unavailable or very busy – or, of course, if the trainee has particular personal issues about asking for help. This is obviously an immensely complex issue and therefore not all aspects can be discussed here.

> Clients may project their unwillingness to take responsibility for therapy on to the clinician being a trainee.

> As a trainee Counselling Psychologist, I am into my seventh year of training in psychology but when clients read that I am a Counselling Psychologist in training, they may believe I have had very little training and wish to see a more experienced practitioner.

How would you deal with a query from a client who was engaged in therapy about your level of training and competence to practice?

BOUNDARIES, CONFIDENTIALITY AND ISSUES OF DISCLOSURE

Confidentiality, boundaries and issues of disclosure are subjects that many trainees reported struggling with in some way. These complex issues are discussed at length by Koocher and Keith-Spiegel (1998). Dilemmas associated with working in a multidisciplinary team were another – trainees reported instances of clients being discussed informally by members of the multidisciplinary team. They also expressed concerns (particularly in primary care contexts) about the security of notes and clinical information. Several trainees reported finding what appeared to be 'fuzzy' boundaries, extremely un-containing in this environment. Although other trainees reported excellent practice in multidisciplinary teams with clear and open communication channels and where everyone considered the best interests of the client.

> I'm aware that supervisors are sometimes faced with the dilemma of whether information divulged in supervision should be passed on to the

manager, e.g. a counsellor struggling because of a bereavement. As a therapist (and trainee supervisor) I learnt the importance of having an explicit contract and checking the boundaries if I were unsure.

Self-disclosure was also mentioned. There were varying views about this, probably reflecting different theoretical models. It seemed that trainees at the start of their training found it harder to deal with being asked to self-disclose than more experienced practitioners.

My client asked me directly if I had a family as the material we were working with related to difficulties my client was experiencing with her children. I really struggled to deal with this; lots of different thoughts went through my mind about how to answer. I don't think I dealt with it very well, but think I will be better prepared should this happen again.

What are your thoughts about therapist self-disclosure? What factors do you think influenced your answer? What kind of information do you keep in your clinical notes? Are they purely factual, or do they contain clinical opinion, or are they interpretative or a combination of the three? You have been seeing a client for three months and they demand to see their notes. What would you do?

CONCLUSION

This chapter has attempted to reflect a range of trainee perspectives on professional and ethical practice issues. As mentioned in the introduction, it does not attempt to be conclusive, but to share the views of trainees from a range of institutions and courses who participated through completing questionnaires or taking part in focus groups or seminars. It is hoped that the issues raised will assist the reader in thinking about some of the professional and ethical dilemmas that can arise in training and beyond. The chapter also made some suggestions about how some of these issues may be integrated into training and offered reflective questions in relation to a number of the issues raised. If you are a trainee or inexperienced practitioner you may find it helpful after reading this chapter to make a list of the ethical and professional practice dilemmas you are worried about encountering and discuss them with a colleague or seminar group. You might also wish to consider what guidelines, policies or legislation are appropriate to your work? How can you ensure you are informed about updates? The codes of ethics are available to assist you and regular or specific updates may be issued; these are generally available from your professional organisation or via their website.

REFLECTIVE QUESTIONS

1   By what methods do you ensure that you uphold and monitor your own professional and ethical standards?
2   You know that your clinical supervisor had a recent bereavement and seems to be unavailable to you in supervision sessions. What would you do?
3   A client tells you he committed a serious crime but was never caught for it. What would you do?
4   A colleague tells you 'in strictest confidence' that she is now dating an ex-client.

The author would like to thank the many trainees who gave so generously of their time either in completing questionnaires or through participating in focus groups at various institutions in several countries.

REFERENCES

Aljunied, M. (2002) Paper presented at the Professional Ethics Across National Boundaries: Seeking Common Ground symposium, International Congress of Applied Psychology, Singapore, July 2002.

Bond, T. (1993) *Standards and Ethics for Counselling in Action*. London: Sage.

Bond, T. (2000) *Standards and Ethics for Counselling in Action*, 2nd edn. London: Sage.

Clarkson, P. & Pokorny, M. (eds.) (1994) *The Handbook of Psychotherapy*. London: Routledge.

Cooper, G. F. (1992) Ethical issues in counselling and psychotherapy: the background. *British Journal of Guidance and Counselling*, 20(1), 1.

Cross, M. (2004) The person in ethical decision-making: living with our choices, in R. Tribe & J. Morrissey (eds.), *The Handbook of Professional and Ethical Practice*. Hove, UK: Brunner-Routledge.

Cross, M. C. & Papadopoulos, L. (2001) *Becoming a Therapist*. Hove, UK: Brunner-Routledge.

d'Ardenne, P. & Mahtani, A. (1999) *Transcultural Counselling in Action*, 2nd edn. London: Sage.

Gottleib, M. C. (1994) Ethical decision-making, boundaries, and treatment effectiveness: a reprise. *Ethics and Behaviour*, 4, 287–293.

Guy, J. & Liaboe, G. (1986) Personal therapy for the experienced psychotherapist: a discussion of its usefulness and utilisation. *The Clinical Psychologist*, Winter, 20–23.

Halewood, A. & Tribe, R. (2003) What is the prevalence of narcissistic injury among trainee counselling psychologists? *Psychology and Psychotherapy: Theory, Research and Practice*, 76, 87–102.

Herlihy, B. & Corey, G. (1992) *Dual Relationships*. Alexandria, VA: American Association for Counselling and Development.

Jenkins, P. (1996) *False or Recovered Memories? Legal and Ethical Implications for Therapists*. London: Sage.

Kitchener, K. S. (1984) Intuition, critical evaluation and ethical principles. *The Counselling Psychologist*, 21(3), 43–45.

Koocher, G. P. & Keith-Spiegel, P. (1998) *Ethics in Psychology*. New York: Oxford University Press.

Leach, M. (2002) Paper presented at the Professional Ethics Across National Boundaries: Seeking Common Ground Symposium, International Congress of Applied Psychology, Singapore, July 2002.

Morrissey, S. (2004) Teaching ethics for professional practice, in R. Tribe & J. Morrissey (eds.), *The Handbook of Professional and Ethical Practice*. Hove, UK: Brunner-Routledge.

Palmer Barnes, F. (1998) *Complaints and Grievances in Psychotherapy: A Handbook of Ethical Practice*. London: Routledge.

Patel, N., Bennett, E., Dennis, M., Dosanjh, N., Mahtani, A., Miller, A. & Nadirshaw, Z. (2000) *Clinical Psychology: 'Race' and Culture: A Training Manual*. Leicester: BPS Books.

Pettifor, J. (2002) Paper presented at the Professional Ethics across National Boundaries: Seeking Common Ground Symposium, International Congress of Applied Psychology, Singapore, July 2002.

Prevention of Professional Abuse Network (POPAN) Network Annual Reports, 1 Weevil Court, Weevil Rd, London SW8 2TG.

Schoenfeld, L. S., Hatch, J. P. & Gonzalez, J. M. (2001) Responses of psychologists to complaints filed against them with a state licensing board. *Professional Psychology: Research and Practice*, 32(5), 491–495.

Seymour, D. (2002) Paper presented at the Professional Ethics Across National Boundaries: Seeking Common Ground Symposium, International Congress of Applied Psychology, Singapore, July 2002.

Shillito-Clarke, C. (1996) Ethical issues in counselling psychology, in R. Woolfe & W. Dryden (eds.), *The Handbook of Counselling Psychology*. London: Sage.

Spinelli, E. (1994) *Demystifying Therapy*. London: Constable.

Tribe, R., Weerasinghe, D. & Cockburn, L. (2004) Ethical dilemmas when working overseas. Presented at the DECP Conference, Paris.

Appendix: List of resources

American Psychological Association
http://www.apa.org

Australian Psychological Society (APS)
http://www.aps.psychsociety.com.au

British Association for Counselling & Psychotherapy (BACP)
1 Regent Place
Rugby CV21 2PJ
Email: bac@bac.co.uk
http://www.counselling.co.uk

British Confederation of Psychotherapists (BCP)
http://www.bcp.org.uk

British Psychological Society (BPS)
St Andrews House
48 Princess Rd East,
Leicester IE1 7DR
Email: psychologist@bps.org.uk

European Association for Counselling (EAC)
PO Box 52659
145 03 Drossia Attica
Greece
http://www.eacnet.org/

United Kingdom Council for Psychotherapy (UKCP)
167–169 Great Portland Street,
London W1N SB
http://www.psychotherapy.org.uk/

Websites

http://www.counsellingcharity.freeserve.co.uk/
http://www.psychnet-uk.com
http://www.questions.co.uk
http://www.uktherapists.com

Index